·mediately

COMMUNITIES

COMMUNITIES

ESSAYS IN THE SOCIAL HISTORY

OF

VICTORIAN WALES

IEUAN GWYNEDD JONES

Gomer Press
1987

First Impression - 1987

ISBN 0 86383 223 7

© Ieuan Gwynedd Jones

*Printed in Wales
at Gomer Press, Llandysul, Dyfed*

I ALUN

CONTENTS

PREFACE

Like the collection of essays on the social history of Wales published in 1981 under the title *Explorations and Explanations* the essays brought together in this volume are reprinted from a variety of publications. These are identified in the text. Two were given as lectures and subsequently published in pamphlet form by the institutions which so kindly invited me to deliver them. Some were written for historical journals, others for learned societies. Nevertheless I hope that they possess a fairly uniform style of presentation, and I have standardized the notes and in some cases added references. The critical reception accorded to the first volume encourages me to believe that the conclusions I propose are helpful in the understanding of Welsh society at the most critical period in its development.

The over-arching theme of this volume is the ways in which communities were made in the mid-nineteenth century and the major forces which went into the making of them. All the essays examine specific communities of more or less size, rural and urban. The essays in Part 1 on the building of Anglican churches are included not merely because the social history as distinct from the architectural history of church building is a much neglected field, and in order to stress the importance in Welsh social and religious history of the reform and revival of the Anglican church, but also for the reason that the study of individual acts of rebuilding expose the underlying social realities of the places in which they took place and the motivations and preconceptions of the individuals and groups concerned in them. The building of a new church or the rebuilding of an old one, like the building or rebuilding of a chapel, served to increase a community's awareness of itself as a community, and this was as true of the emergent urban settlements in industrial Flintshire or in the town and valley of Aberdare as of the deeply rural parishes of Cardiganshire or the different urbanity of its rural towns.

Though church and chapel building sharpened denominationalism and refined the awareness of political differences, the sheer numerical strength and apparent invincibility of competing religious organizations and their spontaneous and reactive appearance in the earliest and most crucial stages of community growth suggests that organized religion as a whole, whatever the differences in theology and conceptions of church government contained within it, was a primary social force in the making of new communities. It was the virtually universal acceptance of this primacy by the irreligious as well as the committed which enabled organized religion to function as a stabilizing force in society at times when so much conspired against the achievement of good order, and at a time when most of these communities lacked even the most rudimentary institutions designed to supply these needs. So powerful was this attachment to religious denominations, so singular the loyalty to the moral imperatives for which they stood, that Welsh religious communities performed miracles of generosity in taxing themselves in order to provide English immigrants, whom they believed to be religiously deprived, with religious institutions such as they themselves possessed. They believed that religious benevolence of this kind was a prudent measure in the face of the threat to the integrity of Welsh communities posed by the encroaching alien culture of the English immigrants. In so doing they consciously put the values of religion above that of language and thus hastened the processes of cultural change. But these processes resulted in gain as well as loss, and in the circumstances of economic growth and urbanization without precedent in respect of its speed and unforseen social consequences people on both sides of the linguistic divide considered the primary need to be the protection of the integrity of their communities whatever their linguistic mix. And gradually consciousness of class rather than of ethnicity came to be seen as their distinguishing characteristic and as a positive gain.

It is an illusion to believe that the processes by which communities were made in rural areas were entirely different from those operating in industrial areas as if the former were somehow insulated from the latter. Especially it is the relative simplicities of their social structures and their shared religious culture that needs to be stressed. It was these which made the transition from one to the other intelligible for the thousands of migrants who made the journey from country to town, and it was these which came to be expressed most completely and, for a time, most satisfyingly in a common political culture.

*   *   *

I wish to thank the following for permission to reprint; the editors of *Journal of the Flintshire Historical Society, Journal of the National Library of Wales, Ceredigion: Journal of the Cardiganshire Antiquarian Society, Llafur: Journal of the Society for the Study of Welsh Labour History,* the *Welsh History Review:* Paul H. Ballard and Erastus Jones, *The Valleys Call* (Ferndale, 1975), the Torfaen Museum Trust, and the University College of Swansea. I thank Professor Harold Carter and the Department of Geography at the University College of Wales, Aberystwyth for the map.

In addition to the staff of the National Library of Wales and of the Hugh Owen Library at Aberystwyth, I wish to thank the Librarian of the Cynon Valley Libraries, Aberdare for so readily supplying photographs and other research material, and the Librarian of the Lambeth Palace Library and the Secretary of the Incorporated Church Building Society for permission to quote from papers in their possession. Behind all the essays, as of the collection itself, lies the critical appreciation of my wife and son. To them I give my special thanks.

ILLUSTRATIONS

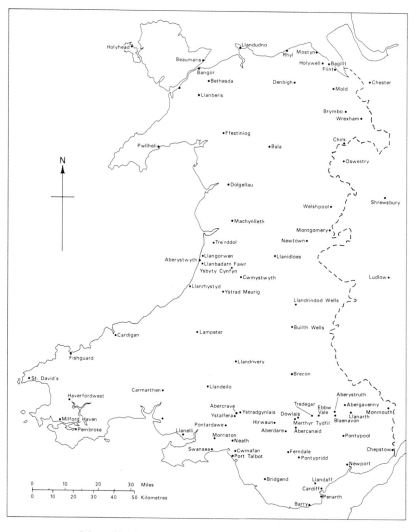

Map of Wales showing places mentioned in the text.

Part 1

Building Churches

CHURCH BUILDING IN FLINTSHIRE
IN THE MID-NINENTEENTH CENTURY*

It was at the thirty-third annual general meeting of the Incorporated Society for Promoting the Enlargement, Building and Repairing of Churches and Chapels, in May 1851, that the Bishop of St. Asaph, after a characteristically eloquent and enthusiastic speech by the Bishop of Oxford, drily remarked that he could not believe that a church which had been so active in erecting places of worship as the Church of England had been, could have the judgment of the Almighty impending over it. There present, he said, were six bishops each of whom had consecrated one hundred new churches, and that therefore, whatever reasons there might be for alarm, he could not help trusting that the providence of God was over the country for good. The Bishop of Lichfield observed that he had consecrated upwards of sixty new churches in seven years, and not to be outdone, the Bishop of London added that his number was fast approaching to two-hundred. The Archbishop of Canterbury (Sumner), coming at the tail-end of this catalogue, modestly offered the information that during the twenty years of his episcopate at Chester [1828-48] he had consecrated 235 churches in that diocese. [1] Whether the providence of God operated in strict conformity to the rules of arithmetic, or whether a contrite heart and a broken spirit are not truer indications of religious growth are questions that, for the moment, I shall avoid. Certainly, much of Victorian religiosity was based on the former assumption, and it was this endless fascination with the quantitative aspects of organized religion that fuelled the arithmetic war of high Victorian times. In themselves, the facts about church building, like the facts about its counterpart, chapel building, are remarkable enough. As indicators of Victorian religiosity and more, as evidence of profound social changes, they are even more remarkable, and it is with an eye for social significances that I wish to study this great movement of church building and reconstruction, this insatiable, compulsive need to provide Anglican places of worship within the diocese, and more particularly, within the ancient county. I shall do so under four heads: What was done? When was it done? Where was it done? and How was it done? before finally asking, Why was it done?

What was done?

Church reconstruction involved a number of distinct, though related areas of activity. These were, first, the building of new churches, the repair and reconstruction of old ones, the enlarging by repewing and refurbishing of churches, the planting of mission churches (including prefabricated iron churches), second, the provision of parsonages and, finally, the building of schools. All these diverse activities, without exception, involved three layers of ecclesiastical authority: the Church Building Commissioners (from 1818, and before that in all probability the Board of Queen Anne's Bounty), the diocesan hierarchy, and the parish. Some of the connections between these were contingent, others necessary. The contingent ones arose from the need, which was almost invariably to case, to obtain funds from central authority (the Church Building Commissioners) to assist in the rebuilding, and to provide endowments or augmentations where these were deemed necessary. There were great national societies which existed to assist in these directions also, and later I shall describe their role. Necessary connections were those laid down by statute and ecclesiastical law, and no building, rebuilding or repair, however humble, could proceed without an exact concordance with the law. Because of this nexus of law and the existence of a complex bureaucracy in the Church, both at the centre and in the diocese, it is possible to study the physical evidences of reconstruction in some detail and it is the existence of adequate sources which enables the historian to establish the relative importance of these distinct area of activity.

The most spectacular aspect of reconstruction was the building of entirely new churches. In England and Wales as a whole no fewer than 2,381 additional churches and chapels were erected with the aid of the Church Building Society, and to this figure must be added those new buildings put up by private individuals, corporations and industrial companies. In Wales, an additional 827 churches and chapels (including mission churches) were built between 1831 and 1906.[2] The stock of churches in St. Asaph more than doubled, rising from 151 to 326—an increase of 175. But however great this increase in the building of new churches, the repair and enlarging of old ones was even more spectacular and, taken over the period as a whole and the country as a whole, not a bit less important. If we take the activities of the Church Building Society as an indicator, then out of a total of about 900 grants, 800 were for repairs and rebuilding and refurbishing, etc.[3] Again, it is necessary to point out that these Society statistics do not include the rebuilding, repair and refurnishing, which was carried out without recourse to public charities or governmental aid[4]—and the Faculty Books (authorizations for work to proceed) show that there was an enormous amount of work of this kind proceeding—so that we must conclude that, in general, this constant work on the fabric and furnishing of the churches contributed far more to the outward and physical state of the Anglican church than did the building of new places of worship. For reasons that we shall discuss later, this proportion of new churches to buildings repaired and refurbished in this diocese was rather different, the proportion of new churches being greater. In the county of Flint the relation was almost one to one—twenty-nine new churches to thirty restored. But whatever the ratio, in scarcely a parish in the diocese was there no building or restoration or repair of some kind or another, and it is difficult for us now to imagine the transformation that this must have involved in the appearance of places, towns, villages, and landscapes. As we shall see, this was not an unexpected bonus, an unforeseen by-product, of the developing programme: on the contrary, it was of the very essence of the movement, for it was the conviction of the protagonists of church building that propriety and decency in ecclesiastical appearances led inevitably to the moral improvement of the localities concerned.

Secondly, we must not ignore the rebuilding and provision of parsonages. Many were old thatched cottages or small farmhouses, and by the 1870s, at least in St. Asaph, most of these had been replaced by new and sometimes quite splendid buildings. This is a theme to which I shall return.

Finally, the third element was the provision of schools. The National Society existed independently of the Incorporated Society and was older by some seven years, but from the foundation of the latter in 1818 they had been closely associated, if only as the chief beneficiaries of the funds collected by means of the Royal Letters. From about the end of the '30s, the connection became less adventitious as it came to be realized that 'wherever a new Church [was] built, the establishment of a School [was] almost sure to follow'; which pragmatic consideration came to be enshrined in the principle that the school was a necessary appendage of the church and that national education was hallowed and blessed by the prayers of the Established Church[5] It is interesting to observe that this pattern of growth—first the church and then, as an appendage, the school—was the exact opposite of the morphology of Nonconformist growth, where the establishment of schools normally preceded that of the chapel. The Anglicans built a church and hoped to fill it: the Nonconformists gathered the congregation first, who thereupon provided themselves with a building. Observe also that what may for Anglicans have been originally fortuitous soon became necessary, what was at first adjunctive and adventitious became typical, and that finally what was necessary and typical came to be enforced as such. In this way the Church was enabled to advance its stone and mortar outposts on both flanks, and the result can be seen in town and country in the close juxtaposition and, more often than not, in an architectural harmony of the three symbols of a settled Anglican parochial ministry—the church, the parsonage and the school.

When was it done?

In the speech from which I quoted in the beginning, Bishop Vowler Short 'presumed that there was never a time since church building began' when so many churches had been built.[6] He was probably right, and contemporaries thereafter expended a great deal of ingenuity in turning a presumption into a certainty. Someone calculated in 1861 that of the 12,000 churches standing in 1850 in England and Wales, 8,000 had been built before the Reformation, 1,500 between the middle of the sixteenth century and 1800, 500 between 1800 and 1830, and 2,000 (2,029 to be exact) between 1830 and 1850.[7] More precise figures were provided in the 1851 Census of Religious Worship. Basing his statistics on the admittedly incomplete returns from the parishes, the official responsible for that report calculated that there were 14,077 churches *and other buildings* belonging to the Anglican church, and of these 9,667 had been built before 1801. Of the remaining 4,410, 55 were added in the first decade of the century, 97 in the second, 276 in the third, 668 in the fourth, and 1,197 in the decade 1841 to 1851. That left 2,118, but he assumed that all but 60 or 70 of those were pre-1800. So the result is the same in round numbers: 500 between 1800 and 1830 and 2,000 between 1830 and 1850.[8] This was an enormous growth, but what I wish to emphasize is the varying rates of growth—or the spectacular increase in the rate of growth. Thus, about five or six churches per annum were built between 1801 and 1811, nearly ten per annum in the decade 1811-21, and nearly twenty-eight per annum in the decade 1821-31. Then comes the great leap forward. In the fourth decade of the century, an average of sixty-seven churches per annum were being built, and in the last decade 120 per annum.

The peaks of building activity came in these central decades of the century—roughly the first three decades of Victoria's reign. Between 1840 and 1876, in England and Wales, the Anglicans built 1,727 new churches and rebuilt or restored, with consequent enlargment, 7,144 old churches. The total cost was estimated at £25,548,703.[9] The activities of the Incorporated Society show clearly the enormous work involved. Between 1840 and 1868 the Society gave grants for the building of 1,094 new churches and chapels, for rebuilding 632 old churches, and for enlarging 1,922 churches. The total of grants distributed for these purposes was £786,208. The decline in the peak years in the building of new churches came after 1854. There was a recovery to something like average rates of building in 1859-60, but thereafter there was no growth and the numbers of new churches built fell off slowly. The same was true of the investment in rebuilding and enlarging, and although relatively more of the Society's declining resources was diverted to rebuilding, repairs and enlarging, it is clear that by the '70s the golden years were over. Hence, for purposes of analysis we are dealing with a movement which was most active and productive in the four central decades of the century from 1830 to 1870.[10] Those were the decades of what Anglicans had come to think of as their own distinctive mode of revival.

The chronology of new building, repair and enlarging in Flint and in the diocese reproduced this national pattern. It starts in the county early in the 1820s with the building of two new churches, namely, St. Matthew's, Buckley, and the new church in Broughton, both in the parish of Hawarden, and both destined to become district churches. There is then an interval of twelve years during which only the cathedral undergoes repairs and a school is built. Then suddenly, starting in 1835, there is a spurt of building which persists until 1847. During those eleven years ten new churches were erected, namely, Rhyl,[11] Pontblyddyn in 1836,[12] Connah's Quay 1837,[13] Gwernafield 1838,[14] Bagillt 1839,[15] Bistre 1842,[16] Penmynydd (Pentrobyn)[17] and Llanfynydd in 1843,[18] Mostyn 1845,[19] Rhes-y-cae in 1847.[20] There then followed an interval of five years until 1852 when Gorsedd was built[21] and Brynford[22] in 1853. Bodelwyddan was erected seven years later, in 1860,[23] a second church in Rhyl,[24] followed by Prestatyn[25] and Eryrys[26] in 1863 and Rhydymwyn[27] in 1864. Sealand church was built in 1867, Greenfield[28] in 1871, Croes Ati (Flint)[29] in 1872, and finally, Caerfallwch (Rhosesmor)[30] and Bettisfield[31] in 1874. To all intents and purposes the building of new churches had been completed. The chronological pattern of the very substantial restorations and repairs was exactly the same: and it should be borne in mind that most of these restoration involved virtually the destruction of the old church, as in Ysgeifiog in 1837,[32] Northop, in 1840,[33] Whitford in 1843 and 1846,[34] Cilcain in 1845,[35] Gwaenysgor in 1846,[36] and Nerquis[37] and Flint[38] in 1847. Grants from the Incorporated Society—in some respect the most sensitive index of change—confirms that chronology.[39] By the last quarter of the century the characteristic form of building was the missionary centre, either semi-permanent or temporary, and an increasing use of school-rooms and other secular buildings for religious purposes—a development which would have been frowned upon in traditional circles earlier in the century. No less than thirty-one such buildings or adaptations of existing buildings were licensed between 1870 and 1896.[40]

This chronology undoubtedly reflected national movements in the cycle of church-building and restoration, but it would be a great error to conclude from this congruence that the role of the lesser part was passive to and wholly receptive of the larger. For the social forces, both economic forces and spiritual or mental influences, operated equally in Flint as elsewhere. Of the economic forces the most invincible was population change, and there are three aspects of this that are relevant. First, the increase in population. In England and Wales it more than doubled between the censuses of the period we are dealing with, increasing from 10 millions in 1811 to 22.7 millions in 1871, and by 1881 it was almost 26 million. In Wales the increase was of the same order: from 587,000 to 1,572,000 in 1881. An increased population required increased provision. But second, this increase took place at varying paces at different times. Nationally, the increase between 1811 and 1831 was at the rate of just under two millions between censuses, but after 1831 until 1861 the decennial increases were of the order of 2½ millions. Then between 1861 and 1871 the increase was 2¾ millions, and between 1871 and 1881 an enormous 3¼ millions.[41] In Wales there were critical differences and variations in the *rate* of increase in each decade: the rate remained high up to 1841, then fell very suddenly to only a half of what it had been in the early decades, only to rise very sharply in 1871-81 and so to the end of the century.[42] But the Flint pattern of increase did not conform either to the Welsh or the national pattern. Between 1801 and 1811 the rate of increase was 16.4, in the next decade 17.3, after which it fell to, and remained at, just over 11.0 for the next two decades to 1841. Thereafter the fall was spectacular. Between 1841 and 1851 the rate was only 1.8, in the next decade 2.3, between 1861 and 1871 it rose to 9.4, falling back again to 5.6 in the decade 1871-81. Up to the decade 1831-41 the county as a whole gained population at a very high rate: indeed, during the first two decades its overall growth rate was almost as high as that of Glamorgan and industrial South Wales. Between 1821 and 1831 the percentage increase was 17.3, and it remained at over 11.0 for the next twenty years, until 1841. The next decade saw an almost cataclysmic fall of less than 2 per cent, and it rose slightly between 1851 and 1861. Recovery came powerfully in the next ten years when the percentage rose to 9.4, falling again to 5.6 by 1881. In the period of this study, therefore, there were three quite distinct phases in the population history of the county, namely, forty years of rapid growth to 1841, then twenty years of virtual stagnation to 1861, followed by twenty years of growth again but this time on a more modest scale. Third, it is vastly important that we understand the rapidity with which changes in population took place in the rural area of counties as well as in the mining and manufacturing regions. The decennial statistics are much too crude to do more than suggest the magnitude of change, and they do not record the rapidity and utterly unpredicted and unforseen nature of these changes. The population, rural and urban, was mobile. People came and went, formed communities, appeared settled, only to disappear as unpredictably as the clouds over the hills.

Yet despite this mobility and apparent propensity for sudden change, there was one persistent element of growth, and that was the continued appearance of new urban area. With the development from the end of the eighteenth century onwards of mining and manufacturing industries on the coal measures along Deeside in Whitford, Holywell and Flint parishes, in Mold, Hawarden and Hope, so there occurred transferences of population within these parishes. Agricultural workers moved into the new towns or congregated in those corners of these huge parishes where there was a demand for labour, and though the pattern of industrialization changed with great rapidity, the processes of urbanization on the coalfield in the Deeside parishes of Hawarden, Holywell and Whitford persisted, bringing to old towns and to new towns a sense of permanence and of relative stability. In the inland parishes—in upland Mold, Halkyn, Hope, Cilcain and Ysgeifiog—lead-mining diversified a poor or even marginal agricultural economy, in some places producing characteristically industrial townships. In such parishes population remained more mobile than elesewhere, and the economy created a class of workers which was both agricultural and in-

dustrial—men and women who moved between both occupations as demand required, or farmers who became leadminers without relinquishing their agricultural occupations and
pursuits. Concurrently with these changes in the economy and
the consequential shifts in the distribution of populations was the
appearance of a distinct kind of town—the seaside town, the
north coast resorts. Their growth was explosive and their
morphology unique. So it was that within this cycle of
population change, and chronologically the product of the first
period of massive growth which lasted until the mid-forties, new
towns had appeared: Buckley and Broughton and Pentrobyn in
Hawarden parish, Bagillt, Greenfield and Connah's Quay and
Brynford in Holywell, Bistre, Gwernafield and Pontblyddyn in
Mold, Llanfynydd in Hope, Rhes-y-cae in Halkyn, and Rhyl in
Rhuddlan. In addition, some villages had grown into small
towns or become the nuclei of circumambient lead-mining
settlements: Cilcain, Llanasa and Gorsedd come in this
category.[43]

In addition to the fundamental chronologies imposed by
demography and economy there is another chronology against
which Anglican reconstruction must be studied, and that is the
over-arching one of the growth of religion in general.[44] If, to
begin with, we confine ourselves to the numbers of places of
worship, we find that a total of 146 places were added to the
county stock in the course of the half-century between 1800 and
1850. The Anglican contribution to this total was 13, or just
under 9 per cent. Looking at the chronology of this growth, 96 or
almost two-thirds of the total were built between 1825 and 1850,
the years of highest growth being between 1822 and 1841.
During that nineteen-year period no fewer than 89 places of
worship were added and of those only 8 were Anglican. By the
time the Anglicans had begun to build in 1836, already the
Independents had built 8 chapels, the Baptists 10, the Calvinistic Methodists 35, the Wesleyan Methodists 29, and the
various Methodist off-shoots 11. In other words, the religious
complexion of the county and its denominational pattern had
already been determined before the Established Church had
begun to adjust to the self-same forces that were producing a
flowering of unofficial, anti-establishment religions. As we shall

see, this was a powerful element in the motivations of the
Anglicans and a factor of the highest importance in determining
the manner of their reaction.

Where was the rebuilding and reconstruction done?

We have now partly answered this question. In principle, the rebuilding and reconstruction was an organized response to a perceived need, though as I shall show later the motivations behind
this were anything but simple, for there were separate and distinct compulsions at work operating outside the accepted par-
ameters of need. The need was a constantly growing deficiency
in church accommodation and the men who perceived the need
were the Evangelicals. The founders of the Church Building
Society—the so-called Hackney Phalanx—argued in their petition to Lord Liverpool's government in 1817 that it was notorious that sufficient:

> Places . . . do not exist . . . in the great Parishes which
> surround the City of London or in many other populous
> Cities and Towns of this Kingdom. We believe we are
> correct when we state that in Fifty Parishes in or near the
> Capital there are more than a Million of Inhabitants and
> that all the places of Public Worship in those Parishes be-
> longing to the Establishment are not capable of containing
> One Tenth Part of that Multitude.

Only Parliament could supply the wants of the inhabitants
'beyond the Power of private and parochial Contributions'.[45]
The government's eventual response was the Act of 1818 establishing the Church Building Commissioners who were made responsible for the application of a parliamentary grant of one
million pounds towards the building of new churches according
to principles laid down in the Act. The Act confined their activities to parishes of more than 4,000 population, and it was the
growing realization of the enormous extent of the need, not only
in the metropolis and in large manufacturing towns, that determined the Evangelicals to keep their Church Building Society in
being. Year after year it was this apprehension of the challenge

of increasing numbers that kept them active as members of the Society and as a pressure group acting on government: ' . . . who that looks at the increased and increasing population of the country, can suppose that there are not thousands and tens of thousands for whom Church accommodation remains yet to be provided?' they asked in 1824,[46] and in 1825, after the government had given an additional half-a-million pounds to the now bankrupt Commissioners, the theme was the same:

> It may perhaps be supposed, that in consequence of Parliament Grants, the exertions of the Society can be dispensed with. This however by no means follows . . .[for] this Society adapts itself to the exigencies of every parish, be it more or less populous . . .[47]

and if there had been in the first decade of its existence a suggestion that its exertions would be temporary only and that the need would shortly and inevitably be met, no such illusions remained by the thirties:

> And when the growing population of the county is considered, when additional houses and cottages are seen to spring up in almost every town and every village, can it be doubted that the want of Church accommodation will, ere long, be felt in many places where it does not at present exist?[48]

By the 1850s an expanding need of massive, if not despairing, proportion darkened the future as the Society saw with astonishment the opening up of new mining and manufacturing districts in hitherto wholly unprovided places, like Cwm Rhondda[49] very few of which had been endowed by the Ecclesiastical Commissioners.

Hence, the constant refrain in applications to the Church Building Society by bewildered and astonished incumbents was of hitherto empty parts of their parishes suddenly filling up with people, of settlements and townships developing, as in Gwernafield, at a 'distance of three miles in a hilly country with indifferent roads render [ing] attendance at the parish church almost impracticable'.[50] Two local examples will suffice. The vicar of Cilcain, writing in 1845, explained that when the church was last repaired:

> It would appear that the Parish was then but thinly inhabited, and that it was an agricultural district, soon afterwards however discoveries of lead ore being made in our lime stone rocks, the state of things assumed a different aspect. Miners congregated from other places, and the inhabitants themselves such as were labourers, and farm servants becoming miners and small adventurers secured a little capital and built themselves cottages and cabins as they could along the side of our mountain waste . . . This influx of population and the inhabitants of the newly erected cottages were entirely unprovided with church accommodation . . .[51]

The second example, from the parish of Halkyn, illustrates the problem faced by the Church equally vividly. The incumbent described Rhes-y-cae as a remote corner of his parish where by reason of extensive mining a considerable population had congregated. It was two miles distant from the parish church:

> separated from it by a bleak and dreary mountain across which no regular road has ever been formed in this direction and the surface of which is so broken up by mines and quarries as to render the passage over it at all times difficult, and in fog, tempest, and darkness absolutely dangerous. With the exception of a few small farmers [the population of about 1,000] consists entirely of operative miners and their families and thus cut off, to a great degree, from all communication with their parish church . . .[52]

Such examples could be multiplied, for they are typical of conditions in all the large parishes where industry and commerce were changing the ancient order of things. Building and reconstruction took place where the need appeared at the time to be greatest, that is to say, first of all and mainly in the mining and manufacturing districts, where entirely new settlements had been recently formed and were still in process of development. Where population had expanded in or around old existing towns, or within easy reach of the old parish churches or ancient chapels of ease, these were reconstructed and enlarged so as to increase accommodation and provide free seats for the poor. St. Mary's, Flint,[53] for example, was taken down and rebuilt in 1847-8, St. Peter's, Northop,[54] was nearly rebuilt in 1840, and Nerquis Chapel [5] greatly enlarged in 1847.

How was it done?

This question leads us into the heart of the matter, for it is in the way that the necessary funds were raised—or, indeed, failed to be raised—that some of the essential characteristics of the particular communities and of society at large are most clearly revealed. Earlier I alluded to the magnitude of the building programme undertaken in the course of some forty or fifty years. According to Sir Robert Peel, the Prime Minister, no less than 525 new churches had been consecrated between 1835 and 1843.[56] A Parliamentary return of 1876 gives the total number of churches built since 1840 as 1,727, and the total of churches rebuilt as 7,144. the total cost was given as £25,548,703,[57] This latter return gives the numbers for Wales as 637 churches built and restored at a cost of £318,362.[58] How was this money raised? Basically, it came from two main sources, from central funds and from the localities themselves, and to a consideration of this funding I now turn.

The central sources of possible assistance consisted of the Church Building Commissioners (after 1866-7 taken over by the Ecclesiastical Commission itself), and the Incorporated Church Building Society. In effect, the personnel of these two great bodies were the same—the Executive Committee of the Church Building Commissioners wearing different hats and meeting in a different place[59]—and their function was to disperse grants from public funds and from charitable sources in such a way as to respond to the growing demand and also, if this were possible, in accordance with agreed principles. It is important to note that the pattern of financing and the relative share that came jointly from the Commissioners and the Society changed very remarkably from about 1830 onwards. Between 1800 and 1830 the proportion of moneys coming from public sources was in the region of 40 per cent, that is, £1,200,000 from public sources and £1,800,000 from private benefactions. But between 1830 and 1851 public grants rarely exceeded about 8 per cent, that is, public grants rarely exceeded £500,000 while private benefactions amounted to about £5,500,000.[60] The Church Building Commissioners alone spent over one million pounds between 1818 and 1823, but thereafter their individual grants were never on the same generous scale as after 1818, so much so that after 1830 the cost of the building and restoration programme was largely financed by the localities themselves. Between 26 March 1840 and 20 December 1852 the Commissioners reported that a total of £1,007,840 had been spent on erecting 273 churches and chapels, of which sum £871,502 had been raised by voluntary subscriptions, local rates, etc. In other words, 86 per cent of the sum expended was raised by voluntary means. During that period of twelve years, 14 churches were built in Wales at a total cost of £38,655, of which £31,064, or 80 per cent, was raised in Wales itself. Six of those churches were in the diocese of St. Asaph, costing a total of £15,092, of which £12,372, or 82 per cent, was found in the parishes concerned.[61] By 1876, when the total expended had risen to £408,371, the proportions had risen to no less than 97 per cent,[62] so that even though Anglicans were certainly privileged in that the worshippers did not have to find the total costs of building or reconstruction, the proportion not found by them was really very small. It is nevertheless worth bearing in mind that although the amount contributed from public funds was small, relative to the total sums involved, the actual sum could be of critical importance to the often poor and struggling parishioners in their financing of what would probably be the largest investment they were ever likely to make.[63]

The Incorporated Church Building Society was the exact contemporary of the Church Building Commissioners but its function was to assist in the provision of church-room in places which fell outside the scope of the first of the Church Building Acts—parishes, that is to say, of less than 4,000 population, but suffering from extreme insufficiency with regard to accommodation and likewise in great need of pecuniary aid. Also, the Society was not only or primarily concerned with building new churches: restoration and enlargement, repairing, and the enlargement of existing churches by repewing or the erection of galleries, none of which could be aided out of the parliamentary grant, became the major preoccupation of the Society and the objects to which its benevolence were directed. Judged by the number of churches it helped to put up and the increased provision that it was instrumental in creating, the Society was enormously successful. In the first fifty years of its existence it had made 5,303 grants, of which 1,461 had been for aid for the erection of 1,461 churches and chapels, and for rebuilding and enlarging 3,842 existing churches. By this means the Society claimed to have obtained 1,402,587 additional seats, of which 1,073,773 were set apart for the poor. The total sum disbursed by the Society in grants was £754,493.[64] The diocese of St. Asaph received 98 grants amounting to £13,132. During that same period, as we have seen, the total amount of money expended on church reconstruction in he diocese was £408,371. Of that sum £5,265 was disbursed among thirty-two places in the county. This was a generous contribution, but in proportion to the sums actually spent on the churches it was small, for the total money expended on those thirty-two places assisted by the Society was not far short of £59,000.[65] Hence, the financing of church building and restoration was very much the achievement of the parishioners themselves. A county and a diocese so closely associated with the Society from its earliest days realized fully the expectation of the Society that its main function would not merely be to assist with money but also, and more importantly, to stimulate and to direct local benevolence.

It is interesting to note that the average grant to churches in St. Asaph was higher than in the other Welsh dioceses, with the exception of Llandaff where it was slightly higher.[66] There was nothing adventitious about this, and certainly it had nothing to do with the fact that the 2nd Lord Kenyon was one of the Society's leading figures until his death in 1854. St. Asaph and Llandaff received on average higher grants and proportionately more of them because it was in the heavily industrializing parts of Wales that the need was greatest. As we have already remarked, the need was particularly great in the vast upland parishes where new populations had been formed away from the old parish churches. The Society took seriously its obligations to assist in making the 'Act for making better provision for the Spiritual Care of Populous Parishes' (6 & 7 Vict. c. 37 (1843)) as effective as Sir Robert Peel had designed it to be. [66] By this Act the Ecclesiastical Commissioners were given powers similar to those of the Church Building Commissioners to divide parishes, but while the latter could only assign new parishes to new churches, the Ecclesiastical Commissioners could assign new districts to incumbents, the incumbents to hold services in licensed places until the church was built. Under this Act, seven new districts were formed in 1844[68] and another—Rhes-y-cae—in 1848.[69] To give some examples: the Revd. C. B. Clough, the energetic vicar of Mold, who was the progenitor of church reconstruction in Flint and who, as Archdeacon of Mold from 1844, exerted a tremendous influence beyond the confines of his own parish, wrote as follows to the Church Building Society in March 1839: 'We have in the parish of Mold a very extensive & populous district at a considerable distance from the Parish Church, from whence scarcely any one out of 2,000 Souls attend our services, . . .' 'The state of the district', he added in a later letter, '. . . is really lamentable'.[70] He was given £250. Clough's two other churches, Pontblyddyn (1836), and Gwernafield (1838), were intended for similar, lead-mining populations, and were put up for extraordinarily small cost, more than half of which, in each case, was contributed by the Society and Commissioners.[71] Rhes-y-cae was planned for an extensive mining population two miles from the parish church, and like all the others of a similar kind built in this first period of reconstruction, was given generous support and immediately designated a district church.[72]

The size of the parishes and the often great distances between their churches and the new centres of industrial populations were not the only, or even the primary, difficulties that had to be surmounted. Rather, it was the poverty of the mass of the population superimposed upon a social structure, the main feature of which was the lack of powerful and rich and resident gentry families. To give some examples: in Ysgeifiog the largest proprietors were Lord Fielding and E. M. V. Mostyn who owned 789 and 573 acres respectively, and Hugh D. Griffiths who owned 845 acres. The average size of holding was only about seventeen acres. The pattern was similar in Halkyn where the Marquis of Westminster was the largest landowner with 508 acres. Apart from Sir Piers Mostyn, David Pennant, Esq., and Ralph Richards, Esq., there were no great landowners and no medium ones—or small proprietors in Bateman's definition—either in those parts of the parish of Holywell where the new settlements were, that is to say, in the townships of Coleshill, Bagillt, Brynford, and Greenfield. The same was true of the industrializing parts of Mold, Nerquis, Hope and Whitford. The pattern is basically the same throughout these parishes, namely, large numbers of proprietors and the land divided into minute holdings.[73] By contrast, Hawarden parish was virtually all owned by the Glynne family.

This distinction between parishes having large, resident, gentry families, and those with few or none is important because of the role that such families were expected to fill—and which, by and large, they did fill—in what was increasingly becoming a deferential society. As the leaders of society and the natural allies of the Established Church, they were expected to be charitable to the poor and to help to provide for their spiritual needs. The church was the bastion of order, the exemplar of the divine governance upon earth, the source of all sound public and private morality, and her clergy looked to the wealthy and powerful for support. As the reconstruction movement gained momentum and became more fashionable, so the contributions of the gentry were easier to obtain. But if the parishes lacked wealthy gentry families, they were forced to have recourse to methods of raising the necessary cash, such as by means of church rates, that were counter-productive, and indeed such as to encourage the growth of unofficial and despised forms of religion. Judging by the returns of 1856 [P.P. 1856 XLVIII (343)] Flint was very dependant on these increasingly difficult ways of raising money for the repair of the fabric. Of a total amount of £1,200 raised by church rates in 1853-4, only about £60 came from other sources—including gentry benefactions. Conscientious refusal when grafted on to poverty could become irresistible in the end, and always a source of hatred. As the incumbent of Hope reported, £6 was the average raised each year 'from scanty donations grudgingly given, and painfully and laboriously collected'. Where gentry influence and benevolence were forthcoming, there one would find costly and rather splendid churches being erected or expensive works of repair and preservation being carried out. Consider the investments made by the Glynne of Hawarden family between 1816 and 1859. St. Deiniol's church in Hawarden was repaired in 1816 at a cost of £1,416, repaired again in 1855-6 in neo-Gothic style when expensive new benches were put in instead of the old pews, the chancel reseated and the windows filled with stained glass. Finally, it was rebuilt after the fire of 1857 at a cost of £7,000. The architects were not local men but fashionable and expensive ones like Harrison of Shrewsbury, G. Gilbert Scott and G. E. Street. In addition, the family built St. Mary's, Broughton at a cost of £1,100 in 1824, the elaborate and beautiful St. John's, Penmynydd in 1843, and they were instrumental in persuading the Church Building Commissioners to put up St. Mathew's, Buckley, at a cost of £4,000.[74] Landed proprietors were prominent in some other parishes and districts, though none of them on the scale of the Hawarden family, in Bodfari, Brynford, Eyton, Llanfynydd, Mostyn and Nannerch.[75] This was particularly the case in the second half of the century as, for example, in 1872-4 when Bettisfield was provided with a church at the sole expense of Lord Hanmer.[76] Where gentry influence and benevolence were not forthcoming, then the churches that were erected tended to be utilitarian, indifferently designed, unprepossessing and badly built. Thus, two of Archdeacon Clough's three churches, namely Gwernafield, which was built at a cost of £764 in 1838, and Pontblyddyn built for £790 in 1836, had to be rebuilt in 1861 and 1865 respectively. His third church at Bistre was assisted by the Church Building Commissioners and cost £1,250, which was probably why it stood the test of time. One wonders whether the ancient and venerable ruin of Ysgeifiog would have been demolished if there had been local gentry in the parish interested in antiquarian values and associations and prepared to spend money on its restoration? As it was, the rector found it impossible to say when a new church can be complete if left to [the parish's] own resources—and I much fear that Benefactions from the Landowners will not raise a large sum, as they are all of them absentees . . . Were they resident the object of their benevolence would be more immediately in view.

£160 was the most that he could collect from them towards and estimated cost of £1,061.

When to this was added poverty, then church reconstruction made heroic demands on the faith as well as the pockets of its advocates. As we have already observed, the parishes which lacked a resident gentry class were precisely those upland parishes where lead-mining provided a precarious income, or was a source of additional income, for the peasantry and immigrant labourers. How could money be raised from these? 'A large majority of the labourers are almost in a state of starvation', wrote the rector of Ysgeifiog in 1831. 'Several have been at my door this day asking for some employment and offering to work at 6d per week . . . It is not merely poverty but misery in the extreme, such as I never before witnessed, and of which you can have no conception'. 'So much', he said, 'for the poverty of the poorest place in Wales'. Seven years passed before the church was built.[77] Ysgeifiog was not unusual: conditions there were duplicated in other neighbouring parishes and districts—in Rhes-y-cae, in Rhydymwyn, in Tremeirchion, Gwernafield and Gorsedd—and continued in these mining and manufacturing districts well into the century. Of Rhes-y-cae, for example, the rector of Halkyn wrote in June 1844, 'from the non-residence of the different landed proprietors, and the total absence of any even moderately wealthy people in the district, I apprehend much difficulty in collecting sufficient funds'. A year later he was still short of the target of £668, and the building had to be shortened in order to make the necessary saving.[78] Hence the importance of the grants given by the Incorporated Building Society and the often crucial gifts from the Diocesan Building Society, which in the early years of the reconstruction campaign made grants of £2,350 to the churches in this category.[79]

Why was it done?

Church reconstruction was an extraordinarily complex movement, and it is a very difficult and hazardous task to disentangle
or to distinguish clearly the different motives and compulsions at
work in the hearts and minds of so many different kinds and conditions of men. For men and women from all ranks of society,
from the top almost to the bottom, were involved. Aristocrats,
wealthy business-men and industrialists, men from the learned
professions and from the churches, were moved to give of their
riches and their talents along with common and working men,
some of whom were only partially literate and who could give
only their pennies or contribute to a church-rate. To what extent
were these, at all those different levels, commitments to a cause?
At what point in time did religious conviction give way to mere
fashion, or concern for the religious well-being of the poor
become merged in the pride of a community in the quality of its
buildings? To what extent was fear as well as love involved, and
at what stage was utility overtaken by aesthetics? Those are
questions one should try to answer, but at the risk of over-
simplying I want to indicate what I think were some of the main
motivations at different times in the history of the movement.

At first, in the infancy of the movement and before reform had
become formalized and institutionalized in the Ecclesiastical
Commission and its attendant auxiliary agencies, such as the
Church Building Society and the Pastoral Aid Society, fear of
the social consequences of irreligion was primary motive. This
was the language of the address to the nation drawn up by the
Church Building Society as its first public act:

> . . . they who are of opinion, that no remedy has been pro-
> vided mored effectual, for the evils to which human life is
> exposed, than the exercise of a rational piety and a sound
> instruction in the doctrines and duties of Christianity, will
> find little reason to wonder, that in the circumstances
> which have been here described, pauperism, vice, and
> depravity should abound; that impiety and disloyalty
> should be widely diffused; crime increase; and the voice of
> human law appear often to be raised in vain. [80]

The address finished with an appeal for friends and support from 'all who are justly alarmed at the consequences that may ensue, if so large a portion of the community continue to be without the means of obtaining Religious Instruction'.[81] Profligacy and insubordination, public calamity and individual misery, a million of the people of England living in the grossest ignorance, prey to evil and designing men, their minds corrupted by unbelief and atheism, ripe for rebellion and insurrection—this was the image that alarmed the God-fearing gentlemen upon whom the Church Building Society relied for its funds. Nor was this spirit confined to the disordered times of depression after the ending of the Napoleonic Wars, or to the period of political unrest in the years running up to Reform and afterwards in the decades of renewed working-class agitation for better political representation and social improvement. It was the Chartist Rising of 1839 which had awakened Sir Thomas Phillips to the threat of social order implicit in the appalling conditions being created in the south Wales coalfield by industry, and the Education Reports of 1847 that turned him into a campaigner for church extension and the provision of church schools in the diocese of Llandaff.[82] The memories of 1839 remained vivid and the alarm that he and his fellow magistrates then felt never completely died away:

> Bristol, Newport, Nottingham Castle—the flames which consumed our homesteads, and destroyed that corn which a bounteous Providence had supplied for our sustenance —the recent design to fire the metropolis and to murder that civil force by which the peace of a great city was preserved—are ominous warnings to us of a social condition full of peril.

Thus Sir Thomas Phillips in his book in 1849 and thus also the tenour of his thinking when he became a member of the Church Building Society in 1850.[83] And thus also, by implication, the young Bishop Sumner of Llandaff in 1827 when he bade goodbye to Evan Jenkins, whose new church at Dowlais he had just consecrated: 'I leave you as a missionary in the heart of Africa'.[84]

Closely associated with this in the minds of a majority of churchmen was alarm at the growth of unofficial forms of religion, both Roman Catholic and Dissenting. These religions were to be deplored almost as much as infidelity itself: indeed, in Wales it is probable that Unitarianism was the next worse thing to atheism. They were to be deplored because they inculcated a wrong political morality and questioned the right of the Established Church to a monopoly of the benefits that the connection with the State was believed to confer. Roman Catholicism in Wales was being recreated as a church in the first half of the the century, and its constituency was drawn mainly from the Irish immigrants, the poorest, most hopeless and despised communities in the new towns and industrial districts.[85] Dissent had long since become the religion of the lower classes and its very existence among the multitudes whom the Church now sought to attract threatened all that was held to be vital and necessary to the proper functioning of the Church at the level of the local community—the institution of the parish, control over all the *rites de passage* of the community, and its claim to a monopoly of education.

> . . . Popery is rearing its head, with power to subdue the weak and ill-instructed, and act to seduce the unwary [while] a latitudinarian spirit of indifference to articles of faith and modes of worship, opens to both superstition and unbelief a ready access among those who make boast of their civil and religious freedom.[86]

From the standpoint of the Establishment, Popery and Dissent were not so very different and posed a threat to her hegemony, especially when, as was increasingly happening, men of substance and or rank and station were successfully seduced. Hence the reaction of county society when the church at Pantasaph, originally intended by its founders, Lord and Lady Fielding, as a district church, was transfered to the Roman Catholics on their conversion. Most of the north Wales aristocracy, with a most unusual promptness and unanimity, contributed generously to the £10,806 raised for the building of St. Michael's, Brynford and St. Paul's, Gorsedd.[87]

St. Michael's Brynford.

St. Paul's, Gorsedd
The combined cost of these two churches was £10,806.
from D. R. Thomas, History of the Diocese of St. Asaph.

In Flint, Dissent was more of a challenge than Popery, though it would be easy to exaggerate distrust and hatred of the Nonconformists as a motive. It is extraordinary how, in their negotiations with the authorities, incumbents seemed totally to ignore the existence of Nonconformists, and one is left to infer their presence in a parish only from the reluctance of an incumbent to raise a church rate. An exception was the rector of Ysgeifiog who was very sceptical about getting large numbers in his congregation. Three-quarters of the parishioners were Dissenters.[88] 'We have Calvinists, Wesleyans and Baptists in abundance, very civil and decent in their conduct. Many of the followers of Mr. Wesley attend but never join us at the Altar'.[89] Very sensibly—and by implication in criticism of some aspects of church extension—Williams attributed the weakness of the church in the parish not to an inadequate building or even the extent of the parish but to the consequences of a dual absenteeism—that of the incumbent and of the landlord for over a century.[90]

Any realistic view of church extension therefore would be sceptical of the certainty of its advocates that the provision of a building and a supply of free seats for the poor was all that was required to bring in the congregations. Year by year the Church Building Society produced its figures showing an astonishing growth in the number of free seats provided for the poor. The equation was much too simple: an increased population needs increased provision. But what about man-power? What about pluralism, and non-residence, and the long after-taste of nepotism? It was some years before the authorities recognized the interconnections between edifices and man-power. It was a long time also before they acknowledged that the problem of non-attendance was merely or solely an urban problem. As we have seen, it was to the new urban areas and expanding old ones that the aid was going and the additional churches being erected, but it was a grave error to believe that it was there that the need was greatest. As the rector of Ysgeifiog had noted, it was in the rural parishes from whence the people migrated that the fundamental weakness lay, and that this weakness was symptomatic of the alienation of the common people from both church and gentry. And when it was pointed out to the advocates of church extension that, after all, people were not attending the new churches or filling the pews and benches in the reconstructed ones, the facts were disputed or glossed over or explained away. Said the Bishop of Oxford (Wilberforce) in 1851:

> . . . when we are taunted with the observation that, after all, our new churches are not filled, our answer is, 'Who ever expected they would be?', that is to say, in any given period of time . . . did any person expect that these churches would be filled at once by a people who are not accustomed to the blessings of pastoral superintendence, who never received scriptural instruction at home, who scarcely ever heard a church bell . . .?[91]

This judgment, based on observations of attendance in London, did not apply in Flint where the new district churches were well attended by congregations almost certainly not to be classed with those of Bethnal Green. But relatively the Anglicans were in a minority, and everywhere it was Nonconformity that had succeeded. Whether the church would succeed in altering the balance in its favour would depend not on more churches but on more evangelically-inspired men to serve those that already existed, and if necessary outside an outmoded parochial system.

For church building and restoration by the 1860s, in Flintshire as elsewhere, had become a fashion. It was noted as early as 1840 that one of the main tasks of the Church Building Society was to act as a catalyst and stimulant to local bounty. Its influence was leading 'individuals of wealth and station to build, mainly or entirely, at their own cost, and on no mean scale, edifices to the honour of God',[92] and it is noticeable that from about this time applications to build new churches grew relatively larger. It was about this time also that aesthetic and liturgical considerations became more prominent in the movement. The Society issued 'Suggestions and Instructions to Persons Engaged in Enlarging of Building Churches or Chapels' in 1842, coming down emphatically in favour of Gothic styles and earnestly recommending that 'good ancient examples should be followed'. Instructions regarding the placing of the altar 'two or more steps above the floor of the chancel, which should itself be

raised a step or two above the floor of the nave', and the position-
ing of the font, which had to be of stone 'and large enough to
admit of the immersion of infants', and with 'sufficient space for
the sponsors to kneel', show the influence of new liturgical ideas
and an emphasis on propriety and ceremonial.[93] In Flint these
aspects of the movement culminated in the building of Bodelwyddan in 1860 at a cost of £35,000.

The fact that motives were mixed, religious conviction,
idealism and a concern for beauty operating along with fear,
cynicism and pride, should not be allowed to detract from the
enormous achievement of the church builders. Perhaps the early
Victorians were naïve to attribute the peace and order which
prevailed in England and Wales in 1848 'when other states and
kingdoms are torn by internal convulsions and lawful government shaken to its foundations' to religious influences then per-
meating society through the new churches.[94] But we can
probably go along with Bishop Wilberforce's rhetoric when he
said:

> not only is the moral and religious character of a neigh-
> bourhood altered by the erection of a Church, but there is a
> marked improvement in its social and domestic state, and
> even in its external appearance. Invariably, as soon as a
> new church is erected—even, in some instances, before the
> roof is put on—the houses in the neighbourhood are
> repaired and whitewashed, the children become more tidy
> and orderly, and generally a more decent appearance is
> manifested among the people.[95]

A church, solidly built, using the best of materials, designed by
architects alive to its symbolic significances, and flanked by
parsonage and school, was bound to exert a profound influence
on the neighbourhood in which it was planted. And equally, the
restoration of a ruin could not be ignored by a community
familiar with its dilapidations. But likewise it would be naîve to
attribute too much to the movement. After all, church restoration was a part, and a part only, of a much greater movement
which involved the chapels of diverse denominations and the
meeting-places of sects. Looking at the expansion of both church

St. Margaret's Bodelwyddan was built by Lady Willonghby de Broke
at a cost of £35,000.
From D. R. Thomas, Diocese of St. Asaph.

and chapel in the county we can surmise that perhaps they were both on the same side even though at the time they seemed to each other to be divided. Both church and chapel ultimately looked to the perfection of Christians in an un-Christian society, and it ill behoves us who cannot find the money even to take down and reduce into picturesque ruins the redundant churches our fathers built, to belittle their efforts. Perhaps the last words ought to be those of Bishop Short with whom I began. 'It is wise', said this old Tory, 'to consider what is within and what is beyond our power. Clearly it is not within the power of any one generation to alter the tone and temper of a country, and to do the work which has been neglected for 300 years: but if it pleases God to enable us, by increased exertions, to raise that tone and temper even in a comparatively small degree, I believe a work will have been effected far beyond any numerical account.'[96]

NOTES

*First published in *Journal of the Flintshire Historical Society* xxix (1979-80)

[1] Incorporated Church Building Society, 33rd *Annual Report* (1851), pp. 12-13; A.G., Church Building, Past and Present'. *The Church Builder,* II (March 1862), 40-3.

[2] Royal Commission on the Church and other Religious Bodies in Wales, P.P., 1910, XIV, 130.

[3] I.C.B.S., op. cit., pp., 156-7.

[4] In 1890 the Annual Report emphasized the catalystic work of the Society and the way it stimulated local benevolence and effort, and pointed that there were many instances 'of late (of) individuals of wealth and status, mainly or entirely, at their own cost, and on no mean scale (erecting) edifices to the honour of God which may be the witness to future days, that the spirit of piety and charity which animated our forefathers, is not altogether extinct among their children'. *Report* (1840), p. viii.

[5] I.C.B.S., 21st *Annual Report* (1839), pp. xi-xii.

[6] idem, 33rd *Annual Report* (1851), pp. 12-13.

[7] *Church Builder,* op. cit., pp. 40-3..

[8] *Census of Great Britain 1851: Religious worship: Report and Tables* (1853), pp. xxxix-xli.

[9] P.P. 1876, lviii (553).

[10] See Table 1.

[11] *Church Builder,* (March 1862), 40 Lambeth Palace Library, I.C.B.S., R/Box 1 (1834-7); N.L.W. Church in Wales, SA/Bounty 136; D. R. Thomas, *A History of the Diocese of St. Asaph* (1874), pp. 303-6.

[12] I.C.B.S., G/Box 2 (1836-38), *sub* Gwernafield; Thomas, op. cit., pp. 610-11.

[13] I.C.B.S., G/Box 3 (1826-37, 1839-40) *sub* Northop; Thomas, op. cit., pp. 481-2.

[14] I.C.B.S., G/Box 2 (1836-38); N.L.W., Churh in Wales, SA/Bounty 41; Commissioners for Building New Churches, 19th *Report* (1839); Ecclesiastical

Commissioners R.O., Summary Book, f. 236; Royal Institute of British Architects MS. CBC 5729, Folder 16; Thomas, op. cit., pp. 606-7.

[15] Church Building Commissioners, 21st *Report* (1841); E.C.R.O., Summary Book, f. 274; Thomas, op. cit., p. 472.

[16] I.C.B.S., File 4785, B/Box 6 (1839-43); Church Building Commissioners, 23rd *Report* (1843); E.C.R.O., Summary Book, f. 307; Thomas, op. cit., pp. 605-6.

[17] I.C.B.S., H/Box 3 (1843) *sub* Hawarden; Thomas, op. cit., pp. 590-1.

[18] I.C.B.S., 2nd series, 1842; Thomas, op. cit., p. 597.

[19] I.C.B.S., 2nd series, 1845; Thomas, op. cit., pp. 493-4.

[20] I.C.B.S., 2nd series, 1844-48; Thomas, op. cit., p.465.

[21] IC.B.S., 2nd series, 1851; Thomas, op. cit., p. 492.

[22] I.C.B.S., 2nd series, 1851-4; Thomas, op. cit., p. 473.

[23] Thomas, op. cit., pp. 276-8.

[24] ibid., pp. 304-6.

[25] ibid., pp. 298-9.

[26] ibid., p. 626.

[27] ibid., p. 461.

[28] ibid., p. 474.

[29] ibid., pp., 485-6.

[30] ibid., p. 828.

[32] Reverend William Williams to Secretary, dated 7 April 1831, I.C.B.S., Misc. Box 1, 1830-7; Thomas, op. cit., pp. 494-5.

[33] Reverend Henry Jones to Secretary, dated 7 January 1839, I.C.B.S., N/Box 3, 1839-40; Thomas, op. cit., pp. 479-80.

[34] ibid., p. 488.

[34] ibid., p. 453.

[36] ibid., p. 290.

[37] I.C.B.S., 2nd series, 1839; Thomas, op. cit., p. 608.

[38] Reverend J. B. Brown to Secretary, dated 1 August 1844. I.C.B.S., 2nd series, 1844-9; Thomas, op. cit., p. 483.

[39] See Table I.

[40] N.L.W., Church in Wales, SA/DA/1-59.

[41] For the population statistics see B. R. Mitchell and Phyllis Deane, *Abstract of British Historical Statistics* (1962), *passim.*

[42] The decennial rate of increase was as follows: 17.9 in 1801-11; 13.9 in 1811-21; 15.7 in 1821-31; 11.2 in 1831-41; 10.6 in 1841-51; 9.6 in 1851-61 and 11.2 in 1861-71.

[43] K. Davies, 'The Growth and Development of Settlement and Population in Flintshire, 1801-1851', *Flintshire Historical Publications,* 25 (1971-2), 62-97 and '1851-91', 26 (1973-4), 144-69. W. T. R. Pryce, 'Migration and the evolution of culture areas: cultural and linguistic frontiers in north-east Wales, 1750 and 1851', *Trans. Institute of British Geographers,* 65 (June 1975), 79-107; idem.

[44] The analysis is based on the returns in Ieuan Gwynedd Jones, *The Religious Census of 1851. A Calendar of the Returns Relating to Wales,* Vol. 2 North Wales (1981).

[45] I.C.B.S., [MS.] Minutes of Proceedings Prior to The Establishment of the Society, draft of Petition (no date, [May 1817]).

[46] I.C.B.S., 6th *Annual Report* (1824), p.2.

[47] I.C.B.S., 7th *Annual Report* (1825), p.2.

[48] I.C.B.S., *Annual Report* (1833), p. 12.

[49] I.C.B.S., *Annual Report* (1852).

[50] Reverend C. B. Clough, vicar of Mold, to I.C.B.S., 2 May 1836. Cf. also Reverend H. Jones, Holywell Vicarage, to same, 17 February 1857, regarding Brynford; Reverend Thomas Wynne Edwards, Rhuddlan, to same, 17 March 1834,

regarding Rhyl; Reverend R. Briscoe, vicar of Whitford, 28 April 1842, regarding Mostyn; Reverend Maddock Williams, rector of Halkyn, to same, dated 3 June 1844, regarding 'a remote corner of his parish abutting on the parishes of Cilcain and Ysgeifiog where by reason of extensive mining considerable population is congregated' (i.e. Rhes-y-cae).

[51] Reverend Thomas Evans to Secretary, 24 June 1845, I.C.B.S., 2nd series, 1845-6.

[52] Reverend W. Maddock Williams to I.C.B.S., 3 June 1844; I.C.B.S., 2nd series, 1844-8; Thomas, op. cit., p. 465.

[53] Thomas, op. cit., 483-6; I.C.B.S., 2nd series, 1844-9.

[54] N.L.W., Church in Wales, SA/Bounty/123 (19 June 1826) and / 124 (2 November 1866); I.C.B.S., N. Box 3, letter dated 7 January 1839; Thomas, op. cit., pp. 478-82.

[55] I.C.B.S., 2nd series, 1846; Thomas, op. cit., pp. 608-10.

[56] House of Commons, 5 May 1843, *Hansard,* 3rd series, lxviii, 1291.

[57] P.P., 1876, LVIII (125 & 1251), *passim.*

[58] ibid., Summary for Wales, pp. 1-2, for St. Asaph, pp. 61-2.

[59] For the work of the Ecclesiastical Commissioners see G. F. A. Best, *Temporal Pillars Queen Anne's Bounty, the Ecclesiastical Commissioners, and the Church of England* (1964), *passim* and for the Church Building Commissioners see M. H. Port, *Six Hundred New Churches. A Study of the Church Building Commission and its Church Building Activities 1818-56* (1961). The 1876 Returns referred to above for St. Asaph diocese do not distinguish sources of money contributed from outside the diocese.

[60] *Church Builder,* op. cit., p. 42.

[61] P.P. 1852-53, LXXVIII (125), 'Accounts of the Sums expended under the direction of the Commissioners for Building Churches'. The churches were as follows: Bagillt 1841 (cost £1,827.15.5), Cwmaman 1842 (£1,075), Bistre 1843 (£1,091.9.3), Denbigh 1843 (£3,599. ◊ 7.2), Cardiff 1844 (£5,723.16.0), Newtown 1846 (£4,836.17.9), Llangyfelach 1847 (£1,600), Pontfadog 1848 (£849.0.11); Merthyr Tydfil 1848 (£4,109.10.11); Pembroke Dock 1849 (£3,773,13.0), Skewen 1851 (£1,050), Llanelli 1851 (£2,460.2.8), Gwersyllt 1852 (2,404. 10. 10), and St. Woolos 1852) (£2,700).

[62] Total expenditure £408,371 between 1840 and 1875; contributed by I.C.B.S. £9,357. Note that the total expenditure *excludes sums* of less than £500.

[63] Examples of the actual financing of individual projects are given below, pp. 000-000.

[64] I.C.B.S., 50th *Annual Report* (1868), p. 15.

[65] These statistics are based on the Reports of the I.C.B.S., the Minute Books of the Church Building Commissioners and Thomas, op. cit.

[66] Grants to Welsh dioceses up to an including 1868 were as follows: St. Asaph, 98 grants amounting to £13,132: £134 average; Bangor, 100 grants amounting to £9,208: £92 average; St. David's, 203 grants amounting to £20,970: £103 average; Llandaff, 116 grants amounting to £15,946: £137 average. Based on List of Grants, *Report* for 1868, p. 126.

[67] On the Act see Best, op. cit., pp. 357-9.

[68] The districts and the parishes of which they were formed were as follows: Bagillt (Holywell), Connah's Quay (Northop), Mostyn (Whitford) and Bistre, Gwernafield, Nerquis and Pontblyddyn (Mold). Census of 1851, Population, Welsh Division, p. 91. P.P. 1852-3, LXXXVI.

[69] Rhes-y-cae was formed out at Cilcain, Halkyn and Ysgeifiog.

[70] I.C.B.S., Lambeth Palace, B/Box 6, 1839-43, C. B. Clough to Secretary, 7 March 1839 and 8 April 1839.

[71] Clough to I.C.B.S., 2 May 1836, Lambeth Palace, G/Box 2, 1836-38; Thomas, op. cit., pp. 606-7 and 610-11.

[72] Reverend W. Maddock Williams to I.C.B.S., dated 3 June 1844 et seq., I.C.B.S., 2nd series, 1844-48; Thomas, op. cit., p. 465.

[73] The above is based on an analysis of the Tithe Surveys and Apportionments. See also the articles by Davies and by Pryce cited above, and John Bateman, *The Great Landowners of Great Britain and Ireland* (1883), edited by David Spring (1971), p. 513.

[74] Commissioners for Building New Churches, 3rd *Report,* 1823. The cost to the Board of erecting the chapel was £4,051.15s 0d.

[75] The list of major benefactions in the diocese is as follows: Bodelwyddan, £35,000 by Lady Willoughby de Broke; Abergele, £780 by Jones Bateman; Betws and St. John's, £2,560 by the Coed Coch family; Trefnant, £4,200 by the Mainwaring family; Llanddulas, £6,000 by R. B. Lloyd Hesketh; Llanelian, £535 by the Coed Coch family; Llanddewi, £2,700 chiefly by Mr. Sandbach; Llysfaen, £2,300 chiefly by Mr. Hesketh and Mr. Wynne; Llanbedr, £3,100 by J. Jesse; Llanfair porch, £3,200 by Mr. Owen; Rhydymwyn chancel, £3,500 by P. D. Cooke; Pentrefoelas, £2,300 by the Foelas Hall family; Penmynydd, £3,100 by Sir Stephen Glynne; Mold chancel, £6,500 by J. Wynne Eyton; Llansantffraid Glyn Dyfrdwy chancel £2,100 by Lloyd Rhaggatt; Llanuwchllyn, £2,100, half by Sir W. W. Wynn; Pool Quay, £3,100 by Lord Powis; Llwydiarth, £1,200, half by Sir W. W. Wynn; Erbistock, £3,500 by Mrs. Gerardot; Rossett, £2,600 by J. Townshend; Tallarn Green, £800 by Lord Keynon; Bettisfield, £6,000 by Lord Hanmer.

[76] Thomas, op. cit, p. 828. The architect was G. E. Street, who designed the new Law Courts in London (1868), the new nave of Bristol cathedral and who carried out extensive repairs at York Minster and at Salisbury and Carlisle cathedrals (*c.* 1871).

[77] Lambeth Palace, I.C.B.S., Ysgeifiog X Y Z and Misc. Box 1, 1830-37, Reverend Williams Williams to the Society, 4 July 1831, 15 March 1831, 7 April 1831, and 7 July 1837.

[78] Reverend Maddock Williams to I.C.B.S., dated 3 June 1844 and 6 March 1845, Lambeth Palace, I.C.B.S.

[79] St. Asaph Diocesan Society for Promoting Building, Enlargement and Endowment of Churches and Chapel *Reports* 1835-38. The income of the Society was as follows: 1835—£1,945.12.0; 1836—£2,196.2.5; 1837—£2,602.14.11; 1838—£467.7.0. See also Bishop Joshua Hughes, *Charge at his Second Visitation* (London, 1874).

[80] Society for Promoting the Enlargement and Building of Churches and Chapels, [First] *Annual Report* (1819), p.11.

[81] ibid., p. 14.

[82] For Sir Thomas Phillip's role in church extension in Llandaff see Wilton D. Wills, 'The Established Church in the Diocese of Llandaff, 1850-70: a study of the Evangelical Movement in the South Wales coalfield', *Welsh History Review* 4, no. 3 (June 1969), 235 *passim.*

[83] Sir Thomas Phillips, *Wales* (1849), pp. 491-2. He spoke in the annual general meeting of the Incorporated Society, 21 May 1851. *Report* for 1851, p. 13.

[84] Quoted by G. H. Sumner, op. cit., pp. 122-3.

[85] See J. Bossy, *The English Catholic Community 1570-1850* (1957): John Hickey, *Urban Catholics: Urban Catholicism in England from 1829 to the Present Day* (1967).

[86] I.C.B.S., *Annual Report* (1851), p. 10.

[87] On these two churches, with the names of the principal contributors, see Thomas, op. cit., pp. 473-4 (Brynford) and pp. 492-3 (Gorsedd).

[88] Williams to I.C.B.S., dated 18 April 1831, Lambeth Palace, I.C.B.S.

[89] ibid., 12 March 1844.

[90] ibid., 7 April 1831.

[91] I.C.B.S., *Annual Report* (1851), p. 13.

[92] I.C.B.S., *Annual Report* (1840).

[93] I.C.B.S., *Annual Report* (1842), pp. 50-1.
[94] I.C.B.S., *Annual Report* (1848), pp. 10-11.
[95] I.C.B.S., *Annual Report* (1852), pp. 13-14.
[96] ibid., p. 14.

CHURCH RECONSTRUCTION IN NORTH CARDIGANSHIRE IN THE NINETEENTH CENTURY*

At the consecration of Llanddeiniol new church in October 1835 the Reverend John Hughes, vicar of Llanbadarn Fawr (and later Archdeacon of Cardigan) preached from the text 'Surely I will not go into the tabernacle of my house, nor go up into my bed; I will not give sleep unto mine eyes, or slumber to mine eyelids, until I find out a place for the Lord, an habitation for the mighty God of Jacob' (Psalm 132,$^{2-5}$).^{1} In the course of his sermon the reverend gentleman drew analogies betweeen a Jerusalem bereft of its temple and a deanery of Llanbadarn Fawr sorely lacking places of worship and he could, given the circumstances, be forgiven his rhetoric and rhodomontade. In fact, if there was one thing the deanery did not lack in the 1830s it was places of worship, and the Victorian era in this district was an era of extreme religiosity. As we shall see, churches were added from time to time, but basically what we have to observe during that period is the reconstitution of church life, its inward adaptation and its outward reconstruction in the face of changing circumstances.

It would not be difficult to show that this part of Cardiganshire was in some important yet mysterious respects deeply religious. The contribution of Cardiganshire as a whole to the religious life of Britain has been enormous, and one which is probably almost as old as the coming of Christianity itself. The furthest ecclesiastical point in the vast parish of Llanbadarn Fawr—sixteen long and heavy miles from the parish church—is the chapelry of Yspyty Cynfyn with its ancient church set like an exotic jewel in a Celtic stone circle. The name Llanbadarn itself sends the mind reeling back through the centuries to its foundation in the Age of the Saints and to its role as a cathedral and abbey church under the native dynasties, while the name 'Yspyty' reminds us of the existence of that indigenous Cistercian House of Strata Florida whose influence, cultural and religious, on this part of its domaine was immense throughout the centuries. One thinks of the Methodist Revivals of the eighteenth century, and it is a peculiarity of that extraordinary continuing experience that one of its epicentres was at Llangeitho, and that the southern part of the county, within the immediate influence as it were of that little village, continued to spawn a succession of revivals long after the other religious centre at Trevecca had lost its heat and been dampened in the formal life of an academic institution. And not only the southern part of the county. The most astounding revival of Victorian times in Wales began only a few miles from Aberystwyth at Tre'rddol and Ystumtuen, Bontgoch and Pontrhydygroes, and Yspyty Ystwyth in 1858-9. And the last great Welsh revival—that of 1904-5—likewise began in the southern seaside parishes of the county.

We might allude also to other remarkable facts to show the religious vigour of these parts. Here is the home of Tractarianism in Wales, and Llangorwen was the first Tractarian church in Wales.[2] Indeed, the *Ecclesiologist* proclaimed it to be 'a church as it should be . . . One of the most complete and successful imitations of ancient models that the present age has produced'.[3] It was no accident that it should have been founded in that parish and I hope to show that much that was chacteristic in its worship was already present in the worshipping customs of many other churches. Then, going off in another direction, one could point to the long and honourable educational activities of churchmen in these parts. Ystrad Meurig in the north of the deanery, was famous for its grammar school long before and long after Bishop Burgess founded Lampeter in 1826. Indeed, one wonders where the Anglican Church would have recruited its priests in Wales if it has not been for the readiness of north Cardiganshire men to enter the church. Archdeacon David Evans (a Llanrhystud man) in his *Recollections* published in 1904, actually list 59 men who had to his knowledge entered the ministry from that one parish in his own lifetime, and the Rev Lewis Evans, vicar of Llanbadarn Fawr, told his cousin, Isaac Williams, of Cwmcynefin that 'there are more young men educated for Holy Orders from Llanfihangel Geneu'r Glyn and neighbourhood than any other given locality in Wales'.[4] One would need to know what was the quality of the education they received, but the fact that Rowland Williams—'Bunsen's reviewer' in *Essays and Reviews*—was Vice-Principal at Lampeter from 1850 to 1862 should give us pause, as also should the fact that it was still customary for young men who could not afford the £50 fees of Lampeter to go much more cheaply to Ystrad Meurig or (sometimes the best alternative) to a Dissenting Academy.

I stated at the beginning that the main problem facing the church in the deanery was not merely or mainly a shortage of churches. This was certainly the case when the movement for reform of the church began in the early 1830s. The main problems then and for a considerable time after were the inexorable facts of dilapidation. With the exception of the Chapel of St. Michael's in the borough of Aberystwyth and new buildings to serve new districts, such as Llangorwen (1841), Elerch (1868), St. Mary's Aberystwyth (1873), Penrhyncoch (1881) and Trinity (1886),[5] the activity was confined to re-building or reconstructing existing churches or, in a few cases, carrying out extensive repair works. Dilapidation was the curse of the church in North Cardiganshire. This was true throughout rural Wales, as the Incorporated Church Building Society had come to recognize by 1851. 'Many of the churches in Wales are in a much more dilapidated condition than any in England, and yet, like those in the latter country, are susceptible of complete restoration'.[6] Of the 14 churches and chapels in the deanery in the early 1830s, no less than 12 were either completely rebuilt or otherwise heavily restored on account of the desperately poor state of the fabric. 'Damp and uncomfortable', 'in a state of disrepair', 'very dilapidated'—these are the reasons one finds in Vestry Books, in Faculties petitioned for and granted, and in articles of consecration.[7]

This raises some interesting questions. To what extent were these churches *in fact* as bad as they were stated to be? There is always a subjective element in judgments of that kind, and fashion and changing sensibilities exert an influence. The Visitation Queries and Answers, both Wardens' and Ministers', often give the impression that all is well with the fabric, yet a few years later a church has disappeared and a new one built because of the alleged dilapidation, dampness or inconvenience of the old. There is no denying that most were in a very bad way. Archdeacon David Evans in his book of recollections[8] describes how cold and uncomfortable was Llanrhystud, with its shuttered windows, its earth-floor 'mixed with the bones of our ancestors', its few pews and cruelly hard benches. Moreover, they had been like this for many, many years, and one suspects that they were no worse and no better at the beginning of the nineteenth century than they had been at the beginning of the eighteenth. One would not wish to play down the dilapidations endemic in the churches of the region, but at the same time one might suggest that the sudden and sustained burst of restoration should be regarded as an indicator of a deep change in fashion. People's apprehension of reality changes, as does their ideal of religious behaviour. That is to say, church restoration is a symptom of cultural change—of rejection of the old and the acceptance of the new.

One sees this from time to time in the petitions for faculties for reconstruction. What exactly is meant by 'Unfit for divine service' in the Llanddeiniol petition of 1833?[9] Or old St. Michael's in 1831—when at the previous episcopal visitation the wardens declared the building to be satisfactory?[10] One suspects that incumbents were looking for ways of getting rid of the old box pews in order to replace them with benched open pews. By the mid-Victorian years this is quite clear. Llanilar was entirely reconstructed in order to make it possible to perform modern liturgical forms of service. 'Pews badly made originally, now out of repair, uncomfortable to sit in and most inconvenient for kneeling—a general wish on the part of the congregation for open seats and a better arrangement of the whole internal fittings, especially, of the chancel. The space around the altar being so limited by the pews . . . as to render difficult a reverent receiving of the Holy Communion; and above all, to render the building generally more worthy of them to whose service it is dedicated'.[11] Here we have a religious or liturgical revolution, with its popular undertones, demanding a reconstruction of the internal arrangements along more democratic, or religiously equal, lines. But Mr. Parry of Llidiarde, the local squire, insisted on a first choice of eight sittings for himself and four of his servants! The plans for the new church at Yspyty Ystrad-meurig were criticized for leaving too narrow a step at the altar for the priest to kneel at.[12] That was towards the end of the century and by then the aspirations and changing fashions of the few at the beginning of the century had become the accepted norm of the many.

Equally an obsession with Victorian clergymen and laymen was the pressing need to provide accommodation where it was needed. This was a problem aggravated by the enormous size of the parishes. The 14 churches served an area of 174,000 acres. Llanbadarn Fawr itself covered 52,750 acres, Llanfihangel Geneu'r Glyn 32,825, and Llanfihangel y Creuddyn 22,553. The boundaries, of course, were medieval and represented the enclosing of territories sufficient to provide the incomes for incumbents (and in some cases for the appropriators of the livings, for there were no rectories, as we shall see). For centuries these vast hill parishes had supported their sparse pastoral populations and the parish churches and the few chapels of ease had supplied such means of grace as was demanded. Demand changed in response to the operation of two main forces, the one physical, the other spiritual. The first was the growth and the redistribution of population, and possibly it was the redistribution which was of most immediate relevance to the clergy.[13] The villages, especially those in the valley bottoms and in the coastal region almost certainly expanded, but much more serious was the appearance of entirely new communities settled around the lead-mines. Most of these were situated in areas very distant from the parish churches, as in Cwmsymlog, Goginan, Ystumtuen, Cwm Ystwyth, the hinterland of Talybont, and Elerch, and other places. There was an obvious need for chapels of ease in strategic places. The other factor was equally powerful, namely, the demand being made for the means of religious worship. The Nonconformists were the quickest off the mark: indeed, it was they, and particularly the Calvinistic Methodists, who created the demand in the first place—who stimulated that enormous hydroptic thirst for spiritual things which periodically exploded in revivals and which by mid-century had resulted in an extraordinary chapel-building activity throughout the deanery. In an area exactly continuous with the deanery there were by 1905 no less than 105 chapels and schoolrooms.[14]

Hence the response of the church from the 1830s onwards. Capel Bangor, built in exactly the style of Eglwysfach, was opened in 1839 to accommodate the growing communities of the neighbourhood, mainly leadminers from nearby Goginan and the slopes of the Ystwyth. Llangorwen in 1841, as is well known, was *sui generis,* but it is important to note that the petition of Matthew Davies Williams of Cwmcynfelin and Wallog pleaded the inadequate means of religious instruction to the demands of the populous and increasing parish of Llanbadarn Fawr.[15] St. Peter's, Elerch was built by Lewis Gilbertson and his family for the same reason—the means of religious worship being inadequate in a valley busily being exploited for its lead.[16] St. Mary's, Aberystwyth was built for the Welsh population—to enable the authorities to achieve what was always a major aim of the Welsh hierarchy in the Victorian church, namely, to keep the two languages separate.[17] St. Matthew's, Borth was opened in 1879—in this case a direct response to the building of the railway and an investment in seaside-resort business.[18] Penrhyncoch, consecrated in 1881 was situated like a Norman castle at the ancient crossroads into and out of the mine-bearing valleys.[19] Finally, Trinity in Aberystwyth in 1886-8,[20] and the new St. Michael's in 1890.[21] Of these, Eglwysfach (in 1855), Elerch (1868), Trinity (1887) and Penrhyncoch (1901)[22] were made into District Chapelries, so that by the end of the century the deanery had no less than 18 places of worship and in addition was holding services in some other unconsecrated buildings, such as the school at Penparcau.[23]

None of this undoubted increase in efficiency was accomplished without cost, and here the church faced what was undoubtedly its greatest obstacle, poverty. Apart, perhaps, from the town of Aberystwyth itself, the deanery was probably the poorest part of the county and one of the poorest in Wales. Its economic resources were small and the wealth that was produced exceedingly unevenly divided. 'The inhabitants of the parish', wrote the incumbent of Llanafan, Rev. D. E. Jones to the Church Building Society in December 1836, 'with the exception of a few persons hereinafter named, are persons of low and narrow circumstances in life, being either employed in the mine works, or as labourers under Agriculturists of the neighbourhood. The seven or eight farmers in the parish are of limited means, excepting one Proprietor . . .'[24] Dr. Turner, the Medical Officer of the Privy Council reported in 1866 that 'the children pine for want of food as soon as weaned', and gave it as his opinion that were it not for the prevailing mild weather the people would all die.[25]

Poverty of the masses, however, was something distinct from the poverty of the Church: the two were linked only in that their causes were not singular but common, and insofar as the Church, given the prevailing religious climate of Nonconformity, could not look to the general population for assistance. It could look only to its own resources and to the assistance it could expect from its natural allies, the gentry. These latter, where they were patrons and impropriators, in any case had a legal obligation as well as a religious duty to assist. In North Cardiganshire, as in the county generally, lay patrons outnumbered ecclesiastical patrons but by no stretch of the imagination can they be said to have fulfilled their duties with a proper regard for the spiritual welfare of their inferiors. The advowsons of new churches were always kept within the church itself or vested in ecclesiastical persons.[26]

Much more serious was the poverty due to the alienation of tithes to laymen. There was only one rectory in the deanery worth only £93: all the livings were impropriated and only one of these to an ecclesiastical corporation—the end result being the same, of course. The most notorious of the lay impropriators was the family of Chichester from Devonshire, who owned the tithes of no less than nine of the parishes. From these he derived £5,411 annually in tithes. The total income of the incumbents of those nine livings was £1,127—an average of £125 p.a., ranging from a high of £221 to a low of £88. Most of this income came from Queen Anne's Bounty or from parliamentary grants: Chichester's contribution in fixed stipends (payable out of his £5,411 from tithes) amounted to not more than about £60 or £70 per annum.[27] So far as I have been able to discover J.B.S. Chichester gave not a penny to any of the work of reconstruction and renovation and repair.[28]

Chichester influence on the deanery was therefore or critical importance and had maleficent effects. It was poverty caused by his depredations that was the underlying cause of the far too numerous pluralities that existed. Eight of the livings were plural livings,[29] and not until towards the end of the century had this necessary evil been removed and each parish provided with its own resident priest. It accounted also for the poor state of the fabric to which we have alluded, and when one considers the great amount of money spent in the restorations and rebuildings we can appreciate that for this to have happened while the deanery was steadily being milked of its substance by Chichester must have involved a tremendous effort on the part of clergy and laymen. Local gentry were very generous, especially the Pryse family of Gogerddan: the Powells of Nanteos less so, perhaps: they insisted on the full market price when negotiating the transfer of the land to the Ecclesiastical Commissioners for the third St. Michael's. But the bulk of the money in the outlying parishes came by voluntary subscriptions, by grants from the Church Building Society, and from the profits of various fund-raising community actions. After 1856 the raising of Church rates was no longer attempted in the deanery.[30] A few figures will show what was happening. In the deanery as a whole between 1840 and 1876 a total of £19,660 had been spent on church building and restoration, and of this sum no less than £19,170 had been raised by voluntary subscription, £285 from the Church Building Society and £200 (at Llancynfelyn) by a church rate (in 1834).[31] So, this poor county accomplished what was virtually a complete rebuilding and restoration programme out of its own resources, and when we consider the enormous amplitude of Nonconformist places of worhsip going up at the same time, or themselves being rebuilt and restored, it will sufficiently be understood that my original claim about the religiosity of the county holds good.

The fact that two of the new churches were virtually erected, furnished and partially endowed by private families does not affect the argument. Llangorwen and Elerch were wholly untypical in their origin and style. They were certainly deeply untypical of the prevailing theological climate of the deanery. The Rev. Owain Jones has argued in his book on Isaac Williams and in his articles on Tractarianism that there was little that was accidental in the location here of these Tractarian churches but that, on the contrary, there existed a powerful tradition, albeit confined to a few families, of High Churchmanship dating from the Jacobitism of the early eighteenth century.[32] The evidence he adduces is not entirely convincing. A study of the Visitation Returns for the whole century indicates that by the early nineteenth century at least (returns of 1807) institutions such as monthly communions, more than one service per Sunday, weekday services, and services (sometimes with communion) on the main festivals were pretty common. This reflected not a High Church tradition but a strong evangelical one and was probably as much a response to Methodistical demands for the regularity of the sacrament as an inbred High Churchmanship. Moreover, what on the surface appear to be Tractarian innovations on deeper reflection turn out to be unconscious survivals from the Roman Catholic past. It is necessary always to remember that religious development always produces its own forms of social competition, and there is no doubt that this provided a powerful motivation in the reconstruction movement. I have illustrated this theme from the history of the rebuilding of the second St. Michael's, and there is no need to amplify here.[33] Nor should one forget that once the physical presence of the Williamses and Gilbertsons had been removed the churches they had built and endowed soon reverted to a more socially acceptable style of public worship. Some differences remained and traditions survived, but they were minor and quite superficial. Today, we can admire and be thankful for the buildings: but buildings alone cannot perpetuate a revolution.

We can therefore understand the true significance of the movement as a whole in the Victorian era. Mainly, I think, it was highly symptomatic of a profound change in the church's conception of itself. It started as a church in a very religious society, the causes of whose religiosity are probably to be found deep in the social changes being endured by the people as a whole, and in organized movements standing outside and often in opposition to it. It had contributed much to the religious life of the county, but the initiatives had moved elsewhere. It had been slow to analyze the nature of its role in a society which demographic and economic forces were rapidly changing, and slow to adapt even when the consequences of these changes became apparent. It ended by being a church virtually on the voluntary principle, and so far as its social role was concerned not very different from that of the chapels. This, after all, was a reflection of the deep community of the region itself. There is something slightly grotesque in the idea that a few wealthy men could come into this ancient county from outside and by introducing a new theology change its nature in a generation or so. Methodism was an indigenous thing: that was its strength, and its values were those of the people among whom it spread. In the end it is people who make theology.

But finally, it ended as a church most beautifully equipped in its fabric. We should think not only of the great architects: of Underwood, Butterfield, Ritchie and Seddon: we should think also of the common people who so readily responded to a religious ideal of decency, modesty and quiet, assured beauty. Looking at Elerch Church who can fail to see how richly Butterfield must have responded to the genius of the place? Its harmony goes deep and there is a powerful repose in the way that it lies on the land. North Cardiganshire imposes itself on its buildings, and in the end it is people and history that remain.

NOTES

*The article was first published in *The National Library of Wales Journal* XX No. 4, Winter 1978.

[1] N.L.W., SD/C/119. Draft consecration dated 6 October 1835.
[2] On Tractanarianism in Wales, see O. W. Jones, *Isaac Williams and his circle* (London), 1971) and the same author's article 'The Mind of Robert Raikes', *Journal of the Historical Society of the Church in Wales,* XVIII (1968). See also D. Eifion Evans, 'Mudiad Rhydychen yng Ngogledd Sir Aberteifi', *ibid., iv*(1954), pp. 45ff.
[3] Quoted in O. W. Jones, *op. cit.,* p.96.
[4] *ibid.,* p.104.
[5] For details of the building and consecration of these churches see N.L.W., SD/C/150 (Llangorwen, 16 December 1841), SD/C/76 (Elerch, 29 June 1868), SD/C/11 (St. Mary's Aberystwyth, 3 June 1873), SD/C/224 (Penrhyncoch, 14 June 1881), SD/C/8, 9, 11 (Holy Trinity Aberystwyth, 10 August 1886, 29 November 1888 and 31 May 1899). For St. Michael's, Aberystwyth, see below pp. 70-87.
[6] Incorporated Church Building, *Third Quarterly Report,* 1850-1, pp. 11-12.
[7] For example, N.L.W., SD/F/330, Llanfihangel-Geneu'r'-Glyn, 8 May 1884 for Vestry Minute; SD/F/450, Llanychaiarn, Vestry Minutes dated 12 December 1877; SD/F/399, Llanilar, Vestry Minute dated 8 May 1873; SD/F/380, Llangwyryfon, for taking down an entirely removing the old church.
[8] David Evans, *Adgofion yr Hybarch David Evans Arch-ddiacon Llanelwy* (Lampeter, 1904), p.7. See also E. D. Jones, 'Some aspects of the history of the Church in North

Cardiganshire in the eighteenth century', *Journal. Hist. Soc. of the Church in Wales*, VIII (1953).

[9] N.L.W., SD/C/120 P.

[10] N.L.W., SD/C/13 s (d), and N.L.W., St. Michael's MSS and Documents, and 1807 Visitation Returns (Wardens') where they return that the fabric is in good repair.

[11] N.L.W., SD/F/399/M (letter dated 2 April 1874).

[12] N.L.W., SD/F/690. Faculty granted 28 December 1897.

[13] Most of the townships into which the large parishes of Llanbadarn Fawr, Llanfihangel Geneu'r Glyn and Llanfihangel-y-Creuddyn were divided lost population during the century. Only the townships where lead-mining was an important sector in the economy showed anything like sustained increases; for example Broncastellan, Elerch, Cwm Rheidol, Melindwr, Parsel Canol, the parish of Llanafan, Llanfihangel-y-Creuddyn Uchaf, and Gwnws.

[14] Royal Commission on the Church of England and other religious bodies in Wales and Monmouthshire, vol. 6,pp. 29 ff. See also N.L.W., SD/S/10/1 'Statistics of Church Work, Finance and Property of the year 1899-1900'.

[15] N.L.W., SD/C/150. Consecration dated 16 December 1841. Among ths inhabitants who signed the petition were Matthew Davies Williams of Cwmcynfelin and Wallog, and his son, Rev. Isaac Williams, who gave the land, part of Nantcellan Fawr farm.

[16] N.L.W., SD/C/76. Consecration dated 29 June 1868. Among the petitioners were Rev. Lewis Gilbertson, Fellow of Jesus College, Oxford, of Cefn-gwyn, whose family gave the land.

[17] N.L.W., SD(C/11. Consecration dated 3 June 1873.

[18] N.L.W., SD/C/27. Consecration dated 15 September 1879.

[19] N.L.W., SD/C/224. Consecration dated 14 June 1881.

[20] N.L.W., SD/C/145. Sentence of consecration dated 30 September 1890.

[22] N.L.W., SD/OC/49 (Eglwys-fach, dated 27 November 1854); SD/OC/108 (Elerch, dated 14 September 1868); SD/OC/148 (Holy Trinity, dated 12 July 1877); SD/OC/163 (Penrhyncoch, dated 10 December 1901).

[23] N.L.W., SD/S/10/1. See also the series SD/DS, from which the chronology and location of the use of unconsecrated places would appear to be as follows: 1834 Rhydmeirionydd (Llanfihangel Geneu'r Glyn); 1839 Aberystwyth; 1842 Borth; 1862 Elerch; 1863 Penparcau; 1863 Penrhyncoch; 1866 Llanafan; 1870 Llanfihangel-y-Creuddyn; 1876 Borth (again); 1878 Llanychain; 1879 Talybont; 1882 Commins Coch; 1822 Llanddeiniol: 1884 Llanfihangel Geneu'r Glyn.

[24] Petition from Rev. D. E. Jones to the Incorporated Church Building Society, dated from Llanafan 27 December 1836, File No. B2225.

[25] Seventh Report of the Medical Officer of the Privy Council, with Appendix, *Parliamentary Papers,* 1865, XXVI. i. p.498.

[26] In 1835 the position was as follows: the Bishop exercised the patronage of 4 livings, a vicar of 1, and Brecknock Collegiate Church of 1; lay patrons owned the advowsons of 7 livings, and the inhabitants of a Chapelry 1 other. In 1900 the position was as follows: the Bishop was patron of 8 livings, a vicar of 1, ecclesiastical persons of 2, lay person of 5, and the inhabitants of a chapelry of 1. *Royal Commission on the Church of England,* vol. 5, p.190.

[27] For details of incomes, appropriations etc., consult Ecclesiastical Duties and Revenues Report, 'P.P., 1835, XXII, Table No. 4, which gives the values etc. as at 31 December 1831. For the ownership of tithes around mid-century see 'Tithes commuted and apportioned . . . distinguishing those assigned to Clerical Appropriators . . ., P.P., 1848, (298); details for all the parishes can be found in summary form in Ieuan

Gwynedd Jones and David Williams, *The Religious Census of 1851, A Calendar of the Returns Relating to Wales* (Cardiff, 1976), *passim.*

²⁸There is evidence that he positively refused to subscribe to the parish church of Llanbadarn Fawr: see Rev. David Evans, incumbent, to the Incorporated Church Building Society dated from Llanbadarn 28 June 1837. Also, same to same, dated 12 March 1838 where he states that Chicheester had not deigned to reply even though the chancel was in a bad state of decay.

²⁹In 1835, Chichester was the impropriator of Eglwys-fach, Llanafan a'r Trawsgoed, Llanbadarn Fawr, Llanddeiniol, Llanfihangel Geneu'r-glyn, Llanfihangel-y-Creuddyn, Llangwyryfon, Llancynfelin, Llanilar, and Llanychaearn. All these, with the exception of the first and last, were held in plurality.

³⁰'Return of the amount of Church Rates received and expended by Churchwardens in the years ending Easter 1832, 1839 and 1854', P.P., 1857 (Session 2), XXXII (88), and 'Return of the names of all parishes in cities or parliamentary boroughs . . . in which (during the last fifteen years) Church Rates have been refused, and since that time ceases to be collected', P.P., 1856, XLVIII (319).

³¹'Returns showing the number of churches . . . which have been built or restored at a cost exceeding £500 since 1840', P.P., 1876, LVIII (125 and 125 I).

³²O. W. Jones, *op. cit.,* pp. 92 ff. See also D. Eifion Evans, *art. cit.*

³³see below pp. 70-85.

THE REBUILDING OF LLANRHYSTUD CHURCH*

For most denominations in most places throughout Wales in modern times capital investment in religion has invariably involved deficit financing. Loans and borrowings, mortgages and an anxious preoccupation with the flow of money have been the inevitable concomitants of religious adherence. Debt, when kept within reasonable bounds, has been regarded generally not with distaste but accepted as eminently respectable, at once the indicator of relative success, the cement in the community, and the strongest argument for community survival. Whatever might be the motive to invest, and whatever forms that investment might take as, for example, the decision to build a church or chapel, to rebuild and enlarge an existing one, to add a schoolroom or vestry, install an organ, or beautify the fabric, the commitment once undertaken would be a continuing one, and thereafter come to constitute a primary element in the life of the community concerned. This is true whether the community were church or chapel, for the difference in organization between the two was not, as polemicists on both sides tended to argue, as between voluntaryism on the one side and of national endowment supplemented by legally enforcible systems of local taxation on the other, but of the relative degrees of voluntaryism in both. This was increasingly so from the mid-century onwards. By then, the £1,500,000 voted by parliament for the building of new churches in populous places had been used up—Old St. Michael's, Aberystwyth, had benefited from this to the tune of £1,289 in 1832—and contemporaneously, the traditional forms of local taxation for ecclesiastical purposes—the Church Rate—was increasingly coming under attack.[1] The Established Church, as a direct result, was becoming more 'voluntaryist' in its outlook, more dependent than it had ever been before on the philanthropy of its members. Well might Bishop Ollivant of Llandaff declare in 1854 that 'There is no Church on earth more dependent on the voluntary principle than the Church of England was'.[2] The bishop, of course, was thinking of the situation primarily in his own diocese, where 'spiritual destitution' was at its sharpest and the need for church reconstruction greatest. There the situation was of recent growth, for in Llandaff, as in other populous dioceses, the appalling in-adequacy of church provision was the product of migration into the mining and manufacturing districts, the overwhelming of old provision by the new potential demands. But there was also another side to the way in which churchmen regarded spiritual destitution and church extension, namely, a still dimly appre-hended suspicion that the roots of the trouble lay deeper back in time and in regions untouched by industrial development and urban growth, that is to say, in the deep rural parishes, in the countryside. If the problem in the rapidly expanding towns was a lack of churches, in the countryside it was dilapidation that caused concern, ruined and ruinous churches, cynically-re-garded advowsons, over-large parishes, endowments diverted from religion, and weary and disillusioned pastors. How to deal with this complex situation posed enormous difficulties: how in fact it was done in one small, rural parish is the purpose of this paper.

*   *   *   *   *

Llanrhystud's problem was relatively simple. It was not 'spiritual destitution' in the sense of a lack of provision for religious worship. The four Calvinistic Methodist chapels, the one Baptist, and the parish church between them offered accom-modation for nearly 1,400 people—this in a parish of only 1,516.[3] To this total the church contributed 120, but there is no evidence that this was not considered to be sufficient, and long before the middle of the century the overwhelmingly Methodist character of the parish had been well established and come to be accepted. Nor was the fact that all the church room was approp-riated, that is, allocated to the exclusive use of named indi-viduals or families leaving only a little free space under the tower for the use of children, regarded as a grievance. Llanrhystud's problem was simply that the church building was in a ruinous condition, dilapidated and depressed. From time to time repairs had been attempted, the latest in 1839 when £12 had been spent in an attempt to repair the roof. It may be that the contemporary print of the old church (Plate I) exaggerates the

Old Llanrhystud Church.

The new Church.

air of romantic decay, but it certainly does suggest that the roof threatened to collapse at any moment, and that large-scale restoration might be necessary. In this Llanrhystud was typical of many parish churches in rural Wales, all crying out for the same remedy.[4]

The fact that there was no spiritual destitution as such in the parish made the problem not easier to solve but more difficult, for it meant that the parish could not make any claim on ecclesiastical resources centrally administered, such as those of the Church Building Commissioners. The parish was thrown back on its own resources, and the story of what then transpired must be read against a background of a parish strained to the uttermost to provide itself with what the Fifteenth Homily called 'a convenient place to resort to, and to come together, to praise and magnify God's holy name', like unto a house 'having all things in order, and all corners sweet and clean . . . well adorned, with places convenient to sit in . . . kept clean, comely, and sweet'. For Llanrhystud was a relatively poor parish, embarking on the largest, financially the most exacting, undertaking ever contemplated in its long history, at a time when there can have been scarcely any surplus available for common use. Consider for a moment the people of the parish, their numbers, occupations, and probable incomes. In 1851, when the decision to build was taken, they numbered 1,516, of whom 712 were men and 804 women. If we exclude children under twelve years as being too young to contribute substantially to the labour force—though this is a very conservative estimate of the working age, for the census enumerator described the ten year old son of Pentreafter as a shepherd—the working population is immediately reduced by 480. Exclude again the aged, say, over 60 years (there were only 13 aged 80 years and over), and you exclude another 125. Deduct the 14 paupers aged 12 years and over, and the so-called 'poor women', and we are left with an effective working population of not more than 900 people—that is, men, women and children over twelve and under sixty years of age. The new church would have to be paid for from the surplus production of these.

Who were these people? What occupations did they follow? How did they support themselves and their children, the

widows, orphans and the hopelessly poor? All, with the exception of the 12 mariners and some of the craftsmen employed
in building and repairing ships, were either directly or indirectly
farmers, rearing live-stock and tilling the land. The largest
single occupation group were the farmers: 127 heads of families
were thus described. In addition, there were 67 labourers
(including agricultural labourers), a groom, a woodsman, a
stone-setter, and a shepherd (the ten-year-old boy), all of these
living in their own houses and most of them, though not all,
cultivating small plots of land. The labour force was made up of
the families of the farmers themselves, supplemented by a total
of 151 resident servants (74 male and 77 female). Scattered
about the parish, though mainly concentrated in the village,
were the craftsmen—the blacksmiths (9), the saddlers (2), the
carpenters (9), masons (8), the glazier, and the painter. There
were the trades using the products of the land, like the spinners
(7), the wool-carders (3), the tucker, and the stockinger. There
were the makers of clothes, such as the tailors (5), the dress-
makers (5), the shoemakers (13). The villages contained three
shopkeepers, a butcher, a hatter, and a tea-dealer, and in
addition there were three inns. Finally, there were ministers of
religion, the sexton, and the policeman.[5]

How well off were they? We can only surmise that they were
on the whole pretty poor. Consider the facts from which we can
infer an answer. The vast majority of the farmers were tenant
farmers. There was only one estate, organized as such, in the
parish, and that—Mabws—was only 2,021 acres. S. D. Davies
of Moelifor owned about 870 acres, and the Hughes family of
Alltlwyd 536 acres. To all intents and purposes there was only
one large proprietor and, judged by county standards, he was of
a minor magnitude. What is important to consider is the way in
which the 8,491 acres of cultivated and cultivable land was
divided out among the farmers. The Tithe Survey of 1841
depicts a parish morcellated into a patchwork of very small farms
and holdings. If we take the total area held by farmers of more
than ten acres, we find that there were no less than 139 of them,
giving an average farm size of about 54 acres. But the bulk of
these—84 of them—were well below the average size of 68 acres,
14 of 120 acres, 5 of 180 acres, and there was only one farm of

more than 250 acres. In addition, there were the smallholdings, more than 40 of them of an average size of 6 acres. These, as we have already observed, belonged to craftsmen, or were held by labourers, agricultural or otherwise, or attached as grazing to the inns. Many of them, no doubt, had originated as 'tai un-nos', particularly in the north west of the parish. The pattern of land-owning and of land-holding and usage was, in fact, very similar to that described by Dr. Dafydd Jenkins, and I suspect that it would not be difficult to distinguish the various categories of holdings according to his classification.[6]

Inevitably for the bulk of the community this was a sub-sistence economy. Money would play a relatively minor role in the complicated nexus of economic and social relationships in it. Yet money was necessary part of the working of the parish. Rents had to be paid in cash, and so did the local taxes. The Poor Rate—the heaviest financial obligation of the parishioners—for the year 1850-51 amounted to £545.9s, raised by four rates of 6d in the pound.[7] It is interesting to note that Llanrhystud Mefenydd—the coastal area, including the village and the best agricultural land—was assessed at 9d for one of these rates. The Poor Rate, of course, was administered centrally by the elected Guardians of the Aberystwyth Union, and a proportion of it would have been spent within the parish, for example, maintain-ing the 31 paupers. Money for other, purely parochial purposes, was raised annually as it has been from time immemorial. Highways not under the control of Turnpike Trusts required to be maintained, bridges kept in repair, the overseers' expenses covered, and above all, the church and church-yard kept in a state of repair. Repair of the church required its own special rate and it was customary for a special rate of 1d to be raised as and when required. Finally, there was the burden of tithes, which had been commuted for a rent-charge of £620 payable annually, the vicar's share of this being £170. Thus, local government of one kind and another made considerable financial demands on the parishioners, and one suspects that the extraordinarily complicated system of land-holding—the morcellation or farms, the complex renting out of fields to neighbours by even minor farmers—was determined not only by farming needs, but also by the necessity actually to raise cash for these parochial purposes.

It was thus a poor community already pressed for ready money which undertook this relatively enormous commitment to rebuild its parish church. How did the parishioners go about it? The decision was taken by the vestry, in which the leading figures were the vicar, the two churchwardens, and the leading farmers. The incumbent of the vicarage of Llanrhystud and the rectory of Rhosdie was John Lewis, a native of Llangwyryfon, who had been appointed to the living by its patron, the bishop of St. David's, in 1834.[8] In 1851 he was fifty years of age and lived at Rhiwgoch with his wife, six children, four farm servants, a dairy maid, and a housemaid—a household, it should be noted, containing as many servants as Mabws. As livings went in Cardiganshire it was rather above the average, being worth £170 a year (excluding other minor source of income) which was the amount allowed him by the appropriators, the Precentor and Chapter of the cathedral, out of the £620 for which the tithes were commuted.[9] As vicar, he was the ecclesiastical ruler of the parish and presided at the vestry meetings. Assisting him were the two wardens, elected annually by the parish, who were therefore men of quite considerable influence with whom he would have to co-operate closely and without whom nothing of importance concerning the ecclesiastical government of the parish could be done. In 1851, these were Richard Thomas, one of the village shopkeepers, and Evan Herbert of Brynffosydd, a farmer of 60 acres, the farm being rented of the Reverend James Morris.[10] These two had been wardens for a number of years and had been responsible for raising and spending a penny rate (which brought in a little more than £9) on the church fairly regularly during that period. The last rate had been raised in March 1851 shortly before they had been confirmed in office.[11] These ordinary meetings of the parish seem never to have been heavily attended, and it does not appear that the most substantial families put in regular appearances.

The decision to rebuild was taken at a special Vestry held on 30 April 1851 when it was 'unanimously resolved that the present church being in a dilapidated state and not fit to be repaired, it should be pulled down and re-built—and that the Parish should contribute £500 to be raised by a rate during the present year and the remaining Four Hundred Pounds to be borrowed and repaid by annual instalments of no less than One Hundred Pounds to be levied on the Parish by rates'. It is interesting to note that a specific sum of £900 is mentioned, and in the absence of further information one must assume that this was based on some kind of estimate of the cost of rebuilding supplied locally, or else was thought to be the greatest sum which the parish could be expected to contribute. The Diocesan Building Society was not formed until 1883 so that there was no local body possessed of the essential expertise to whom the Committee could have turned.[12] To get the sum proposed into perspective one has only to recollect that £560 was what was currently being levied for the Poor Rate, so the parish were committing themselves to a sum equal to the Poor Rate with the additional sum of £110 per annum over a period of four years. At that same meeting John Hughes, Esq., of Alltlwyd, the vicar, Mr. Davies, Ffynonhywel, Mr. David Jones, Tregynen, and Mr. Davies, Pentre Mawr, along with the two wardens, were nominated as a Building Committee. John Hughes, as the squire of Alltlwyd, was obviously the most influential person on the committee, and it is likely that it was his drive and generosity which made the rebuilding possible. The absence of any member of the Mabws family is striking: Captain Phillips, the head of the family, was to take a minor part in the closing stages of the proceedings, but initially he appears to have had nothing to do with it. David Jacob Davies, of Pentre Mawr, a farm of 110 acres, was a Llanddeiniol man married to a Llanrhystud woman who appears to have settled in the parish some ten years previously. The important thing to note about him is that he was a Methodist. William Prydderch, the Methodist minister lodged in his house, as did John Roberts, a teacher in the British School. This requires to be stressed as illustrative of the unanimity of the parish with regard to the project, and the readiness of Nonconformists to tax themselves heavily on behalf of a church from which they were formally separated. David Jones, of Tregynan Isaf, a farm of 150 acres, was a widower aged 64 years who may (on the tenuous evidence of a very common name) have acted as a church-warden in the past.[13]

This Building Committee now worked very quickly—so quickly that one suspects that much of the forward planning had already been done, probably by Mr. Hughes and the vicar, before the meeting of the vestry. First, the wardens would have petitioned for a faculty to rebuild: these documents have not survived: and for a licence to perform divine service in the schoolroom in the interim. This latter was granted on 24 July.[14] Second, fairly firm decisions on the size and type of building to be erected must have been taken, an estimate of the costs, and an architect chosen. It is clear that it was a simple rebuilding that was envisaged: the old church would be taken down and rebuilt substantially in its old form, consisting, as it did, of a nave, chancel, tower, porch and belfry.

The architect chosen was Richard Kyrke Penson. This was a very remarkable choice. Thirty five years of age, he had only recently settled in Oswestry after training in London, where he became F.S.A. and F.R.I.B.A., in this following his father, Thomas Penson, F.R.I.B.A., the Wrexham architect. He had already achieved some distinction as a painter, and was founder-member of the Water-colour Society. Later, he was to be responsible for rebuilding many Cardiganshire churches and houses, among them Llanfihangel-y-Creuddyn, Llanilar, the National Schools at Aberystwyth, alterations and additions to Bronwydd, and Llidiardau, the new residence for F. R. Roberts near Aberystwyth. But at this point in his career he was relatively unknown, and it may have been through his father, who was Surveyor for the central Wales counties, that his name was brought to the attention of the Building Committee. The rebuilding of Llanrhystud church undoubtedly helped to establish his reputation.[15]

From the beginning, the Building Committee relied a great deal on the Incorporated Church Building Society. Founded in 1818 as 'The Society for Promoting the Enlargement and Building of Churches and Chapels', and incorporated by Act of Parliament in 1828,[16] it was the premier voluntary Church of England society, one of three philanthropic organizations authorized to issue the Queen's Letters (the successor to the Royal Briefs) in support of its fund-raising activities. In 1851 its resources were strained to the uttermost, and in that very same

month when Llanrhystud's case came before it it was preparing
to petition the Queen for permission to issue her Letter directing
collections to be made in churches in its behalf.[17] Between 1829
and 1851 the Society had made grants totalling £1,835 to
Cardiganshire churches, so that its operations were well-known
and well-publicized. Its secretary, the Reverend John Bowdler,
was the son of the famous John Bowdler, one of the founders of
the Society, and nephew of the even more famous, if not
notorious, Thomas Bowdler, whose expurgated edition of
Shakespeare had given the phrase 'to bowdlerize' to the English
language and who had lived for many years before his death at
Oystermouth, Swansea. John Bowdler was a typical Evangelical
churchman, deeply involved in the philanthropic movements of
his age, an unbending anti-Tractarian, and an outstanding
example of the new ecclesiastical bureaucrat which church
reform was producing at that time.[18] There were two reasons
why the committee should have turned to the Incorporated
Society. First, because they hoped for a grant in aid, and second,
because the Society could give them expert advice at all stages in
what was an undertaking of major importance. Perhaps it was
advice that was most needed in the early stages—advice, for
instance, as to where to raise a mortgage and on what terms.[19]

By the end of May Penson had visited Llanrhystud and had
sent his plans and estimates to the Society, which was followed a
few days later by a formal application for a grant by the vicar.[20]
Penson's plan was for a church in the Decorated style, consisting
of nave, chancel, vestry and porch, with a tower, a bell-turret
and a spire. It was designed to provide seating for 174, all of
them appropriated, with additional space for 72 children under
the tower. If the vicar's calculations as recorded in his application were correct, this represented an addition of 54
seats—though according to his second application a year later
the old church had contained room for 160, of which 60 were
free. The estimate for the cost of the building and fittings was
£1,630, plus the architect's fee of £80 and £52 for the clerk of the
works—a total of £1,762 or £1,732 after deducting £30 as the
value of the old materials. Well might the vicar plead for a
generous grant from the Society. The total moneys received or
promised to date was only £960—£500 from the rates and £460

in subscriptions—leaving a deficit of £772. Of the money sub-scribed, John Hughes of Alltlwyd had given £200, the bishop £100, and the remainder in smaller sums collected locally or given by well-wishers such as the Reverend Sir George Prevost, the eminent Tractarian and friend of Isaac Williams who was known to John Hughes.[21]

The Committee of the Society, having studied the plans and considered the correspondence decided on 23 June to make a grant of £50 towards the cost 'on condition that additional accommodation for 126 persons be obtained including 72 seats for the use of the poor for ever'.[22] This was by no means a very generous grant, and the local committee could not have been particularly impressed. The Society, however, were certainly impressed by the case itself, and in their Third Quarterly Report they drew attention to it as illustrating perfectly the basic problems of rural religion and the need for substantial aid for such places—more than the current state of their finances permitted. 'Many of the Churches in Wales are in a much more deplorable condition than any in England, and yet, like those in the latter country, are susceptible of complete restoration. *The Church of Llanrhystud . . .* is now in a very dilapidated state', with the drawings of the old church and the projected new one illustrated vividly both the problem and the possibilities.[23] These illustrations and this publicity, however, had quite unexpected results: they came into the hands of two important figures in the church at that time, namely, the Reverend John Allen, Arch-deacon of Salop, and the Reverend Isaac Williams, vicar of Stinchcombe, near Dursley. The latter's concern is understand-able. He was a leading Tractarian, it is true, but on the issue of church-room Tractarians and Evangelicals saw more or less eye to eye, and his criticism of the projected building was, first, that it was too small for a parish of 1800 people, and, second, that the rules of the Society were being contravened insofar as all the seats would be appropriated. Isaac Williams had gone so far as to inform the vicar that he would assist them 'only on the sup-position of there being room for the poor and [would] do nothing for them unless this object were provided for'. Coming from the famous son of a powerful local family—the Williamses of Llanrhystud and Cwmcynfelin—this was a serious blow to the

Building Committee, and more importantly reminded the
Church Building Society of Rule 8 of their 'Laws and
Regulations' which stated quite unequivocally that 'no grant be
made unless *one half*, at least, of the increased area and accommodation proposed, be secured for additional free and
unappropriated sittings for ever'.[24]

The other objection—that of Archdeacon Allen—was perhaps
less fundamental but was even more bothersome. John Allen
was one of those archetypal mid-Victorian churchmen—of
good, landed family, highly educated, extremely well-connected, zealous in all good works, the apotheosis of the new
managerial type of archdeacon. He was the personal friend of
bishops, poets, writers, architects, politicians, and in ecclesiastical affairs, therefore, one whose views could not be ignored,
least of all by a philanthropic society so dependent upon the hierarchy for its success. To boot, he was a Welshman, and his
objection was to the style of building proposed for the new
church. 'You must know', he wrote, 'that I am a Welshman,
and miserably dilapidated as I doubt not that Llanrhystyd
church is, yet what person with any sense of fitness and local
character can view without regret the proposed transformation
that your paper depicts so vividly?—cannot the old Tower be
retained?—must it be pierced with freestone windows of the
newest pattern of sham antique? *Why*, the proposed restoration
appears like the last erection of Turnham Green or some other
sub urban school or the revival of Gothic architecture, instead of
being fitted for the bluff position of the old weather-beaten and
venerable structure. The prettiness of the ornaments of the wall
of the chancel arch and the affectation of buttresses for the
support of the new porch seem to be, for such a situation, considering what at present exists, absolutely detestable'. Beneath
this fine aesthetic rage, of course, were some hard, combustible
motives which the Society could least of all afford to neglect and
which its secretary would warm to, namely a distrust of the
Gothic revival as an expression in stone of Anglo-Catholicism,
and a concern for prudence in money matters. Preserving the
ancient character of Llanrhystud would perhaps (though he did
not say this in so many words) preserve the parish from the infection of Llangorwen, and 'save the outlay of much needles cost

. . .' Penson's design, he added, with more bitterness than charity, would be 'an enduring monument of [the parishioners'] having more money than wit'.[25]

This protest against the destruction of a genuine antique in order to erect a sham antique was not to be ignored, and Bowdler was clearly shaken. With Allen's permission he sent his letter to an architect in whom the committee of the Society (and Allen) had every confidence—namely, to James P. Harrison, one of the leading ecclesiastical architects of the time, much employed by the Society. Predictably enough, Harrison agreed with Allen. He could see no good reason, when funds permitted, why experiments in building *new* Welsh churches should not be attempted, but in the case of Llanrhystud he felt that 'the old Tower . . . would feel both indignant and uncomfortable in its English clothes. A pyramidical Tower does not require buttresses and its very form guides the eye with sufficient grace & ease to the point of an ordinary Welsh spire'. The bellcote he thought pretty and appropriate on the old building but pretentious on what was virtually a new and much taller building. There were other criticisms too; the gables did not suit the elevation, and the sides of the porch roof rose above the eaves of the nave, and he was doubtful whether the old church could ever have had a spire. Harrison sent a sketch of his ideal for the new church, and when this was forwarded to Allen it was received with rapture—'a work of real genius'. Unfortunately, this sketch has not survived, and we are left wondering what Llanrhystud would have looked like if Harrison had had its way.[26]

Copies of this correspondence—without, of course, disclosing their origin—were sent to Penson who, in his characteristically brusque way dismissed then out of hand. Had Harrison known that the floor of the church would have to be raised by at least four feet he would not have gone on about the elevations, and the archdeacon should not let his feelings for things Welsh run away with his judgment. 'With the exception of the Bellcott no building [i.e. the exisiting building] can be poorer in an Ecclesiological sense, and I really cannot persuade myself that one ought to tread in the steps & adopt the uncouth ideas of the rude village masons who built so many of the Welsh Churches when their dilapidated state renders it indispensable to restore them rather than to reconstruct them'. On a more philosophical note, he could not agree that while it was generally accepted that a church should reflect the character of a district it should not equally be acceptable that a church should give character to a district. Allen would accept none of this and could see no prospect of agreeing on any point with a man who insisted on pretty details and who was blind to the beauty of Harrison's sketch. Let Penson read T. (*sic*) G. Scott's, *Plea for the Faithful Restoration of our English Churches,* and in the meantime he would withdraw from the contest. [27]

In the event, Penson's designs had to be altered, but not on grounds of aesthetics. It was Isaac Williams's point about free accommodation—with which Allen heartily concurred—which weighed with the Society, and six months later new plans were submitted by Penson. It was substantially the old building but with a South Aisle added in order to provide free sittings for an additional 141 adults and 114 children. [28] The new church was thus to be double the size of the old one, not at the request of the parishioners, not in reponse to actual parochial needs, but merely in conformity to currently accepted doctrines in high places. It was increasingly becoming apparent that the original objective of church extension as practised in the early decades of the century—to remedy spiritual destitution—was being displaced by a mere competitive urge to out-do the dissenters. For the parishioners doubling the size of the church meant a relatively enormous increase in costs. The new church was now to cost an estimated £2,207, plus the architect's commission, etc., amounting to £160—a total of £2,367. By March, the vicar had collected promises of £1200 in addition to the £500 to be raised by a rate, so that he was left with a deficiency of £645. In a sense, it was the Church Building Society which had been responsible for this unexpected and unwelcome additional expenditure, and they recognized this by voting a grant of £160. But it is clear also that the parishioners were very perturbed by these developments, and possibly also resentful of the fact that decisions of such fundamental importance were taken without consultation. The Building Committee was thus very vulnerable, and at a vestry in July they solemnly gave a guarantee, carefully recorded in the Minute Book and signed by all four members, that they would not involve the parish in any expenditure on the new church over and above the £500 voted in April 1851. 'We will', they declared, 'protect and indemnify the said Parish for all claims and demands whatsoever which may be made upon it in respect or by reason of the re-building of the said Church'. In these circumstances, and bearing in mind that one of the Building Committee was a Methodist deacon it is not surprising that the good will of the parish should have shown signs of strain. Church rates were ever the Achilles heel of church extension.[29]

For the time being, however, all was well, and the foundation stone was laid by the vicar on Tuesday, 11 October 1852. The builder chosen by the committee was Thomas Roberts of Llanstephan, Carmarthenshire, who signed a bond to complete the building by 1 September 1853. There was a penalty attached for non-completion of contract, but as no date had been specified in that particular document, there would be in fact be no means of enforcing it. Nor it is clear that the contract was such as to allow his dismissal by the architect who, of course, was finally responsible for the building. Meanwhile, the vicar was hard at work trying to raise the additional money required. He now acted on the vestry resolution of 30 April 1851 to raise an additional £400 by mortgaging the rates, and a rate of six pence in the pound was voted at a vestry in October to enable them to borrow this sum as soon as possible. The local gentry were also brought into parish affairs more closely: Captain Phillips of Mabws began to attend the parish meetings in November, by which time also the Lloyds of Bronwydd and the Williamses of Cwmcynfelin were being asked to exert their influence.[30]

The reason for this was three-fold. First, by late summer of 1853 it was becoming obvious that the builder was not going to complete the work by the specified date. By then, some of the Building Committee, though not all, had lost confidence in him. This was a very serious matter for the vicar. Not only did they have no church but the raising of funds was made more difficult: in a parish where Anglicans were in a minority it was important not to lose the impetus given by the original enthusiasm. But second, John Hughes of Alltlwyd, the chairman of the committee and the church's main benefactor, had died. His death came at the crisis in the rebuilding for, third, the architect and the builder had fallen out. It is highly improbable that Penson had chosen Thomas Roberts in the first place: there are ominous indications that he was the nominee of his friends on the committee. However that may be, by mid-November relations between them had become so bad that Penson had resigned. He had already hinted to the Society that this might very well be the outcome. He had accused Roberts of certain malpractices, of refusing instructions, of acting in defiance of instructions, and of playing off one faction against the other on the Building Committee. The Society, he averred should support him and the vicar by threatening them with the loss of the grant unless the contractor worked strictly according to the plans and specifications. Roberts should be dismissed immediately. But it was Penson who went, not the builder.[31]

The vicar was now in desperate straits. Winter was approaching and the church only half completed: the building was not roofed and work on the spire had been suspended. He himself had every confidence in Penson and was unwilling to proceed without him, and this was also the opinion of Thomas Lloyd of Bronwydd and Isaac Williams. But this was not the opinion of a majority of the Building Committee: they wanted to choose another architect, or failing that, wanted the Society to choose one of their own architects to arbitrate. Penson's allegations against Roberts were quite specific: contrary to instructions he had used timbers for the roof 'off the ground'; the roof had been up 'for months' without a single slate being laid with the result that the stonework within the church was dripping with water; the Bath-stone dressings had not been cased up against damage by the weather and other accidents; materials had either not been ordered on time or been allowed to lie about deteriorating. He had consulted his solicitor on the builder's contractual responsibility, had given him and the committee due warning, and had resigned (along with the clerk of the works) only when the committee had over-ruled him and instructed Roberts to proceed.[32]

For his part, Roberts was equally certain that the allegations made against him were unfounded, and on the face of it it is extremely unlikely that he would deliberately defy the one man who could block his periodical payments. His situation was also pretty desperate: he had received no money and had been unable to pay his workmen for three or four months. He made a special visit to London to deliver a plea from the committee for the appointment of another architect, but to no avail, and early in December he wrote to Mr. Bowdler pleading for some action. 'I have applied to the Llanrhystud Committee for my install-ments until Mr. Penson Resigned he had the Blame as he Refused to come to the work now it is the Society for not naming one in his place . . . I am the person who Suffers . . . Mr. Lewis and Mr. Penson has Refused to send me what fault is on the work I have their Refusal in writing'. Compared with the polished professionalism of Penson there is an air of puzzled and pathetic innocence about the letters of Roberts, but it is obvious also that the somewhat haughty and cosmopolitan architect had more than met his match in the rustic parishioners of Llan-rhystud and the county builder of Llanstephan.[33]

Faced with this deadlock the Church Building Society was forced to act on the request of the committee, and late in December, with the agreement of Penson, they invited Henry Kennedy to report on the state of the building. Kennedy was architect to the Bangor Diocesan Building Society, a man eminent in his profession, and acceptable to both sides. He invited Penson to join him in the inspection, and Penson agreed, but at last minute withdrew on the advice of the vicar who, wisely enough, judged that his presence would be resented and might be made a pretext for refusing to pay their expenses. But he was able to consult Mr. John Lloyd who had been clerk of the works until his resignation in October 1853.[34]

Kennedy's Report, dated 27 January, was far more en-couraging than the Society had been led to expect by Penson. Exposure to the rigours of two winters had not affected the masonry, and the Bathstone dressings had not cracked. The builder, by some strange misconstruction of the drawings had inserted only two belfry windows in the tower instead of the four required by the architect, and the corbels under the mouldings at the springing of the spire had also been omitted but subsequently inserted, so far as he could tell, in a satis-factory manner. The only real criticism he had to make of the masonry concerned the way the spire had been constructed.

Evidently stone from the beach had been incorporated at its base, and this, with some doubt as to the quality of the mortar used, and insufficient scaffolding which was not in position when he made his inspection, led him to judge that the spire was probably unsafe. Because the roof timbers had already been stained he was unable to pronounce categorically on their quality, but since they had been erected under the supervision of the Clerk of the Works he was prepared to pronounce them satisfactory. But some of the roof timbers were deficient in thickness, and he thought the builder should make an allowance for this. He thought the slating was efficiently done, though he drew attention to the fact that the rows had not been marked out very straight and that the ornamental ridges had not been put on with sufficient precision. He had some minor criticisms to make of the plastering, lead flashing and guttering. He refused to arbitrate on the question of the non-completion of the contract within the specified time, 'the causes given being so various and contradictory'. As a way out he suggested that since the building was now virtually complete it would be unnecessary to employ an architect to supervise what remained to be done, and that the task should be given 'a competent, non-professional person (say a respectable builder) residing in the neighbourhood', and that finally a dignitary of the Church should be asked to certify completion.[35]

This was an eminently satisfactory report, precise in its criticisms, wise in making recommendations which avoided all possibility of recrimination or involvement in parish politics. A copy was sent to the vicar who immediately called a parish meeting. Twenty-four parishioners attended and, with Captain Phillips in the chair, Kennedy's recommendations were accepted. But the vicar's troubles were by no means at an end, and again money was his preoccupation. It was now necessary to raise more funds, and it was resolved to borrow an additional £300 at 5 per cent of Mr. David Davies, Rhydias, to be repaid in three annual instalments of £100 together with interest. Even with this sum safely accounted for, there would still be a deficiency of £300 exclusive of an estimated £88 for furniture and fittings. More immediately there were Mr. Kennedy's expenses amounting to £18.18s which, although reduced from their

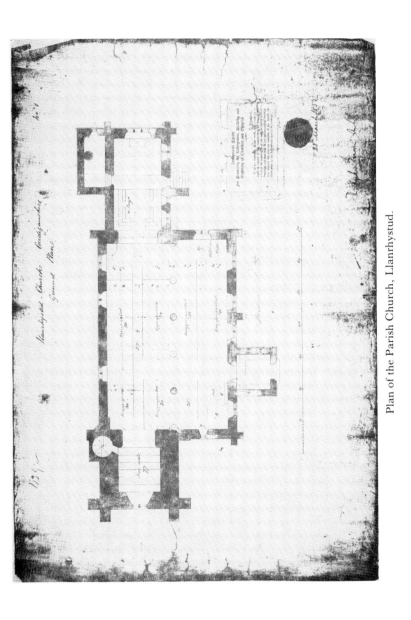

Plan of the Parish Church, Llanrhystud.

original £21 in response to the vicar's desparate importunities, had to be settled without delay. The Society paid his fees, but he utterly refused to allow the settlement of his expenses to wait on the result of a bazaar at Aberystwyth!

These negotiations were highly embarrassing to the vicar as to all concerned for the sufficient reason that Kennedy's association with the church was not likely to cease with his inspection. The Society's rules laid down that any grant voted would become payable only on production of a completion certificate signed by the architect, and the vicar was in a quandary as to who should now certify in order to gain the grant. Kennedy had suggested that a church dignitary should do so, but as late as August Mr. Bowdler was sticking to the letter of the law and demanding that Penson should do so. With a debt of £350 hanging over him the vicar pleaded with the Society and with influential friends that Kennedy should be again called upon to sign: 'I should prefer paying Mr. Kennedy a 2nd visit than that there should be any risk about the grant. I am sufficiently involved already without risking that also. Pray, can you do anything for us among your rich friends—I want at least £350 independently of the grant'. Eventually, in October, this was allowed, and Kennedy came down to make another inspection. There were still minor things to complete, and he left the certificate of completion in the hands of Captain Phillips who was to deliver it to the Society when these had been done. Meanwhile, on 19 October 1854, the church was consecrated by the bishop, and a few weeks later the Completion Certificate returned. All that now remained was to pay the builder the balance due to him, but alas, there was yet another rule which had to be satisfied before the grant could be paid, namely, the production of a ground plan setting out the location of the free accommodation. By now, the vicar was in a state of distraction: he had no plans; Penson had them; they must write to him. But Penson was seriously ill, and it was late in November before the seating plan reached the Society [Plate 3], and only after another short and sharp letter from the vicar was the cash forthcoming. With what relief must John Lewis have written out a receipt for £160 on 8 December![36]

Only one more thing required to be done, and that was to receive the Society's plate recording their grant and the conditions under which it was given. Few people now, perhaps, as they read that iron plate on the north wall of the porch, realize what a labour had been involved in the re-building. Behind its iron print, as I have tried to show, lies a story of great effort and considerable sacrifice on the part of a whole parish. Opinions may differ as to the appropriateness of the architectural style of the church; we may side with Allen or with Penson as to the propriety of its spire and its decorative buttresses, or we may regret that strident arguments about ecclesiological niceties should have silenced the instinctive good taste of an ancient community. But in the end it is not the structure alone that survives to gain our admiration and excite our wonder: rather is it the consistency of effort which was involved and the coherence of a small community in which good neighbourliness counted for more than sectarian zeal. Twenty years previously, the building of St. Michael's Chapel, Aberystwyth, had ended in bitterness and denominational strife. Llanrhystud had taken on a far greater burden than the parishioners of that town, and had carried it through with dignity, good-sense, and tolerance. Those who laboured in the parish, alike with those who gave them assistance from afar, are long since silent and laid to rest. We who inherit the beauty of their labour can but pay tribute to their faith and dedication.

NOTES

First published in *Ceredigion: Journal of the Ceredigion Antiquarian Society* VII, No 2 (1973)

[1] Parliament granted £1,000,000 in 1818, and £500,000 in 1824.

[2] Speech following the consecration of St. Fagan's new church, *Cardiff and Merthyr Guardian,* 4 August 1854. On the building of this church see above, pp 000-000. For similar statements, see *Yr Haul,* Gorffennaf, 1851, and Sir Thomas Phillips, *Wales* (1849), p. 176.

[3] Jones and Williams, *The Religious Census of 1851.* (South Wales) pp. 528-30 1851. The return for the parish church is missing.

[4] "Many of the churches in Wales are in a much mor dilapidated condition than any in England, and yet, like those in the latter country, are susceptible of complete restoration". *Third Quarterly Report,* 1850-51, pp. 11-12.

[5] This analysis is based on the enumerator's returns for the 1851 Census: PRO, HO 107/2485.

[6] Dafydd Jenkins, *The Agricultural Community in South West Wales at the Turn of the Twentieth Century* (Cardiff, 1971). See also C. J. Lewis, 'The demographic structure of a

Welsh rural village during the mid-nineteenth century', *Ceredigion* V, (1970), pp.
290-304, and Colin Thomas, 'Rural society in nineteenth century Wales: South
Cardiganshire in 1851', *Ceredigion*, VI, (1971), pp. 388-413.

[7] Form C.

[8] N.L.W. MSS. SD/P/1893; P.R.O. HO 1071/2485. For John Lewis, see Benjamin
Williams (Gwynionydd), *Enwogion Ceredigion* (1869), tt. 156-7.

[9] Samuel Lewis, *Topographical Dictionary of Wales*, (edn. 1848).

[10] N.L.W., Llanrhystud Vestry Books, 24 April 1851, and Tithe Survey, op. cit.

[11] Vestry Books, op. cit., 21 March 1851.

[12] Delyth Jones, 'Some Social and Economic Problems of the Church of England in
the Diocese of St. David's 1800—1874', unpublished M.A. thesis (Aberystwyth), 1972,
p. 220.

[13] HO 127/2485; I.C.B.S., File 4392, J. Lewis to J. Bowdler; Tithe Survey.

[14] N.L.W. MSS. SD/DS/30, petition for licence dated 9 July 1852.

[15] Frederick Boase, *Modern English Biography*, vol. VI (reprinted 1965), p. 103;
obituary in *The Builder*, 3 July 1886 and 5 June 1886: D. H. S. Gamage, *An Architectural
Account of the Churches of Shropshire* (1894), vol. 1; *Journal of the Royal Institute of Architects*,
vol. V (1886-7), p. 20. Among his other buildings in Wales we might mention St.
David's, Carmarthen, church and vicarage; St. Peter's School, Carmarthen; St.
Peter's Llanelli; Cockett Church, Swansea; the National School, Swansea; rebuilding
of Mumbles Church; additions to Kilvey Church; restoration of Llanrhidian Church;
Pen-maen Church; Morriston Church; and churches at Amroth, Angle, St. Petrox,
Roche, Rosemarket, Llanddarog, Llanedi, Llan-llwch, Llandefaelog, Bettws, Mathri,
Merthyr, Llanglydwen, and many others in Denbighshire and the border towns.

He was currently engaged on St. John Baptist, Pont-fadog (1852-53), in place of its
original architect, Wegenhert, who had gone bankrupt. See W. H. Port, *Six Hundred
New Churches* (1961), p. 172. His father was the architect for a number of commissioners'
churches in ales, among them St. David's, Denbigh (1850-51), Holy Trinity, Gwersyllt
(1845-47), St. John, Rhosllannerchrugog (1852-3), and St. Peter, Swansea (1856).

[16] 9 Geo. IV. cap. 42.

[17] I.C.B.S., Minute Book 14, 23 June 1851 for the final draft of the petition. Lord
Palmerston took a very dim view of this method of begging, and this was the last
occasion for such a petition to be made. For the government's view, see the
correspondence in PRO, HO45/8806/1-11.

[18] For the Bowdlers, see D.N.B., and for a memoir of the Rev. John Bowdler, see
Church Builder, I (1862), pp., 26ff.

[19] Vicar to I.C.B.S., File NO. 4392, 12 May 1851. Loans could be obtained from the
Public Works Loan Commissioner at 4 per cent interst repayable over ten or twenty
years, on the security of a rate.

[20] *ibid.*

[21] *ibid.*, vicar to Bowdler, 3 June 1851; Penson to *idem*, 31 May; Form C and receipt
dated 4 June 1851; 'Prevost to Bowdler, 23 May 1851.

[22] I.C.B.S., Minute Book, 23 June 1851.

[23] Third quarterly Report for the session 1850-51, *Church Building Society*, No. 11
(August 1851), pp. 3 and 12. The drawings are reproduced herewith, Plates 1 and 2.

[24] Isaac Williams to CBS, 12 March 1852. For Isaac Williams see Benjamin Williams,
op. cit, tt. 242-4, *Dictionary of Welsh Biography* (1959), and O. W. Jones, *Isaac Williams
and his circle* (1971).

[25] Anna Otter Allen, *John Allen and his Friends* (n.d.); R. M. Grier, *John Allen, Vicar of
Press and Archdeacon of Salop* (1897): I.C.B.S.; File No. 4392, Allen to Bowdler, 22 August
1851.

[26] Basil F. Clarke, *Church Builders of the Nineteenth Century: A Study of the Gothic Revival in England* (1938): I.C.B.S., Allen to Bowdler, 22 and 26 August 1851; James P. Harrison to Bowdler, 29 August 1851; Allen to Bowdler, 6 September 1851.

[27] I.C.B.S., Penson to Bowdler, 8 September; Allen to Bowdler, 16 September 1851; George Gilbert Scott, *A Plea for the faithful restoration of our ancient churches* (1850). This latter pamphlet was published by the author "as likely to do some little towards stemming the torrent of Destructiveness, which, under the title and garb of "Restoration", threatens to destroy the truthfulness and genuine character of half of our ancient churches" (p.2). Scott held, as a guiding principle, "that *individual caprice* should be *wholly excluded* from restorations" (p. 31), and quoted with approval Petit's "is it either kind or prudent to disregard that *admonitus locorum,* which may exercise a more powerful influence than we imagine in attaching our countrymen both to their Church and institutions" (p. 34). Allen may have had the name wrong, but no more powerful advocate of his point of view would have been found. On (Sir) George Gilbert Scott, see Clarke, *op. cit.,* and Sir Nicholas Pevsner, *Some Architectural Writers of the Nineteenth Century* (1971).

[28] Grier, *op. cit.,* p. 150; I.C.B.S., Minute Book, General Committee, 15 March 1852.

[29] Application Form C, received 4 March 1852. N.L.W., Llanrhystud Vestry Minute Book, 30 April 1851.

[30] Vestry Minute Book, 15 October 1851; Vicar of Bowdler, 26 August 1853; Vestry Minute Book, 15 October 1852.

[31] The plaque on the south wall of the church records his generosity: I.C.B.S., Joint letter of Building Committee to Bowdler, 22 November 1853; Penson to Bowdler, n.d.; and same to same, 7 December 1853.

[32] I.C.B.S., vicar to Penson, 23 November 1853; Building Committee to Bowlder, 22 and 30 November 1853.

[33] I.C.B.S., Building Committee to Bowdler, n.d., but probably December 1853: Thomas Roberts, from Llanstephan, to Bowdler, 10 December 1853.

[34] I.C.B.S., Minute Book 14, 19 December 1853. On Kennedy's work in north Wales, see Herbert L. North, *The Old Churches of Arllechwedd* (Bangor, 1904), Harold Hughes and Herbert L. North, *The Old Churches of Snowdonia* (Bangor, 1924), and M. L. Clarke 'Church Building and Church Restoration in Caernarvonshire during the nineteenth century', 22 (1961), pp. 20ff; Penson to Bowdler, 19 June 1854.

[35] I.C.B.S., Kennedy to Bowdler, 27 January 1854.

[36] Vestry Book, 10 February 1854; printed *Appeal,* dated 11 May 1854; Kennedy to Bowdler, 10 February 1854. Vicar to Bowdler, 13 February 1854; Kennedy to Bowdler 22 February and 10 July 1854; vicar to? 25 July 1854 (forwarded by recipient to Bowdler); Completion Certificate dated 7 November 1854; Lewis to Bowdler, 2 December 1854.

RELIGION AND POLITICS: THE REBUILDING OF ST. MICHAEL'S CHURCH ABERYSTWYTH AND ITS POLITICAL CONSEQUENCES*

In the early decades of the nineteenth century, during the first stages of attempts to reform the Church of England, the building of parish churches and of chapels intended for public use was, as often as not, a hazardous business not to be undertaken without some calculation of their social, as well as their financial, costs. Indeed, in the case of churches or chapels built with the aid of the funds voted for that purpose by parliament in 1818 and 1824 and administered by the Church Building Commissioners,[1] finance was not necessarily the main preoccupation of their promoters for most, if not all, of the money came from the central fund. The church at Buckley (Flintshire), built in 1821-2 at a cost of £4,052, was paid for entirely out of the first parliamentary grant.[2] This was the only Welsh church financed in those early euphoric and generous years of the Church Building Commissioners, and their subsequent operations in Wales were never on the same scale of magnanimity. The second parliamentary grant of half a million pounds in 1824 was administered much more carefully. Thus, Abersychan received a grant of £1,745 towards its total costs of £2,245, and, as we shall see, St. Michael's, Aberystwyth, £1,289 towards a total expenditure of £3,788.[3] Later on in the decade the Commissioners were, on the whole, even more careful, in some cases, positively parsimonious. In 1837 Bedwellty, where the need was so great, was given a grant of £1,042 towards the costs of £3,061 for the church at Tredegar, St. Woollos, Newport, £1,350 out of a total cost of £5,024, and St. David's, Carmarthen, £1,106 towards its cost of £4,106. Right at the end of the decade, in 1839, Glyntaff, Eglwysilan was given £414 (total cost £2,500), Brymbo, £600 (total cost £1,180), and Gwernafield, Mold, £300 (total cost £1,600).[4] The size of the grant from central funds could be of critical importance socially, for the insistence of the Commissioners that no church or chapel could be erected until the total costs had been covered—including the conveyance to them of any land—meant that the promoters would be compelled to rely upon local resources. This invariably involved an appeal to the parishioners which might, or might not, be succesful in raising the projected fund. Where it fell short, as often happened, it was possible, by proper legal process, to borrow a sum on the security of the rates or even, in the case of a re-building, to raise a specific sum by means of a rate. Moreover, all churches when built required to be kept in a state of repair and properly maintained. This also required, or might require, the raising of a rate from time to time. Indeed, the 1818 Act required parishioners to maintain not only the old, but also the new, church (after twenty years) by means of a church rate.[5] Almost inevitably, therefore, issues of the highest significance, involving religious and political principles, might be raised and the community split into warring factions. How such a situation could arise and develop, and how it could permanently affect the political life of a small town, is the purpose of this study.

$$* \qquad * \qquad * \qquad *$$

The chronology of church extension in Aberystwyth, and the four distinct stages in the rebuilding of the chapel of St. Michael's, suggest that its promoters proceeded with great caution.[6] It was in July 1820 that the first moves were made when Job Sheldon, the mayor, consulted the Shrewsbury architect, Edward Haycock, regarding the possibility of enlarging or rebuilding the existing chapel.[7] This was an auspicious time for such an undertaking, and probably no architect in Wales was more able to advise than Haycock. The parliamentary grant of one million pounds was inviting, and raised the possibility of avoiding the depressing delays in raising money which had retarded the building of the first chapel. Haycock was heavily employed by the Church Building Commissioners at the time and as familiar with their ways as any layman could be expected to be. He advised the rebuilding of the old chapel, enclosing with his letter a sketch of a proposed elevation. But there the matter rested and five years were to pass before anything more was attempted. This second stage was characterized by a sudden burst of activity and an attempt to involve the whole of the town in the project. On this occasion, beginning in April 1825, the vestry was involved.[8] The leading proponent of extension was John Hughes, one of the wardens, and it is important not to confuse this layman, a solicitor and land agent, with the Reverend John Hughes who has hitherto been regarded as the initiator and inspirer of the movement.[9] A few months after the annual vestry, this John Hughes, acting apparently in his official capacity as warden, wrote to the Church Building Society to ask whether they would assist financially in the event of a decision being taken to enlarge the existing building. In his letter, John Hughes drew attention to the lack of church room as being "a source of great inconvenience and complaint" in a town which had outgrown the facilities provided when the existing church had been built forty years previously.[10] The reply must have been encouraging, for at a special vestry held a month later a decision was taken to rebuild "upon a larger scale".[11] Finally, on 22 September, a building committee was formed and an appeal launched.

There is insufficient detailed evidence surviving to enable us to be categorical about the nature of the movement at this stage, but enough survives to highlight some of its major characteristics. In the first place, it is not clear that the rebuilding was expressive primarily of the new evangelical movement within the church at large and in the Chapelry of Aberystwyth in particular. Thus, it has been assumed by previous students of the movement that the turning-point in the church-life of Aberystwyth was the powerful influence of the evangelical Reverend John Hughes. But at this time John Hughes was the curate of Deddington, near Oxford, where he was making a name for himself as a fervent 'Puritanical Welsh preacher':[12] it was not until 1827 that he was appointed to St. Michael's.[13] Moreover, this does less than justice to Reverend R. Evans, incumbent of Llanbadarn Fawr, who had been closely associated with the first stage of the movement and who had written in June 1820 to the Church Building Commissioners to ask for their assistance.[14] It seems unlikely that the vicar of Llanbadarn Fawr was animated by much evangelical fervour. He was certainly a pluralist, being at the same time vicar of Llanrhystud and Rector of Rhostie.[15] In his letter of 9 June 1820 to the Commissioners it is the competition from the growing bodies of dissenters rather than 'a lust for souls' which get pride of place in his submission. 'Most of the poor people,' he complained, alluding to the growth of the town and its inadequate church room, 'finding no room in their town chapel are tempted to stay at home or go to a conventicle on the Lord's Day'.[16] This was a familiar enough observation and typical of the reaction of clerics overtaken by events but, as we shall see, there were few indications that the Nonconfmormists were in fact growing at the expense of the Church. The Reverend John Hughes was therefore not the initiator of the movement for church extension in Aberystwyth, and his religious zeal, when he finally arrived in 1827, was channelled into a movement which already existed and along courses which had already been cut by others.

For, in the second place, it is the strongly secular nature of the drive of church extension in these opening stages which is striking. The emphasis in the correspondence between the promoters on the one hand, and the Church Building Commissioners and the Church Building Society on the other, is on the size of the rapidly growing town, its rising importance as a sea-side resort, and the alleged inadequacy of its church accommodation. They estimated the population 'at 5000 and upwards': in fact, the town did not reach that figure until 1851: twenty years earlier it was 4,128 and in 1821 3,556 only.[17] The town was certainly growing fairly rapidly, but at no point in its history did it grow as rapidly as the towns in the mining and manufacturing districts or the large towns and cities of the country for whose benefit the parliamentary grants of 1818 and 1824 had been intended. Under the Act of 1818 grants out of the fund were to be given only to parishes of over 4,000 where there was no church room for a quarter of the population. It was specifically designed to aid the church in those areas where accommodation was non-existent, or geographically remote from new centres of growth, or where existing accommodation had been overwhelmed by the flood of numbers. Finally, the new churches were intended to accommodate the poor. It was on these grounds that the Commissioners had rejected the petitionary letter of the Reverend Richard Evans in 1820, and it is easy to understand why the promoters five years later should tend to exaggerate the religious problems facing the church in the chapelry and obscure what were probably the basic underlying motives of the movement.

From its inception the movement was directed by the town oligarchy. The building committee of 1825 consisted of some of the leading professional and business-men of the town. It was headed by a banker, whose firm handled the accounts, and included a surgeon, a land-surveyor, a draper, a tanner, a captain in the militia, and a solicitor.[18] Members of the corporation were closely involved: indeed, it might very well have been a sub-committee of the unreformed corporation in much the same way as the Improvement Commissioners later tended to be. Politically, some of these men called themselves Liberal, and indeed, it was their influence in Aberystwyth which ensured that the Gogerddan family was able to dominate the Cardiganshire borough seat in the name of the Liberals. But in the practice of politics within the town itself they constituted a self-perpetuating oligarchy which the commissioners under the Municipal Reform Bill regarded as little less than a scandal. The Job Sheldon, mentioned above, had been mayor seven times in 15 years, and was to be mayor five times yet again.[19] The court leet, in which was vested the government of the town was in fact controlled by a small group of individuals who in turns filled the main offices and profited themselves and each other by the spoils of office. The local gentry had been effectively excluded from town government, or rather, had come to accept the necessity for a purely bourgeois government as the price for the unswerving support of the burgesses and the town elite at parliamentary elections. Pryse Pryse of Gogerddan supplied the non-resident burgesses from among whom the mayor could appoint the court jury and whose compliancy and obedience were assured. In return, Pryse Pryse could rely on merchants and solicitors to turn out a solid vote in his favour on election day. This alliance with Gogerddan was purely fortuitous in its origin and was maintained for motives of expediency only. Pryse Pryse's record in parliament showed him to have been a Whig who moved gradually in Liberal directions, but there is no evidence that this had anything to do with the political opinion of his Aberystwyth constituents.[20] 'Siop-fawr' politics was characterized by an absence of ideology, a pathological fear of change, and an enervating desire not to offend one's fellow-burgesses. It is difficult to discover any social differences between the so-called Liberal members of the corporation and the Tories, and it is the absence of 'reformers', or of any radical element, among them that is significant. There was therefore no party of change and, until the reforms imposed upon the government of the town by the Municipal Corporations Act, there were few indications that one would develop. Nor were there, in what was still a market-town and small port with scarcely any industrial base to its economy, any significant pressures from within the community making for a reformist tradition. Apart from the large land-owners with estates in the region, the wealthiest families were land-agents, a few lawyers, and other professional men whose interests were closely bound up with the landowners and the townspeople at large. Tradesmen, shopkeepers and innkeepers were prominent in the social life of the town, and it was these, whose prosperity depended upon the expansion of the town as a watering-place, who were most likely to provide a reformist leadership in years to come. By the middle of the century they were doing so, giving an impetus to sanitary reform and improvement under the 1848 Health Act for example,[21] and it is this class which provided the back-bone of Nonconformity in the middle decades of the century and eventually of Noncon-formist Liberalism.

In the 1820s and early 1830s, however, no one could have pre-dicted that this would be the case. Nonconformity, like the church, exhibited few of the characteristics of an expansionist, missionizing evangelicalism. Of the four congregations of Non-conformists only the Calvinistic Methodists were flourishing. They had recently built their second 'Tabernacle' in 1819 and were shortly to rebuild in 1832, this time on a much larger scale with seats for 1200. In addition, they had 'branches' in various parts of the town and its environs.[22] The two Dissenting congre-gations were in a much less flourishing condition. The Inde-pendent chapel in Vulcan Place was a monument to the extra-ordinary individual efforts of the minister, Azariah Shadrach, who built the chapel between 1821 and 1823 without, it seems, any financial assistance from his small congregation.[23] Nor were the Baptists any stronger. Writing towards the middle of the 1830s the Baptist historian, David Jones, doubted whether the membership at that time was any greater than it had been in 1819,[24] suggesting that baptisms during that period only just kept pace with losses. Like the Independents, the Baptists were heavily indebted to the labours of their most remarkable minister in the early years of the century, and Samuel Breeze is remembered above all for his extraordinary fund-raising gifts—gifts which he exercised on behalf of the congregation with most noticeable success at a distance from his home town.[25] The Wesleyan Methodists were almost as weak. Aberystwyth became a circuit-centre in 1807, and two years later their meeting-house was registered, this remaining their home until the building of a new chapel on a new site in 1879. If their history at Aberystwyth resembled that of the denomination as a whole in Wales, then the 1820s were years of unspectacular growth and of enhanced respectability.[26] Certainly, after 1832 there were Wesleyan Methodists on the town council, and Aberystwyth never became a stronghold of any of the various secessionist Methodist denominations, such as the Wesleyan Reformers.[27] This is not surprising, and it should be noted that the reason lay not in the strength of the parent denominations but in its relative weakness. Conspicious by their absence as an organized body also were the Unitarians. Powerful and politically active in the south of the county in Aberystwyth they were represented by only a few, isolated families. Hence it was that in these early decades of the century Nonconformity in Aberystwyth was virtually synonymous with Calvinistic Methodism. It was the strongest denomination numerically and almost certainly socially as well. It was a denomination busy establishing its credentials in the town, eminently respectable, attracting a large proportion of the 'shopocracy' and tradesmen. It felt itself to be distinct from the church,[28] but not in violent antipathy to it, and in its political attitudes no more disposed than the Wesleyans to be more than vaguely 'neuter' or mildly Liberal.[29] There were good reasons 'to humbly hope', as their Appeal on behalf of the building fund for their new chapel put it in 1818, 'that friends in connection with other denominations of Christians in Aberystwyth will in this instance overlook minor differences and join a helping hand in this necessary work'. With the experience of

Breeze and of Shadrach in mind it must have been to church
people that this was primarily directed, and in fact the names of
prominent Anglicans are to be found in the list of subscribers.[30]

The Appeal issued by the St. Michael's building committee in
1825 strengthens this impression of a mainly secular drive
behind the re-building. It has the grandiloquence of an official
document and is couched in that semi-legal jargon so beloved of
officialdom: the burgesses could have been forgiven for believing
that this was an 'actum' of the corporation. Its avoidance of any
religious language whatsoever effectively removed from it any
taint of denominationalism, and its reference to the aid expected
from the Church Building Commissioners should a sufficient
sum be forthcoming from the inhabitants must as effectively
have appealed to their civic pride. The subscription list tells
the same story. By the time it was closed three years later nearly
£2,005 had been promised—a very considerable sum in the
circumstances. The list of names was headed by the local landed
proprietors, who together promised well over half the amount
promised. The local impropriator of the living—J. P. B.
Chichester—was conspicious by his absence. These are
followed by the professional men and the three clergymen, and
finally the tradesman and shopkeepers. Most of this latter group
seem to have contributed—un-named contributors of under £5
amounted to £120—and this, in itself, is evidence of the secular
nature of the drive, for many of them must have been dissenters
from the church. A church building not only commensurate with
the size but also symbolic of the rising importance of the town,
especially during the 'fashionable' summer months, was what
was needed, and for most of the business community this
consideration at that early stage may have transcended the sectarian, or even the religious, one. The physical need for more
church-room was by no means self-evident, as we have indicated, nor was it necessarily admitted on all sides. Some, no
doubt, read the Appeal with a jaundiced eye. A few years later it
was observed that the existing chapel was 'large enough to
contain more people than are in the habit of attending there,
except during two or three of the summer months.'[31] But that
was written under the strain of events which the Building Committee had hoped to avoid, and for the moment all would agree

that the provision of a fashionable church was *sine qua non* in a
rising seaside resort priding itself on its increasing attractiveness
to English gentry and middle-class families. Pride and self-
interest were as much involved as religious conviction and
spiritual need. After all, by the mid-forties the Welsh Nonconformist denominations would also begin to supply splendid new
chapels for their English visitors.[32] Hence, by the end of 1825
the essential decisions had been taken. Land had been procured
by the simple expedient of persuading Sir Uvedale Price, whose
seaside home, Castle House, lay close by, to reliquish his lease
on a plot of corporation land near the old cemetery.[33] The architect had already submitted a design for a building providing
room for 1,500, and Richard Jones, a local builder, had submitted a tender of £3,250.[34] The Church Building Commissioners had promised £1,000, and had themselves suggested
an approach to the Church Building Society,[35] and since these
latter were 'the Commissioners in the guise of a Church, as
distinct from a State, society'[36] there was no reasonable doubt
that the rebuilding could now proceed.

In the event, nothing more was done for nearly four years, and
then most of the negotiations with the ecclesiastical authorities
had to begin again. It is important to discover what accounted
for this delay. There is no doubt that money remained a major
preoccupation, and that the early summer of 1828 the building
committee had come to the conclusion that the church as
planned in 1825 could not now be built, and that the size of the
edifice would have to be reduced to 1,100. But the grant of 1825
from the Church Building Commissioners had been conditional
on providing sittings for 1,500, and it is clear that they were very
reluctant to make the same grant for a smaller building.[37] Yet,
without this grant of £1,000 the building committee could not
proceed, for by 1828 it was perfectly clear that, despite further
attempts to raise more money, the most that would be forthcoming in cash at the time was £1,100. There could be no
guarantee that the remaining £900 would be collected. The
existence of a parliamentary grant did not necessarily make the
situation of the promoters easier, for though there was a source
from which they could hope to draw, its existence tended to
restrict the flow of voluntary giving and to make even nominal

churchmen more calculating than they might otherwise have been. The second parliamentary grant of half a million pounds had been made in the teeth of opposition, and the party spirit thus engendered had by no means been confined to London and the great provincial towns: it interpenetrated the parochial troubles of small towns like Aberystwyth as well. From the point of view of the promoters who were mainly, as we have seen, members of the ruling oligarchy, it was absolutely essential to raise money without recourse to the rating system. Any proposal to borrow on the security of the rates, for instance, must be avoided, for to do so would endanger the non-controversial nature of the undertaking. Hence, the Commissioners, having agreed to the smaller building, the building committee made desperate efforts to call in the outstanding moneys. By June 1829, a further £400 had been collected, making it possible to send £1,500 to the Commissioners, leaving another £700 to be raised in the following six months. With the £100 promised by the Commissioners this would bring them to within £700 of the newly estimated costs of £3,200.[38]

This is where the Church Building Society came in. Acting on the suggestions of the Commissioners in 1825, John Hughes began what was to prove a long negotiation and which was to result in a grant of £400 being made on 28 December 1829.[38] The Society could impose its own conditions; in particular, it could insist that a half of the additional seating provided should be free—403 as against the 396 proposed in the application form—and much ink and energy was expended on this detail. The Society grant still left the committee short of £300, and evidently attempts were made to persuade the Commissioners to find this. But the latter were adamant, pointing out that they had already deviated from the strict interpretation of the 1818 Act in making a grant at all.[40] It was in the course of this correspondence that they made the fatal suggestion that it was open to the parish, under certain circumstances, to 'raise a Rate to repay the expenses of building a new chapel'. As we have seen, this was exactly what the building committee hoped to avoid, and throughout the remainder of the year they redoubled their efforts to collect the money so enthusiastically promised five years previously. Not until late in February was the required sum raised and, the Church Building Society's grant having been made over to the Commissioners, tenders were invited in February and the foundation stone laid in 9 June 1830.[41]

The actual building took two years, and though the inhabitants must have been pleased with what they saw going up, the building committee do not seem to have been entirely happy with the result. In particular, the church lacked a steeple. The Reverend John Hughes was still angling for additional funds to provide this deficiency, 'the want of which will be a material deduction from the beauty of the edifice'.[42] But the Society was not to be drawn: they existed for more important purposes than supplying expensive steeples in watering-places. So the building went ahead without its steeple but with the understanding that this could be added should the funds be forthcoming, and by June 1832 the building was complete and ready for occupation.

Then the unexpected happened, and the whole character of the operation changed, and with it, the internal social relations of the town. Part of the building plan involved the construction of a wall or terrace on the west side of the church to protect the building against the sea. This wall would have run alongside a strip of land bordering the whole site, about 28ft wide, which had been reserved as a roadway from the Castle grounds to Castle House on the west side and which had not therefore been conveyed to the Commissioners.[43] The west and southern elevations of the church were therefore very near to the sea and extremely vulnerable to the ravages of the waves. The Reverend Hughes, by now the chairman of the committee, was warned in June by the Commissioners that the completion of the wall according to the original undertaking was an essential part of the contract, and subsequent letters made it clear that until this had been satisfactorily completed the new church would not be consecrated.[44] This was no minor task to be hastily put up and then forgotten, for according to plans submitted by Mr. Clinton, the clerk of the works, it would cost £200.[45] The Commissioners, quite properly, regarded it as an essential part of the church building, but they also made it perfectly plain that not a penny would be forthcoming from them. This put the building committee into a panic. How were they to collect the money? It had been difficult enough to gather in the subscriptions which had been promised in 1829[46]; to ask for more was out of the question. There was only one alternative left—a church rate, but one fraught with unforseen circumstances and from which un-told bitterness in the future was to flow.

The fatal decision was taken in a general vestry on 19 July 1832, when it was resolved to adopt Mr. Clinton's plan, and further 'That instead of making a rate expressly for the purpose of building the Church Yard Wall it is advisable that the next Church Rate made by the Church Warden be augmented to one shilling and Six Pence in the pound and that two-thirds thereof be applied in building the new wall and the wardens are hereby requested forthwith to publish a vestry for the purpose of making sure a rate'.[47] In this way it was hoped that simply by augment-ing the normal rate, never in the past objected to by the rate-payers, the additional sum would be raised without trouble. This resolution was signed by the incumbent, the two wardens, and five others, but according to a later report was not a unanimous decision but passed on a majority vote. At the vestry called for the following week this resolution was confirmed, and signed by all seven persons present all, with one exception, having been present at the first vestry.[48] The exception was Edward Locke, the Custom House keeper. Events now moved very rapidly. There would appear to have been 'a general reluctance' on the part of the inhabitants to pay the rate and, constantly prodded by the Commissioners to get the work completed, and wishing to hasten the consecration, the wardens thereupon summoned some of the defaulting ratepayers. The resultant case before the county justices, chaired by the young Evan Matthews Davies, of Tanybwlch, was something of a *cause célèbre*, for the wardens had chosen to summon five Nonconformist ministers, including the three resident ministers of the Independents, Baptists, and Wesleyans (the congregation at Tabernacle was served by itinerant preachers). These were Azariah Shadrach, William Evans and E. Edwards. Also summoned was John Matthews the younger,[49] the land surveyor, draper, burgess and leading member of the town, who was also, like his father, a prominent Calvinistic Methodist. The conduct of the magistrates was alleged to have been disgraceful, in particular, no regard being paid to the plea of the defendants that the rate was illegal being in respect of property not belonging to the church and on unconsecrated land. All the defendants refused to pay, and their goods were distrained upon and auctioned for the recovery of the rates owed.[50]

The consequences of these events on the development of political parties and the growth of opinion in the town and locality were crucial and critical. Convinced that a miscarriage of justice had taken place it was resolved at a public meeting, chaired by William Locke and addressed by John Matthews, to seek counsel's opinion. Thirty one ratepayers contributed to the cost of this operation. At this meeting, resolutions were passed calling for an examination of the church-wardens' accounts for the past six years, deploring the arrogant and insulting behaviour of E. M. Davies, viewing with indignation the selcting of dissenting ministers 'to be the victims of the persecution' of the wardens, lamenting the past indifference of the inhabitants of the town to vestry proceedings, and calling upon them to attend all meetings of the vestry in future.[51] This latter point, was, of course, the crucial one. And the response was immediate. As we have seen, only eight people (including the incumbent and the two wardens) had attended the first of the July vestries and only nine the second. In October a total of 117 cast their votes, and a resolution for a repeal of the church rate was lost by only one vote.[52]

Until the application of the Municipal Reform Act to the town three years later the vestry was virtually the only governmental body in which the ratepayers at large could have a democratic voice. Municipal reform, including the adoption of an Improvement Act, made possible an extension of popular participation in local government, but the felt need to participate ante-dated such externally-imposed measures and stemmed directly from the sense of outrage generated by the events of 1832-3. The grievances of the Dissenters and of those Anglicans who sympathised with them, were real and painful: their religious leaders had been persecuted and justice abused for party and sectarian ends. Henceforth, there were reformers in the town, and the chapels would become the forcing-houses of Liberal opinion and the bases for the organization of political groups whose object-

The new St. Michael's Church, showing Castle House, the castle, and the retaining wall.

ives transcended the merely local and parochial. The Church Rate case altered fundamentally the religio-political imbalance of Church and Dissent, in particular by radicalizing the traditionally conservative Calvinistic Methodists. Church and Dissent now confronted each other where before they had tolerated, with mutual respect, each other's presence. In future, church-rates would be fought and carried, as the incumbent of Llanbadarn-fawr expressed it, 'against the powerful opposition of the Dissenters'. In 1856 they were made voluntary.[53] But that interval of twenty-four years had been a period of political education, with the result that the Liberalism of the parliamentary politics of the mid-century in Aberystwyth was not, as it had been hitherto, a purely nominal and conventional thing. It was Welsh Nonconformist Liberalism, as typified, for example, in the life of John Matthews, junior, the organizer of the Nonconformist Liberal break-through at the election of 1868.[54]

Thus it came about that the church wall was built, and St. Michael's opened for public worship on 27 July 1833 and consecrated the following September. In money terms it had cost £3,788 plus £338 for the wall. In social terms its cost was incalculable. A small sea-port, beginning to adjust itself to its new found role as a sea-side resort and unremarkable for the quality of its political life, was riven by controversy and torn by seemingly incompatible beliefs. Organized religion had become a matter not only of spiritual values but also of political attitudes and convictions. Anglicanism had become identified with despotic and irresponsible government, Nonconformity with liberal democracy. Leaders had arisen who would henceforth be identified with the party of change. Suddenly, absorbed as it has been with its own parochial affairs almost to the exclusion of the great issues of the day, Aberystwyth understood what national politics were about and the meaning of political principle.

NOTES

*First published in *Ceredigion*. VII, No2 (1973)

[1] 'An Act for Building and Promoting the Building of Additional Churches in Populous Parishes', 58 Geo. III, C. 45. For the work of the Commissioners consult M. H. Port, *Six Hundred New Churches. A Study of the Church Building Commission and its Church building Activities* 1818-1856 (1961). See also, in general, Owen Chadwick, *The Victorian Church*, 1, (1966), pp. 24 et. seq.; G. F. A. Best, *Temporal Pillars, Queen Anne's Bounty, the ecclesiastical Commissioners, and the Church of England* (1964), *passim.*

[2] Third Report of the Commissioners for Building New Churches, 1823, and R.O. Summary Book, f. 13. See also M. H. Port, *op. cit., p.138.*

[3] For Abersychan, see Twelfth Report, 1833, and E. C. R. O. Summary Book, f. 184: for Aberystwyth, see Thirteenth Report, 1833, and Summary Book, f. 189.

[4] For Bedwellty, see Seventeenth Report, 1837, and Summary Book, f. 217; for St. Woollos, Newport, *ibid.,* and Summary Book, f. 218; for Carmarthen, *ibid.,* and Summary Book, f. 218; for Eglwysilan, Nineteenth Report, 1839, and Summary Book, f. 235; Gwernafield, *ibid.,* and Summary Book, f. 236, and Brymbo, *ibid.,* and Summary Book, f. 238. See also 'Account of the Sums expended under the Directions of the Commissioners for Building New Churches since 15 May 1837', PP. 1840, XXXIX (262).

[5] Owen Chadwick, *op. cit.,* p. 85.

[6] For an account of the various chapels built, see George Eyre Evans, *Aberystwyth and its Court Leet* (1902), pp. 33-52, and Clare Taylor, 'Brief Aspects of the History of St. Michael's, Aberystwyth', *Ceredigion*, VI, No 4 (1971), pp. 415-421.

[7] N.L.W., St. Michael's Manuscripts and Documents, A2/12, Edward Haycock to Job Sheldon, 22 July 1820. On Haycock's reputation, see John Louis Petit's remarks on his design for St. David's, Barmouth, in *Remarks on Church Architecture* (1841), II, pp. 47-8 and 143, referred to by Sir Nikolaus Pevsner, *Some Architectural Writers of the Nineteenth Century* (1972), p. 96.

[8] N.L.W., St. Michael's Vestry Books, April 1825, and Evans, *op. cit.,* p. 46.

[9] See, for example, Evans, *op. cit.,* p. 45 who confuses the two men.

[10] Lambeth Palace, File 676, A Box 1; letter from John Hughes to the Secretary, dated 19 July 1825.

[11] Vestry Books and Evans, *op. cit.,* p. 46. It should be noted that the 1818 Act expressly forbade the parliamentary funds being used for enlarging existing buildings.

[12] Sir George Prevost, *Autobiography of Isaac Williams* (1893), pp 42-3, Benjamin Williams (Gwynionydd), *Enwogion Ceredigion* (1869), pp. 97ff.

[13] Clergy List, 1851 *sub.* Llanbadarn-fawr; Church in Wales Records, N.L.W. SD/SC/786-8 and SD/SL/3.

[14] R. O., Minute Books of H. M. Commissioners for Building New Churches, vol. III.

[15] Reports from the Commissioners appointed to consider the State of the Established Church, with reference to Ecclesiastical Duties and Revenues, P.P., 1835, XXII, Table IV, pp. 328-9 and 338-9.

[16] Church Building Commissioners, Minute Books, vol. III.

[17] Census of 1851.

[18] Evans, *op. cit.,* p. 46.

[19] Reports of Commissioners appointed to inquire into Municipal Corporations.

[20] For the political representation of Aberystwyth, one of the Cardiganshire boroughs, see David Williams, *The Rebecca Riots* (1955), pp. 8-11. There is a slightly scurrilous but interesting analysis of Aberystwyth politics on the eve of municipal reform in *The Welshman*, 15 January 1836.

[21] On this, see the correspondence in P.R.O. H.O. 13/2 and N.L.W. Aberystwyth Corporation Records.

[22] Evans, *op. cit.*, pp. 67-9, and Evans Evans, *Y Tabernacl, 1785—1935* in *Adroddiad am 1934-35* (1935), t. 53ff.

[23] T. Rees and J. Thomas, *Hanes Eglwysi Annibynnol Cymru* (1875) IV, pp. 132-3.

[24] David Jones, Caerfyrddin, *Hanes y Bedyddwyr yn Neheubarth Cymru* (1839), t. 106.

[25] *Ibid.*, p.100.

[26] A. H. Williams, *Welsh Wesleyan Methodism* (1935), pp. 118-9; Evans *op. cit.*, p.73.

[27] A congregation of 'Free Methodists'— probably belonging to the Wesleyan Methodist Association—began in 1842. Evans, *op. cit.*, p. 73.

[28] At the secession of 1811, a Calvinistic Methodist, Mr. David Jenkins, felt so strongly on the critical issue of holy orders that he built a chapel in Baker Street for the use of those who believed, as he did, that only episcopally ordained priests could legally officiate at communion, or indeed, ought to be permitted to do so. This attempt at conservative reaction failed, and in 1816 he rented the building to the Independents. Rees and Thomas, *op. cit.*, IV, p. 132.

[29] In 1836 the two Wesleyans elected to the new town council were accused of trying to avoid making a critical political decision by remaining neutral. *The Welshman*, 15 January 1836.

[30] This is printed in Evans, *Aberystwyth and its Court Leet*, pp. 68-9. See also Evan Evans, *op. cit.*, t. 56.

[31] *The Welshman*, 30 November 1832, letter signed 'Ratepayer'.

[32] The Wesleyans began in 1844 (rebuilt in 1869), the Methodists (Bath Street) in 1867, the Congregationalists in 1866, and the Baptists in 1867.

[33] N.L.W. 1805 E, f. 32; St. Michael's Documents A1/9.

[34] Church Building Commissioners to Haycock approving the tender, St. Michael's Documents A2/13.

[35] Same to John Hughes, 2 June 1825, *ibid.*, 'A1/43.

[36] M. H. Port, *op. cit.*, p. 108.

[37] Church Building Commissioners to John Hughes, 2 June 1828.

[38] Same to Building Committee, 12 June 1829 and J. Hughes to I.C.B.S., 20 June 1829, N.L.W. St. Michael's Documents, 3/35.

[39] This correspondence is to be found in *ibid.*, and in Lambeth Palace, I.C.B.S., A Box 1, File 676.

[40] Church Building Commissioners to John Hughes, 30 October and 12 December 1829.

[41] N.L.W. MS. 7963 E, f. 34.

[42] Rev. John Hughes to I.C.B.S., 1 Sept., 1830.

[43] *The Welshman*, 26 October 1832.

[44] C.B.S. to Rev. John Hughes, 22 June, 21 August, and 12 September 1832.

[45] Some of the correspondence with defaulting or tardy payers is preserved among the St. Michael's Documents.

[46] *The Welshman*, 26 October 1832.

[47] Matthews Papers, N.L.W. MS. 8326 E, f. 13.

[48] *Ibid.*, *sub.* 26 July 1832.

[49] *The Welshman*, 26 October 1832, and St. Michael's Documents, N.L.W.., 8326 E, f. 22. For John Matthews Junior, see D.W.B.

[50] *The Welshman*, 26 October 1832.

[51] Drafts of the resolutions and the names of proposers and seconders are to be found among the St. Michael's Documents, and in NLW. 8326 E, ff. 48, 106, 107 and 109. They are printed in 'Ratepayer's' letter, *The Welshman*, 26 October 1832.

[52] *Seren Gomer,* Tachwedd 1833, t. 343ff. carries an editorial on Church Rates in which it points out that some English places have refused to pay for fifteen years, that this attitude is now spending to Wales, and instances Aberystwyth as a recent example.

[53] Return of the names of all parishes in cities or parliamentary boroughs . . . in which (during the last fifteen years) Church Rates have been refused, and since that time have ceased altogether to be collected . . . P.P., 1856, XLVIII (319), p. 208.

[54] See the present author's 'Cardiganshire politics in the mid-nineteenth century', in *Explorations and Explanations,* pp. 165-192.

THE BUILDING OF ST. ELVAN'S CHURCH, ABERDARE

On the 11th December 1849, the Reverend John Griffith, vicar of Aberdare, wrote a long and somewhat impassioned letter to the secretary of the Incorporated Church Building Society. It was long because he had much to say about the social conditions of the parish, and it was impassioned, if not a little petulant, because it seemed abundantly clear to him that that august body, charged as it was with alleviating spiritual destitution wherever it might exist in England and Wales, was in danger of getting its priorities wrong. It may be that the young and eager incumbent of this turbulent parish was too acutely aware of the challenge of spiritual destitution in his own locality to be anything but partial in his judgement, but the statistics set forth in the Annual Report of the Society which he had been studying and its assessment of the extent and location of current needs could certainly have indicated that such a parish as his and such a diocese as Llandaff were indeed missing out in the urgent matter of church extension. In the forty years of its existence the Incorporated Society had made nearly 3,000 grants totalling almost half a million pounds, but of this quite prodigious total the diocese as a whole had received less than £9,000, and the parish of Aberdare nil. "I think it is time", he wrote, "that you gave Wales a turn", and his letter was an argument in favour of starting with Aberdare.[1]

This reproach was scarcely merited. The Society, despite its statutory privileges (it had been incorporated by Act of Parliament in 1828), its enjoyment of the highest degree of royal patronage, and the right which it enjoyed to issue the Queen's Letter in support of its operations, was nevertheless a voluntary society dependant upon the philanthropy of individuals and religious organization for its funds. These it dispersed not in order to initiate the expansion of church accommodation in particular places but mainly in order to encourage such initiatives by supplementing the charitable efforts already in being. If church accommodation were to be increased in Aberdare the parishioners would have to raise the bulk of the money. There was no other source, and even the Church

Building Commissioners could be expected to contribute only a relatively small sum. John Griffith was perfectly aware of this, and his original intention in writing to the Society had been simply to explain why he thought it was not expedient at the present time to appeal to his parishioners on behalf of their fund. The Queen's Letter would have to go unread. As he explained, when he had entered into his benefice three years previously there had been school accommodation for only 120 children: as a result of his efforts this had been expanded to 1,1000. All the money for this had been raised locally and it was unlikely that more would be forthcoming just yet. But the fact of "spiritual destitution" remained, and the expansion of school accommodation under the auspices of the National Society, though a necessary beginning, could not be an end in itself. As with all religious denominations in the mining and manufacturing districts of England and Wales, the pattern of growth was first the school and only then the church or chapel. It was this second and more difficult stage that concerned him now, and he could not but be gloomy and frustrated as he outlined the situation as he saw it for the benefit of the Society. Had he been able to foresee the trials and tribulations that lay ahead he would have been gloomier still.

What irked the vicar was the knowledge that, so far as he could tell, the Society's funds seemed to be going into parishes far less destitute than his own. "Spiritual destitution" could be measured numerically and expressed in arithmetical terms as the relation between the number of souls and available accommodation. Indeed, this was the only way, however rough and ready, in which a centralized agency could establish priorities. There was very little accurate information to go on. Officials relied for most of the basic information on the Ecclesiastical Revenues Commission Report of 1835 which, as they realized, was often defective and anyway out of date, and it was only the chance correspondence of local enthusiasts for their work which could provide the detailed statistics they required.[2] The annual report in the hands of the vicar made much of parishes of 5,000 souls with seating accommodation for only 600: but Aberdare had a population of 13,000 and only 250 seats. And this understated the true position for, as he later wrote, the

population was nearer 14,000 and the sittings only 176.[3] To
make matters worse, and a consideration of the highest
relevance to the Society, this population was growing, as had
been the case since the early 1840's, at almost 1,000 a year,
while the accommodation in St. John's remained static. Even
more serious was the fact that all the 176 seats available in the
parish were appropriated, that is to say, were the private
property of named individuals or offices and therefore, to all
intents and purposes, unavailable for use by other individuals.
In no other ancient parish in the diocese was the problem of
spiritual destitution, in this Anglican sense of the term, so stark
and brutal. Well might the Rev. John Griffith stand appalled
at the magnitude of the problem it posed. "There is no place
like it", he said, "unless it be San Francisco."[4]

There were two further factors complicating this already unprecedented example of spiritual destitution. The first Aberdare
had in common with most other mining districts of recent
growth, namely, what the vicar still regarded as the uncivilised,
lawless and turbulent, nature of its society. Strikes and disturbances, and serious exhibitions of uninhibited violence were
common. Only a fortnight previously a ten-week strike of
colliers had ended and already a new one had begun, and
"whether it will end quietly God only knows." Strikes and lock-
outs were to be deplored not only on account of the violence and
brutal behaviour which sometimes accompanied them; even
more alarming to the thoughtful observer was the irreparable
harm they could do to the social fabric.[5] The town was
beginning to know itself as a town, beginning to observe itself
objectively, and starting to take the first hesitant steps to provide
itself with communal facilities. It had begun to look to its roads,
to the drainage of parts of the town, was establishing a gas works,
building schools, thinking of enclosing land for a park, and
generally aspiring to self-government. Strikes and disturbances
destroyed not only the image of the place, but did considerable
damage to social relations. Above all, they reduced the supply of
money available for improvement both at the level of the individual household and at that of local government. That there
was poverty and physical destitution in Aberdare no one could
deny, but it was nothing to compare with the abject, hopeless,

despairing kind endemic in the great centres of population in England. Poorly paid ministers of religion of all denominations could be forgiven for taking a jaundiced view of a working population in conditions of full employment whose average household incomes far exceeded theirs. It was not only or mainly low wages which made Aberdare relatively poor, but the trade cycle aggravated by intermittent strikes and disturbances.[6]

The other factor was unique to Wales and present in one of its acutest forms in Aberdare. This was the problem of the two languages. There is no doubt that Aberdare was overwhelmingly Welsh at the time the vicar was writing his letter. The families flooding into the valleys whether they were bilingual or not (and probably they were mainly monoglot Welsh) required their religious services to be in the Welsh language. But St. John's was to all intents and purposes an English church. This was not the fault of John Griffith, for he was not a free agent in the ecclesiastical government of his parish. The chief ratepayers—the ironmasters and some of the colliery proprietors—were English. It was these who had appropriated the seats in the church and these, assisted by an English-orientated middle-class, who dominated the vestry. Hence, as the vicar explained shortly afterwards in his evidence before the Episcopal and Capitular Revenues Commission (1850) and again before a Select Committee of the House of Lords on the Means of Divine Worship in Populous Places (1851), he was obliged, if there were to be any Welsh service at all, to hold it, "at an hour which is most inconvenient to" the Welsh worshippers, that is to say, "in the afternoon, when the generality of Welsh working people go to lie on their beds." As one workman had remarked, "A man must indeed have a love for the gospel to go to worship at such an hour."[7] Without their own church building providing services for them in their own language the Anglican cause in Aberdare would languish and die. Whether or not they were misguided in thus insisting on the use of their own language was beside the point. But we may observe in passing that language had a distinct and vital role to play in the creation of a working-class consciousness. The working-classes of northern England, it was observed, clung stubbornly and irrationally to their own distinctive and "barbarous" accents and speech idioms: Welsh working men had even more justification for clinging tenaciously in their own insecure communities to their infinitely richer and more precious heritage of a distinct language. [8]

The response of the Society to the vicar's letter was immediate and favourable. In the event of a new church being built they would provide a grant-in-aid and make their other resources available. It now lay with the vicar and his parishioners to make a decision and present their plans. This was the crucial stage in the movement for church extension in the parish, and the vicar was faced with a potentially difficult and complicated situation. First, he would require a site as near the old church and the centre of the town as possible, precisely, that is to say, where land values were high. Fortunately, his late patron, the second marquess of Bute, who was the major landowner in that part of Aberdare, had promised to provide land for a church four years previously when he had given land for a parsonage. [9] The trustees of the estate honoured this promise, and a site overlooking the old church and dominating the centre of the town was given. Later, as we shall see, the conveyance of the site to the Ecclesiastical Commissioners was to cause the vicar and his wardens infinite trouble, but for the time being all was well.

The second obstacle the vicar could expect to encounter was much more formidable, namely, the absolute necessity of carrying his parishioners with him. Much would depend on the state of relations between Anglicans and Nonconformists, and since the latter were in a majority and led by such redoubtable champions as the Baptist minister Thomas Price of Calfaria, and politically-minded colliery owners and shopkeepers, it was by no means certain whether the necessary tolerant cooperation would be forthcoming. The memory of the vicar's "treacherous" evidence before the Education Commissioners of 1847 was still fresh in people's mind, and it was still possible for the embers of resentment to be fanned into a blaze of anti-church hostility. In the event, there was no opposition and no hostility. In April, 1850, the vestry, in which Thomas Price was a leading figure, agreed the normal church rate of one penny in the pound, and later (24 July) a parish meeting specially convened agreed that church accommodation was insufficient and that steps

The newly built St. Elvan's Church rising above the 'Rising Sun.'
Photo: Cynon Valleys Libraries, Aberdare.

should be taken for the erection of a new church.[10] As the *Cardiff and Merthyr Guardian* reported, there was "but one feeling throughout, and that was the kindliest possible towards the Church, as well as the liveliest sense of the duty and the necessity of providing more church room." Nearly £1,000 was promised at that one meeting, before any formal appeal had been made, and it is significant that much of this was made up of relatively small sums.[11] The vicar could not have expected such a favourable response, for the people of Aberdare were perfectly aware that the church in their parish was potentially extremely rich. The rectorial and vicarial tithes were commuted for a rent charge of £352 per annum, but of this very substantial sum £342 was retained by the impropriators, the dean and chapter of Gloucester. The whole income from church property in the parish was only £10, and it was only after long negotiations, conducted for the most part on the side of the vicar in the columns of *John Bull,* that the impropriators had reluctantly given an additional £20 towards the cost of employing as curate for three years. Even more of a scandal was the fact that the impropriators, headed by the dean (the brother of Lord Dynefor), were leasing the most valuable parts of the glebe for the ridiculously low rental of about £150 to £200 and a fine of £108.10s. every seven years. It was well-known that the 30 acres of glebe should produce £1,500 a year as building land and that mine royalties could produce an income of around £33,000 per annum. Lord Bute got 1s. a ton in royalties: why not the Church? "The abuse of this property is the constant talk of the parish: if I ask for any subscription from gentlemen, towards schools or anything else, they always say, 'There is plenty of Church property. Why is not that applied to this?'"[12] Had the voluntaryist Nonconformists wished they could surely have made of these facts a major justification for opposition. In fact, one had to search the files of *Y Diwygiwr,* the monthly journal of the Independents, edited by David Rees and published in his home town of Llanelli, for any murmurings of dissent. Yet even the carping letters published in that periodical could not conceal the fact that even Hirwaun, that stronghold of Nonconformity, responded generously to the appeal.[13]

There are several possible explanations for this happy state of affairs. At the level of highest generality we can see that spiritual destitution was a fact of life in Aberdare which all religious denominations recognized, which none could ignore, and to the alleviation of which all were equally committed. The market was unlimited, free trade the accepted philosophy, and the rewards beyond price. Religious "protectionism" simply did not exist, and what an observer called y *farchnad rhydd mewn eneidiau* ("free-trade in souls") was the order of the day. At the level of practical operations the vicar kept it so. He had learned his lesson in 1847, had come to respect his adversaries even to the extent of sharing many of their basic pre-suppositions, and he acted with diplomatic finesses in his relations with them. Neither in his private letters to the Society, nor in the more public evidence he gave before various commissions inquiring into the religious conditions of his parish and region, did he attack Nonconformity either as a religious or a political movement. He believed ardently in the Church and accepted as a guiding principle of ecclesiastical reform the ancient tradition that the mission of his Church was to all men, that the parish as an ecclesiastical unit was his responsibility, and that it was his duty to provide accommodation adequate for all, irrespective of creed, language or wealth. Finally, at the level of community responsibility and civic virtue, he knew that in building a splendid but unostentatious edifice, the church would set standards of architectural excellence in the rapidly growing town, and become a source of pride not only to church-people but to the inhabitants of the valley as a whole.

He was planning for a building to accommodate 800 persons, and the architects of the Incorporated Society (as of the Church Commissioners) reckoned that a building of that size, "of a plain but correct style" could be erected for about £3,000, depending upon the locality. The vestry held on 28 January 1851 decided to build to a design submitted by the architect Andrew Moseley of London, and accepted an estimate for £3,225 for the cost of building (excluding fees, etc., amounting to £275). The building would provide a total of 752 sittings of which 510 would be free. It was to be Early Decorated in style, cruciform in shape, consisting of nave, chancel, side aisles and transepts, with a tower and spire, and north and south porches. The timbers were to be of Baltic fir, the roof timbers ornamented, the pillars, arches, lintels, etc., of Bath stone, the guttering of heavy lead, and so on.[14] Strangely enough, no one questioned the estimate. The Society's architects accepted the design more or less and agreed his estimate even though the alterations they suggested increased rather than decreased the cost. It was not until the contractor's tender from the firm of Strawbridge, Bristol, was received in February that drastic action was taken to reduce the estimate. Strawbridge's tender was for £4,685, and the Society's architects were hard put to reduce the final estimate to £3,019. The thickness of the walls was reduced by 6 inches all round, the south door and porch and the south transept left out, the height of the nave reduced, the amount of Bath stone severely limited, and most ornamentation removed.[15] In fact, St. Elvan's was to be a much plainer church than Moseley had planned or the building committee had envisaged.

This reduction in the probable cost must have been welcomed by the vicar and his committee, for otherwise they would have been left with an impossible deficit such as the Church Building Commissioners would never sanction. At the time of the original application the local committee had raised £1,900, leaving a deficiency of about £1,000. To this the Church Building Commissioners were prepared to contribute £250, and the Incorporated Society £400. It is interesting and instructive to note the pattern of philanthropic giving which the building called forth. The bulk of the money was raised within the parish, and only to a lesser extent (if we exclude the Bute estate) in the diocese. The largest givers were the Abernant Iron Company (£105), and J. Bruce Pryce of Duffryn (£100). There were six contributions of £50, including those of Thomas Wayne, H. A. Bruce, G. R. Morgan (Gadlys), William Thomas, the Court, Merthyr, and David Davis, the coalowner (and Nonconformist). The two valley surgeons gave £30 each, as did Morgan Williams, the registrar and old Chartist leader. There were numerous contributions of £15 and under, including most of the leading tradesmen, innkeepers, agents and so on—men whose names constantly recur in the religious and political annals of the valley. Diocesan philanthropy was represented by the bishop

(£50), the vicar (£60), the bishop's son (£10), the archdeacon (£10), and the rector of St. Nicholas, H. A. Bruce's cousin, (£5). Most notable of all was the £50 donated by the newly-formed Llandaff Church Building Society—or, to give it its full title, the Society for Providing Additional Pastoral Superintendance and Church Accommodation in the Diocese of Llandaff. Formed in October 1850 largely as a result of the efforts of Archdeacon Thomas Williams whose *Charge* of 1849 and subsequent *Open Letter* to the bishop had demonstrated the extent of spiritual destitution in the diocese, the Society had already raised a capital sum of over £4,000 by the time St. Elvan's had been started. It liked to think of St. Elvan's as its own particular church, the first-fruits of its efforts to stir the consciences and open the sewn-up purses of that rich but irresponsible class, the ironmasters and coalowners.[16] But it was due mainly to the indefatigable vicar of Aberdare that the funds for the new church continued to flow, and St. Elvan's is a monument to his reforming zeal, his evangelical ardour, his commitment to the people of the valleys, and to the generosity of his parishioners.

And truly, he required to be zealous and indefatigable, for almost as soon as the building was completed the troubles that beset him multiplied. Money was a constant source of worry. St. Elvan's was opened for public worship on 30 September 1852, and as Mr. Boyle, the senior trustee of the Bute estate remarked when he visited it, it was to be admired as an "ornament of ecc-lesiastical art not to be equalled in the principality."[17] So it was, but ornaments of ecclesiastical art cost money, and the original estimate had been far exceeded by the contractor. Soon the vicar was pleading with the Society for the payment of their grant of £400. The church had already cost them more than £4,000, excluding £100 for a heating apparatus, and £185 for a small organ. By July 1853 he was in desperate straits. The contractor's bill was no less than £5,293—an impossible sum. Mr. Moseley's estimate of work done was for £3,995, and arbitrators had come up with the figure of £4,147. Evidently the contractor held out for his price, and was threatening the vicar with an action which could be avoided only by payment into court of the sum of £1,270. By August, £4,300 had been paid. but the possibility of a court action for payment of the remaining

£1,000 still hung over him. The vicar had already borrowed £1,400, but despite his appeals and those of the churchwardens and a testimonial from the bishop, not until August was the grant paid over and the vicar relieved of the worst of his embarrassment.[18]

The explanation for this curious attitude on the part of the Incorporated Society lay in two quite separate difficulties which had arisen between the vicar, the Bute estate and the Ecclesiastical Commissioners. The first was—or appeared to be—a relatively simple matter. To whom would the patronage of the church belong? Obviously, no one had thought of this, and since the original intention had been to build a new church to *replace* the old one, the question would not have arisen. Since 1846 the patron of the benefice had been the marquess of Bute: it had been the second marquess who had persuaded the original patrons, that is to say, the dean and chapter of Gloucester as patrons of the mother church of Llantrisant, and the vicar of Llantrisant as patron of the chapelry of Aberdare, to transfer the patronage to himself in return for an augmentation of £85 per annum for the newly created vicarage. The Incorporated Society as well as the Ecclesiastical Commissioners had to be satisfied on this matter because in law a patron had duties as well as rights, in particular, duties regarding the upkeep of the fabric which he shared with the parish. Now that an *additional* church existed, would the young heir, when he entered into his inheritance, accept the increased responsibilities which patronage implied? Would he exercise a right of appointment to the new church? Who could tell?—for the marquess was only two years of age. The vicar's solution was simple: he proposed that St. Elvan's should be regarded as a supplementary parish church. He was confident that the ratepayers would grant a rate towards maintaining the fabric of the new as well as the old church, and that for purposes of appointment the patronage should be vested in him as incumbent to be exercised in consultation with the bishop. He was certain that the marquess, when he came of age, would agree to this arrangement and consent to the binding of the incumbent's successors to maintain it. In the event, St. Elvan's became a curacy under St. John's. Had anyone been able to foresee that the third marquess would become a Roman

Catholic on reaching his majority it is virtually certain that different arrangements would have been made. As it was, the vicar now had his two churches in the town of Aberdare, and his dream of having a separate building for his Welsh parishioners had been realized.

The second difficulty was much more complicated, and since it was largely a matter for lawyers, involving protracted negotiations between the Bute estate and the Ecclesiastical Commissioners, it nearly drove the vicar to distraction. It was accepted that the land on which St. Elvan's stood had been given by the Bute estate, but it was a condition of consecration that the land should be conveyed to the Commissioners. Difficulties arose over two matters. In the first place, there seemed to be a doubt—it is hard to see why—in the minds of the Commissioners as to whether a conveyance by the Bute trustees would be good in law. When satisfied on this point, they wanted an assurance that the minerals under the plot would not be worked. The right to work the underlying minerals in the vicinity of the church was already leased to David Davis, the colliery proprietor, and the suggestion to the Commissioners that the conveyance should include the underlying minerals as well as the surface area was tantamount, according to the vicar, to requiring an additional £3,000 from lady Bute who had already contributed £500 to the church. The Bute estate was ready to give a guarantee that the underlying minerals would not be worked, but the Commissioners insisted on a hard and fast conveyance in fee simple. This was a matter for lawyers and involved technicalities beyond the capacity of the vicar to understand. For two years the negotiations dragged on, the church meanwhile remaining unconsecrated, and it required the personal representations of powerful local men, such as G. T. Clark of Dowlais, and Crawshay Bailey of the Aberaman iron works, to the senior trustee of the Bute estate to persuade E. P. Richards, his south Wales agent, to finalize the matter late in 1853.[19] But St. Elvan's existed, a splendid building set on a hill and not to be hid. It was in use, and the ivy-clad church of St. John's below it rang again with the sounds of an ancient language so apt for praise and adoration. Already the vicar had turned his attention to the spiritual destitution in other parts of

St. Elvan's Church, Aberdare, Glamorganshire.
Photo: Rock & Co. London.

his parish, and shortly he would have the joy of officiating at the opening of yet another new church, St. Fagans. But it was St. Elvan's which most clearly embodied his ideal of the church in an industrial society, and its existence thereafter ensured that the Anglican church should contribute readily to the developing culture of the town and valley.

NOTES

[1] Lambeth Palace Library, I.C.B.S., Aberdare, First Church, file 4219, Rev. J. Griffith to Secretary dated from Aberdare Vicarage 11 December 1849.

[2] P.p. 1835, XXII, Table IV, pp. 123 et seq.

[3] I.C.B.S., File 4219, Griffith to Secretary 12 December 1850.

[4] *ibid.*, Griffith to Secretary 11 December 1849.

[5] *ibid.*

[6] See above pp. 265-9 for a detailed study of the growth of the town.

[7] Episcopal and Capitular Revenues Commission: Report and Minutes of Evidence, P.P. 1850, XX (1175), Qs. 2923-64.

[8] For further discussion of this point see above pp. 132-5.

[9] *CMG,* 3 August 1850 for a detailed report of the Vestry held 25 July 1850, and *ibid.* 3 February 1851 for the Vestry held 28 January 1851. It is interesting to note that the first move to increase accommodation in Aberdare was at a Vestry on 24 July 1850 with the aim of asking for the assistance of the impropriator of the living, namely, the Dean and Chapter of Gloucester: Aberdare Minute Vestry Minute Book 1843—1904, GRO P/61/2.

[10] For Thomas Price and his role in Aberdare politics see above pp. 264 ff.

[11] *CMG,* 3 August 1850.

[12] Episcopal and Capitular Revenues Commission, 'Q. 2964.

[13] For lists of subscribers see *CMG,* 3 August 1850 et seq.

[14] This is based on correspondence and returns in ICBS, File 4219.

[15] The estimate was reduced by £1606.

[16] See, in addition to the *Open Letter* and *Charge* of 1849, *Substance of Speeches delivered at Bridgend and Newport . . . 1850* (London) 1850).

[17] *CMG,* 2 October 1852 for an account of the opening ceremonies.

[18] ICBS, Griffiths to Secretary, 29 July 1853 and 25 August 1853.

[19] This analysis is based on the correspondence in ICBS File 4219 and on papers in the archives of the Church Commissioners, London.

Part 2

Communities

THE SOUTH WALES COLLIER IN MID-NINETEENTH CENTURY

In the mid-nineteenth century the town of Cardiff and the cathedral town of Llandaff were undergoing an architectural transformation involving artistic embellishments that were to be the wonder of the time and which remain to delight and astonish our own generation. The rebuilding of the cathedral church, the rehabilitation of the castle and the rebuilding of Castell Coch could not but have had profound implications for the rapidly growing communities of south Wales. They must be seen against a background of valleys being denuded of their vegetation, of hills being turned inside-out as the teeming thousands laboured like termites to produce the incredible wealth thus being displayed in arrogant profusion. At the other end of the scale from the priceless, exotic fantasies of the castle and the marquess's other residences and follies, must be put the new frontier towns and villages, and the ill-designed, hastily built and amenity-lacking collections of colliery houses where lived the families whose labour produced the wealth. Socially perhaps the outstanding difference between the third marquess and his father must lie in the quality of their alienation from the communities which they were largely responsible for calling into being. Unlike his father, the third marquess was not directly involved as entrepreneur in the industrial life of south Wales, and by the time he had reached his majority and entered into his inheritance, conditions had so changed politically that it was no longer feasible to control in an aristocratic fashion the political development of the towns and territories over which he was overlord. The father built docks and railways, apportioned leases, set rents, and agreed royalties: the son built castles and landscaped parks, and reigned rather than ruled in those areas where his influence was commensurate with his royalties. The social distance, therefore, between the third marquess and the collier communities of the hinterland of the port of Cardiff increased rather than decreased as time went on, and the consequent confrontation between the two different cultures became more stark and grotesque as the century unfolded. The father, by his extraordinary combination of entrepreneurial skill and aristocratic pretensions, had dictated the slant of social change in Cardiff and its environs: while the son pursued his rarified hobbies and satisfied his aesthetic longings, power fell into the hands of the new bourgeoisie, the coal-owners and shipping magnates and merchants, the creators of the new wealth, the political masters of the town. At the same time the terribly neglected colliery towns and villages were creating their own distinctive communities, producing a unique culture out of their own individual experiences.

The rebuilding of Llandaff Cathedral, similarly, was at the time curiously unrelated to what some observers regarded as the most pressing religious and social problems and needs of the expanding coalfield. The rebuilding precipitated as sharp a crisis as any experienced in the history of the diocese. The poorest diocese in Great Britain—in financial resources, buildings, and manpower—it had been suddenly, in the space of thirty or forty years, overwhelmed by a population explosion greater than that experienced by any other diocese in the kingdom. Even with fairly substantial help from the Ecclesiastical Commissioners its resources in money and men remained hopelessly inadequate. Its patrons among the gentry were relatively few and larger in their promises than in their magnanimity, and the new capitalists of the Hills were either mean to the point of culpability or Nonconformists not over-anxious to rehabilitate an alienated established Church. By the middle of the century the clergy of the coalfield were split into opposing factions—the rich, well-connected, highly educated gentlemen-clergy of the Vale, confronted by a kind of proletarian clergy of the Hills, the latter poor, for the most part ill-educated, with a social status and at an income-level not very superior to that of their Nonconformist brethren. It was the former class of clergy, hereditary landlords some of them (like Bruce-Knight, the Dean of Llandaff) who pressed for magnificence in the rebuilding. It was the poor clergy of the Hills and industrial parishes, led by the Rector of Merthyr, who opposed the scale of the rebuilding on grounds of evangelical need. It is scarcely an exaggeration to suggest that the rebuilding of Llandaff Cathedral in the middle years of the nineteenth century, at a time when the Church was faced with its greatest challenge ever, and in a diocese overwhelmingly Nonconformist when it was not raw with irreligion, was itself symptomatic of the existence of layers of cultural alienation within the society of the coalfield as a whole.

*   *   *   *

It is difficult and dangerous to generalise about the Welsh collier at any time: the communities he created differed substantially from place to place and from time to time. This should not surprise us. Geography has been as divisive a force in the history of south Wales as a unifying one. The steep sides of the valleys, even after the coming of the railways, have always been a hindrance to communication, and one senses that the villages which grew up along their flanks and in the folds of the encompassing hills nourished a strong individuality. Isolation was always a condition of life for these communities, and joint concerns and common interests on social and political questions were invariably friable and grew longitudinally, so that it is "valley" opinion on questions of current interest that one finds rather than a coalfield view.

Taking a wider view, it is necessary to stress that the geological peculiarities of the coalfield militated against uniformity of structure and social pattern. The steam coals are found in the centre of the coal-basin at very deep levels, the bituminous coals along its borders and rim near the sea or in the high plateaux, while the anthracite coals are found only west of the Tawe valley in that region of small farms on the low, wooded hills running down from the great limestone Carmarthenshire Black Mountains. Not until the '80s did the anthracite coalfield develop in a substantial way, by which time the great steam-coal age had entered its prime. The unsuitability of anthracite for smelting; its very specialised market, and the late development of railways in the region meant that its exploitation was never on the same scale as that of other types of coal, and that consequently the growth of communities in that region was more sober and orderly, more integrated into the pre-existing agricultural order, its communities smaller, and its way of life less disrupted by alien influences.

There were great differences, therefore, in the type of settlement in the different regions of the coalfield. Nowhere in south Wales, with the possible exception of Merthyr Tydfil and the port of Cardiff later in the century, was there a truly urbanised proletariat. The degree of urbanization, however, varied greatly from place to place. None of the towns of south Wales was so large as completely to engulf its inhabitants, and in all of them the rural hinterland interpenetrated the urban pattern of settlement. But this is a matter of degree. Within the context of the coalfield itself the distinctions which are socially meaningful are between those towns which supported a variety of industries and those which depended entirely on coal production, and secondly, between those towns with long urban traditions of government and those with little or none. Iron-making, non-ferrous smelting, tinplate manufacture produced relatively diversified communities. Ancient corporate towns (and there were few of these) made it possible for urban growth consequent upon industrialisation to be nucleated both physically and socially around pre-existing centres and institutions. Where, as in Merthyr and, earlier in the century, at Aberdare coal was but one factor in the industrial process, the collier was but one occupation group among many. He was under the social necessity, both within the context of work and of leisure, to see himself in relation to other occupation groups. Group solidarity, in this sense, was a major concern: within the context of work it tied him to the interests of other workers with whom his own interests might or might not coincide. Within the context of leisure it induced him to provide his own distinctive and (often) exclusive means of entertainment and self-improvement—his own pubs, friendly societies, etc. Invariably in such towns colliers tended to occupy distinct areas, neighbourhoods which were regarded as distinct communities. In such towns, also, there existed hierarchies among the different classes of workmen. In the iron-towns, for instance, if we may judge by rates of wages, the collier was midway between the skilled iron-worker and the iron-stone miner.

Occupational diversity—leaving one side the relatively few craftsmen—was entirely lacking in the typical colliery village in the steam coal region. In such places the occupational structure was entirely within one industry, the one pit. But this did not ameliorate—it sharpened hierarchical differences. The collier felt himself to be above the day-wage men—the repairers, riders, hauliers, door-boys, etc—in fact, a skilled man claiming for his work a wage relative to his function. It was the uncontrolled, massive expansion of the labour force which prevented the growth of such feelings and their expression in some corporate form of industrial organisation. A great deal of the literature produced by colliers during these decades is about this—an exercise in self-esteem, the creation of an image of the collier and of his role vis-a-vis other workers and in relation to society at large. Of course, within these one industry settlements there were subtle differences in status—differences which are immediately apparent to the initiated. At first glance the villages appear to consist of monotonous rows of terraced houses, built of locally quarried stone or manufractured brick, but a closer observation will reveal the telling difference: the bow window, the front garden bordered by a wall, the manager's house, the overman'a residence, and so on. Where occupation left little or no scope for the visible expression of individual difference and individual gifts, or no avenue for social aspirations, the collier was not long in creating them.

These new colliery settlements differed from the iron towns also in respect of the opportunities for alternative employment which they provided. The possibility of finding a different job, whether better paid or not, as miner or iron-worker or tinplate worker was completely lacking. And slack times were slack not for one occupation only, or for a particular area of a town, but for the bulk of the population and for the whole community. We should not exaggerate the degree of choice and the availability of alternative work in the iron towns; but however little it was less in the colliery villages of the steam coal area. And as this region came to be exploited intensively, and the valleys to be populated and settled by communities all producing for the same market, so the opportunities for the readily migrant collier to move elsewhere became more restricted.

Physically also, these new villages and towns were different. Merthyr Tydfil in mid-century might appear to the outside observer to be monotonous and drab to a degree, the houses

and shops being uniform in appearance and structure. This
was not in reality so, any more than its class structure was as
simple as some people claimed it was. The discerning observer
would remark on the differences between the types of building—of houses and cottages, shops and chapels, and the public
places, the squares and 'triangles', the back-to-backs, the
thatched cottages white washed as in their original rural
setting, the long terraces of houses. There was in reality great
physical diversity, but it was this which was lacking in the
colliery village. One might distinguish between the original
rows of houses put up by the coal owner or his agent
immediately coal had been struck and the later mushroom-
building of the private speculator, but apart from the few larger
houses of the managerial class, subsequent building was all of a
pattern. When the collier built for himself, and terminating
building societies and building clubs flourished in the valleys,
he put up houses indistinguishable from those of the speculative builder or the houses built for renting by the coal owner.
Poll-stone, with yellow or red brick window and door sur-
rounds, these terraces of houses are bleak and monotonous.
All were nucleated around the newly-sunk pit, and since they
were invariably sunk in the valley bottom development tended
to be longitudinal, running parallel with the railway, along the
road, and beside the river, with colliery tips spilling down the
hill-side threatening to do the lives of the people what they had so
quickly done to the fields and vegetation.

Further west, on the anthracite coalfield, settlements were
entirely different. As a direct consequence of the way in which
they had originated and the relatively slow rate of their growth
there was there a greater degree of integration into the pre-
existing rural structure, and therefore a more direct preservation
of the peasant culture into the new industrial age. Many of these
colliery villages were nucleated around the church, in this
respect being extensions of ancient villages. In others, hill-top
churches became the centres for new developments. In these
cases the original character of the villages was preserved, rarely
engulfed by the inward migration of people, and the old
buildings provided the pattern and the inspiration for the new
ones. This should not surprise us, for migration into these

colliery villages was generally short-distance migration, and the proportion of new-comers lower than that in the steam coal areas. Even when new villages were founded near the sites of collieries the migrant workers did not flood in from the surrounding countryside. Not until the last decades of the century was growth so rapid as to produce towns on the scale of these in the steam coal areas, and when this happened the growth was stimulated more by tinplate undertakings than by coal mining. In the anthracite area, therefore, urbanisation was at its least significant. A sizeable proportion of the colliers were never entirely dependent upon their wages: they were also farmers, small-holders for whom work in a colliery was welcomed as a means of supplementing an inadequate income from farming. The multiplication of small collieries, usually drifts, over a large geographical area in a region of marginal hill-farming was not conducive to the growth of large urban settlements or to the creation of an industrial proletariat. The colliery *village* was typical of this region, and the rural 'mores' were preserved in the way of life of the colliers living in and about them.

Another difference between the different regions was the difference of language. The collier was typically a Welshman, but anglicization affected the whole of the coalfield with increasing strength throughout the period. Immigration from adjacent English counties exerted a powerful influence on the linguistic composition of the coalfield. Anglicization had started in eastern Monmouthshire before the coming of industry to south Wales, though it is probable that heavy migration into the coalfield from adjacent Welsh speaking counties held back the process of complete anglicization until comparatively late in the century. In the early nineteenth century the Monmouthshire coalfield appears to have been Welsh in its more formal social life, probably more so in the Hills than in the developing steam-coal areas in the southward-running valleys. The Glamorgan coalfield was certainly Welsh for very much longer, and this includes the older iron towns which had from their beginnings experienced an influx of skilled and unskilled English workmen. As late as the 1880s it is probable that the whole of the coalfield was Welsh in its language and in the institutions the people created for themselves, and that this institutional life was strong enough to absorb the English-language culture of the migrants from England. Even in Merthyr in the 70's it was necessary for English lecturers and politicians to have the service of interpreters. Further west, Welsh was exclusively the language of common discourse. As the century advanced, however, the tide of anglicization flowed more strongly. Educational policy, the prestige-value of English and, above all, sheer indifference resulted in Welsh becoming the language of a minority and tending to be confined to institutions and to areas of experience which were themselves rapidly losing their prestige and relevance.

Structural differences such as these cannot be ignored because they underlie basic themes in the social development of the region. The formal politics of the coalfield, for instance, is unintelligible unless we take account of the fact that until 1885 all the new urban development was taking place outside the parliamentary limits of the old boroughs. The failure to create any effective trade union organisation covering the whole of the coalfield until after 1898 is another example. It was these structural differences, likewise, which determined the preoccupations of the colliers in the different areas, for it was these which controlled the pattern of his work, the types of social discipline to which he was subjected, the conditions of his labour, and the quality of his personal life as reflected in his leisure activities. And they help to explain why socialism came so late to the coalfield.

What then were the colliers' preoccupations? How did he regard himself in the society of the coalfield? His immediate preoccupation, naturally enough, was in his labour, its conditions, and its rewards. Judging by what he himself wrote about these aspects of his life and from the way in which he conducted his relations with his masters, he had a high regard for himself, for his skill and intelligence, his courage and endurance. Indeed, he could scarcely undervalue these characteristics for they were developed to a high degree by the nature of his job. Whether he worked in level, drift or pit his tasks demanded considerable intelligence and self-assurance as well as physical strength. The techniques of working the coal could be acquired only with long practice, and almost uniquely in this occupation his survival depended utterly on the method used to extract the coal, to stand timbers, and other multifarious aspects of his craft. He spent at least twelve hours of every working day in constant danger of his life from falls or explosions, and the best collier was he who learned to respect his environment and to understand its silent ways. He needed to be strong, with great powers of endurance, and while preserving his individuality, the integrity of his stall, he had to respect the rights of others, for not to do so might lead to disaster. Everywhere he learned the craft the hard way. Officially or not there was a kind of apprentice system and ideally, however he hated the memory of it, his working life would have begun as a lad of ten or eleven years sitting for twelve hours each day at the ventilation doors listening for the sound of the journey of trams and watching for the glimpse of another human being in the dim light of his candle. Ben Davies, a poet of no mean stature, wrote about such experiences in his memoirs.

"Carchar rhyfedd oedd hwn i blentyn y mynydd. Cofiaf yr oriau unig yn y gongl gerllaw'r drws. Ai awr heibio weithiau heb i mi weled na chlywed neb. Edrychwn i'r tywyllwch bythol ar bob llaw. Rhoddai fy llusern bŵl ddigon o olau i mi weled y tywyllwch. Clywn sŵn y diferyn unig yn disgyn—fel ticiadau hen gloc araf yn y pellter—yn myned i gyfeiriad arall. Os cofiaf yn iawn, dim ond rhyw bedair siwrnai yn y dydd ai heibio i mi yn ystod deuddeg awr. Deuai hiraeth poenus arnaf ar adegau am y caeau, a'r defaid, a'r bryn, a'r mynydd. Ar awr o syched angerddol byddwn yn portreadu dylif croyw, eirias "Ffrydiau Twrch' gerbron fy meddwl, ac yn meddwl fod yr haul yn tywynnu ar y caeau—a ninnau yn y dyfnder du. Yr oedd pruddglwyf yn fy nghalon bob awr. Gyda mynwes drom lwythog yr awn i lawr y pwll bob bore—ac un ochenaid hir ddistaw oedd y diwrnod ar ei hyd. Nid oeddwn yn gallu chwerthyn yn y dyddiau hynny. Methwn a mwynhau nos Sadwrn na'r Sul, am fod bore Llun a'i garchar du a'i safn yn agored ar fy nghyfer''.
(*Darn o Hunangofiant*).

'A strange prison was that for a child of the hills. How can I forget the lonely hours in a corner by the doors? Sometimes an hour would pass without the sight or sound of a solitary human being. I would gaze into the blackness that surrounded me. The pool of light shed by my lamp was sufficient only for me to see the darkness. . . A painful longing would sometimes assail me for the fields, the sheep and the hills. In the hour of greatest deprivation I would paint before my eyes the crystal clarity of the mountain stream at its source, and imagine the sun shining on the fields—and me buried in that grim blackness. My heart was heavy with sadness each day. With a heavy, laden breast I would go down each morning—the day was one long sob. I could not laugh in those days. And Saturday night and Sunday morning were without pleasure for me because Monday morning with its black prison and gaping jaws waited to engulf me.'

It is now wonder that the favourite verse form of the Welsh collier was the nature lyric: unnatural darkness opened their eyes to natural beauty. Other boys, as a visitor observed in 1851, took to their work 'a farthing's worth of happiness in the form of a piece of chalk', and covered their doors with their recollections of life above ground. In both types of reaction art made bearable what must have been almost intolerable to the boy and brutalizing for the man. Alternatively, the boy learned his craft with his father or close relatives, and there were tasks of astonishing severity which only he could perform. It was his task in some places to drive ventilation shafts two or three feet in diameter through the rock or coal from one heading to another. His job too, to help fill the drams, loading the large in such a way as to obviate the production of small coal for which the men were not paid. Stepping timber was a highly skilled job, calling for a sure eye and hand, and a respect for the materials, both the wood itself and the rock it was designed to support.

A major preoccupation of the colliers was in the conditions of their labour and, in particular, in the question of safety. Conditions varied, of course, from district to district and from mine to mine, but from the time of the sinking of pits in the central coalfield to the deep steam seams conditions worsened.

Pen-y-Graig Exposion 1880

The down-shaft explorers descending.
Photo: National Library of Wales

Explorers crawling between the fallen debris and the roof.

Bringing the dead from the bottom of the Shaft.
Photo: National Library of Wales.

Carrying the dead through the village of Trealaw.
Photo: National Library of Wales.

Technically, there were improvements: in ventilation, in winding mechanisms, for instance; but the tally of disasters over and
above the less publicized toll of individual lives and limbs,
showed how inadequately the industry was responding to the
increasing demands and responsibilities now being placed on
it. 914 men and boys were killed by explosions alone in
Glamorgan between 1844 and the end of 1871—an average of
about 32 lives per year. In 1865, 159 lives were lost in the coalfield and another 120 the following year—or, as the annual
report of the Inspectorate put it, 1½ lives per 100,000 tons of
coal raised.

The men were aware of all these adverse conditions, obviously, and a great deal of their leisure time was spent discussing the question of responsibility for safety—the role of the
collier himself, of the master, and of the government. Indeed,
in the late 50's and 60's, even before the terrible Blaenllechau
(Ferndale) disaster of 8 December 1867, when 178 men and

boys were killed, safety and conditions generally were matters of primary concern. No local eisteddfod was complete without a topic dealing with safety or some aspect of mining being set for one of the prize essays, and the periodicals and newspapers circulating in the area abounded with articles on such matters. Nor was discussion the only evidence of concern. The strike of 1867, for instance, which must be regarded as politically the most important movement on the coalfield between the disturbances of the early decades of the century and the great strikes of the early 70's, was mainly about safety and conditions of work. Wages were of secondary importance: it was human dignity and questions of justice which were uppermost in the minds of the colliers. Ostensibly about wages, a threatened reduction of 5 per cent, the strike was really an attempt to prevent the proprietors, acting in unison, from introducing the Double Shift system of working in place of the Single Shift system universal in south Wales. The proprietors proposed to force the change on the colliers by legislation if possible, but in the short term, by exploiting the depression and offering a smaller reduction in wages in return for the adoption of the new system. It is quite clear that the men were not concerned about the reduction: they struck against the new system being imposed on them. It is not easy to appreciate why they refused to go along with the masters: the proprietors' arguments made good economic sense, and certainly made for better conditions of safety. The men successfully upheld their refusal because they considered the new system to be an unjustified interference with their traditional methods of working, because they were not convinced that safety would be enhanced, because the system entailed a disruption of family and community life, and above all, because it would bind them even closer to an industrial discipline which they resented.

Throughout this period this sense of outraged justice is a permanent element in the men's apprehension of their situation. The great strike of 1857 illustrates this. Again ostensibly about wages, the strike was really about industrial relations and social attitudes. The men knew that a reduction was inevitable: they read the financial columns of the newspapers carefully and thoroughly. What they resented was the atmosphere in which negotiations were carried on—the lack of respect shown to them as men, responsible heads of families, the assumption that the masters knew best, the arrogance of imposing the burden of depression upon the class least able to carry it, and without prior consultation. 'We would have preferred death to the abandonment of our principles', they said.

Gathering Shingles for Fuel.
(Illustrated London News, 1873.)

On the topic of wages, it is the moderation of the men that is remarkable, their rationality and evident readiness to listen to the arguments of the masters and to carry on the discussion with them in their own terms. One is impressed by their knowledge of market conditions, their critical use of current economic doctrine, their ability to marshal evidence and present a case. Their acceptance of the market and of current economic explanations was complete, and even when they were disposed to reject some of its implications as contrary to their sense of justice and humanity they rarely if ever put forward Utopian schemes of economic and social reform. They were aware of their essential role in the economic processes, thought of themselves as the primary producers of wealth, did not resent or distrust the profit motive absolutely as a sufficient incentive. What they claimed was a fair deal, and they took industrial action, formed combinations, usually to protect themselves against exploitation and when they considered their conditions to be desperate. One is struck too by the modesty of their demands. These rarely went beyond the claim that the arduous nature of their work, its skill, and the danger involved, and its primary contribution to the creation of wealth, should be rewarded, in a manner that would ensure them a sufficiency of shelter, food and clothing with a surplus to pay for the education of their children and for their leisure activities. Of course, this was a subjective valuation, but its objective elements were sufficiently well understood. It meant, firstly, judging themselves against the rural societies out of which they had emerged, and only secondly, against the rewards enjoyed by the proprietors. They knew that their standard of living was considerably higher than that of their rural counterparts, and they were easily persuaded to protect that higher standard by appropriate industrial action whenever the unilateral action of their masters threatened it. The migration to the coalfield was a response to an attraction, a means of escape from the miserable conditions, in terms of the primary needs of life, of the rural worker. He took pride in his house, in its comfort and its appearance, and he valued a woman for her ability to organise his home life and possessions. Indeed, he was glad to give up part of his paternal authority in return of the qualities he con-

sidered essential. He loved to surround himself with possessions, pieces of furniture and articles of decoration which
symbolised for him his emancipation from one kind of
thraldom. He took pride in his clothes, and possessed as a
social necessity, as a mark of his integration into the community, Sunday-best clothes which were as different from his
workday clothes, and as distinctive, as his after-work clothes
differed from his tough working trousers and shirt. 'Dillad
parch' (respectable clothes), whether he was a chapel-goer or
not, were a sign of solidarity with his fellows. Similarly with his
food. Physically, he needed food rich in protein—
which is why he consumed great quantities of fresh meat,
cheese, bacon—and was a beer-drinker rather than a spirits
man.

Another of his preoccupations was the way in which he
received his wages. The 'long pay', involving weekly or
fortnightly 'draws' and often associated with Company Shops,
was universally resented. Truck Shops as such were not necessarily a grievance where they existed: opposition to them was as
often as not fomented by traders, the shopkeepers, who stood to
gain most where they were abolished. When conflict within
settled communities took place on the issue of Truck it was
sometimes the case that the working class were on the side of
the masters and against the middle-class traders from whose
depredations and adulterations they suffered anyway. As consumers, they understood their situation well enough, and their
attitude to government legislation was one of mild cynicism.
They preferred to operate within a free market provided it were
genuinely free, and they were far-seeing enough to realise that
improved communications and ease of travel might in the end
bring a greater degree of emancipation than either Anti-Truck
organisations of the platitudinous aspirations of legislators.
What they valued most was the right to act independently of
the masters and their social superiors in those aspects of social
welfare in which there was, or might be, a concealed element of
truck—for instance, in the medical services and the schools
organised by the proprietors. It does not follow that because
they objected to weekly amenity deductions they were therefore
opposed to medical and educational facilities. It was simply

that they resented the autocratic attitudes and the paternalism of the masters. Communities in which co-operation increasingly flourished, among which Friendly Societies and building clubs, Sunday Schools and chapels multiplied, could be excused for believing that they were perfectly capable of organising such amenities themselves.

When we consider the leisure preoccupations of the colliers we can see to what an extraordinary extent the characteristic institutions of the coalfield were their creation. Whether we think of the religious institutions or the secular ones—and in both this distinction more often than not distorts the nature of both—of the chapels and Friendly Societies, the Sunday Schools and the 'eisteddfodau' and 'cymanfaoedd ganu', the literary societies, etc.—we cannot but wonder at the energy and purposiveness with which they set about creating agencies of community life according to some inner compulsion and clearly apprehended objective. Two observations should be made in relation to these. First, what was achieved was almost entirely the result of their own efforts. Time and again in the writings of the colliers themselves, or of their own intellectual elite, the ministers, the point is made that the neglect of the masters in respect of the education, morals, and religion of their workmen was if anything greater than their neglect of their physical condition.

> ''Mae cyfoeth meistri gweithfeydd Cymru yn ddiarhebol, gan mwyaf wedi ei gasglu trwy lafur y gweithiwr. Yn ngwyneb y fath olud sydd yn eu meddiant, gellir yn briodol ofyn iddynt, Pa le mae yr annedd-dai cyfleus a'r gerddi ffrwythlon sydd ganddvnt ar gyfer eu gweithwyr? Pa le y mai y clafdai a'r elusendau ar gyfer y claf a'r dinodded? Pa le y mae y banciau cynilo a'r llyfrfaoedd? Pa le mae y darpariaethau sydd gan feistri Cymru er . . . difyrwch iddynt ar eu horiau hamddenol? Ychydig iawn, a dim mewn llawer cym'dogaeth. Mae y dosbarth gweithiol wedi eu gadael yn hollol iddynt eu hunain yn y pethau hyn, ac i'w hadnoddau eu hunain o ran y meistri''. (*Gardd y Gweithiwr.* Eisteddfod Ystalyfera 1860).

'The riches of the Welsh coalowner are legendary, and for the most part consist of the profit gained on the hard labour of the colliers. Considering that they possess such wealth, is it not allowable to ask them, Where are the convenient dwellings and gardens provided for the workmen? Where are the hospitals and alms-houses for the sick and needy? Where are the savings banks and libraries? Where are the means provided by the masters for their workmen during their leisure hours? Very little, and literally nothing in some localities. The working class has kept itself entirely independent in these things and to their own resources so far as the masters are concerned'.

The exceptions to this indictment of the whole coalfield are very few indeed. The works schools, the reading rooms, the few churches erected by the patronage of the industrialists were rarely in colliery towns and villages. Mostly the patrons appear to have been ironmasters of an evangelical frame of mind and a pathological fear of radical excess, as in Merthyr Tydfil, or Ebbw Vale, Cwmafon and Maesteg. The colliery proprietor, whether English or Welsh, with a few notable exceptions, was curiously unaffected by any philanthropic motive of a public kind, and peculiarly insensitive to the socially imposed duties which deference implied. Voluntaryism was the hallmark of the characteristic institutions of the coalfield, and this was not entirely due to a simple determination among the colliers to preserve their independence for it was partly imposed upon them by the indifference of their economic masters and social superiors. Social conditions thus reinforced an ideal which they found elsewhere—in their experience of religion and in their political traditions and preconceptions.

The second thing to note about their leisure pursuits is that the time at their disposal was very limited and that they had very little energy left to spare. The work-day was one of about twelve hours, extremely arduous, and spent in conditions which tended to sap the spirit as well as to destroy physical strength. One collier writing in the early 1870's calculated that out of each day a man had barely three hours in which to pursue his individual or group interests. This seems to have been accepted as a basic fact of life: not until the '80's was there pressure for a shorter working day, and Mabon's Day, when it came, was as much an economic as a social measure, designed to keep up prices by reducing production as well as to make it possible for miners to attend to union affairs. It scarcely required middle-class agitators to explain to the colliers that excessive physical exertion in almost inhuman working conditions led to an abuse of the little leisure they had. They were aware of the connection and deplored the effects: but they were surely right in putting the blame for, for example, excessive drinking on the lack of decent facilities for doing otherwise. What we need to bear in mind is the astonishing range of cultural activities created by them, and developed out of such an unpromising background—that the literary societies, the eisteddfodau, the Friendly Societies and chapels were created despite a milieu calculated to brutalize and to reduce common humanity into a state of abject servitude.

That it did not have this effect in south Wales was due primarily to the high value which the colliers placed on their own institutions. Of these the most prestigious and effective were the religious ones, the complex interweaving organisations Nonconformist chapels inherited from the immediate past. Nonconformity had become the religion of the coalfield in the half century or so preceding the great expansion of coal-mining which began in mid-century, and the new collier communities entered into this great inheritance and made it the basis on which to build the most characteristic aspects of their new culture. It is clear that their Nonconformity was a positive thing, embraced as a matter of principle, involving a rejection and an affirmation—the rejection of established churches and the affirmation of dissenting attitudes in political as in religious life. This is revealed when we examine the denominational pattern of the coalfield. Over the coalfield as a whole the older dissenting denominations predominated, a predominance even more marked in the most heavily industrialised localities. The religion of the coalfield therefore was not merely Nonconformist, it was distinctively dissenting, with the various brands of Methodism—Welsh Calvinistic Methodism and Wesleyan

Methodism with its various off-shoots—somewhat in a minority.

It seems trite to remark that what these denominations had in common was their denominationalism, but it requires emphasis, for nothing is more striking that the comparative failure of various sects in south Wales. The Mormons were virtually the only viable and growing sect but in 1850 they had only about 4,500 members and were no longer growing at the pace of a decade earlier. Not the rejection of the world, therefore, was the ideal of the religious collier, but its acceptance as something given, to be modified and changed through the means available to him. That he was typically a dissenter made him aware of his history, and nothing is more important than the extent to which the denominations strove to understand the origins and developments of these religious organisations. Histories of religion, of the various denominations, of individual chapels, of leading personalities abounded and underlying the incessant doctrinal disputes a desire to adapt ancient dogmas to the current situation, It is not clear that the rejection of the Established Church, which was undoubtedly one important factor in the growth of Nonconformity, involved a rejection of the 'religion' of that church, of its basic dogma and theology. The Welsh Calvinistic Methodists, whose movement lay at the centre of religious expansion, constantly asserted that this was not the case, and the quarrel between Dissent and Anglicanism, at least until the coming of ritualism and Anglo-Catholicism, was likewise not about theology. It was the evangelicalism of all religious persuasions which was the keynote of the religious life of the coalmining communities in mid-century. The rejection had been for secular reasons and on largely secular grounds and pre-dated the coming of industry. The economic hold of the church on a tithe of farming incomes, its association with the landed gentry, its grip on the administrative and legal machinery of town and country—probably these had been the operative reasons. Dissent offered an alternative mode of religious organisation, more congenial as a creed and more adaptable as a form of social organisation. However middle class dissent may have become after 1860— and the extent of this had probably been exaggerated—it had retained as central in its experience its embryonic democratic forms, and it is these which were open to adaptation in the totally new societies of the coalfield and in which in one form or another, they came to have a central formative place. It was this old tradition of political thinking and of constitutional political activity which was taken over and transformed by the new working classes. At the level of the community it gave scope for personal initiative and provided what secular society did not provide, namely, a basic education in literacy and the possibility of status needs being satisfied.

This leads us into the extremely dark area of the education received by the collier, his response to what was available, and the quality of what was offered. One needs to be on one's guard against accepting uncritically the information and judgements to be found in the Blue Books of the period, in censuses and the like. Most of these reports documenting the extent of illiteracy and ignorance were prepared by Englishmen whose objectivity was more apparent than real and whose presuppositions made them totally to ignore areas of educational experience foreign to their experience. For these, education for the masses was conceived of as a primary means of social control and as often as not they attributed behaviour which they could not understand and of which they did not approve to lack of appropriate educational agencies. Thus, the picture which emerges from Tremenheere's report of 1840, which was prepared immediately in the aftermath of the Chartist march on Newport, is one of undiluted savagery, ignorance, and bestiality, with the prevalence of the Welsh language singled out as a major hindrance to social improvement. The 1847 Reports on the whole of Wales seemed scarcely to modify those conclusions. Counting attendances at Day Schools and accepting Day Schools as the norm inevitably meant ignoring layers of education which were extremely important in, and which made rich contributions to, those same communities. One would not deny the extremely unsatisfactory nature of the means available for secular elementary education in the first half of the century, but one should insist that the educational heritage of the collier in mid-Victorian Wales was considerably

The Colliers Sunday.
(Illustrated London News, 1873.)

Coal Famine at Merthyr. 'A Penn'orth of coats'.
(Illustrated London News, 1873.)

richer than the facts and figures collected by commissioners would seem to suggest.

In particular they almost certainly failed to do justice to the contribution of the Sunday Schools. If we accept that standards in Day Schools, where they existed, were bad, we need not accept a wholly sceptical attitude towards the Sunday Schools. As its very lowest, the chapels at least provided more or less appropriate places for educating people. Their schoolrooms, where British Schools did not exist, were superior as buildings to the bulk of places otherwise available. Nor is it realistic to fault the Sunday Schools on the restricted nature of their curriculum. They were highly successful in teaching people to read, and in this respect it is salutary to recall that the tradition of literacy was not one painfully achieved in recent years but was as old as Griffith Jones's Circulating School tradition of the previous century. The system was different: the ideal of universal literacy remained, and the achievement of the eighteenth century was not forgotten. We should realise also that the educational ideal and method of the Sunday School was comprehensive in the sense that it was intended not only for the individual but also for the family. Parents received their education at the same time, in the same place, and largely by the same method as their children. It is not surprising that the chapels should think of themselves as educational establishments, and that this should be reflected in the pathology of their growth. In expanding communities such as were typical of the coal-field, the growth-pattern is not of a chapel producing a school as an off-shoot, but almost exactly the reverse. When chapels sent out off-shoots—and this was the normal method of propagation—they established first schoolrooms, then chapels, the timing and costing of the latter being the responsibility of the new religious, educational community. As the century advanced, and as the British School movement expanded (individualistic chapels remained reluctant to give up their rights) these school rooms came to provide Day School facilities as well. Many ministers supplemented their stipends in this way; for generally the coalfield ministers earned about the same as the colliers who subscribed to their keep. In a chapel society there was but little need to stimulate a demand for education: basic literacy, which was the achievement of the chapels opened eyes to its worth, created a demand for its realisation, and made possible the creation of an educated elite among the colliers themselves upon whom the communities relied for leadership. For they were supported, as I have suggested earlier, because they were not wholly 'religious' institutions. Architecturally this was the case. Unlike the Anglican churches which were designed for fairly complicated and exclusive liturgical purposes, they had many other functions to perform which might be regarded, and were so regarded by their critics, as secular. Politics, for instance, or lectures, eisteddfodau and concerts, penny readings, adult education classes, and the other multifarious activities of communities not yet provided with appropriate amenity buildings. Until the end of the century and beyond, only the public houses offered alternative accommodation. Precisionists might deplore the blurring of the edges between the religious and the secular, the sacred and the profane, but for the vast majority of people the question simply did not arise, for the social aspects of religion were inescapably present, and the processes by which society came to be secularized not yet apparent in their operations. If religion appeared to suffer from contact with the secular, it could be argued that the secular gained by the intermixture of religion. If religion took on a political tone, politics adopted the language, much of the feelings, and some of the techniques of religious organisations.

The other solidly present institution in which the collier indulged his few leisure hours lay at the other end of the pole—namely, the pub. Colliery pubs, like the chapels, were buildings of great simplicity, and sometimes of comparable size. They were organised around two sets of essential rooms, the bar with its associated lesser rooms, and the upstairs 'long room'. The bar, or tap-room, long in relation to its breadth was provided with wooden benches along the walls. Privacy, always at a premium, was provided in smaller rooms with tables, and therefore well-adapted for the committee meetings of the various organisations, lodges, Friendly Societies, and so on. Most pubs were associated with one or more of the numerous Friendly Societies, and the long rooms were

Amusements of the colliers:—Stepping.
(Illustrated London News, 1873.)

intended for the formal gatherings of the lodges. Temperance Societies, of course, used the chapels, but so did the others, including embryonic chapels who used the long rooms of the pubs. Of course there was a clash between the two ideas of private and public life represented by these institutions, but it is possible that the antithesis between 'chapel-people' and 'pub-people' had been exaggerated. Welsh colliers seem to have been overwhelmingly in favour of the Sunday Closing Act of 1881, but this did not prevent them from taking advantage of loopholes in the Act. As the millennial tinge of the earlier Teetotal movement faded and was replaced by a greater confidence in conventional political machinery, so the working classes came to absorb more middle-class ideals of respectability into their way of life and perhaps outward conformity became the norm of behaviour. The trouble was that there were no centres for recreation between these antithetical poles, and this remained a grievance of the first order. The frequent, often excessive, overcrowding of houses, the universal keeping of lodgers, meant that privacy was at a discount, and while no normal collier regarded his home as his castle, it might very well become a place merely to eat and sleep in, recreation being sought elsewhere. It was only the evangelical, middle-class teetotalist who failed to see this. Most chapel-going colliers were far more realistic in their understanding of the situation and far more liberal and less censorious in their attitudes to drink. It was men like these who consistently advocated the construction of better housing for the collier. Houses should consist of a bedroom for each child, there should be a commodious living-room with a kitchen attached, and a separate room where the head of the household and the eldest children could spend their leisure. In addition, there should be a garden, and this kind of improvement, concentrating upon the family and the home, would do more to cut down excessive drinking than all the exhortation of moralists and any amount of legislation.

The Strike in South Wales: Interior of a colliers cottage.
(*Illustrated London News*, 1873.)

These were literate communities, therefore, with a deep understanding of themselves, and however tough some aspects of the general culture of the coalfield may have been, there was a well-nigh universal acceptance of the role of the chapel and of the values for which Nonconformity stood. It appeared to them that it was religion which had civilised society, religious institutions self-created and voluntarily sustained, which had provided the outstanding agencies of change, and it is clear that even though they may have attracted only a minority into active membership their pre-eminent role was accepted and recognised.

One other institution must be mentioned as typically a product, in its most popular form, of the culture of the coalfield, namely, the eisteddfod. The importance of this institution is that its history in the nineteenth century illustrates better than anything else the ways in which a chapel-orientated working class culture appropriated an essentially aristocratic and medieval literary tradition and transformed it into something very different. The eisteddfod, in its original medieval and its Tudor rehabilitated form, a structured guild-like meeting of poets under the patronage of the aristocracy, had been resurrected at the end of the eighteenth century under the guidance of emigré London Welsh Societies. It was a typical product of the radical romantic revival of those decades, and was devoted to the perpetuation of the ancient bardic traditions and the study of Celtic or British antiquities in general. Insofar as it availed itself of the patronage of the gentry it still retained its aristocratic tinge, but with the alienation of the higher gentry from Welsh culture generally it had lost its aristocratic *raison d'être,* and the impress given to it by the radical literatures of the revolutionary decades of the early part of the century meant that its aristocratic pretensions were formal and deferential only. One link between the radical political and philosophical tradition of the eighteenth century and the radicalism of the following century is thus to be found in this remarkable institution. By the mid-nineteenth century it was a highly democratic and popular institution. Every locality, every sizeable chapel in the coalfield, organised its eisteddfod as part of the annual round of its week-day activities, and there is no exaggerating the prestige and honour, both on a local and national scale, which was attached to the winning competitors.

The eisteddfod had significant social functions, notably educational, to perform. First, it was popular. It is true that all eisteddfodau had their patrons, and in the coalfield these were normally coal-owners or other notables. But the role expected of these patrons was circumscribed, and only on the relatively rare occasions when they were Welsh did they contribute more than their prestige and benefactions. Second, they were literary organisations mainly. Singing, particularly choral singing, developed later with the spread of the tonic sol-fa system, and never displaced the literary competitions in public esteem. Third, it is necessary to stress the extent of the commercial and economic connection between the eisteddfod and the business of publishing. All local eisteddfodau were reported at great length in the local newspapers, denominational and other magazines which abounded in the coalfield and, increasingly from the 1860's onwards, volumes of transactions containing the prize poems and essays along with detailed adjudications were published. Thus, the eisteddfod gave the common man who aspired to learning, who had mastered the art of self-expression, both an audience and a cheap way of reaching that audience in a prestigious way.

It is obvious that the study of these published transactions and other reports of eisteddfodau affords a primary way of entering into the culture of the coalfield. In them we can observe working communities united by their largely self-shaped religion, educating themselves, under the leadership of their most intelligent and gifted members, by means of the literary traditions of the past. There is something slightly grotesque in the sight of colliers and other workmen struggling to master literary forms rescued from an obscure and remote past, of highly technical forms of prosody being bent and tortured in the effort to adapt them to the task of expressing the ideas of a culture wholly foreign to their originators. But this is where the fascination of such a study lies, and it enables us to see to what an extent there developed that traffic with the past without which consciousness of nationhood is impossible. It was out of such efforts concentrated within such institutions that the demand for a better system of education grew, and it helps to explain why an industrial working class should have been so united on the need for a system of higher education. While such institutions were lacking the chapel and eisteddfod pre-eminently made possible an enormous expansion in the scope of adult education. The titles given to these eisteddfodic transaction are revealing in this context. The Transactions of the Ystalyfera Eisteddfod of 1861, for instance, carries the title *Gardd y Gweithiwr* or *Workingman's Garden*—and a more appropriate title one could not hope to find. The papers in English and Welsh show the enormous preoccupations of the colliers with art, and philosophy, and current affairs, and reading them one soon comes to the conclusion that the last thing one could accuse the colliers of was a romantic failure to face up to the realities of life. If anything, it was here in the eisteddfod that the working man discovered his self-consciousness and adapted himself intellectually and critically to his situation. And one should add, that the eisteddfod was a means of absorbing those tensions within society between the religious and the secular, and within society as a whole, without which they might have torn themselves to pieces in mutual hatred and distrust.

This brings us to the last of the aspects of the life of the collier, an aspect which sums up the whole, namely, his politics. An essay in one of the volumes of eisteddfod transactions already alluded to illustrates clearly the generally accepted ideas and preconceptions of the time. It is entitled 'An essay on the most effective means of protecting the social rights and well-being of the worker' and it was written in 1860/61. The author divides his essay into two parts. First, he discusses the external means necessary and, second, the private, individual, moral means to be practised in the life of the worker. Under the first he puts a better representative system, the reduction of indirect taxation, freedom from the extra-industrial activities of masters, involving the ending of Truck and of social services tied to the place of work, a justly ordered and regulated market for household commodities, the disestablishment of the Church of England because of its perpetuation of injustice and antipathy to social progress and, finally, a free, secular educational system such as would equip the worker to

The Colliers Saturday Night.
(Illustrated London News, 1873.)

Conference between Iron Masters and Workmen.
(Illustrated London News, 1873.)

resist oppression, to defend himself, and to demand his rights. Among the private, individual means he puts most emphasis on self-improvement, and he advocates obedience to the laws of the land, the eschewing of violent ways, and a determination to avoid all actions contrary to the common good. It is the conventionality of this essay which needs to be emphasised. It is a statement of principles generally accepted and current in the coalfield. It is not a revolutionary document, but on the whole assumes that the normal democratic processes of government and the system of representation underlying it must be accepted until such a time as they could be changed by lawful and peaceful means. There were some colliers who regarded such a statement, despite its stong overtones of the Charter, as naive, but in this chapel-dominated society such moderate views as these prevailed.

That was in 1861, twenty years or more after the 'time of troubles', to what the gentry referred to as 'those very foolish and unmeaning but savage and disgraceful affairs', the riots of 1816 and 1831 and the Chartist risings of 1839 which made the name of Merthyr and the ironworks districts 'a synonym for armed rebellion and barbarous violence'. High-minded moralists and established politicians were constantly lecturing the men on these themes and in those partial and prejudiced terms. From the point of view of the men, those times were indelibly a part of their political tradition. Those times had provided them with a martyrology, taught them the value of education and of purposive, systematic organisation. Nothing in their subsequent history had amounted to a repudiation of the Charter; on the contrary, Chartist organisations continued. O'Connor was venerated and the old leaders, both nationally and locally, held in high esteem. The *Northern Star* and the *People's Paper* circulated widely, and there was always a ready welcome for the visiting lecturer. Violence was abhorrent to them, and it is simply not true that riotous behaviour was a characteristic of working class political activity in the coalfield. It is the quality of ordered, coherent organisation for attainable ends which is striking. The millennial sound is subdued: there is no expectant waiting for the trumpet call: it has been replaced by a more orchestrated if mundane harmony. Nor is

the comparative lack of disturbances to be attributed to the
effectiveness of policing methods and the planting of barracks
at strategic points. Soldiers drafted into the coalfield at the time
of Chartist risings were still there, and magistrates remained
almost as hyper-sensitive as ever they had been. But this in
itself was a grievance, deeply resented. The lack of civil
disturbance is to be attributed rather to the quality of leadership which the men produced themselves. Their attempts to
organise themselves in trade unions provided a real discipline,
and the variety of forms which these attempts produced is
notable not for its immaturity and lack of grasp but as evidence
rather of the enormous difficulties of a physical kind which they
encountered. Chapel going or, at its lowest, the acceptance of
the ethos of the chapel, was likewise a political education, and
it was probably through the chapels and through participating
in the constant work of the Libeartion Society that men learned
the techniques of party organisation and of ordered public
pressure on government.

Thus it comes about that even in politics it is the maturity of
their achievement that is striking. The study of elections on the
coalfield in the '50's and onwards to the end of the century
confirms this. Excluded from the reformed franchise they were
yet an essential factor in the politics of the region. Committees
of the unfranchised, run by old-Chartists and the organisers of
trade unions and leaders of Friendly Societies as well as by
ardent members of the Liberation Society, were always to the
fore, so that even parliamentary elections became an education
for them to be turned, when the time came, to their own
advantage. In the campaigns of 1868, for instance, they had
their own separate organisation, distinct from those of the
established parties, and designed as a political extension of
their industrial organisation to campaign on issues distinct
from those of official Liberalism, and they startled the political
world by getting rid of a representative in whom they had no
confidence. And when, in 1885, the franchise and redistribution Acts brought the necessary changes, they promptly
returned their first working-class M.P.—William Abraham
(Mabon) than whom, in Victorian Wales, none was more

typical of the total culture the collier had created in south Wales.

The social and political history of the collier communities of south Wales in the early decades of the twentieth century contrasts almost violently with what we have attempted to depict above. The development of a powerful trade union, the growth of the Labour Party to predominance in both local and national politics, south Wales 'a hot-bed of socialism'—aspects such as these highlight the enormous differences in the social and intellectual climate between the one period and the other. Yet it is the continuities which impress the student, and no one who has studied the period as a whole can resist the conclusion that much that was most characteristic in the more recent experience of the coalfield was implicit in this earlier period. But it deserves to be studied in and for its own sake. The almost unique creation by a sadly mis-used and abused people of truly radical democratic communities under the very walls of the castle at Cardiff and the cathedral at Llandaff deserves our closest and most attentive study.

THE VALLEYS: THE MAKING OF COMMUNITY

I start with Aberfan and Merthyr Vale, at a point in time just one hundred years ago when the industrial developments which were to give them birth had scarcely begun, and in a part of the valley between Merthyr Tydfil and Pontypridd as yet unblemished save for the canal, the railway, and the heavily polluted river. In its origin and growth as an industrial settlement and in the ways in which it became a self-conscious, highly articulated and rich community, Merthyr Vale was characteristic of the industrial towns and villages of the second growth which at that time, and with increasing speed in the following decades, were to transform the valleys and moorlands of the coalfield and indeed the whole of Wales itself. Merthyr Tydfil, the archetypal iron-town of Wales, at the head of the valley a few miles away, was itself at that time scarcely a hundred years old. Anyone over thirty years of age could remember the coming of the railway up the valley, and some old men could claim to be as old as the canal. Time had passed quickly, but like the scale of the industrial changes against which it was measured, it had not been so fast as to obliterate the memory of the old. That was to be the danger inherent in the scale of the growth about to begin: the waste from the new pits would threaten not only place-names but the folk memories and history embodied in them. A few miles lower down was Pontypridd at the confluence of the Tâf with the Rhondda, still uncertain of its destiny or its identity—Newbridge or Pontypridd, rural or industrial? There also growth had been rapid and within the memory of man, and there too it had not been such as to alienate or dispirit its inhabitants.

> Pwy a ŵyr eto pa waith
> Heb ei orffen yn berffaith,
> A lunir i'w ddadlenu,
> Mwy i fod na dim a fu?
>
> Gwella gwna gwlad ein tadau,
> Ei llwybr rhydd—gwella i barhau:
> Gwella nes gwella pob gwall,
> Anturiaeth heb bwynt arall.[1]

Even as the poet sang thus in 1864 in praise of Cwm Rhondda and its collier the sinkers were busy in ever-deepening pits at Ferndale and many other places away from the areas of primary exploitation around Dinas and the Lower Rhondda, and at that very time the pit at Merthyr Vale was being sunk. A new era was about to open.

*   *   *

There are bascially two ways in which we can study the nature of the communities of the coalfield which now began to be settled. We can look at them from the outside, observe the physical evidence of their growth, and we can attempt to look at them from the inside. The first is the method of the economic historian, of the geographer, the demographer, and the sources which these specialisms use are quantitative, measurable. The second is the method of the anthropologist and is concerned less with measuring than with depicting and understanding, and its field of study is social relations and consciousness. The social historian is neither one nor the other, but both, and in what follows I propose to attempt to bring these two approaches together. I shall do so not by giving a version of the history of the Valleys, but rather by trying to see what elements were of permanent importance in their composition, how their origins determined their eventual shape and character.

Let us look first at the dimension of time, the chronology of their appearance. I have already suggested that Merthyr Vale, though only five miles distant from Merthyr Tydfil, was separated from it by a great distance in time. Merthyr Tydfil, though young in age, was very old in experience. In the eighty odd years of its existence as an iron-town its people, immigrant or native, had endured a transformation in their lives such as no community had experienced before. They had suffered the whole trauma of unrestricted capitalistic development, and the shape and character of the town had been dictated by no considerations beyond those of the commercial needs of its great ironmasters. It was the product of a laissez-faire going far beyond the merely economic and commercial, but extending to the uttermost relations in society, and inasmuch as private

Cardiff Castle: the smoking room.

The Kitchen at 71 Monk Street. *Photo: Cynon Valleys Library.*

morality is affected by the physical conditions of life, into the
most intimate and private relations of individuals. Sewage disposal, adequate water supplies, privies, do not of themselves
ennoble a people: but their lack degrades individuals, tends to
debase communities, and makes it infinitely more difficult for
higher standards of civilization to be reached. The new valley
towns escaped this dark side in the experience of the older communities, for by the time they were appearing some of the
harsher side-effects of laissez-faire were being mitigated and
some of its consequences alleviated. The new towns would face
tremendous problems, but they would not be entirely or exclusively the products of the uneven conflict between profit and
people, capital and community, and there would be enhanced
opportunities for their inhabitants to shape their own lives and
to create communities more agreeable to their own aspirations.

This can be illustrated by reference to Merthyr Vale. It first
emerges into view in May 1869 when the General Board of
Health received a petition signed by 88 ratepayers praying for
the separation of the southern part of the parish from the
Merthyr Tydfil Local Board of Health.[2] This latter had been
in existence since 1850, and since 1858 had been raising and
spending very considerable sums of money on the provision of
water supply, mains sewage, and certain other basic improvements in the district.[3] This is not the place to deal in any detail
with these, except to make this point; that almost all these
improvements, particularly the key one of the supply of
water—for without this waste disposal was bound to be in-
efficient—had been either directly or indirectly hindered or
even opposed by some or all of the ironmasters. Their grip even
on the supply of health-giving and health-preserving amenities
was well-nigh invincible, despite the statutory powers available
to the Local Health Board. It seems to me to have been a
decision of the highest importance by the London Inspector of
the General Board of Health to recommend that the petition
should be rejected. He very quickly discovered that the petition
had been got up by the firm of Nixon, Taylor and Cory who
were at that time sinking the pit which was to bring the village
into existence. In 8 to 9 years there would be a population of 5000,
but it was admitted by the Company that during this interval

they intended "doing as little as possible in the way of Sanitary Works". The Inspector continued, "As the interests of Messrs Nixon, Taylor & Cory are by far the largest in the Vale part of the District, it may, I think, be fairly assumed that if any local authority were hereafter formed there, it would be completely under the influence and direction of that firm".[4] We may be libelling the memory of those gentlemen, for we have no means of knowing how they would have acted, but we can be fairly certain that they would not have erected a garden village in Merthyr Vale. Nor, of course, did the Merthyr Tydfil authority envisage any such plan: but at least Merthyr Vale when it came to be built was supplied from the beginning with plentiful supplies of clean water and an adequate sewerage.

This applied to most colliery villages of the post 1858 period. The vast majority were planted within the boundaries of existing local health authorities and so far as the basic needs of sanitation were concerned had to abide by the statutory requirements of the various Health Acts. By the standards of our own days these requirements were minimal; but the people who inhabited the new villages judged according to existing standards and not by some ideal vaguely in the future. There is no question but that these new places springing up in the first surge forward of the steam coal industry were far healthier places than the older iron and coal towns of the first half of the century. After the legislation of 1875/6 and before the flood tide of immigration twenty years later many of them improved still further, and by then also other social legislation, such as educational reform, had come to reinforce the self-help efforts of the communities themselves to raise standards of living.

This meant, also, that the enormous upsurge in house-building which took place on the whole provided houses which were a great deal more adequate and built to higher standards Than what had been typical of the older housing. The noisome courts, the rows of low cottages with only one entrance and minute windows, the backs-to-backs, were gone for ever. Topography, the availability of land, the economies of scale and, above all, the pace of development dictated the prevailing physical shape of the communities. There is no evidence that this was ever resented by the inhabitants, and there is evidence that these streets constituted neighbourhoods, distinct nuclear communities of their own in which close personal relations could freely develop. Nor do the houses at this stage in their development appear to have been over-crowded. That was a phenomenon of the unprecedented expansion of these self-same villages later on in the century. Already by 1870 some of the housing being put up for colliers in the Rhondda repro-duced the evils of the old iron-towns.[5] Again, I would stress that overcrowding is a relative term and that we should avoid transferring our own notions into the nineteenth century. Families were large, probably intentionally so, and acted as a kind of natural mechanism in a family's confrontation with the harsh realities of economic survival. A large family, given reasonable luck, was a better insurance against old age than anything a Friendly Society could provide.

It is a fair inference that these new colliery settlements must have been relatively attractive to the worker. The demand for labour in such a labour-intensive industry continued unabated and insatiable with the opening of so many collieries. It is a mistake to think of the collier as essentially immobile, attached to his patch like a peasant. The typical picture of the collier of the 'sixties is of a strong figure of a man leaning on his tools, pipe in mouth, with his pack on the platform awaiting a train to yet another job. It is clear that Blaenllechau (Ferndale) and other places being opened up in the Rhondda at this time were being colonized by Merthyr and Aberdare men, even as the Aberdare villages had been colonized in the first instance from Merthyr. When Blaenllechau exploded in 1867 and again in 1869, killing a total of 225 men and boys, it was Merthyr and Aberdare that mourned. Later, with the second stage of expansion, they came from far and wide, though mainly from Wales, but by this time, I would argue, the original inhabitants had laid down sufficient social capital to leave their stamp on the places, to impose patterns of behaviour into which the newcomers would fit.

It is astonishing how quickly this could and did invariably happen. The sequence of settlement of colliery villages located at any distance from large existing town or villages followed patterns which were everywhere the same. Wooden shacks, or

Capel Bethel, Georgetown.

Capel Ebenezer, Trecynon, Aberdare, 1815.

houses, or barracks would first be erected for the contractors and the men engaged in sinking the pit or driving the slant. Since the sinking of the shaft could take many years (seven in the case of Merthyr Vale), these might often take on a semi-permanent character. House-building as such would begin only when the owner was virtually certain that his venture would be a success. This often meant a further delay, particularly in regions of heavy geological faulting, so that something like frontier-settlements, hideous to behold, and inhabited by a type of navvy, would develop. At the remote tops of valleys and on the moorlands these might remain long after their original justification had passed away. Thus Dafydd Morgannwng comments bitterly on the barracks built by David Davis of Blaengwawr in 1862 for his original workmen, but which in 1874 were "rhy wael o lawer i ddynion sydd yn llafurio yn galed ym mherfedd y ddaear" (far too poor for men who work hard in the bowels of the earth)[6] There would then follow the building of permanent houses, and it is vitally important for my argument to emphasise that this was rarely done by the colliery owner. Occasionally the company might do so and in some cases thus lay down acceptable standards which would thereafter by emulated by other. David Davies, of the Ocean Coal Co. did this at Treorchy, for example. This meant that the typical collier was not a tenant of his industrial master. The vast majority of houses were built by speculative builders for sale either to individuals or to building clubs. Most of what we know about these terminating building societies and clubs dates from the period after 1878 when plans and drawings had to be deposited and approved, but there is evidence that they existed from a very much earlier period, at least as early as 1848. They appear to have been entirely *ad hoc* ventures organized by small groups of men, a kind of cooperative self-help indicative of the urgent need which the majority of men had to own their own houses. This is very different from the pattern of ownerhsip in Merthyr, where the ironworker and ironworks' collier or miner was typically a tenant of his master. House-ownership of this kind and on this scale, or even tenancy to a kind of *rentier* class, gave stability to a community and created grades of respectability within it which would otherwise be absent.[7]

David Watkin Jones
"Dafydd Morgannwg."

Griffith Rhys Jones
"Caradog."

William Williams
("Carw Coch",) 1808—1872.

Photos: Cynon Valleys Libraries.

What was lacking in villages so quickly gathered together in those ways were public buildings. Yet again one is astonished at the speed with which chapels, for example, were erected. Four years after the sinking of the pit at Ferndale the Baptists had built a chapel with seating for 600. A year later the Independent chapel was opened, the Calvinistic Methodists opened theirs three years later, and the Wesleyans theirs in 1871. Four chapels with seating for 2,200 within less than ten years and before the township was half-built! Apart from anything else this represented an enormous investment in money and effort and is eloquent testimony to the existence of shared values which must have given a cohesive force to the community by contributing richly to its inner, intellectual, cultural life. Looked at in a wider context both of time and place we can see that this primacy given to religion was a factor of inestimable importance in the life of the country as a whole, in the total culture of which these communities were a part. It is undoubtedly true to observe that the pattern of religious worship so characteristic of Wales in the second half of the century had been established in the first half, even by the early 1830s, but it is as certainly misguided to believe that the pattern once established should therefore be secure and immutable. We need to recognize the social crisis involved in the new expansion, appreciate the upheaval that accompanied it, the psychological stress for countless families and individuals uprooting themselves and settling into utterly new, often alien and sometimes repulsive surroundings. These were years of critical importance therefore in the history of Wales as a whole, and the fact that the period as a whole, right to the end of the century, was not violent and brutal but relatively ordered and peaceful was eloquent testimony to the wisdom and self-sacrifice of these earliest settlers and to their determination to adhere to the values and aspirations of their fathers and to keep intact what they regarded as the highest expression of community-religion and culture.

The chapels were vital ingredients in community in many other and complex ways. They produced the leaders in society, the intellectuals, the artists, the organizers. They educated the people, provided schools, books and reading matter, raised

Ferndale Colliery, Rhondda Valley, South Wales, The Scene of the explosion in 1867.　　[*London Illustrated News*]

platforms for the eloquent, gathered audiences for anyone with
anything to say, and opened villages to the cultural riches of the
past and contemporary world. But in addition to all this, or
rather, as a by-product of this internal discipline, the chapels
broke down the stifling isolation with which so many of these
settlements were afflicted. Typically, Welsh collier religion was
a full-blooded denominational type religion: there were, on the
whole, few sectarian elements left in it. It was not the religion
of the lonely, it was not introspective, did not encase its adherents in a dualism of other-worldliness, or confine them
within the low horizons of the hills. The Welsh ministry was far
more settled than it had been half a century earlier when it had
resembled a vast inchoate missionary movement. But even so,
there was restless, complicated movement of ministers within
the denominations, and this was a great integrating factor in
the whole adding enormously to the self-confidence and pride
of the individual places. The denominations were organized,
however loosely, from within, and each congregation knew
itself to be an essential and equal part in some larger county-
wide and country-wide organization. At a lower, though more
practical level, the chapels united adjacent villages in a common culture through the agency of preaching festivals, cymanfaoedd canu, choral and other concerts, temperance organizations, eisteddfodau, and so on, all highly competitive, but all
organically united. This, I think, needs to be stressed, for it is
a common culture that we have to explain, and community,
not isolation, that we need to stress.

I have put leisure before work, but of course, the *raison d'etre*
of these communities was labour, the production of coal. Inner
disciplines may in the final analysis be more important in
explaining the inner life of a community than externally imposed disciplines, but there is no ignoring the fundamental
importance of the work-place in the life of the community. The
basic rhythms in the life of the colliery villages were imposed
upon it by the industrial process, and ultimately by the trade
cycle. The one was regular, measurable and known, the other
unforseen, uncontrollable, fortuitous, massively and in-
corrigibly a presence. The one determined the physical movement within the village, the daily treck of the men in common, to

their place of work before the rising of the sun and their joint, regimental return after it had set. The activities of the household likewise revolved around the imperious note of the colliery hooter, the wife as subject to it as her husband and working children. And when the trade-cycle silenced the hooter, the whole community as a community, suffered in its silence.

But the discipline of the colliery worked within the community at profounder levels even than that. The nature of the work itself encouraged a sense of community. Brutally dangerous and hard, the collier at his work-place could survive only in cooperation with his fellows. There can be no such thing as an individual collier: there can only be communities of colliers, all inter-dependent, breathing the same inadequate air, relying upon their joint skills, all subject to the same instantaneous disaster. Equality for such is not an abstraction: it is a fact of life, and transferred to the larger community of the world outside it produces a natural, unselfconsious democracy. It is not strange therefore that the forms of political organization and ideology of these communities should be profoundly democratic and that they should be prominently present. I have already mentioned the chapels, but one must add those agencies of joint good, those cooperative, collective organizations which existed from the beginning, spontaneously extensive of the discipline of work. I refer to the innumerable friendly-societies, the clubs, trade-union branches (even before the regional and national organizations), and, in the case of the pubs, spontaneously reactive to the same disciplines. Moreover, I would suggest that the scale of the industrial processes and the size of the villages and towns encouraged such developments. By continental standards the collieries were small, averaging perhaps work-forces of about 500—and although this made for fragmentation and for at least a generation militated against the creation of powerful working-class organizations on the coalfield at large, it certainly made possible face to face relationships and community solidarities such as would have been impossible in larger undertakings or in great towns.

I have argued that these communities were inherently democratic. It is necessary to stress that they were "political" communities as well—a fact often forgotten by those who define politics in ways which exclude all but the parliamentary side of it. So far as the rhythms of political activity are concerned, the parliamentary ones were the least important. Far more vital to ordinary people were the administrative activities of Poor Law Guardians, of local Boards of Health, and so on. Until, and even after, the Suffrage Act and the Redistribution Act of 1884/5, the franchise in local affairs was much wider, and it was here, rather than in the infrequent parliamentary contests that the ordinary ratepayer and house-holder learned the realities of political organization. This, based in his experience of Friendly Society, trade union, club, chapel, made him think of the local government changes of the end of the century as his heritage. It is a well known fact that the Labour Party captured Wales in its local government first, and only then in its parliamentary representation.

One final word on this theme. We are certainly justified in thinking about these communities as "working-class". This was emphatically true in the sense that they were almost exclusively inhabited by working-class people. But this does not mean that they were uniformly so, or that there were not status differences as between individuals and groups. Some occupations carried a higher status and commanded a higher respect than others. Relative positions in society were keenly recognized and aspired to. And their rarity increased their value. If we may cite Ferndale again. Its four chapels would demand a diaconate of not less than 50, and in addition they would have Sunday School superintendents, 'codwyr canu', precentors, teachers, etc., and the roles for women would be numerous and heartily competed for. As society became more highly organized additional roles would be created, many of them of a secular kind. One has only to look at reports of funerals of popular figures to see the force of this.

Much more difficult, and a topic for extensive research, is the existence of class consciousness. There is no doubt that the essential preconditions were present on a massive scale, and there is evidence that as time went on the term "dosbarth gweithiol" (working class) was becoming heavy with technical overtones, carrying connotations suggesting that workmen

Tip girls leaving the Dowlais Works.

(Illustrated London News.)

Tonyrefail c. 1863.

were becoming conscious of the underlying conflict of interests between capital and labour, and an understanding dawning of their place, as a class in society, in the historical process. But I would hasten to add that there was little "scientific" about this understanding. The vast bulk of the people found the increasing orthodox radicalism of Liberalism sufficient. Their intellectual roots were in the chapels: they accepted individualism, self-help, and competition, and while they admired their own forms of collectivism they had a hearty distrust of the collectivism of the state. The increasing preoccupation of industrial workers from the mid 1870s, as reflected in their writings for the periodical press and in eisteddfodic transactions with social questions common to them all, such as housing, health, education and well as wages and industrial relations, is eloquent testimony to a quickening awareness of class consciousness. It was out of this culture that the militancy of the turn of the century grew.

I turn now, and finally, to the question of language, and I want to put it where it belongs, in this context of consciousness. The settlements that we are thinking about were Welsh in their origin and, I suspect, remained Welsh for far longer than we imagine. The original settlers, as I have indicated, moved into the newly-colonized districts from existing centres, attracted by the relatively higher wages being offered, for obviously it was to the advantage of the coal-owners to attract as many experienced miners as possible. The nature of Welsh population movements ensured that subsequent immigrations would consist of Welsh-speaking Welshmen and their families. Yet from their beginning there was the sense of crisis, that the language was in danger. And so it was. The whole weight of educated, bourgeoise opinion, was against the survival of the language. Progress was the prerogative of English, for the English language contained the secrets of finance and commerce, of economics and the new social science; it was the language of law and the institutions, and of political debate: it was the language pre-eminent in the world, it was proclaimed by Englishmen, of creative literature, of poetry, of drama, the novel, and of philosophy: and at the level that hurt most, it was the language of management. One could read this kind of argument in scores of different publications, ranging from the satire of *The Times* and the *Quarterly Review,* through the howling mirth of *Punch,* to the smug eloquence of the canting *Eclectic Review.* More precisely, one could hear and read Welsh intellectuals and educational experts repeat the same sad advice—the Rev. Dr. Lewis Edwards, for example, or Sir Hugh Owen. Even the eisteddfod pundits welcomed the inevitability of the coming demise of the language. Why then did it not die? Why did it survive so long in these collier communities? Some experts on population movements argue that its survival was a function of migration, that it lasted only as long as the pump remained primed with newcomers. That is a part of the explanation, but it confuses life and commodities. I would argue that, while the economic historians' arguments are valid as to the necessary conditions, the real reason must lie in the collective will of the people themselves. The fact is that the vast majority of people, the ordinary folk who inhabited these communities, stuck to their language. And why? Because it represented the essence of community to them at the critical periods in the histories of those communities. It was unthinkable that their chapels should be other than Welsh, and in places where the flow of English immigrants seemed to threaten this Welshness they built separate chapels for the newcomers, much as the Anglicans, faced with the same problem, aimed to provide distinct churches for the two linguistic communities. It is a *fact* that Welsh is the language of heaven! It was accepted without question that Welsh was a barrier to lax morals and evil customs, that as one moved nearer the English border and the predominance of the English language that the people became more and more degenerate. The Welsh language protected the people against slavery and oppression: it gave the worker a dignity which his English fellow-worker could not possibly have. And because only the worker, as distinct from bourgeois intellectuals and middle-class traitors, alone kept his language, the worker had become the inheritor of the past upon whom had fallen the age-old duty of preserving the country's independence. Without the Welsh worker, said Dewi Afan (a collier turned minister) Wales would be like a large fair room occupied by oppressors.

Byddai Cymru heb ei Gweithwyr
Fel ystafell eang fawr
Gyda channoedd o ormeswyr
Yn cydwelwi hyd ei llawr;
Byddai'n gyrfa wedi'i hatal,
Trengai ei hurddasol fri;
Colli'r engyl sy'n ein cynnal
Fyddai colli'i Gweithwyr hi.[8]

From this it follows that the institutions in which the Welsh language lived should have had a prestige higher than that accorded to any other, and that the bard should have come to occupy a status in society as high as any that society could accord him. Think of those hundreds and hundreds of *noms des plumes* which appear in the papers and magazines. It requires a real effort of imagination to appreciate the situation, but there is no doubt that this level of literary achievement and the social relations which it created were of enormous importance within the colliery towns themselves. The eisteddfod, the chapel, the friendly society, the pub were genuinely the creations of a working-class culture providing for itself by itself and with a breath-taking confidence taking over the cultural-literary role of an aristocracy.

No communities such as were these, existing sometimes on the very edges of survival, threatened with the degradation of excessive labour, plagued by endemic sickness, knowing poverty—poverty, as Sir John Simon said, "not merely as subject of physical privations: but poverty as complicated with the caduity and helplessness of ignorance . . . (and) as susceptible of deepest heartache when the pomps and luxuries of civilization seem to deride it"[9]—communities like this need above all self-confidence. Community for them is not some kind of product of conditions—it is the condition of existence.

NOTES

[1] Llewellyn Jones, Trecynon, *Llawlyfr ymarferol mwnwyr a glowyr Deheudir Cymru, gyda chyfeiriadau neillduol at weithiau Cwm y Rhondda* (Aberdar (1864)).

[2] P.R.O. MH13/125. The documents are printed in A. H. Williams, *Public Health in Victorian Wales. Correspondence from the Principality to the General Board of Health and the Local Act Office 1848-1871,* (Cardiff, Board of Celtic Studies, 1983), pp. 999 ff. Copies of this work may be consulted in the libraries of the constituent colleges of the University of Wales and the copyright libraries.

[3] For detailed discussion see below pp.

[4] Williams, op. cit., pp. 1058-65.

[5] See the evidence of Dr. T. J. Dyke in the First Report of the Sanitary Commission, PP 1868-9 XXXII (4218) Qs. 6329 et seq., and in the First report on the Housing of Working Classes, PP 1884-5 XXX (4402), Qs. 12, 974 et seq.

[6] Dafydd Morgannwg, *Hanes Morgannwg* (Aberdar 1874), tt. 224-5.

[7] See Philip N. Jones, *Colliery Settlement in the South Wales Coalfield 1850-1926* (University of Hull, 1969), and Esmond Cleary, *The Building Society Movement* (1965).

[8] *Fy Ngwanwyn* gan Dewi Afan (David Michael), (Aberdar, 1873), t. 43.

[9] Sir John Simon, *English Sanitary Institutions* (1890).

THE VALLEYS IN THE MID-NINETEENTH CENTURY

When I last had the honour of addressing this Conference I took as my theme—or rather, I was given as my theme—'The Valleys: the making of a community', and for the purpose of the talk I focussed upon Aberfan and the communities to the south and the west of Merthyr Tydfil. Today, it seems to me, I should focus on the Monmouthshire valleys and that string (if not garland) of towns stretching westwards from Brynmawr with their pendant townships running away in valleys towards the sea in the south. Alas, this is an enormous task and the kind of research into their individual histories and into the history of the region that one thinks to be desirable has only just begun. Not that these places have been neglected: on the contrary, their inhabitants have always been distinguished for their keen historical interests, and no generation has been without its historian. For the period that I shall be talking about one thinks of Edmund Jones ('Yr Hen Broffwyd') whose *Historical Account of the Parish of Aberystruth* was published in 1779 and his *Relations of Apparitions in Wales* in 1780—the latter being not the farrago of nonsense that some critics say it is but an essential source for the understanding of the culture of the pre-industrial inhabitants of this area. Then there is my name-sake, Ieuan Gwynedd (Evan Jones), who wrote a life of Edmund Jones in 1850, and David Morris who published his *Hanes Tredegar* in 1868 which was followed in 1884 by the remarkable *History of Tredegar* of the Powells, father and son. There are numerous topographical accounts, descriptions of iron-works—William, Coxe, Malkin and many others—and eisteddfodic transactions and Welsh language magazines abound in histories of the individual places, towns, chapels, churches, societies. 'Myfyr Wyn' (William Williams) *Atgofion am Sirhywi a'r Cylch,* gathered by Myrddin Lloyd from *Tarian y Gweithiwr,* or Eiddil Gwent' (David Morris) who published his *History of Tredegar* in 1868 and left much more unpublished for in instruction and delight of the historian. And there are many of that heroic kind whom we could name—iron-workers, cobblers, colliers, ministers. I mention them at the beginning not merely for sound academic reasons—begin always with the historiography of your field—but also in order to put ourselves in perspective. We are not starting something new but entering into a rich and honourable tradition. No historian, least of all the local historian, can afford to be arrogant in the presence of the past.

But a great change has come over the writing of the history of these places, and it is due to a number of factors. First, there is what we can without distortion or exaggeration properly call 'the opening of the archives'. Parish registers, the census material, the ever-increasing and ever more rich and complex statistics about demography are all easily available in County Record Offices, and even computer science is now at the disposal of the local historian. Then there are the quarries of documentation in central archives—Poor Law, health, government, and public order, education, religion, the economy—an untold wealth of source material undreamed of by our predecessors. Then second, there are the new institutions, such as the Record Offices with their archival expertise, and the university departments in south Wales where, every encouragement has been given to studies of localities such as this. So we have works of a very different character from the earlier ones, books such as *A history of Ebbw Vale* by Arthur Gray-Jones or that of Oliver Jones (one of the very richest of histories). Above all, there are the books and articles of that master of the Home Office sources, Dr. David Jones of Swansea, and the works of Dr. Gwyn Davies and Dr. Siân Rhiannon Williams. All of these make use of a multiplicity of source materials that simply were not available to that earlier generation. It is these two factors in combination—the tradition of history writing and the new sophistication in methodology—that gives ground for hope that we are entering into a new period of local history studies. I cannot possibly in the time I have at my disposal do more than indicate in a very rough and ready fashion the kind of conclusions we can now confidently assert about the past of this region, and in so doing perhaps indicate some of the themes and problems to which we might with profit direct our attention.

The period you have asked me to talk about is a very short one in the chronologies of valley history, only a generation or

so, about half the life-time of a healthy, not over-worked man
or woman of the time. There is a definite unity about the
period, and contemporaries felt this even at the time and
certainly when they looked back on it from the hurly-burly of
the eighties. 'Mid-Victorian', it is called, 'the age of prosperity', 'the age of equipoise'. We should certainly ask whether
the prosperity existed, whether the calm was not an illusion,
the equipoise a delusion: that is what history is about. But we
note what contemporaries thought. They looked back at the
radical thirties, most of them with relief, and if times were still
difficult at least the hungry forties were over. Above all, they
were aware that they were entering into a new era, an age of
endless improvement both physically and morally, and it was
this that gave them what to us seems to be an astonishing self-
confidence. It is on this period of about twenty-five years from
1850 to c. 1873/74, that I want to concentrate, and I propose to
to do so by examining first, the main features of the economy,
secondly the population of the region, thirdly its social
structure, fourthly its religious and cultural life and finally its
political life.

I. Economy

There are two important observations that need to be made
about the economy of the district as a whole during these
decades. First, there is the familiar one concerning the changes
that took place in the relative importance of iron production
and of coal mining for export. The iron industry by the early
1850s was being challenged by the faster-growing, more concentrated, more favoured Cleveland iron industry, so much so
that Welsh workers had begun to migrate there in considerable
numbers: indeed, Monmouthshire was a favourite recruiting
region because of the Welsh connections of its managerial staff.
The Welsh iron industry could not compete successfully
because so many of the factors of production favoured the
Clyde-Middlesborough region: raw materials, proximity to the
sea, good communications and ample capital for investment.
But, of course, the decline of the south Wales industry was only
relative: in 1850 there were 55 furnaces producing 173,000 tons
of pig iron which was about one quarter of the total production

Ebbw Vale.

of south Wales. Some works were to close in the '50s, but the Ebbw Vale Works, including Sirhowy, were very efficient under the management of Abraham Darby, and by 1855 the Ebbw Vale Company had absorbed the Victoria Ironworks (in 1848), the Abersychan Works (in 1852) and other works at Pontymoel and Pontypool (in 1855). They were responding to the market by perfecting their technology: steel making, using a process invented by Parry, the works Chemist in 1854-5, was introduced before Bessemer perfected his converter, and the Company were very quick to adopt this very efficient method of steel-making in 1866-8. The Age of Steel came early to the valley and provided a base for the continuance of the iron tradition for yet another century in at least one of the valleys.

The shift in the economy which was in due course to completely transform the society of the valleys came with the rise of the coal industry. This gain was relative. It was certainly the case that coal production was an ancillary to iron production in the first half century or so of iron-making; in the 1840s, for example, it is estimated that three tons of coal were needed to produce by hot blast one ton of pig iron and a further one and a half tons of coal for converting the pig iron into bar iron. Cold blast furnaces required more. Hence in 1850 the iron works would have used about 800,000 tons of coal. There are no exact figures, but it is probably safe to assume that the ten major iron works were together using about a million tons of coal a year.

But this was not the sole market for coal. There was an expanding coast-wise trade and a less significant foreign trade developing. In 1850, 552,000 tons of coal were shipped from Newport, one quarter of it being to foreign parts. Newport in the 1840s, it needs to be remembered, shipped more coal than any other south Wales port. Nor must one forget the domestic consumption of coal in the industrial settlements. It is impossible to calculate this household consumption, but if we assume that the average household consumed about eight tons a year then total consumption would have been not less than 100,000 tons per year in the region of our study.

The 25 years that followed saw a decisive shift in these over-arching relativities. Ironworks' demand for coking coal fel steadily, partly by reason of increases in efficiency but mainly as a consequence of the depression which set in after 1860. By the early 1870s the prosperous times were over and the iron industry had ceased to expand: indeed, ironworks from Hirwaun to Clydach and from Beaufort to Pontypool were closing. Thirty years earlier this would have had a disastrous effect on the coal industry: as we have seen well over half of total production was consumed in the furnaces: now, by the middle '50s and early '60s it made little difference, for the coal age, based on an insatiable world-wide demand for steam-coal had arrived. The railways, which made the exploitation of the coal possible, and which were themselves enormous consumers of the commodity they carried, by 1859 snaked up every valley and connected them to each other and to the main ports in a web of iron and steel.

Although by the '70s the coal industry was poised to exploit a market entirely distinct and separate from the markets of the iron-masters it is important to note than in the period we are concerned with the iron-works were themselves the suppliers of the new markets. Until the opening of the steam-coal age it was the bituminous coals that were in demand and this was a demand that the iron-master were very ready to satisfy. Hence, in the early stages of the transition to the age of coal the iron-works played an important, indeed a leading role, in the development of the new trade. This was because they were always free to enter the trade in export coal simply by releasing supplies whenever it was in surplus to their requirements. But already in the '50s they were producing over and above their needs specifically for this growing market.

Nevertheless, there were vast differences between the two related undertakings. In respect of their capital requirements the ironworks by the second decade of the century were monsters of consumption and formation. In 1817 the capital of Tredegar stood at £120,000. The Blaina and Cwm Celyn Works required an investment of £250,000 to bring them to production, the Victoria Works £300,000, and when the Rhymney Iron Company was formed in 1837 it had a capital of £500,000: and by 1854 no less than £700,000 had been invested in it. Collieries on the other hand required very little capital: small capitalists could embark on the enterprise. Thus the total value of Hafodyrisclawdd Colliery, bought by Thomas Powell in 1840 was £2,200. When the Argoed Colliery, one of the richest and most profitable in Monmouthshire was opened in 1812 the capital invested was £3,000. £7,500 to £10,000 was reckoned to be the sum required to open a typical south Wales colliery in the early decades of the century, and as late as 1848 very large undertakings such as Aberbeeg required only £20,000 or so. The reason for this difference can readily be understood. Iron making was an extremely complex industrial process requiring relatively expensive machinery and always remaining labour intensive in the running. But the collieries were small in respect of the numbers employed, unsophisticated technologically, consisting for the most part of levels driven into the coal in the sides of the steep valleys.

There is no need to point out the importance of those differences sociologically. Ironworks produced large urban settlements which very soon became permanent and forward-looking. Collieries created unformed, miscellaneous small settlements nucleated (if that is the word) around the colliery itself. Permanence was not of their essence: the facts of geology reinforced the uncertainties of the market. Then, also, the industrial complexity of the ironworks required a complex society to maintain it in production. Far from being simple and elementary the work force of the iron towns was variegated and diverse, bringing into being a multiplicity of trades, crafts, technologies within the works, and a large and growing variety of men and women to serve the domestic and the cultural needs of the town inhabitants. Not so the collieries. By comparison they were simple and uncomplicated both at the point of production and in the community of place. Hence, to sum up: while the old basic iron production continued to support the towns on the coalfield, increasingly the demands of a changing export market called forth the creation of entirely different kinds of community which were largely independent of them.

II. Population

I wish to make one or two general points about the population history of the valleys. The first is related to what I have just said and concerns stability and instability of populations in

different parts of the region. Now as we all know, the population of the north-western, industrial parts of the county increased very considerably in the first forty years of the century.
Let us take the Registration District of Abergavenny which
included the heavily industrialized parts of the county, namely,
Blaenavon Sub-district, Aberystruth, Tredegar, and Bedwellty.
The rate of increase for the District was as follows: to
1811—60%: to 1821—39%: to 1831—32%; and to 1841—
65%. In the next three decades the rate fell sharply to 16%,
13% and 11%. So there is a clear pattern: very high growth
rate (60%) between 1801 and 1811, and the same high rate
between 1831 and 1841. In between, in the two decades 1811 to
1831 the rate was less by a half (about 30%). Finally, in the
period I am discussing the rate of increase falls very sharply
and continues to fall until the end of the century. The percental
rate of change is shown on Graph 1.

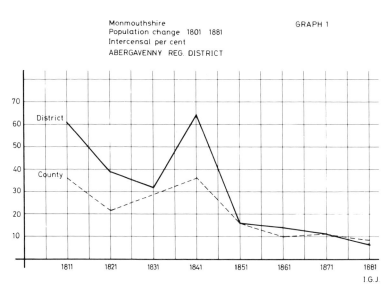

Monmouthshire
Population change 1801 1881
Intercensal per cent
ABERGAVENNY REG. DISTRICT

GRAPH 1

I.G.J.

The population of the District was growing very rapidly, of
course. This is shown on Graph 2. It is a remarkably even and
regular growth, from 17,000 in 1801 to 79,000 in 1881, with
the highest growth occurring in the decade 1831 to 1841.

Population change   1801 – 1881   GRAPH 2.
ABERGAVENNY DISTRICT   '000s

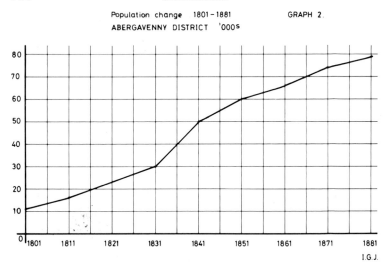

I.G.J.

Population change in Monmouthshire subdistricts   GRAPH 3.

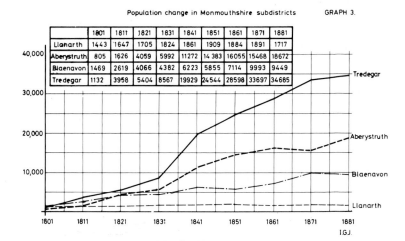

	1801	1811	1821	1831	1841	1851	1861	1871	1881
Llanarth	1443	1647	1705	1824	1861	1909	1884	1891	1717
Aberystruth	805	1626	4059	5992	11272	14 383	16055	15468	18672
Blaenavon	1469	2619	4066	4382	6223	5855	7114	9993	9449
Tredegar	1132	3958	5404	8567	19929	24544	28598	33697	34685

I.G.J.

Graph 3 is included to illustrate a point of fundamental importance, namely the difference in the growth profiles of the
different parts of the District. Llanarth was a wholly rural area,
its parishes supporting a peasant population. The graph shows
only a marginal growth up to 1851 followed by an equally
marginal decline in the next 30 years. Contrast Llanarth with
Tredegar. Growth for the first 20 years is of the same order as

that of Llanarth. It then begins to rise at a slightly steeper rate until the take off in the decade 1831-41 which is sustained for the rest of the century.

This contrast between patterns of population growth between the rural and the industrial parts of the county is of the highest importance. It is, for example, what determined the character of settlement, the nature of government and above all, the cultural differences between the different regions. What was vitally important was the rate of growth—or the percentile difference from decade to decade. Graph 1 shows how much more violent the rate of change was in the District than in the county in the 20 years after 1831. The curve for the District shows how very sensitive the population of the industrial parishes were to the market. If, as is shown in Graph 4, the characteristic of the rural districts was the marginality of the rate of change in the industrial districts it was the magnitude of the fluctuations in the rate that is the main characteristic. Graph 5 shows this clearly. With the exception of Abergavenny which consisted mainly of agricultural parishes and only of pockets of mining and manufacturing activities, all the Sub-districts have this characteristic of violently fluctuating rates of population change in the first half of the century. Take Tredegar. Between

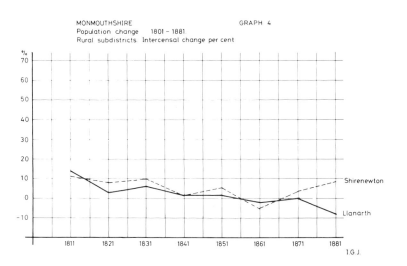

MONMOUTHSHIRE
Population change 1801 – 1881.
Rural subdistricts. Intercensal change per cent

GRAPH 4

I.G.J.

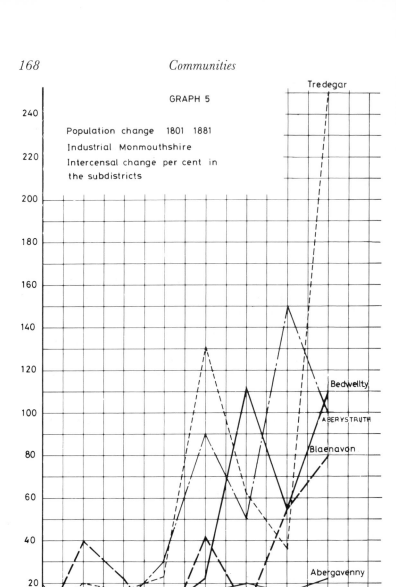

GRAPH 5

Population change 1801 1881
Industrial Monmouthshire
Intercensal change per cent in
the subdistricts

Tredegar

Bedwellty

ABERYSTRUTH

Blaenavon

Abergavenny

I.G.J.

1801 and 1811 its population grew by 2½ times, between 1811 and 1821 by only one-third, by two-thirds in the next decade, doubling in the next, and then between 1841 and 1851 the growth rate falling again to only one-third. What they all have in common, with the possible exception of Blaenavon, is the relative evenness of growth after 1851. This, as will be seen from Graph 3, would appear to apply also to a typical area of colliery developments—namely Mynyddislwyn.

Generally speaking, therefore, the characteristic instabilities of population growth—characteristic of all mining and manufacturing districts in the first half of the century—had given way by the 1850s to greater regularities. For about three decades in succession population grew at roughly the same rate. And that was important in the apprehension of these communities of themselves.

But decennial figures can only give a very rough guide to actual population movements. Ten years, or even three or four years, might be enough to witness both the rise and dissolution of a place. This leads me to elaborate on another characteristic feature or difference within the manufacturing districts themselves—a difference which was very pronounced in the years we have in mind. It is this. There were basically two kinds of settlement developing on the coalfield during those years. The iron towns were now towns in a recognizable way such as had not been the case a few decades earlier, and although the market was beginning to turn against their product there was no suggestion that their economic base would collapse. They were rich towns, permanently planted at the heads of the valleys. But what about the colliery towns that were beginning to appear lower down the reaches of the rivers and towards the centre of the basin of the coalfield? Until the steam-age had come in its fullness they were characterized by an even greater fragility than had been the lot of the iron towns. They were almost literally encampments, as in Flint, and their inhabitants knew that they had in their places no abiding city. Later I shall argue that this impermanence, this dependence upon chance or forces beyond human control—geology, the trade cycle, contrary winds in the channel, inadequate ports and communication—helps to explain much in their physical shape, their

architectural styles, and above all, the community arrangements of their inhabitants.

III. Society

Bearing in mind the complexities in the economic structure
of the county it is probably a delusion to imagine that one can
think of one social structure—one model of society applying
equally to the whole of the region of study. Within the region
there was an old borough town, Abergavenny, an administrative and legal centre, commercial and market centre, and
likewise to the north and south, around the fringe of the area
there were similar old market towns, corporate boroughs, the
homes of gentry families. But most characteristic of the region
were the new towns, the industrial towns, the manufacturing
conglomerates at the heads of the valleys, heaving with people,
defying description, impossible to categorize. And finally there
were the scores of small, impermanent, often evanescent settlements, places of minimal organization, only loosely bound to
their larger neighbours, remote in style and ethos from the old
corporate towns. What social model will cover this complexity?
Nevertheless, there are some guidelines that can be discerned.

For there did exist a social hierarchy. At the top were the
landlords, the old landed proprietors. They were at the top of
the pyramid for two not unrelated reasons. First, they were
large landowners in the district and second, they had been
there before industry came. The fact that they were not the
largest landowners in the iron districts themselves was less important than the fact that their holdings elsewhere in the county
were so large. The proprietors I have in mind were the Nevills
of Abergavenny, the Duke of Beaufort, the Morgans of
Tredegar Park, and the Marquis of Bute. The latter is an
example of a proprietor who had little land in north Monmouthshire but enormous influence and prestige nevertheless.

The proprietors were involved in the iron district not as
industrialists directly but as rentiers, owners of royalties, of
tolls and wayleaves; Sir Charles Morgan's Golden Mile is the
perfect example of the latter. The Duke of Beaufort was
reputedly receiving almost £2,000 per annum in rents and
royalties from an area that had yielded only £20 twenty years

earlier. Sir Benjamin Hall, who received £1,350 per annum from Victoria sold his rights in 1848 for £55,000. When Sir Charles Morgan leased land to Thomas Prothero in 1840 for a colliery his royalty was fixed at 1*s*. 2*d*. per ton with a guaranteed annual return of £700. As early as 1833 Sir Charles Morgan was said to be receiving £3,000 per annum in tolls from his Golden Mile. So even though the ancient landed families were not themselves entrepreneurs they profited greatly from mineral workings and urban rents: the new houses they built themselves in mid-Victorian times were not built or maintained on the profits of agriculture.

Below the proprietors were the entrepreneurs. These were the men who had ventured their money and skills and literally created the towns. Such was Crawshay Bailey, the Harfords, the Kendles, the Halls. As a matter of fact these, individually and certainly collectively, were far richer than the ground land-lords in the valleys. When they leased land for furnaces they took the surrounding land as well for minerals, tipping and urban developments with the result that they were the largest owners of property.

Then there were the coal-owners, entrepreneurs on a much smaller scale but in the sector which was soon to become the predominant one in the economy. Such were Henry Protheroe, Edward Williams, Thomas Phillips, Thomas Powell and many others.

At this point I should warn against too rigid a classification, for the industrialists either were or aimed to become land-owners in their own right, to have the style and port of gentle-men. The Bailey family achieved this by the 1850s, and the Hanbury family of Pontypool as early as the middle of the previous century. It was done by making a lot of money, buying an agricultural estate at a distance from the works and then marrying into the gentry. This usually took a generation or so, but they all tried and most succeeded, including the coal proprietors. One can admire the houses they built themselves by taking 'Bargain Breaks' in the very numerous county hotels in the Usk and lowlands! So there was a blurring in the con-ventional boundaries between the social strata and, as is in-variably the case, the possession of ample money makes upward mobility possible: financial liquidity kept them buoyant! But in any case, in the valleys themselves it was the entrepreneurs who were at the top of the ladder, and no one denied them their right to occupy it. The towns and villages owed their prosperity to them: it was on their skill, their foresight, their understanding of the market that everything depended. They might copy the style of the gentry, but in their works and among their own peers and workforce they were princes exercising whatever degrees of power were necessary for their own good, and, *ipso facto,* the good of all.

Everyone else, including the few remaining small landowners or freeholders, were more or less dependent upon them. It was the nature of the link of dependence that effectively determined the structure of the rest of society. That dependance was the social expression or the expression in social terms, of the economic power of the industrialists both as individuals and in combination. The masters—iron-masters and coal-masters alike—owned, either as individuals or as corporate bodies, all the means of production and they displayed that power and exercised it conspicuously. It is not strange that the generality of people, of their dependents that is to say, seemed to have believed that they actually controlled the whole system. It must have been difficult for people who were familiar with power thus personalized in one man or in a dynasty to abstract the man from the system and to account for it theoretically. It was the fact of power held in this way and of dependence experienced in that way that legitimized the exercise of power and authority, even as the authority of the landowner was legitimized by tradition. It also seemed to be legitimized by law. It was the entrepreneur class, assisted by the few land-owners but increasingly by the clergy, which monopolized the magistracy, so that the administration of the law of the land came to be confused in the minds of common people with the administration of the works. It took a long time for these feelings to be broken down and it was in the middle decades that this process of education and enlightenment began.

The link of dependence to which I referred was more or less strong depending on one's relation to the masters. In the early decades of industrialization there were very few in this class, but as the works achieved permanence and as stability came to the valleys and towns so there arose men whose rare and special skills gave them a degree of relative independence. Within the works themselves by the mid-century there was a well-defined managerial class. The mid-century saw the emergence of the general manager, particularly as the works became joint-stock concerns (and the owners tending to live at a distance) and too large for old styles of management to be applied. Under the general manager was a whole gamut of salaried posts: under-managers, mineral surveyors, engineers, draughtsmen, accountants, cashiers, clerks. There were 49 agents in Aberystruth in 1841 and 29 in Bedwellty. In the towns professional men and shop-keepers, tradesmen, craftsmen and local government officials emerged whose special skills or degree of education or relative wealth weakened the chain of dependence. It is common to call this a middle class, and maybe it was, and if so a middle class which was itself very stratified. Its social characteristic, by reason of its own hierarchical structure, was to have links with both the masters and with the amorphous body of workmen. They were of crucial importance in the provision of a political culture in the valleys. This is the political class and it was of enormous significance that it was the political ideas and the social objectives of this class that percolated down in the masses below and which under-pinned thereby mid-Victorian political stability. Their very existence was a factor limiting the power of the upper class of entrepreneurs. The fact that by the mid-century they were no longer being recruited from England but were largely Welshmen, locally trained and educated, made the lines of communication between them and the workmen below them more natural and spontaneous. The 1847 Education Commission Report is surely misguided in this respect.

Finally, the workmen, though they appear like a *lumpen-proletariat* were themselves distinguished into different groupings. Relative skill and different wage rates, for example, in the domain of work put some men higher than others. But culture stratified them also. The rôles played by men and women in working class organisations gave to some a higher esteem than to others, and where esteem of this kind coincided with an element of financial superiority based on technical skill then an upper class of workman was produced.

It was the mark of this population that it was constantly being renewed by immigration. The reasons for this are complex. For one thing the population of the works could not successfully reproduce themselves in numbers sufficient to maintain the workforce. Natural increase was very high, but so was the death rate, especially that of small children (table 1). The population was constantly recruited from outside therefore. Secondly, the works were increasing in size. For example, in 1809 Beaufort employed a total of 250 men. By 1850 one rolling mill alone at Tredegar provided work for 500. Similarly, the collieries were getting relatively larger, and by the '70s when the pits were being sunk into the steam coal seams, very much larger.

TABLE 1

Fertility Rates: births per 1,000 females aged 15 to 44

	England & Wales	Bedwellty
1841	135.2	200.5
1851	144.3	189.2

Crude Death Rates 1841—1851

1841	32.0
1842	21.7
1843	19.3
1844	28.2
1845	24.6
1846	26.8
1847	30.7
1848	26.6
1849	33.8
1850	25.3
Mean	26.5

Mean for England and Wales	22.3

The recruitment was from outside the area. In Bedwellty in 1851 40% of the population was from Monmouthshire, the remaining 60% came from outside. Roughly the same proportions applied in Man-moel, though it was much lower in Uwchlawr-coed. In the two main parishes of Bedwellty/Aberystruth in

The Bedwellty Colliery, Tredegar, Monmouthshire, the scene of the explosion in 1865.

Funeral of the colliers killed by the late explosion at Tredegar. *(Illustrated London News 1865.)*

1851 10% of household heads were locally born, 10% in adjacent parishes, 7% in the county, 22% in Glamorgan, 27% in the rest of south Wales, 4% north Wales, 12% Hereford and the border, 6% England, 3% Ireland. So not less than 79% of household heads were Welsh-born. No less than 83% of wives were Welsh-born—a very sensible discrimination! This appears to have been the pattern until the population explosion of the end of the century when the old regularities of settlement were finally obliterated. But in our period immigration was not of that order and the effect of the movement of population into the area was to reinforce the linguistic and cultural bonds with an ancient past.

IV. Culture and Religion

This leads me into my fourth point for discussion. Earlier I remarked that the statistics of population movement that we have for the early part of the century are very crude and unreliable, but it is virtually certain that quite quickly in the second and third decades of the century the processes by which this part of the county bordering on England and those Welsh counties which had been anglicized since the seventeenth and eighteenth centuries, were reversed. It seems pretty certain that the consequences of industrialization were 'cymricization'; the industrial valleys became predominantly Welsh. Two sets of related facts support this view. One is the enormous popularity and strength of the eisteddfodau and other literary movements based mainly on the Welsh language and dedicated to the preservation and use of the Welsh language. There was the Cymreigyddion y Fenni, for example, and the numerous branches and off-shoots that were planted in the north of the county. Of course, the eisteddfod in the early days of its resurrection used both languages on the platform and in its literary competitions, but there is no doubt that it was the Welsh element that was given the greatest prestige. It was also a kind of aristocratic institution and literary clergymen took the head in its public appearances, but effectively it was a democratizing institution, one in which ordinary men of unusual gifts could be judged by their peers and hope to have their works published. The north Monmouthshire valleys were the heartland of that re-vitalized welsh culture. Consciously re-vitalized, I should say. Read the *Welsh* local histories and mark the difference between them and the conventional English ones. Coxe saw barely 500 inhabitants in the empty wastes: 'Myfyr Wyn' and 'Eiddil Gwent' looked on families and farms whose individual histories they knew and whose culture they understood and loved. The second piece of evidence is the religious history of the county at large and of the northern valleys in particular. Here what is significant is the pattern of denominationalism. In the industrial parts of the county it is the old dissenting nonconformist denominations that provided most places of worship and attracted most worshippers. These very numerous chapels all traced their descent from the gathered congregations of the hills whose history went back to the seventeenth century. It is likely that many of them by the early stages of industrialization were English in language. This was most certainly true of the various Methodist denominations, including Welsh Calvinistic Methodist churches. There was no linguistic difference between the churches founded by Howell Harris and his followers in eastern and northern Gwent and the churches founded by the followers of Wesley. But by the middle '30s the linguistic difference was the major factor separating the two communions. Why was this? Because of the nature of immigration. Welshmen from Ceredigion and Carmarthenshire, from Montgomeryshire and the uplands of Breconshire brought *Welsh* Calvinistic Methodism with them, and their coming swamped the indigenous Calvinistic causes. The Wesleyans became a Welsh denomination about the same time: in the first decade of the century a Welsh Wesleyan missionary was compelled to preach in English because there were no Welsh people to preach to, and the cause he founded was English. Ten years later Welsh causes had been founded in Nantyglo, Varteg (1829), Ebbw Vale (1830), Rymni (1837), Pontypool (1839) and in Cendl, Brynmawr, Tafarnau Bach and Pontlottyn. Dr. Siân Rhiannon Williams's work shows how closely the fortunes of the Welsh chapels were bound up with immigration from Welsh Wales. Of course the process was not as simple as that. Welsh chapels were also sources of anglicization as was the Sunday School from a very early

Capel Salem, Senghennydd, 1899.

period in some places. Nevertheless, this quarter century that we are concerned with is important as the period which reaped the results culturally and religiously of the constant immigration into the valleys from Welsh Wales.

In this respect it is very important to stress again, but within this argument about culture, the facts to which I have already alluded when talking about the economic history of the period. It was vital that they should have been years of moderate growth, of steady development, rather than the headlong, tempestuous growth of the early years of change. Such a time of over-rapid development would come again to the valleys and this time the old Welsh culture would go under. But at least for a generation there was time for a settling down into a more ordered life, for the creation of new instruments of culture, for education to begin and to be established, for poetry and the things of the mind to exert their benign and civilizing influence. Most certainly religion and industry seemed during these years to be in partnership: contemporaries did not think of this as antipathetic to the true interests of the individual or of society. If religion helped to produce a disciplined workforce, as undoubtedly it did, so too did religion begin to civilize and humanize industry and to create a public conscience on which the politicians would later build. Some people thought at the time that the connection was too close for the integrity of religion: the Rhymney Iron Company not only built and endowed an Anglican Church but regarded the incumbent as no different from an employee, so much so that William Evans, the second incumbent preferred not to live on Company land and moved into the relative immunity and independence of neighbouring Gelligaer. Of course industry wanted stability and order: and the greatest expansion of the Established Church in the valleys came after the political and social turmoil of the 1830s and early 1840s. But everyone, and not only the industrialists, longed for stability. It was for their own good that religious organizations preached the virtues of peace and social harmony. *Sub specie aeternitatis* their stake in society was infinitely greater than that of the iron-masters and coal-owners. Theirs was not an alternative society: it *was* the society.

V. Politics and Order

This brings me to my final point—in a sense the most important because the most comprehensive of the social factors I wish to talk about.

Here again our period was one of transition. This was so in the realm of government, and was due partly to the sanctions of central government and partly it was a response to local needs and pressures. County administration was through Quarter Sessions and with the influx of population the work demanded of the magistrates became increasingly heavy. The magistrates were chosen from among the only class qualified by wealth and status to perform the function—that is, from among the entrepreneurs. Whether the justice they dispensed was even-handed, especially with the multiplication of legislation defining industrial relations between men and masters, was more than doubtful, and from 1829 the call for the appointment of stipendiary magistrates was heard. Petty sessions were expensive, inconvenient and uncertain, and the general inefficiency characterizing the administration of justice locally reflected the disinterest of the magistrates in the work and their readiness to use the position only in order to exercise initiatives in the keeping of the peace.

The other form of local government was the parish vestry. Designed for small rural parishes the vestry soon virtually collapsed under the sheer weight and multitude and complication of problems having to be dealt with. From the beginning the iron-masters dominated this institution as well as the select vestries, not personally but through their nominees. The powers of the vestry were in theory considerable and commensurate with the duties imposed upon them by statute. The upkeep of roads and bridges, for example, the clearance of nuisances, and above all (before 1834) the care of the poor. So far as the first of these were concerned, the iron-masters did as they wished without consultation: no parish vestry was consulted when a master wished to build a road or turn a path into a railway. In this way the parish was becoming irrelevant in the middle years of industrialization. And yet, not entirely so, for the parish preserved those vestiges of democratic government which were to form the basis for the enlargement of public participation in government later in the century.

Government came to be directly involved in local affairs in two general ways. First, the maintenance of public order. In the first half of the century when disturbances threatened the peace the immediate reaction of the magistracy was to try to persuade the government to send in troops. This happened regularly from 1816 onwards and there was constant pressure on government to station troops permanently in these 'black domains'. It was typical of the iron-masters that, although they supported in theory the establishing of a permanent police force, they preferred to arrange things their own way by swearing in their own constables: this was in order to avoid the rating of their property.

Closely connected with that was the influence of government

in the active affairs of the works—the Truck Act of 1831, for example, and the Mines Act of 1842. Though at first honoured as much in the breach as in the observance, they nevertheless created an atmosphere of expectation in the communities concerned that minimal standards of managerial and social behaviour should be respected and, what was to prove more important as the years passed, provided reforming groups with precise legal objectives and a machinery for ensuring the realization of those objectives. Truck would persist where Company power could feed on public apathy: where it was opposed by spirited men it ceased. In those middle decades of the century the companies themselves came to find it expedient to respect the law even if their motives rose no higher than the creation of a public face and a less sinister and dreadful reputation than had been theirs in the previous half century.

But the greatest interference of government came in legislation to do with the most sensitive of social areas—the poor and public health. I will not go into the detail of this legislation—the Poor Law Amendment Act and the 1848 Public Health Act: suffice it to say that both brought fixed procedures into local government and created institutions based on democratic forms of representation. Both these Acts—and the multitudinous legislation that followed both—are of the highest importance in the history of democracy. Not that the changes in attitude were immediate: far from it. Iron-master control was almost complete for many years in the area of the works. Aberystruth and Bedwellty came under Abergavenny Union, but because of their vast social differences came to be organized separately and eventually, in 1848, became a separate Union. But there were now institutions of government in being, elections to be undertaken regularly, the central government satisfied as to the adequacy of arrangements not only for the care of the poor but also for many other aspects of life in these communities. So it was that during these years between 1848 and 1874 the great machine of democratic local government first began to operate. By the time local government had been completely reformed in 1894 the inhabitants of the iron districts had achieved a sophisticated understanding of the political processes and the working classes, in particular, had learned how to exploit them for their own social benefit and eventually to use them as the essential lever in the achievement of their own political emancipation.

I have put local government before parliamentary politics for that was how it was. This is not to say that parliamentary politics were not important, but simply that the vast majority of men in the area could have no hope, even after the Reform Act of 1867, of participating. This huge area of wealth and power and population had no separate representation, such as Merthyr had been given in 1832, and it was not to gain representation until the Third Reform Act and the Redistribution Act of 1884-85, and then on a far more restricted scale than had been anticipated or hoped for.

What did this mean in practice? It meant that the political ideas that were most likely to gain a hearing were those nourished in resentment—the politics of the outsider, of the man with a grievance. Hence Chartism. It was Chartism which had continued to exist as a body of ideas even though it no longer existed powerfully as an organization, and which was being increasingly harmonized into the old traditions of Dissenting radicalism, that provided the ground-work for the new political consciousness of the period. Other societies, political and religious and mixtures of both, toiled in the valleys, and their success or failure was expressive of the extent to which they accorded with the democratic and humane notions of the original combination. The old working-class militancy likewise was diverted into new constitutional channels, and the Scotch Cattle faded into a memory as organized unionism came to be preferred in the valleys and eventually throughout the coalfield. The stability of society, so astonishing in retrospect, owed much to the expansive and expanding economic base which coal and iron provided, but it was the cultural continuities provided by the Welsh language and institutionalized in chapels, friendly societies, eisteddfodau, clubs and sport, which came rapidly to create areas of personal freedom and initiative. These were the essential elements in the Liberal radical democratic political culture of the final decades of the century, and which we, in our turn, can recognize to be in retrospect the most precious part of our inheritance from them.

This lecture was first published in 1981 by the Standing Conference on the History of the South Wales Valleys in association with the Torfaen Museum Trust.

Industrial Monmouthshire has been fortunate in its historians and readers cannot do better than to start with those mentioned in the opening paragraphs of the text. E. Powell, *History of Tredegar* (Cardiff, 1855) and the two Welsh works, D. Morris, *Hanes Tredegar* (Tredegar, 1868) and W. Williams (Myfyr Wyn), *Atgofion am Sirhywi a'r Cylch* (reprint ed. D. Myrddin Lloyd, Cardiff, 1951), though very old-fashioned are delightful to read and full of information not easily available elsewhere for the reason that their authors were often witnesses of the social changes they describe, and the contemporaries of some of the leading actors in events. This tradition of scholarly piety persists and Arthur Gray Jones, *A History of Ebbw Vale* (Starling Press, 1970) is an up-dated version of his pioneering M.A. thesis. The Starling Press has published a number of valuable local histories of the area, including E. E. Edwards, *Echoes of Rhymney* (1974) which I found most informative. The Tredegar History Society was responsible for the publication of Oliver Jones, *The Early Days of Sirhywi and Tredegar* (1969). A classic of controlled reminiscence is Thomas Jones, *Rhymney Memories* (Newtown, 1938, Centenary Edition, Gomerian Press, 1970). Local histories, including chapel histories many of which are in effect histories of whole communities, will be found listed in *A Bibliography of the History of Wales* (2nd edn., 1962) and its supplements in *Bulletin of the Board of Celtic Studies,* XX, XXII, XXIII and XXIV (1963—1972).

The demographic history of the region remains to be written and I have used the decennial Census Reports. The most sophisticated study is the as yet unpublished doctoral dissertation of John Gwyn Davies, 'Industrial Society in Northwest Monmouthshire 1750—1851' (Wales, 1980) and I have relied heavily on this splendid work. Industrial history is best approached via W. E. Minchinton (ed.), *Industrial South Wales 1750—1914* (1969), J. H. Morris and L. J. Williams, *The South Wales Coal Industry, 1841—1875* (Cardiff, 1958), and the old, but very valuable J. Lloyd, *The Early History of the Old South Wales Ironworks* (1906). The recently published *Glamorgan*

County History, vol. V, Industrial Glamorgan from 1700 to 1970
(1980), edited by A. H. John and Glanmor Williams is highly
relevant. Ness Edwards, *The Industrial Revolution in South Wales*
(1924) remains essential reading. Social conditions are
described in numerous articles in academic journals and a few
monographs of which Philip N. Jones, *Colliery Settlement in the
South Wales Coalfield 1850 to 1926* (University of Hull, 1969) is
among the most useful. F. J. Ball, 'Housing in an industrial
colony: Ebbw Vale 1778—1914' in S. D. Chapman (ed.), *The
History of Working-Class Housing: a Symposium* (1977) describes
the growth of a typical settlement, along the lines pioneered by
Harold Carter, *The Towns of Wales* (Cardiff, 1974), and J. B.
Lowe, *Nantyglo Housing and the Crawshay Bailey period 1825-45*
(National Museum of Wales, 1974) their architectural features,
as does the same author's booklet *Welsh Industrial Workers
Housing 1775—1875* (National Museum of Wales, 1977). Mr.
Lowe's captions should be read as carefully as his plans should
be perused. The classic article on the nature of society in the
period immediately preceding the one discussed in this paper is
by D. J. V. Jones, 'The Scotch Cattle and their Black Domain',
in the same author's *Before Rebecca. Popular Protests in Wales
1703—1835* (London, 1973).

Industrial realtions, the growth of trade unions, can be
studied generally in R. Challinor and E. Ripley, *The Miners'
Association: a Trade Union in the Ages of Chartists* (1968) and more
particularly in E. W. Evans, *The Miners of South Wales* (Cardiff,
1961). Further references will be found in J. Morris and L. J.
Williams, 'The Discharge Note in the South Wales Coal
Industry 1841—1898', *Economic History Review,* 2nd series, X
(1957-8). The literature is comprehensively listed in J. Benson
and Robert G. Neville, 'A Bibliography of the Coal Industry in
Wales', *Llafur, 2,* No. 4 (1979).

The political response and the growth of a class consciousness in the region is only now receiving the critical attention it
deserves. Dr. D. J. V. Jones's numerous articles on Chartism,
especially his 'Chartism in Welsh communities', *Welsh History
Review,* 6 (1972-3), the work of Gwyn A. Williams in *The
Merthyr Rising* (1978), and Angela John, 'The Chartist
Endurance: Industrial South Wales, 1840-68', *Morgannwg, XV*

(1971), not forgetting the classic study by David Williams, *John Frost* (Cardiff, 1939), are essential reading. On the nature of politics and political behaviour see Glanmor Williams (ed.), *Merthyr Politics: the Making of a Working Class Tradition* (Cardiff, 1966), and my essay *Health, Wealth and Politics in Victorian Wales* above pp. 322-362 Peter Stead, 'The Welsh working Class', *Llafur,* 1, No. 2 (1973) is a penetrating study over a wider field.

The change in the nature of politics reflected profound changes in society as a whole, and readers should seek to understand the religious and cultural life of the period. This was a culture rich and varied and diverse, and the key to it is the Welsh language. The best available introduction is provided by Mair Elvet Thomas, *Afiaith yng Ngwent* (Caerdydd, 1978). In addition to the bibilography appended to the last mentioned work reference should be made to Thomas Parry a Merfyn Morgan (gol.), *Llyfryddiaeth Llenyddiaeth Gymraeg* (Caerdydd, 1976) which lists most of the authors of the period and critical studies of their works. I have myself tried to see this culture in perspective in 'The Valleys: the Making of a Community' above, pp. 137-157 and, *Communities: the Observers and the Observed.* The Annual Gwyn Jones Lecture (University College of Cardiff, 1985). I have been able to benefit from the yet unpublished researches of Sian Rhiannon Williams into the history of the Welsh language in the region, and I wish to express my thanks to her. Newspapers and magazines circulating in the county, such as *The Monmouthshire Merlin, The Cardiff and Merthyr Guardian, Seren Gomer, Seren Cymru, The Silurian* and *Tarian y Gweithiwr,* are a prime source and all are readily available in Newport and Cardiff reference libraries, as are the county history magazines, such as *The Monmouthshire Antiquary.* There are also are to be found among the Parliamentary Papers the reports of commissions, select committees and such like which proliferated in the period covered in this paper. Many of the books mentioned above refer to the most important of them. Finally, the reader should join a local history class, attend lectures and discussions arranged by the Standing Conference on the History of the South Wales Valleys, and subscribe to *Llafur. The Society of the Study of Welsh Labour History.* In this way he will be kept in touch with current research.

THE SWANSEA VALLEY: LIFE AND LABOUR IN THE NINETEENTH CENTURY*

I am not sure which is the best way to see the Swansea Valley. Some would say that it is best to view it on a fine windy day as you walk along the ridge of Mynydd Marchywel from Plâs Cilybebyll through the green shade of Coed Cwmtawe and straight up, keeping to the ridge along Bryn-ysgallog to the top of Y Darren Wyddon and Farteg Hill. I strongly recommend it as one of the most interesting walks in the district. From the escarpment below Y Farteg you can view the whole length of the trench of a valley from the Glais moraine in the south to the top of Ystalyfera where it broadens between gently curving hills winding up to Ystradgynlais and beyond to Abercrâf and thence up to the slopes of the Black Mountains and that unforgettable parade of westward looking peaks from the Carmarthen Fans to Fan Gyhirych. 'Like to a painted map the landscape lies'. From that vantage point you will see the essential physical features of the valley and the way it is related to the great industrial belt stretching from Swansea to Port Talbot in the east, with the sea and the distant hills of Devon and Cornwall as a timeless backdrop, and how, parallel to it, the adjacent valleys run up from the coast into the high moorlands beyond. You will see how the town of Clydach is crushed into the narrowest part of the valley where the Afon Clydach makes its confluence with the Tawe which is there sharply deflected by Glais moraine. A few miles up the Valley is Pontardawe, also on the confluence of another tributary of the Tawe, and on the other side of the ancient bridge is the village of Alltwen. Then, below you, on the other side of the valley is the town of Ystalyfera widening out into Y Gurnos which lies on both sides of the Twrch where that river runs into the Tawe. Looking down the escarpment at your feet to the alluvial plain below with the regular meander of the river and upwards to the steep, rocky slopes of Allt-y-grug you realise how aptly named was Ystalyfera when it was first settled—Cyfyng, 'the

*The paper was delivered as the first Annual South Wales Miners Library lecture at the library on 22 October 1983 and published in *Llafur* iv, 1 (1984).

Narrows', and if you are familiar with the place you will know that there is a street of houses and a district called Cyfyng where the oldest houses and buildings are to be found. But the most striking feature of that view of the valley is the way in which the pattern of settlement from Y Gurnos down to Morriston is one continuous ribbon of houses occupying a platform or terrace on the precipitous slopes of the western side of the valley. Only at Alltwen and Glais are there villages on the eastern side, and you will notice how on the western side the road and the canal run in tandem, while the railway hugs the slopes of Tarenni Gleision until it crosses into Ystalyfera along a viaduct and so into the Twrch Valley through to Brynaman, Pant-y-ffynnon and mid-Wales, and Llanelli and the main rail routes along the south Wales coast.

Another way of viewing the Swansea valley that I could at one time recommend is from the top of a bus. There was a time when I was expert in this top-of-the-bus-front-right-hand-seat method of locomotion. That was when I made the daily journey over a period of years from my home at Cwmtwrch to College, during which time I suppose that I became familiar with every turn and bump in the road. It would add greatly to the length of this lecture but not materially to its substance if I described the journey, and so I will confine myself to a few relevant observations about some of the characteristic features of the valley as seen from that moving vantage point. I have already observed that from Ystalyfera to Morriston the valley was built up for virtually the whole of the way. This was true also of the few miles along the Twrch Valley to Y Gurnos, except that one was more aware of the nucleation of industrial villages around collieries, tin works or brick works. But the sight which never ceased to gladden my eyes and excite my interest was that which came into view when the bus passed suddenly out of the industrial housing and the relics of defunct tin and brick works, colliery sidings and iron-stone 'patches', over the canal, past the Aubrey Arms and into green, lush parkland bordered with oak and beech with Ynyscedwyn House in the far corner. Here was rich pasture and arable land, the farms and enclosures of pre-industrial times, and the whole scene encapsulated the essential cultural contrast that

Swansea in 1880.

(Illustrated London News.)

gives the Valley its enduring fascination. Then, turning away from the cultivated fields the road ran into the industrial housing once again, with a glimpse of the aquaduct taking the canal over the river, through Ystalyfera, Cyfyng with its small cottages and narrow streets, to Pantêg with its enormous chapel, down through Godre'r Graig into Ynysmeudwy and more industrial ruins and so into Pantardawe. It was the housing that attracted one's attention, rows of early nineteenth century cottages giving way to a ribbon of semi-detached workmen's houses dating from the 1870s, all sash-windowed, their oak-grained and highly varnished front doors opening into well-scrubbed pavements, proclaiming a solid respectability. But one also knew that the older houses clinging to the edge of the narrow road-carrying terraces, low two-storied frontages to all appearance were actually tenements of three or four stories on the valley side, their backsides being cut into the rockface of the terrace.

The other features one could not help noticing were the ubiquitous pubs and chapels. One could not ignore the former because, whether by design or not I cannot tell, those fronting the road were official stopping places for the buses. One caught the bus at the Lamb Inn: it passed the Old Tredegar and the New Tredegar, the 'Sticle', and the Crown and the Aubrey Arms until you stopped outside the New Swan at Ystalyfera—with the Old Swan next door and the Red Cow a bit further on. And so the whole way to Morriston—only to name the pubs one involuntary stopped at is to become dizzy!

Similarly the parade of churches and chapels: St. Peter's, Ebenezer, Temperance Hall, Beulah, Bethel, Capel Newydd, Y Garn, Y Wern, and so on. I am not sure that there were not as many, if not more, chapels fronting the road as there were pubs. Clearly this valley was—and had been—thirsty for things other than beer, though perhaps the clue to the social reality was the balance between the two, more often co-existence than conflict.

I used to wonder, sitting there on the top of the bus with a book half-open on my knee, what would the valley have looked like a hundred years earlier? How had it all happened? Fortunately for us one of the most remarkable men ever to have lived in Cwmtawe and whose long life coincided almost exactly with its urbanisation, put down his memories of it and his impression of its people and its places in a series of articles in the quarterly magazine *Y Traethodydd* in 1865 and 1866. This was Thomas Levi, Calvinistic Methodist minister, who was born just ten years after the battle of Waterloo (i.e. in 1825) at Penrhôs, Ystradgynlais and who died in the middle of the First World War in 1916. He was an ironworker until he was encouraged in his early twenties to enter the ministry, and until he moved to Aberystwyth in 1876 he continued to serve the growing Methodist congregations of the region. He was a man of outstanding talents, a prolific writer, and famous as the founder of the magazine *Trysorfa y Plant* which he edited for fifty years. At its peak it was selling 44,000 copies a month and *Y Traethodydd* and *Y Dysgedydd* were financed out of its profits. He was the father of an equally remarkable son, Professor Thomas Levi, first professor of law at Aberystwyth. Thomas Levi began his description by passing quickly northwards from the centre of Swansea through poisonous smoke and grime and the flanks of Kilvey Hill already denuded of vegetation—he suggested that Glandŵr should be renamed 'Glanmwg'—

'Glandŵr a'r cylch yw'r gwaetha
A'r darth a mwg 'mhob simla,
Aroglau mawr a chymyl du—
Mae'n debyg i Gehenna'.

to Morriston, Ynyspenllwch and Pontardawe, then rapidly up to Ystradgynlais, Abercrâf and Penycae to that spur of the mountain that lies like an arrow pointed in the direction of Swansea from its base high up on the ridge between Bannau Sir Gâr (the Carmarthen Vans) and Llyn-y-Fan-Fawr and Fan Gyhirich. There, about 1200 feet up, sat down and described what he could see.

This again is a familiar place. Some will recall the walk from Tafarn-y-garreg past Y Dderi to Trecastell or, better still, along Fan Hir to Llyn-y-Fan-Fawr. A magically beautiful country, remote, wind-swept, wild. Thomas Levi obviously knew every inch of it, and from where he sat on Cefn-Cûl he could see (you can if you go up there) straight down the valley as far as Abercrâf. Thomas Levi had an eye for two things (apart from the country) namely, farms, the people and their ancestors who inhabited them, and the industrial developments that were then taking place. He knew them all, and some of them are still there. On his right, down in the valley besides the Llanddeusant road, were Blaenau and Blaen-cûl, and on the other side of the river are Llwyn-rhyn and Cae'r helm, Y Dderi, and Tŷ Henri. Then, further down, he could see Glan-Tywynni and Maes-yr-eglwys, Tafarn-y-garreg and the ancient chapel of Callwen surrounded by its meadows and protected by groves of trees. Craig-y-nos rose high above the river to his left, but Madame Patti had not yet discovered this romantic spot and the Castle, in its present form, had not yet been built. And so down the valley, describing the households, giving their histories, quoting the local poets, pointing out ancient earthworks and standing stones, giving places their proper names, and altogether evoking a past that was alive because it was present in the community formed by those scattered farms. That was in the 1860's, but change was in the air—or rather, it was snaking up the eastern flank of the valley in the form of gangs of Irish navvies building the Neath and Brecon Railway. Already they were approaching Pen-wyllt—and I thank whatever powers that be that I worked as a porter-signalman on the railway station Craig-y-nos that they were then building and that I was thus given the opportunity to get to know that wonderful country and to see it mor or less as it had been for two score years or more. At Penwyllt there was silica sand and on the Cribarth, opposite, there were lime-stone quarries to feed the iron—smelting works further down the valley from the canal head at Hen Neuadd. Then, having completed his survey of the upper reaches of the Tawe, Thomas Levi moved down through Ystradgynlais to Ystalyfera, and this time sitting on the roof of Ynyscedwyn House—how this man loved the heights!—he described the view straight down the valley beyond the newly-built steeple of Pontardawe Church to Morriston in its smokey distance. What a pity he ceased his description there, for his third article on the literary and cultural life of the communities shows how precisely he must have

Capel Gellionen, Pontardawe.

known the stages by which this idyllic spot had been transformed into the largest town in the valley. 'I happened to be',
are his last words on the subject, 'on the very spot where,
twenty-five years ago (in 1837), the first blow was struck to
clear away the thornbushes and the weeds from the slope below
the canal to prepare the site for the ironworks. Today', he says
with astonishment and pride, 'it is one of the largest in Wales
and the inhabitants of the place are numbered in their
thousands'. How had it happened? Let us leave old Thomas
Levi on the roof of Ynyscedwyn House and try to find out for
ourselves.

What Thomas Levi had witnessed as a lad of twelve years of
age in 1837 when he saw workmen preparing the site for the
building of the Ystalyfera Iron Works was a turning-point, a
decisive and portentous event in the economic and cultural life
of the Swansea Valley. Incidentally, you can see the remains
of the furnaces that were then built into the slope of the land
below the canal as you approach the first of the roundabouts
that by-pass Ystalyfera on the main Swansea to Brecon road.
The building of the Works was not *the* most portentous event
in the history of the valley, for it was the building of the canal

from Hen Neuadd, near Abercrâf, down to Swansea in 1799 which had made possible the industrial revolution. The opening of the Ystalyfera Iron Works in 1839 marked an advance in the technology of iron production which, in its turn, made possible an enormous advance in the scale of production both of the primary product and of tinplate in that particular part of the valley. The iron industry was no stranger to that region. The neighbouring Ynyscedwyn Works had their origin in the early eighteenth century, and the wooded valleys running into the Tawe, such as the Twrch and the Giedd, had been the sites for smelting locally-mined iron ore from before the memory of man. But Ynyscedwyn had been dependent upon *imported* supplies of charcoal and when this fuel had become hopelessly uneconomic the Works had survived only by using bituminous coals brought up by the canal from the Clydach area. Anthracite coal was being shipped out and bituminous coals imported. The opening of the ironworks was an immediate response to the perfecting of ways of using anthracite in the smelting process and from the beginning, therefore, it could be an almost completely integrated works with the coal and iron mines and the furnaces and foundries and, shortly afterwards, the huge tin-works all under the same management. The owner-manager was J. Palmer Budd and he was almost as original an innovator as the two inventive pioneers, George Crane and David Thomas of Ynyscedwyn, whose technology he adapted and improved. By 1853 he had eleven furnaces in blast, a new forge, and forty puddling and balling furnaces, and he had perfected a way of consuming waste gasès from the furnaces which helped to reduce the above-average cost of production which were the unavoidable concmitants of the geographical situation of the works on the edge of the anthracite coalfield. When Thomas Levi was writing the Ystalyfera works had reached the peak of their prosperity: over 3000 men were employed there with another 1000 on the ancillary sides. Well could this ironworks boast of its achievements and Budd be likened to Guest of Dowlais. In fact, the Ystalyfera Works were comparable not to the Dowlais Iron Company but of the two smaller works of Penydarren or Plymouth both of which by the 1860s had fallen on evil days.

The future lay with steel, and it was works such as the Seimens works at Landore or the two great Merthyr establishments which could afford huge investment programmes that the new technologies called for which survived. In almost every respect Swansea Valley iron would become uneconomic and even the tin-works before long go over to using mild steel.

But that was in the future, and for the time being Thomas Levi's generation could enjoy the expansive and optimistic mood which industrial growth generated. Compared with the massive iron and steel industry on the northern edge of the coalfield that at the top of the Swansea Valley was very small: in the best year (1856) total production in all the works put together (Ystalyfera, Ystradgynlais, Abercrave and Brynaman) was just over 62,000 tons, but the combined output of the Merthyr and district works was over 815,000 tons. Small in relation to the whole, therefore, but of immense importance in the locality and the chief influence determining the growth of population and settlement. 'Iron was King' for the twenty or so years of the mid-century because of the increasing importance of tinplate manufacture in the economy. By the middle of the century two of the eight tin-works in Glamorgan then in production were in the valley, at Ystalyfera and at Pontardawe, and these used the iron-plate produced in the local works— indeed, the two stages in the production of tinplate were under common ownership in both these places. The enormous expansion in the production of tinplate thereafter and the technological changes associated with the use of steel rather than iron led to the foundation not of more integrated works but to the proliferation of small tin-works using imported steel bars. Not until 1890 did Pontardawe go over to steel and by then the Ystalyfera Ironworks had closed. There were tin-works of varying sizes at Ystalyfera (1851), Clydach (1879), Cwmtwrch (1879), Y Gurnos (1880), Ynysmeudwy (1880), and Ynyscedwyn (1901) and, of course, in Morriston. It is probable that one's abiding impression of the valley in mid-century would have been of a string of industrial villages nucleated around tin-works, all of them on the canal, and that it was these manufactories, belching black smoke and emitting those unforgettable acid vapours that was sustaining the economy of the valley.

This would be only partially true, for the coal industry had always enjoyed an independent existence, and from the third quarter of the century, in particular, it produced for an entirely separate market. This was the well-nigh insatiable demand for bituminous coals by the smelting industry in the lower part of the valley from Morriston down to the sea, and a not inconsiderable but steadily growing coastal trade in the same coals. The Graigola vein was widely famed for its steam-raising properties and was heavily exploited on both sides of the valley around Clydach and Glais once the problem of transporting it to Swansea had been solved by the building of the canal and the railway. Anthracite coals were in constant demand also, and it is worth bearing in mind that the specialised market it was ideally suited for in domestic heating, brewing, and lime-burning was more than marginally important in the economy of the valley. The anthracite collieries which were porudcing principally for this market, such as those in the Twrch valley, were relatively large, prosperous and long-lasting. There was never a shortage of Swansea businessman eager to invest in it and when, at the end of the century, demand increased substantially both in the home and foreign markets the little colliery villages which the canal and its attendant tramways had sustained for so long were well placed to take the strain.

*   *   *   *

I turn now to consider some of the outstanding features of the growth of population in the Swansea Valley. Thomas Levi, you will recall, had remarked on the growth of Ystalyfera in a mere twenty-five years from a few scattered farmhouses and cottages into the largest town north of Morriston. First, there is the crude growth of population in the course of the century— that, is for the relevant part of Llangyfelach, Rhyng-dwy-clydach and Cilybebyll, Llangiwg and Ystradgynlais: in 1801 it was just under 3000, in 1891 almost 19,000, an increase of about 610% over the ninety-nine years. But this growth was irregular: 1801-1821 it was under 25%, 1821-1841 it was about 33%, then in the next two decades to 1861 it was about 45%.

Thereafter, the rate of growth was under 6% until the 1880s when it rose to just under 15% before falling again by 1891 to about 7%. So the pattern is clear: twenty years of moderate growth, twenty years of rapid growth followed by twenty years of what can only be described as rampant growth, and finally two decades of negligible growth with a sharp recovery in the last decade of the century.

Clearly this pattern was determined by the industrial changes I have already referred to, and it is reasonable to suppose that this pattern of a doubling of population in thirty years, which was the pattern of change in Glamorgan over the same period, would have been maintained as the century advanced if the original impetus of coal production for shipment down the canal to Swansea had remained unchanged. It was the transformation of the industrial life of the valley on the basis of the new technology and the developments in the iron industry at Ystalyfera and Pontardawe which determined the chronology of growth and the no less catclysmic collapse of that industry in the latter part of the century which accounted for the relative decline.

Morriston.

Detailed figures for the parishes show how sensitive a barometer of industrial change was population change. In Llangiwg, population doubled between 1831 and 1851, doubled again in the next ten years, and then fell back very sharply to under 10% until the recovery in the last decade of the century. Ystradgynlais grew rapidly between 1841 and 1851, this expansion coinciding with the reorganisation of the Ynyscedwyn Ironworks. Then there was stagnation and a loss of population before it picked up again at the end of the century with the advance of the coal trade. 1831-41 was the growth decade in Cilybebyll, and the steady rise in Clydach was due to the increasing production of the Graigola coals.

	1801	1811	1821	1831	1841	1851	1861	1871	1881	1891	1901
Llangiwg	829	1060	1428	1847	2813	4229	7983	8312	9110	9707	12376
Cilybebyll	281	279	327	398	731	982	1346	1650	1940	2006	2463
Ystrad	993	1181	1482	2078	2335	3758	4345	4121	4114	4326	5785
Rhynd-C	722	884	948	1137	1438	1578	1720	2208	3529	4018	4462
	2825	3404	4185	5460	7317	10547	15394	16291	18693	20057	25086

(Est. 1650 for Cilybebyll)

	1801-11	1811-21	1821-31	1831-41	1841-51	1851-61	1861-71	1871-81	1881-91
Llangiwg	27.9	34.7	29.3	52.3	50.3	88.8	4.1	9.6	6.5	27.5
Cilybebyll	-0.7	17.2	21.7	83.7	34.3	37.0	22.6	17.8	3.4	22.7
Ystrad	18.9	25.9	40.2	12.4	60.9	15.6	-5.4	-0.2	5.4	33.7
R.D.C.	22.4	25.5	40.2	26.5	9.7	10.0	28.4	59.8	13.8	11.0
Cwmtawe	20.5	22.9	30.5	34.0	44.1	45.9	5.8	14.7	7.3	25.1

But how fast is fast? It is important to establish some fundamental relativities because there is reason to believe that stability or the lack of stability in the new communities being formed in industrial south Wales was a direct consequence of the speed and regularities of population growth. That is to say, it was a main characteristic of newly-planted industrial settlements that they should be highly sensitive to market changes and that the rise and fall over short periods should be reflected in an almost immediately reactive ebb and flow in the numbers of the population. In this respect the fundamental difference between the new mining and manufacturing districts and the ancient communities of the rural countryside was the lack in the former of the immemorial regularities which could survive even famine and disease and which gave to the latter their settled and permanent nature. Now when we compare the population growth of the Swansea Valley with that in what we might call the region of new growth in the iron districts in Glamorgan and Gwent or in the colliery villages of the steam-coal valleys it transpires that it was on the whole moderate. High rates of growth came in short spurts preceded and followed by longer periods of slower growth. As we have seen, in Ystradgynlais thirty years of relatively rapid growth was followed by population loss and stagnation.

Other relativities are important. Thus the *scale* of growth rarely approached levels reached in the eastern half of the coalfield. The population of the whole valley was still barely 20,000 in 1891, and Llangiwg, where most of the development took place, had only 10,000 by that date. Aberystruth, starting from the same bases as Llangiwg in 1801 had reached nearly 19,000 by 1881 and the Tredegar Sub-district 35,000 in the same period. More to the point, Swansea and Morriston—the area of the Municipal Borough—had almost four times the total population of the valley by 1881 (76,000).

So far I have singled out the relatively modest rate and scale of population growth. Equally important is the observation that the dynamic of this growth was the movement of people into the valley from outside. Hugh Thomas, to whose splendid research I am much indebted, has worked out that by 1841 one-third of the population of Llangiwg were immigrants and that ten years later they out-numbered the locally born (5 to 3). Ten years later two-thirds were immigrants. In 1861 in Ystalyfera nine out of ten heads of household were immigrant, a slightly higher ratio of wives, half the children and three out of four of the lodgers. This pattern may have been only slightly different elsewhere in the valley.

Where did the immigrants come from? Throughout the century it was virtually all a short-distance movement from adjacent parishes in Breconshire and Glamorgan and Carmarthenshire. This is not surprising, for the head of the valley borders on those counties. It was said that the two bars in the George IV Inn in Cwmtwrch were in different counties and the building itself in three!

What of the occupational structure of the population? As one would expect, very profound changes took place in the course of the century. First, there was a sharp decline in the number of people dependent upon agriculture for their liveli-hoods. In 1841 about a fifth of the working population were recorded as being engaged in agriculture. By 1851 this prop-ortion had gone down to 12% and by 1861 it was less than 8%. Coal and ironstone miners who in 1841 constituted 40% of the working population fell by 1861 to about 20%. The proportion of craftsmen rose slightly. The really spectacular growth was in the manufacturing sector. In 1841 iron and tin workers constituted 2% of the workforce, 11% in 1851 and 36% in 1861. By the end of the century there had been another shift with coal miners outnumbering iron and tin workers, especially at the head of the valley, this change reflecting the decline of iron, the effect of the MacKinley tariff and the expansion of the coal industry. There were 1300 colliers in Ystradgynlais and Cwmtwrch in 1895. But the key decades in respect of the occu-pational structure of the valley were the middle years of the

Upper Cwmtwrch.

century. It was then that Cwmtawe took on the character which it has retained into our days, that is to say, a large industrial district with a labour force unequally distributed both geographically and occupationally between mining and the manufacture of tin-plate. It was a working class valley, therefore, in respect of the bulk of its inhabitants.

Before I try to explain what I mean by that let me say first what I take to be the social significance of the factors I have already mentioned. First, they point to a relatively stable society. Taken over the century as a whole we saw that the scale of population growth was moderate. The size of the population, even in the most densely populated parts, was such as could be accommodated fairly easily within the valley. Urban development was longitudinally along the valley from industrial village to industrial village, population tending to nucleate in an orderly fashion at the intermediate points. Old photographs of Pontardawe and Clydach and Ystalyfera and Ystradgynlais do not portray great concentrations of people such as were developing contemporaneously in the colliery towns of Glamorgan or even of old industrial towns like Cwmafan. The rate of growth also made for stability. Apart from parts of Ystalyfera there were none of those explosions of population that were experienced elsewhere in Glamorgan which made a nonsense of the pathetic attempts of local authorities to contain them. And finally, there is the fact that the vast majority of the new population had come only a short distance, rarely more than twenty miles. Distances were not so great as to destroy the social linkages of families: the extended family could be a reality even though the typical household consisted of the nuclear family only.

Adding to this fundamental stability were two cultural forces of the greatest importance, language and religion. Short distance migration with the predominant flow from the west added to and strengthened the cultural homogeneity of the pre-industrial valley. Welsh was the language of the immigrants and the cultures from which they came were not, in some important respects, very different from that into which they moved. It was a condition of survival for the few English people who came in that they should achieve linguistic assimilation:

the Welsh-speaking Bodycombes and Oathericks and Summertons, for example, testify eloquently to the strength of the predominant language. Only at the end of the century did English-language institutions, like chapels, appear and their appeal seems to have been very much to the immigrant middle classes.

Earlier on I said that I wondered whether there were not as many chapels as pubs to be seen from the top of a bus on the journey from Cwmtwrch to Morriston. Certainly, places of worship were very numerous, probably twenty or so in a distance of about ten miles. Much can be learned about the valley from a study of its chapels and churches but I will make only some brief observations. First, that in its formal, institutional religious life it is the overwhelming strength of Welsh Non conformity that is most striking, the Established Church was by no means a negligible force judged by the number of its buildings, for the huge and populous parishes had been divided by the 1860s and provided with district churches and chapels. Clydach could boast one of the earliest of the Church Building Commissioners' churches to be built in Wales, erected and endowed, so it was said at the time 'to combat spiritual destitution'. But they were Anglican and anglicized and widely considered to be little more than monuments to the fame of the local industrialists and sepulchres for their mortal remains.

It was the Independents who were the most powerful and influential of the Nonconformist denominations. With astonishing speed the pre-industrial congregations on the old ridgeways had established daughter churches in the valleys sometimes almost as if in anticipation of the advance of urbanisation, and these in their turn had multiplied. The Baptists had grown in rather a similar way. The Unitarians, likewise, had moved down from the mountain into the valley where their brand of radical theology and politics contributed largely to the intellectual life of the community. But it is worth recollecting that in this respect they were out-flanked by the Swedenborgians who had a congregation, one of the very few in Wales, in Trebanws. When you look at the valley chapels it is worth considering that it was not the old, indigenous denominations who erected the neo-Gothic buildings to be seen, for example, in Clydach but the English-language congregations, and in particular, the Wesleyan Methodists.

Language and religion, indistinguishably dissolving into each other like the elements in a cultural solution, were both of them at one and the same time forces making for the stability of society *and* the most characteristic creation of that society. If, as we have seen to be the case, it was a working-class valley in the sense that the vast majority of its inhabitants were directly dependent upon its industries for their livelihood, it nevertheless needs to be stressed that the working-class character of the valley as a whole was qualitatively different from the working-class character of the colliery villages and towns which were growing up in south and west Wales at the same time. It would be interesting to examine the nature of the differences, and one would need to compare the contrasting styles or modes of urbanism, for example, to establish this, and to delve deeply into their contrasting cultural experiences, for it is the essence of working-class culture that it is self-generated and sustained. Above all, one would need to contrast the different social relations created by different kinds of industries and the influence upon behaviour of different patterns of work and different conditions of labour. One would need to find out how different labour forces perceived their situation in relation to other groups of people, and try to explain why working-class militancy should be endemic in one kind of industrial community and orthodox, conventional political organisation and activity be the norm in another. What can we say about the working-class character of the Swansea Valley?

First, it is worth remembering that some of the pre-industrial structures of society and pre-industrial modes of behaviour survived industrialisation. This is why I have stressed the more-or-less orderly fashion in which population grew and was distributed, and the local and Welsh element within it. The most characteristic feature of the old rural world was the simple division between landed proprietor and farmer, and between freeholder and tenant farmer, with the agricultural labourer at the bottom of the scale. Industrialisation, far from abolishing this stratification enhanced the social superiority of the gentry and the prestige of the farmers who survived. The local

gentry—Aubreys and Goughs and Lloyds and Mack-
worths—however much they might deplore many of the
features of urbanisation, had no reservations about profiting
from it. More so than in pre-industrial times they could afford
the style of gentlemen and the new and enlarged mansions they
built for themselves on the profits of industry and the parklands
they enclosed were the external evidences of the social
superiority they continued to enjoy.

The new industrial proprietors accepted their superiority
and never contested it with them. They aspired to be accepted
among them and they mixed socially on the bench and patron-
ised the same institutions. When it came to the push they real-
ised full well that the essential conflict in society was not
between different kinds of wealth but between those who possessed wealth and those who did not. Meanwhile, they adopted
the style of the gentry and built themselves mansions overlooking their works—Parsons at Ynyscedwyn, Gilbertson at
Llwynderw, Budd at Ynysydarren. Nor did the farming class
disappear. On the contrary, though reduced in numbers they
thrived on the increased production demanded of them and
they slid easily into the role of urban rentiers. It is astonishing
how, in Cwmtawe as elsewhere in industrial south Wales,
farmers seemed to constitute an elite out of all proportion to
their relative riches or to their numbers.

Nor should we forget that there was a strong professional
cláss of lawyers and managers and agents, and it is not fanciful
to detect in the towns and even to some extent in the industrial
villages a segregation of the classes taking place. This was
certainly the case in Pontardawe and Ystalyfera, and even in
the small villages there were colliery or tinplate managers'
houses set apart and a good deal grander than the rest. But the
Swansea valley awaits its Harold Carter. What is certain is
that the trading and shopkeeping class was socially very important. Workmen in Ystalyfera seemed to believe that the
single most beneficial change that could happen would be the
opening of the railway because it would break the trading
monopoly exercised by the shopkeepers in the district.

But the working class was itself a very complex social reality.
Far from being monolithic it seems to me to have been strati-

The Hafod Copper Works, Swansea, 1887.

fied by occupation and wages as well as by life-styles. The main
industries, as I have already noted—the mines, iron smelting,
tinplate manufacture, chemical works, transport—were all
labour intensive but all required a high proportion of skilled
men, and skills and crafts were accorded the respect they
deserved as well as the wages differentials that custom and the
market prescribed. One notices also how important was the
group in most of these industries. This was particularly the case
in the way work was organised in tinplate manufacture where
the division was between the mills and furnaces and the quite
distinct tinning sides, the related groups being paid by the box
in accordance with a customary scale. In the main industries,
also, recruitment was from simple jobs at entry through a
hierarchy of skills in the production teams. Sons followed their
fathers and, in the tinworks, girls their mothers, so that
families were traditionally associated with the same works or
colliery. This interlocking of work and family had the effect of
creating communities of work, that is, communities organically involved as families in the industrial processes. Paternalism, it should be noted, extended throughout society and was
as powerfully present at the point of production as in the
relations which were thought to exist between the owners and
managers on the one hand and the workers on the other. At a
time when many of the mines and tinplate works—all relatively
small—were locally owned and managed these patterns of
labour produced styles of industrial relations and methods of
settling disputes which made industrial unions virtually
redundant and impossible to conceive and localism defeated
the heroic attempts to working class leaers, like Lewys Afan
among the tinplaters, to give them permanence beyond the
immediate grievance.

*   *   *   *

The features of society that I have chosen to discuss—the
growth of industry and the main structural changes that took
place in the course of the century, patterns of population
change, the relative diversity of occupational structure, the
character of immigration, the cultural cohesion and religious

uniformity of the valley—these features help to explain what seems to me to be most in need of explanation, namely, the social stability which persisted beyond the First World War. When one considers what must have been the conditions of life for the vast majority of people—how insecure life was, how bad the conditions were before the public health reforms of the third quarter of the century, how communities were ravaged by disease, how towns were open to the scourge of typhus and sometimes cholera, of the insecurity of labour, of the institutionalised cruelty in the treatment of poverty, old age and small children, and of the deep ignorance about affairs which was the common lot for most of the time and which only the very gifted could hope to escape—when we consider these aspects of life, the standard of living we might broadly call it—it is astonishing that disorder and violence should have been so exceptional. Maybe Cwmtawe was fortunate in its situation: Swansea was a long way off until the coming of the railway, and urbanised Swansea valley kept its distance from what was called 'the metropolis of Wales'. Swansea finance helped to industrialize the valley but Swansea's aggressive middle-class politicans never held sway in Pontardawe or Ystalyfera or any of the other towns. And maybe this worked to the disadvantage of the valley in the sense that its population never received the kind of political education which Swansea's working classes got in its vigorous local political affairs and its experience of parliamentary politics. In local government the valley was united uncomfortably with Neath, and not until 1870 when Pontardawe became a Poor Law District taking in the whole of the valley and having health as well as poverty under its care was the framework for local political activity properly laid. By the time of the great Franchise Reforms of 1884 and the Redistribution Act of 1885 opinion was beginning to be organised and from then on the valley's working-class vote could be decisive in the new constituency of Gower. But it was a Nonconformist Liberal and later a 'Lib-Lab' vote and, of course, it could have been no other. The towns of the Swansea valley had grown principally in those years of prosperity and expansiveness in the middle of the century when the politics of protest and rebellion which had swept through the coalfield in the

1830s was a thing of the past. The Activities of the Anti-Corn-Law League were more to the taste of those who had ears to hear them than the sophisticated ideals of the Chartists, and it is very probable that many who came to settle from the deep rural parts of Carmarthenshire were less concerned with politics, Chartist or Rebeccaite, than with the apparently simple and straightforward and often desparate business of finding work and making a living. It took a long time for the skills of organising and the comradeship they had learned to use to such good effect in Friendly Soiseties and clubs and chapels to be devoted to industrial and political organisations but when the opportunity came with democratic forms of local self-government they were ready to apply them to good effect.

It is not for working-class politics that one looks in the middle decades of nineteenth century Cwmtawe when the lineaments of the society we can remember were laid down, it seems to me, but rather for the way a largely immigrant population from adjacent counties adapted themselves. In doing so they produced communities of an extraordinary creativity and cultural richness. Professor T. J. Morgan in those most sensitive and penetrating studies of the cultural lives of those communities has taught us how to enter into the lives of the people concerned. I think it should be our task to study afresh the ways in which despite—because of—the enormous challenge of the times they built a society which was humane, literate and cultivated in the things of the mind and spirit, and unselfconsciously democratic.

BIBLIOGRAPHICAL NOTE

This lecture is printed as delivered. It was intended for an audience largely unfamiliar with the region, and if it arouses interest in the history of the Valley it will have achieved its main purpose.

An excellent and comprehensive introduction to the larger area is W. G. Balchin (ed.), *Swansea and its Region* (University College of Swansea, 1971). Volume V of the Glamorgan County History, *Industrial Glamorgan,* edited by the late A. H. John and Glanmor Williams (Cardiff 1980) supplies the essential framework and is indispensable. There are very few histories of the Swansea Valley in the English language, but fortunately the best of them is a model of its kind. This is the set of three articles by J. D. H. Thomas, 'The Industrialization of Glamorgan Parish' in *N. L. W. Journal,* XIX (1975-76). This was based on his splendid unpublished dissertation, 'Social and Economic Developments in the Upper Swansea Valley, c. 1770-1880', (M. A., Swansea 1974). For other unpublished dissertations consult Alun Eirug Davies (ed.), *Welsh Language and Welsh Dissertations* (Cardiff 1973), and the book lists which appear at regular intervals in the *Welsh History Review.*

The University College of Swansea published in 1940 a series of scholarly books on the economic and social history of the region and two of these are still worth reading, namely, D. T. Williams, *The Economic Development of the Swansea District to 1921* and A. E. C. Hare, *The Anthracite Coal Industry of the Swansea District.* J. H. Morris and L. J. Williams, *The South Wales Coal Industry 1841-1875* (Cardiff 1958, Paperback edn. 1982), W. E. Minchinton, *The British Tinplate Industry. A History* (Oxford 1957), and Charles Hadfield, *The Canals of South Wales and the Border* (Cardiff 1967) provide the necessary context for more localised studies.

There are a number of valuable local histories in the Welsh language. These include Roger Thomas, *Traethawd ar Ddechreuad a Chynnydd Gweithiau Haiarn a Glo Ynyscedwyn ac Ystalyfera* (Caerdydd 1857), Dewi Glan Twrch (i.e. W. J. Evans), *Hanes Cwmtwrch a Chwmllynfell* (Ystalyfera 1890) and Enoch Rees, *Hanes Brynaman a'r Cylchoedd* (Ystalyfera 1896), and J. E. Morgan (Hirfryn), *Hanes Pontardawe a'r Cylch* (Abertawe 1911). All the above were prize eisteddfodic essays and all contain information not to be found elsewhere. The published transactions of local eisteddfodau always repay study. For example, *Gardd y Gweithiwr: The Working Man's Garden.* Prize Essays at the Ystalyfera Eisteddfod 1860 (Swansea 1861) is an interesting and illuminating source for the opinion of workmen on social issues. There are similar collections for Ystalyfera for 1857 and 1859 and for Ystradgynlais for 1851. When not published separately prize essays etc. were invariably printed in local newspapers or in periodicals circulating in the valley.

The latter, or course, cònstitute a prime source for the local historian. The essays by Thomas Levi to which I refer above are to be found in *Y Traethodydd* for 1865, pp. 236-249, 467-77 and for 1866 pp. 403-20. Valuable source material is to be found in the Library of the University College of Swansea and in the Miners' Library, for which consult the schedules and lists. Particular attention should be paid to the papers of David George Williams of Ystalyfera who was a remarkable historian. The University College Library also had a copy of *Public Health in Mid-Victorian Wales. Correspondence from the Principality to the General Board of Health and the Local Government Act Office 1848-71.* Transcribed and edited with an introduction by Alun Huw Williams (Board of Celtic Studies 1983).

Chapel and church histories can be an important source of information. The most important of these are listed in David Gareth Evans, 'The Growth of organized religion in the Swansea Valley 1820-90', unpublished Ph.D. dissertation (Swansea 1978). There are also a number of good biographies. Examples are Penar Griffiths, *Cofiant Watcyn Wyn* (Caerdydd 1915), W. Thomas, *Cofiant y Parch. Rhys Pryse, Cwmllynfell* (Llanelli 1872), and W. Thomas, *Cofiant John Griffiths, Alltwen* (Llanelli 1855).

The history of working-class organizations in the nineteenth century, Friendly Societies, reading clubs, trade unions is yet to be written. Local politics in the nineteenth century is a field crying out for examination. Pontardawe and district became one of the strongholds of the ILP in the coalfield but its history is yet to be written—though the poet 'Gwenallt' in his recently published autobiographical novel (*Ffwrneisi* (Llandysul 1983)) tried to do so in a more or less fictionalized form. Students of the parliamentary history of the valley have the inestimable advantage of the secure and scholarly framework provided by K. O. Morgan in his *Wales in British Politics* (3rd edn. Cardiff 1983).

The intellectual and cultural life of the valley communities is studied by T. J. Morgan in a number of marvellously rich and evocative essays in his *Diwylliant Gwerin ac Ysgrifau Eraill* (Llandysul 1972) and in his inaugural lecture *Peasant Culture* (Swansea 1962).

THE RELIGIOUS FRONTIER IN NINETEENTH
CENTURY WALES*

The main outline of the story of how the Welsh Calvinistic Methodist denomination came to provide English people resident in Wales with English-language chapels and their own Connexion is well known. Historians who have studied it have been fascinated by the spectacle of Welsh churches, as a matter of policy, setting out to build and endow chapels for people who might reasonably be expected to provide for themselves, and some have been moved to sorrow or satire or just plain mirth as they contemplate the antics of our Victorian forefathers.[1] What I want to do in this paper is to show that the movement to provide English-language chapels ought not to puzzle us; and that what would be puzzling would have been a lack of such a preoccupation in our forefathers. Yet one cannot escape thinking about a movement that touches on all the critical points in the development of society in Wales in the last century. The elements it contains, religion, language and the new social relations generated between them by the economic changes of the century, lie at the very heart of our culture, and it is the nature of these social relations as revealed in this movement that I want to examine in this paper.

There are two major considerations to be established first. It is vital *not* to distinguish as quintessentially different on the one hand the Home Missions of this and other denominations, and on the other the so-called 'Inglis Côs' (English Cause), the movement to provide chapels for English-speaking Welshmen and monoglot English immigrants. It is true that organizationally they seem to be different and that they developed different kinds of machinery in the course of the century is undeniable. It is true also that there is a wide chronological gap between the one movement and the others, between the Calvinistic Methodist 'Society for Promoting Religious Knowledge amongst the Inhabitants of the Marches of Wales' of 1813 and the conferences organized by Thomas Rees, Cendl in the 1850s and in 1860.[2] There may also be a kind of 'class' difference between the two movements, the one being a movement of common people, the other a middle-class dominated movement, although I should myself be very suspicious of such a simplistic explanation without understanding more about what was meant by the opposing terms. But looked at as a whole within the long perspective of the century it is what they have in common that is important and is what requires explanation.

All the denominations, including the Anglican church, were affected: all had their missions and all built places of worship for ethnic minorities, English or Welsh. In this respect, it is not the denominationalism of those years of religious expansion, the contrasts of tradition and of style, that is illuminating of the essential nature of religion but the irrefragable fact that, whether singly or together, as individual religious communities or as mere aggregations of places, they were in a minority. This is the inescapable impression that one is left with when reading the 'cofiannau' of the period—a *genre* not designed to underestimate or to play down the size or influence of men and institutions. This is beautifully portrayed in this *vignette* from Cunllo Davies's *Hanes Hermon Dowlais:*

Efe (sef Thomas Watkin o Ddowlais) oedd yn gofalu am lestri y cymmun, ac i'w ran y syrthiai y gwaith o osod y bwrdd. Am bump o'r gloch, ar Sul cyntaf y mis, gwelid ef yn cychwyn o'i dy yn David Street, a phasged ar ei fraich, o dan ei glogwyn blewog, du, a het sidan ar ei ben—yn cerdded yn araf tua'r Capel. Gwyddai y cymmydogion fod ''y gwr fu dan hoelion'' i gael ei gofio yn Hermon y noson hono, a thawelai y direidus a'r ysgafn wrth weled Thomas Watkin a llestri y tŷ yn dringo at y Capel. Gwisgai ei wyneb ddigrifwch rhyfedd, ac ni fu neb o deulu Aaron yn fwy dwys o ran ei deimlad wrth baratoi yr allor nad oedd yr hen flaenor wrth osod bwrdd ei Arglwydd. Wedi cyrraedd y set fawr lledai y llïain main yn ofalus. Tynai ei law drosto er cael y plygion o hono, a gosodai y llestri yn un ac un ar y bwrdd. Yna, a phobpeth yn barod cerddai i ochr y sêt a chymmerai olwg hir ar y bwrdd gwyn a'r platiau a'r cwpanau; ac os byddai rhywbeth o'i le ail-drefnai hwynt. Wedi cael ei foddloni, codai gonglau y llïain yn orchudd dros y cyfan. Plygai ei ben, a gosodai ei law ar ei wyneb; ac os digwyddai rhywun weled yr olygfa, gwyddent fod Tywysog Bywyd wedi ei wahodd i fod yn Hermon ar doriad y bara.[3]

(It was Thomas Watkins of Dowlais who kept the communion vessels, and to him fell the task of setting out the table. At five o'clock on the first Sunday in the month, he could be seen leaving his home in David Street carrying a basket on his arm under a black woollen cloak, with a silk hat on his head, walking slowly towards the Chapel. The neighbours knew that 'the crucified one' was to be remembered that night in Hermon, and the scornful and the frivolous would fall silent as they watched him carrying his burden up towards the chapel. Grave of countenance no priest was ever more solemn than the old deacon as he lay the table. Having reached the big seat he would carefully spread the white linen cloth over the table, drawing his hand over it to smooth out the folds. One by one he would set out the dishes. Then, when everything was prepared, he would move to the edge of the seat and look long and carefully at the plates and dishes on the white-clothed table, and if necessary rearrange them. Satisfied, he would bring together the four corners of the cloth so as to cover the whole. Then he would bow his head and place his hand on his face: and anyone observing that scene would know that the Prince of Life had been invited to Hermon for the breaking of the bread).

This helps to explain also the millenarian trumpet calls that sound through so much of the literature. Thomas Watkin's favourite hymn was that splendid one which has long since passed out of the repertoire:

> Rowndio caerau Jerico
>   A chyrn hyrddod—
> Seithfed dydd a'r seithfed dro
>   Bron a dyfod!

Fe ddaw'r caearu oll yn rhydd
O'u sylfeini.
'Fengyl Iesu garia'r dydd.
Llwyddiant iddi![4]

(Rounding the towers of Jericho/with the horns of rams—
The seventh day and the seventh time/Almost upon us!
Loosed will all the towers be/On their foundations.
The Gospel of Jesus wins the day/Success be to it!)

It is only minority religious movements, usually conversionist
sects, that are and were millenarian. All the denominations,
also, however long or short their distinctive histories, were
equally the products of an evangelical revival which still operated powerfully if intermittently in the land. Likewise the denominations, whatever systems of church government they
espoused, had all grasped the great Reformation truth that the
instrument of salvation is faith and that faith cometh by
hearing and that in order to have effective hearing it is necessary to have effective preaching. What the benighted border
country wanted was not church government but preaching.
And, finally, because they understood that numerically Christians were in a minority, that as churches they were all evan-
gelically orientated, and that they were commissioned by Christ
to preach the Word, all were aware of and sensitive to the
existence within the country of regions and places where the
Gospel did not run.

All this is merely to say that one of the main characteristics of
organized religion in Victorian Wales was the common awareness of what was called 'religious deprivation'. By that was
meant community or collective ignorance of the truths of
Christianity which could be attributed to a lack of provision of
places for religious instruction and religious worship. This idea
of 'religious deprivation', though it was most intimately associated in the public mind with the reconstruction of the Anglican
Church and its preoccupation with institutional efficiency
rather than revivalist individualism, was by no means confined
to Anglicans.[5] It was not only the Church of England that
thought institutionally. As I shall show later, there were great

Cymanfa'r Methodistiaid Calvinaidd, Calvinistic Methodist Assembly, Bala, June 1820.

differences between the religious provision of the country and the town and it was in the latter where unmanageably large aggregations of people had come to dwell that the deprivation was most in evidence. This was why the 'Inglis Côs' was a feature of the second half of the century and why the Home Missions of the early century changed by the 1880s into movements for the provision of preaching places which differed from the chapels of the 'English Cause' or of the English Presbyterians only in style of preaching and in styles of architecture.

There was a common understanding as to the causes of this spiritual deprivation. 'The great engine of change' was the industrial revolution, and religious organizations were as much subject to its operations as any other organization or any other part of society. This is a vast theme which I shall touch on later, for the interactions between the two forces—between capitalism and religion—were very complex. If religion was shaped by industrial forces so also was the progress of industrialization conditioned by the existence of religion. At this juncture it is only necessary to point to the truly massive scale of the changes that were involved in industrialization. By the 1830s the largest iron industry in the world was located in south Wales and this supremacy was maintained into the second half of the century. Before the end of the century its steam coal industry dominated not only that of Britain but of Europe and the world, and Cardiff was the steam coal metropolis of the world. Of every three steamships on the world's oceans in the decades before the war two would have been running on Welsh coal. Before that had happened Swansea had become the copper-smelting centre of the industrial world, and the new industrial connurbations not only of Britain but of Europe and the Americas were being roofed in Welsh slate.[6] Here was a transformation scarcely dreamt of a hundred years earlier and an exploitation of the mineral resources of the country on a scale such as to defy imagination. And all this was the work of Welshmen! For the growth of population, which had begun before the planting of the new technological industries had kept pace with all this development, and the natural increase of Welsh men and women had been sufficient to provide most of the labour and an increasing amount of the skill required by industry. There

had been no great influx of people from outside until right at
the end of the century and before the First World War and
though there were large numbers of English people settling into
the new industrial and mining areas the numerical superiority
of Welshborn men and women was everywhere evident. Less
than a million at the beginning of the century they numbered
more than 2 millions by the end of the century. And finally, the
concentration of this population on the south Wales coalfield
and in Flint and parts of Denbighshire resulted in the creation
of new kinds of what Victorians called, for want of a better
term, 'populous places', or 'mining and manufacturing
districts'. In addition to this expansion old urban centres likewise grew. These new and expanding places of both kinds
linked together by railways and better road systems, and all of
them creating wealth in undreamed of profusion, however
unequally it may have been distributed, had grown and continued throughout the century to grow by siphoning off the
surplus population of the countryside. In fact, by the last
decades of the century when rapid ocean travel and refriger-
ation brought the prairies and savannahs of the American
continent into the markets of the counties and the shops of the
town, the main economic function of the rural areas had
become the production of people for the mines and ironworks,
for the exploding service and distributive and transport
industries, and for the new servant-employing classes of town
and country.[7]

How did the Welsh religious bodies, react to the transformation of society that this entailed? Was there anything
characteristic in the way they regarded what was happening
such that it helped to determine their reactions or to shape the
ways they adapted as religious bodies to them? I think that
there was, and I wish now to suggest that they apprehended the
changes as a whole on the analogy of a frontier, both a real
frontier and a metaphorical one. They thought in terms of three
such moving frontiers, firstly, the frontier between town and
country, secondly the frontier between Welsh and English and,
lastly, the frontier between religion and irreligion. The nature
of the response they made to change depended largely on their
apprehension of the kind of realities, social and spiritual, which

lay on either side of those three frontiers, and to a consideration
of those I now turn.

*   *   *

In Wales in the nineteenth century, as in Britain as a whole,
the expanding frontier lay in the towns. The population of the
country as a whole doubled in the first forty years of the
century and doubled again to a total of 2 millions by 1901. But
the growth was not regular or even from place to place. Some
counties were losing population from the 1840s onwards and in
some, the process of depopulation having once started, it continued throughout the century. Anglesey and the border
counties of Brecknock, Radnor, Montgomeryshire are examples of these. Between the censuses of 1881 and 1891 all but
four of the counties were losing population, the exceptions
being Carmarthenshire, Denbighshire, Glamorgan and Monmouthshire.[8] These were the counties which had industrialized
in the course of the century—and Flint, though it lost 4% of its
population in that final decade, must be included among these.
In this way the population of Wales was being redistributed. If
one looks at the ancient counties in 1801 one finds that no
single county had more than 12% of the total population and
none less than 3%. By 1851 the distribution changed dramatic-
ally. Glamorgan had one-fifth of the total population and the
percentage of every county with the exception of Monmouth
was less than it had been fifty years previously. By 1881 Glamorgan had one-third of the total population and by the turn of
the century no less than 42%. By that year the percentage
share of Anglesey, Brecon, Cardigan, Merioneth, Montgomery and Radnor had fallen to below 3% of the total. The
country was emptying its people, whether surplus or not, into
the insatiable maws of the industrial south. Indeed, the total
number of people living in industrial south Wales constituted
no less than 57%—more than half of the total population of the
country. Ten years later the population of Glamorgan *alone* was
equal to that of all the other counties with the exception of
Carmarthenshire and Monmouthshire put together.
Industrialization meant urbanization, and what was to be
observed happening was the spread of urbanization, the

moving of the frontier between the country and the town. How to define urbanization is a problem for geographers, but for Victorians it had to do with population size or population density and not of necessity with towns as such. This is an important distinction which we must keep in mind if we are to understand how our forefathers apprehended the problem of this moving frontier. Until industrialization Wales had been a land in which towns, for all their administrative and commercial functions, had been small and sometimes insignificant. In 1801 Swansea was the largest town with 10,000 inhabitants. Merthyr Tydfil had just under 8,000, Carmarthen 5,500, but no other had more than 3,500. By 1851, when large towns were being described as having more than 20,000 inhabitants, there were still only two in that category, Merthyr Tydfil and Swansea, with Newport a close third. It was from about that date, but particularly from the late 1860s and the 1870s that two changes of the greatest significance began, namely first, the growth by immigration of two new categories of urbanized place, the new seaside resorts such as Llandudno and Rhyl, and the suburban growth in the old existing seaside towns, such as Swansea and Aberystwyth; and second, and much more important, the development of densely populated industrial towns and villages in the mining and manufacturing districts which had originated earlier in the century in association with iron manufacturing, and of entirely new ones devoted exclusively to the coal trade. Such places were the mining villages of the north-east, the Llynfi Valley, the Aman Valley and the coal valleys running down from the Blaenau of Glamorgan and Gwent to the sea resulting in the growth on the coast of Cardiff, Newport, Barry, Penarth and the other coal ports.

By the second half of the century, therefore, the town/country dichotomy had lost its essential simplicity and had developed into a highly complex and constantly changing sociological phenomenon. Towns differed radically in their typologies. There were the ancient boroughs—the Norman *bastides*—some of which, like Caernarfon, Flint, Newport, Cardiff, Swansea, had developed into major ports and centres of extractive or metallurgical industries and of manufacturing.

They all had traditions of urbanity and institutions of government, culture and religion which survived as cores of identity and of civilization in the amorphous suburbs which surrounded them and which in the south-east Wales ports were cosmopolitan and culturally complex. Quite distinct from these were the iron towns and villages of the first industrial revolution whose traditions of urbanity were recent but which had become settled and culturally distinctive. Ebbw Vale, Tredegar, Abersychan, Merthyr, the core of Aberdare, and Bagillt are examples of these. Then finally there were the new mining villages and towns, almost all dependent upon the one industry, variegated perhaps by tinplate works, all characterized by very rapid growth and all lacking the social and cultural overheads of the other two types of towns. The Upper Rhonddas, the Llynfi and Garw villages are examples of this development.

The other element in this frontier—the country—needs also to be kept in view as being sociologically far more complex than we might think. Here I need only note the great differences between the settled agricultural villages of the border counties and the great valleys of central and west Wales and the communities of scattered pastoral farms on the mountains. It was a distinction which contemporaries made, especially the leaders of the Anglican reform movement. Many of these latter, including the bishops, were appalled by the problems of the huge mountain parishes, where endowments were inadequate or alienated into the pockets of lay-men or distant corporations, and whose clergy therefore were poverty-stricken, ill-educated and demoralized.[9] But these upland parishes were problems for the Nonconformist denominations too: the missions of the Calvinistic Methodists began in 1813 in Radnorshire. There was also the distinction between farming communities, whether nucleated or dispersed, which lay within proprietorial estates and those which lay outside the immediate jurisdiction and the social controls of landed proprietors. And finally, there were the parishes that were open and those which were closed.

Hence, on both sides of this moving frontier were complex communities of people, but it was in the urbanized regions that the complexities were new, huge and baffling, and it was in them that the challenge to organized religion was at its sharpest.

*   *   *

This is only another way of saying that the frontier between town and country, between agriculture and industry, between rural society and urban society was also a frontier between religion and irreligion and between different kinds of religion.[10] Welsh Victorian religious leaders while recognizing and admitting that this was true of socio-religious developments in England claimed that it did not describe the situation in Wales. As I have shown elsewhere, up to about 1850 or slightly before, the statistics both of chapel accommodation and of religious adherence supported their contention.[11] 'O Gymru, pa le mae dy debyg wlad dan y nef? A pha genedl dan haul a chymaint o ôl crefydd arni, ag sydd ar genedl y Cymru', (O Wales, where is thy like under the heavens! What nation under the sun has so many of the marks of religion as the Welsh?) wrote one religious leader in 1850,[12] and no less a critic of contemporary life than Thomas Stephens of Merthyr could point to the religiosity of the Welsh in 1857 as the unique feature in their culture. 'Mae Crefydd', he wrote, 'a chynnaliad ordinhadau crefyddol yn un o brif neullduolion Cymru: ac oddieithr trigolion Sgotland, y Cymry yn ddiameuol yw y bobl fwyaf grefyddol o fewn cyffiniau Ewrop'.[13] (Religion and the maintanance of religious ordinances is one of the chief characteristics of Wales: with the exception of Scotland the Welsh are undoubtedly the most religious people in Europe.) Nor is it without significance that those words should have been written by a historian, a scholar and keen observer of the contemporary scene, accustomed to weighing up evidence, and from Merthyr Tydfil, the core of the industrial region of Wales. Nevertheless, as early as the 1850s there is an anxious, querulous note in these, by then, clichèd observations. There is already in them a quality of myth, a retrospective longing and a feeling that the old uniformities that characterized some of the essential features of town and country were being eroded. 'Yn yr ardal wledig y cawsom ni ein magu, yr un peth fyddai dweud "Y Gweithiau" a dweud "Merthyr"; ac yr oedd yr olaf yn *noun of multitude,* ac yn gyfystyr â holl weithiau glo a haearn Morganwg a Mynwy. Am gymeriad y lle hwnnw, Merthyr, yr oedd mor ofnadwy ysgeler fel yr edrychid arno megys y drws nesaf i uffern; a'r fath oedd y tebygolrwydd, fel y dyweder i un hen frawd ddarllen un o adnodau y Beibl fel y canlyn: "yr holl annuwiolion â i Ferthyr". I'r Merthyr y byddai sorod ac ysgubion y wlad yn treiglo. Yr oedd Merthyr i Gymru yn gyffelyb i Coventry i Lloegr, neu Gehenna i Jerusalem. Yno yr arlwysai cymdeithas ei budreddi o flwyddyn i flwyddyn.' (In the countryside where I was brought up it was the same to say 'The Works' as to say 'Merthyr': and the latter was a noun of multitude, synonymous with the whole of the coal and iron district of Glamorgan and Monmouthshire. As for the character of the place, Merthyr, it was so utterly atrocious as to be thought to be next door to hell; and so close was the similarity that one old brother was said to have read a verse of the Bible as follows: "all the ungodly shall go to Merthyr." In Merthyr dwelt all the dross and rubbish. It was to Wales what Coventry is to England or Genhenna to Jeruslaem. It was into Merthyr that society poured its refuse from year to year.)[14] That was written in 1860 at the height of the last great classical revival in Welsh religious history.

I do not think that those two sets of statements are essentially contradictory for they draw attention to what was a fundamental determinant of the nature of Welsh society, both rural and industrial, in the nineteenth century, namely, the movement of population from the one to the other. Of course the criminal element and that pitiful residue of society that was a feature of rural as of urban society found its way in the towns, but what Thomas Stephens and his like saw in the mid-century was the hugely successful transference of rural religion into an urban milieu. It was the constant flow of an already religiously socialized people from the countryside which helped to determine the religious character of Welsh industrial towns and which made them so very different from those of England. While it is no doubt true that one of the main characteristics of Welsh religion generally in the first half of the century was its evangelicalism it is extremely doubtful that it was this that accounted for its relative success in the new urban area. It is more likely to have been the fact that country people spontaneously created those institutions which most closely linked them to their rural origins and which might therefore reduce or diminish those feelings of alienation and *anomie* which are inevitably the lot of migrants everywhere and at all times. It is well known that in the new towns immigrants tended to create communities of their own kith and kin and neighbourhoods of settlers from the same country or region of origin. This was true of Merthyr[15] and of the north Monmouthshire iron-towns where there were 'colonies' of Cardiganshire and Breconshire and north Wales people settled into distinct neighbourhoods, and it was probably true of other places as well. Chapels originated in this way and wherever such a chapel was founded so it embodied adaptations of the religious life of the countryside. In times of religious revival they became the nodal points binding town and country in a common religious culture.

It is clear that in the first half of the century the churches as a whole recognized that they fulfilled this role in the rapidly changing societies of the time. The fundamental difference between country and town—the line along which the frontier lay—was the presence in the one and the lack in the other of social stability. It was believed—and there was an element of myth in this belief—that the rural areas were stable and secure in their social relations. Most contemporary observers believed that only very rarely was this stability disrupted, and whatever political radicals might mutter into their beards or write in their periodicals the social bonds of deference and the immemorial customs of the past kept society together. There was continuity, and norms of behaviour common to all ranks were maintained. The Rebecca Riots were exceptions in this respect, and though historians know that there was overt violence—a kind of sub-culture with its own norms existing on the edges of the law—in the rural areas it was the good order, the peace, and particularly the stability that reigned in them that was their outstanding character.[16] Now, in this highly laudable state of affairs the religious denominations of all kinds had played a key role. It was not the product of repression by secular authority or an enforced socialization. The Calvinistic Methodists, for example, always claimed credit for the tranquility of the areas where they were the dominant religion.[17] Their chapels and societies, as indeed *all* chapels and churches, were expressive of the moral unity of society as a whole. 'Yr Hen Gorff' (the Old Body), as it was affectionately known, was never a class religion in the sense that it was expressive of the morality of one social class more than another, for in the country 'middle-class' or 'working-class' were concepts utterly foreign to and contradictory of the fundamental concept of a unitary society. It was this that lay behind the so-called conservatism of Methodists and, when it came to the pinch, of the other denominations as well. And it is this that is most eloquent of the extent to which and the way in which religion had come to be identified with rural society, and I think also that the explanation for the overwhelming predominance of Calvinistic Methodism in the north and the west lies in the way in which it had developed first as a nexus of small communities or 'societies' and only then as a denomination.

The contrast with the urban areas is unmistakable. I have stressed the relative religiosity of the towns. Compared with English cities and towns the Welsh urban areas were astonishingly religious both with regard to the level of provision and of adherence. But comparing Welsh rural Districts with Welsh urban Districts the differences were very wide. Many of the country parishes had more sittings in their places of worhsip than they had population—in the case of some Merioneth and Montgomery Districts as much as 20% more. Even the industrial Districts had room for almost three-quarters or two-thirds or even, at the worst, for more than a half of their inhabitants. There would, indeed, in 1851 have been some justification for the belief that Wales was 'basking in an excess of spiritual privilege'—and that her urban districts were the exceptions that proved the rule about the weakness of religion in urban conditions. But the pattern of adherence tells another story. The towns were certainly well-supplied by mid-century with chapels, but what proportions of their populations were attached to them as members and adherents? What statistics there are are not very reliable but all show that attendances were lower in towns than in the counties and that membership as distinct from adherence showed an even greater disproportion. For example, in 1861 the membership density of the

Calvinistic Methodists in the over 15 year age group in Cardiganshire was 21.1; in Glamorgan it was 4.6: of the Independents 18.5 and 11.6 respectively. And if, in order to avoid the obvious criticism that one should take into account the relative popularity of denominations in the different counties and compare only the strongest irrespective of name, the same conclusion emerges.[18]

But there is evidence enough to show that the churches both individually and collectively, were minority movements within Wales itself, conscious of their numerical inferiority in the face of the indifference or the deliberate hostility of the masses. This was to get worse as the century advanced and as south Wales rushed into its second industrial revolution.[19] In the last half century in Cardiganshire membership continued to grow as a proportion of population despite the continual fall in the population. In Glamorgan the peak of religious strength was reached in 1881; thereafter there was relative decline. Only the Calvinistic Methodists succeeded in keeping pace with population growth—and that was due to the remarkable success of their English speaking churches.[20] It became, therefore, a major preoccupation of all the denominations to push back that frontier of urban irreligion, and universally the means proposed was the provision of places of worship where they were needed and of support for missions to create the need.

*   *   *

Of the three frontiers I have mentioned it was the frontier of language that lay deepest in the consciousness of Welshmen and which was to become the most critical of all as the century unfolded. This was because the Welsh language was bound up not only with national and cultural identity but with the nature, the power and the very existence of religion itself in Wales.[21]

There is no doubt that Welshmen in that silver age of the expansion of religion commonly believed that the extraordinary success of religion among the common people in country and town was to be found in the continued existence of the Welsh language. What for the reformers of the sixteenth and seven-

teenth centuries had been an act of faith, for the saints and
thinkers of early Victorian Wales had become a matter of
observation.[22] It was the Welsh language that had achieved
these great things. This was true, they thought, whether success
was measured quantitatively in the multitudes of believers and
the aggregations of places of worship, or whether it was judged
by the purity of the faith and the spirituality and piety of its
confessors. For all these dimensions of religion—structure,
divinity, morality—had depended upon the existence of the
Welsh language. In no other language could this have been
achieved. Contemporaneously, the Established Church was becoming a minority movement, an alien church, allied to an
aristocracy which was itself being rejected. No one doubted
that underlying all was the providential ordering of history. 'Y
mae rhyw ddiben mawr mewn golwg gan Dduw i ddiogelu y
Cymry a'u hiaith ar eu tir cysefin . . . Pan ymwrthodwn â'n
hiaith bydd inni beidio ag addoli Duw', (God has some great
end in view in defending the Welsh people and their language
in their native land.) wrote R. W. Morgan, Tregynon, and he
went on to declare that the rejection of the Established Church
by the Welsh people was the judgment of God upon it for
having ignored the Welsh language. 'Nid oedd Eglwys Crist
erioed wedi ei sefydlu i fod yn beiriant i ddistrywio ieithoedd a
di-anrhydeddu cenhedloedd'. (The Church of Christ was not
designed as an engine for the destruction of languages and the
dishonouring of nations).[23] However that may be, by the time
he was writing the Church had in fact begun to re-establish
itself in town and country and not the least of its reforms was its
insistence upon the necessity of using the language of the
people in its services.

But this too was a moving frontier. The tide of anglicization
flowed at varying speeds in different places, sometimes pouring
up the valleys and obliterating the ancient landmarks, but
more often lapping over the edges of the lowlands, percolating
quietly and unsuspectingly into the towns and villages. During
the first half of the century, particularly during those crucial
decades of Nonconformist growth between the 1820s and the
mid-1840's it seems scarcely to have been realized to what an
extent the relative position of the Welsh language was chang-

ing. Almost certainly the frontier was apprehended to be where, in a sense, it ought to have been, along the administrative or political frontier. 'Clawdd Offa' was the 'natural' frontier, and there was a kind of condescension in the way that the unfortunate natives of the border counties who had lost the ancient, light-giving, God-carrying culture were regarded. Radnorshire, despite—maybe because of—its glorious puritan past seems never to have been fully accepted into the comity of Welsh counties and the commonwealth of Welsh religious organizations.[24] It was commonly regarded as a backwater, its inhabitants to be pitied—and missionized. Listen to the unconscious arrogance of the prospectus of the second of the Calvinistic Methodist Home Missionary Societies—Cymdeithas Gennadawl Gartrefol—of 1826. 'Mae Corph y Methodistiaid Calfinaidd yn Neheudir Cymru, wedi edrych ar, a gwrando am, ymddifadrwydd eu cymmdogion Saesnig ar y terfynau rhwng Lloegr a Chymru, a rhannau eraill o'r gwledydd o foddion efengyl, er ys llawer o flynyddau, gyd â galar, gofid, a blinder mawr' (For many years the Body of Calvinistic Methodists of South Wales have observed and heard about the spiritual deprivation of their neighbours on the borders between England and Wales with great, anxiety and pain).[25] And they proceeded to establish a Society with the aim of collecting money for the support of missionaries—two in the first place—to work in those benighted regions, in Penybont, Clifford and Hay. Their brethren in north Wales had faced the same challenge thirteen years earlier,[26] so that by 1826 the Calvinistic Methodists were organized to bring the Gospel to tho most unfortunate and pitiable parts of Wales—those which had lost their language. But if there was a little arrogance there may also have been just a touch of irony and a lot of Christian charity, for no literate Welshman in the eighteenth or nineteenth century ever forgot that he owed his religion to Englishmen. This is what they read in the finest of their historians—in Charles Edwards, *Hanes y Ffydd Ddiffuant* and in the ever popular Theophilus Evans, *Drych y Prif Oesoedd* (1716). They were only giving back, with interest, what they had received. 'The jealousy with which the English language was once regarded', pronounced the first editorial in the first number of

The Welsh Calvinistic Methodist Record in January 1852, 'as a medium for setting forth the truths of the gospel, has passed away. Welsh Home Missioners have crossed the border between England and Wales, and are now making known to the Saxon, in his own tongue, "the wonderful works of God". English churches have also been formed in our Welsh towns . . . 'Nor were the Calvinistic Methodists the only denomination to be so moved. The Baptists likewise strove to fill up those interstices in the religious geography of Wales which the Church had so indolently ignored.[27] Further gaps were found at the same time—all in the English-speaking parts of south and west Wales—and the new societies included them in their provinces.

How did the frontier move? The essential predicament of people at the time was that they did not know, and we are little the wiser today.[28] Of one thing they were certain and we can be certain—the language frontier moved as a consequence of industrialization. But the consequences of industrialization operated at different levels. Most obviously, it operated at the level of population movement: the introduction of industry to a place meant an influx of people some of whom—probably in the early stages the entrepreneurially vital part—would be English. In the initial stages of industrialization these English immigrants were relatively few in number. For example, in the ironworks of north Monmouthshire at the beginning of the century the majority of workers were Welsh.[29] The same was true of Merthyr and the Glamorgan side of the iron belt. Not until the end of the century did the English influx become so massive as to threaten the indigenous culture by sheer weight of numbers.[30] But industrialization involves more than the movement of people. It means modes of production, attitudes of mind, the creation of communities stratified in unique ways and geared to serve distant markets. It means discontinuities and disruptions with the past, and above all it embodies values. Now all these things are conveyed, structured, understood and interpreted by means of language, and in the conditions of early industrialization that meant the acceptance of language hierarchies. English was the language of business and of management even if, as remained the case throughout the century in these places, Welsh was the language at the point of production, of labour, religion and the arts. From the acceptance of language domains in an industrializing society it followed that the language of the wealth-giving, power-making, prestige-possessing domain should become the dominant one even though it was an intrusive language. And what becomes of the other? It becomes associated with domains lower in the social and moral hierarchies being created—domains, that is to say, to which no power was attached.

What then did this mean in practice? How did the frontier move? It was not a movement from Welsh to English, the creation of dichotomies, of distinct linguistic communities at first—though it involved that later on—but rather of a kind of bilingual society in which the Welsh understood some English and the English some Welsh. This was true in the 1830s in the Monmouthshire and in the Flintshire iron and lead-smelting and mining areas. This was the frontier zone that people were aware of as moving, sometimes advancing as fresh additions of Englishmen came in, sometimes retreating as the Cardiganshire and Montgomeryshire and Breconshire contingents moved in. Often, even late into the century, one could not foretell what the dominant language in a colliery village might be: it could go either way.

It is enormously difficult for us to comprehend what was involved in such complex language shifts, and it requires a great effort of imagination and of intelligent sympathy to understand what contemporaries made of them.[31] But let us try to assess what were probably the features of it which religious leaders would have identified. First, although they noted the growth of the English increment in the inflow of people into the new and old urban places, the sheer size of the Welsh contribution would have reassured them of the stability and durability of the religious culture which they led. Consider, for example, the history of Calvinistic Methodism in Monmouthshire. Scarcely a chapel in the whole of the county and none in the Blaenau could trace its history back to Howel Harris who had been so active in those parts during his lifetime. All the large and flourishing chapels were founded and maintained by Cardiganshire and Montgomeryshire immigrants, and though the tide

ebbed and flowed Calvinistic Methodism continued to be re-
freshed and invigorated from its roots in the heartland of Welsh
Methodism. Second, it seemed to them that in those conditions, wherever they were reproduced, it was possible to have
the best of both worlds. Let the children learn English, not only
in order to be better equipped for the competitive business of
life outside the chapel—and what Calvinistic Methodist ever
doubted the value of the protestant ethic?—but also in order to
be made free of the classics of English religious and devotional
literature. There were obvious dangers in this attitude, for a
language once learned releases the learner to both good and
evil, and the controls which could be exercised within the
Welsh community were not available to the same extent in an
English milieu. For example, it was not understood that the
very fragility of the Welsh press which made it dependent upon
the patronage of the religious denominations did not apply to
the English-language press.[32] The latter enjoyed not only the
superior prestige of a major language but was also supported
by financial resources which made it independent of the social
controls exerted in Wales and therefore irresistible wherever
and whenever it penetrated the boundaries of Welsh culture
areas.

Hence, thirdly, the well-nigh universal belief that the pene-
tration of English-language culture with all that it entailed in
the way of lax morals, Sabbath-breaking, swearing and
cursing,[33] and such political aberrations as trade-unionism,
could be contained by a policy of adaptation. Welsh religion
must be given an English dress whenever it was necessary. In
bilingual areas the service should become bilingual with the
major role being taken by the dominant language of the
locality. In towns and in anglicized parts of the countryside
chapels must be provided and it was believed that if such
chapels were founded by Welsh mother-churches and maintained in a close connection they would effectively provide
English speakers with an essentially 'Welsh' religion. Both the
English missions and the movement to provide English chapels
were responses to the corruption of Welsh religion by alien
forces, and it was the practical need to maintain Welsh morality on the other side of the moving frontier that was the

dominant motivation in it. 'Carasem yn ein calon pe buasai yr hen iaeth yn gallu dal ei thir hyd ddiwedd y byd yn erbyn yr estrones. Ond rhaid i ni ddarparu ar gyfer pethau *fel y maent,* ac nid fel y dymunem iddynt fod. Y mae achos crefydd yn cael colled ac, o ganlyniad, eneidiau yn cael cam yn yr ardaloedd hynny, o ba rai y mae y Gymraeg yn encilio'. (We could have wished with all our hearts that the old language might hold her ground against aliens until the end of the world. But we must prepare for things *as they are* and not as we might wish them to be. The cause of religion suffers and consequently souls are injured in those places from which the Welsh language is receding). Thus wrote William Williams the secretary of the movement in 1864. Ten years later with the frontier moving even more rapidly and menacingly, he drew the attention of the Calvinistic Methodists to the more rapid response of the other denominations to the same threat, and to the appalling danger that Methodism itself would disappear even from those area where formerly it has been so powerful. 'Da, er lles eneidiau, ydyw fod amryw enwadau ymneullduol ereill yn deall arwydd-ion yr amseroedd, ac yn gwneuthur darpariaethau ar gyfer yr iaith; ond nid ydym, er hynny, yn fodlon gweled Methodist-iaeth mewn perygl o ddiflannu o gymydogaethau lle bu unwaith yn flodeuog, o herwydd esgeulusdra i wneuthur darpariaethau cyffelyb'. (It is good for the salvation of the souls that the other nonconformist denominations understand the signs of the times and are preparing to make linguistic adjust-ments; for our part we are not ready to see Methodism disappear from regions where it once flourished because of our failure to make similar preparations)[34] This was how they saw their predicament and the crisis of their time, and we should not, without hard evidence, accuse those generations of treachery to the language or even of stupidity in the face of events, or, more mildly, of being fools and knaves. We must try to understand their predicament and endeavour to think their thoughts as they grappled with entirely new and con-stantly changing situations.

Of course there were individuals and some societies who read the signs of the times differently and who refused to be deceived by appearances. To these the acceptance of the en-

croachments of the border was the sign of a moral malaise—
selling one's birthright for a mess of potage or consenting in the
sacrifice of the language on the altar of utilitarianism. Or, as
one wrote, 'Nid efengyleiddio'r Saeson yw hyn, ond amcan
uniongyrchol i Seisnigeiddio'r Cymry' (This is not to evan-
gelize the English, but to Anglicize the Welsh).[35] Such was the
freeholder in Bedwellty who refused to sell his land to the ironmasters, or 'Dynolwyr Nantyglo' (the Nantyglo Philanthropic
Society) who, because they believed that industry should serve
man and be preservative and not corrosive of culture set up a
cooperative concern in 1829 in which the Welsh language
should be predominant.[37] But these were exceptional men and
exceptional movements and the majority of Welshmen
accepted all the implications of the fact that industry came from
across the border and that its language was English and necessarily so. The creation of wealth was an English activity.

It was this more than anything that made the situation of
religious leaders so agonizingly difficult. For they were caught
up in a paradox. The mess of potage was needed in the societies
that they were striving to create. Wealth was required to maintain that religious culture in all its diverse aspects in a world
which was being corrupted by that very same wealth. Knowing
themselves to be so weak relatively to the powers of this world
they poured all their resources into maintaining their religious
frontier as the only one over which they had any kind of
control. This meant missions and expanding the outposts of
religion in alien territory—the Methodists' Forward Movement preaching rooms, the halls of the Salvation Army, the
iron churches and the numberless district churches of the
Anglicans. It was all one movement. Religion was more important than race or language, said Dr. Lewis Edwards, and
his son and Dr. Cynddylan Jones and the rest of them encouraged the establishment of English Presbyteries for that
reason.[38] What was the main function of the church—was it to
save souls or to preserve the nation's linguistic heritage?

*   *   *

Looking back from the detached and secular vantage-point
of the present it is easier for us than for our forefathers to see

the interconnection between these moving frontiers. They knew only *their* present and no more that any other generation could they foresee the working-out of those forces which were already transforming both their lives and that nexus of ever-changing communities within which they moved. It is only *we* who can depict the social consequences of the population explosion which came at the beginning of this century. It is *we* who are in a position to assess, or to try to assess, the consequences for the language and for organized religion of a war the nature of which would have been beyond the imagination of previous generations, and it is only we who can trace the effects in Wales of the collapse of the old economic order in the inter-war years. That urbanization and a too-rapid population increase might have deleterious effects on the Welsh language and strain to breaking-point the historic and organic connections between it and the religion they served was regarded as almost inevitable by most people, and it was this universal apprehensiveness as to the consequences of a permanent language shift which accounted for the melancholy which was as a warp to the weft of the optimism so characteristic of the fabric of the age. For they were men of their age, and they had no doubt that as religious leaders they had a prophetic task to preserve and to extend if possible the essentially religious character of the country as they saw it. Hence, their keen sensitivity to the spread of irreligion and secularism and their apparent indifference to the retreating language frontier. But few of them were equipped to think out the relationship between language and religion; there was no theology of Christian nationalism such as is being developed today,[39] and even fewer would have thought this to have been desirable even if it had been possible. All, without exception, believed that it was the religion of Wales that was its distinguishing mark, and it was to the purity and virility of this religion as embodied in the experiences of countless men and women that they devoted their lives. They were not blind to the role of the Welsh language in this: it is simply that they gave the priority to religion and morality. Nor should we forget that they were blind to many other of the connections that religion necessarily has: for example, to the relevance of religion to questions of social inequality, to the widening of the gulf between the classes, to the secular-based radicalism that the working classes were silently embracing; and it is partly to this deficiency rather than to their debasement of the value of the Welsh language that many historians would now attribute the cataclysmic decline of ortho-dox, organized religion and the emergence of a completely secular culture in our land.

NOTES

*This paper was first published in *Cylchgrawn Hanes.* Historical Society of the *Presbyterian Church in Wales,* 5 (1981).

[1] Frank Price Jones, 'Yr Achosion Saesneg' in Alun Llywelyn-Williams ac Elfed ap Nefydd Roberts (goln.), *Radicaliaeth a'r Werin Gymreig yn y Bedwaredd Ganrif ar Bymtheg* (Caerdydd, 1977), tt. 103-31.

[2] For the Calvinistic Methodist societies see John Hughes, Liverpool, *Methodistiaeth Cymru,* III (1856), t. 469 and the works cited by F. Price Jones, *art. cit.* There are some interesting observations on the movement in general in R. Buick Knox, *Voices from the Past* (Llandysul, 1969), pp. 11-12. For the activities of Dr. Thomas Rees see his biography, *Cofiant y Parch. T. Rees, D.D., Abertawy,* by Owen Thomas (Dolgellau, 1888), tt. 192-3.

[3] D. Cunllo Davies, *Hanes . . . Hermon Dowlais* (Bala, 1905), tt. 69-70.

[4] *ibid.,* t. 69.

[5] On the idea of religious deprivation see in general A. D. Gilbert, *Religion and Society in Industrial England. Church, Chapel and Social Change 1740-1914 (1976), passim.,* Owen Chadwick, *The Victorian Church,* Part I (second edn., 1970), R. A. Soloway, *Prelates and People, Ecclesiastical Social Thought in England 1763-1852* (1969), chapt. VIII. For the reactions of the Church in Wales see below, pp. 22-6.

[6] For the industrialization of south Wales see Glanmor Williams and A. H. John (eds.), *Glamorgan County History.* Vol. V. *Industrial Glamorgan* (1981), W. E. Minchinton (ed.), *Industrial South Wales 1750-1914. Essay in Welsh Economic History* (1969), and for north Wales A. H. Dodd, *The Industrial Revolution in North Wales* (1951), R. Davies, 'The Growth and Development of Settlement and Population in Flintshire 1801-1891', *Flintshire Historical Publications,* 25 (1971-2) and 26 (1973-4).

[7] For population statistics and movements see Phyllis Deane and W. A. Cole, *British Economic Growth 1688-1959* (second edn., 1967), *passim.,* B. R. Mitchell and Phyllis Deane, *Abstract of British Historical Statistics* (1971). The key works, in this respect, are by Professor Brinley Thomas, especially his essays in *The Welsh Economy. Essays in Expansion* (Cardiff 1962).

[8] On urbanization see Harold Carter, *The Study of Urban Geography* (3rd edn. 1981) pp. 16-35, and *idem., The Towns of Wales* (Cardiff, 1968).

[9] For example, 'The Church in the Mountains', *Edinburgh Review,* April 1853. Reprinted in J. Conybeare, *Essays Ecclesiastical and Social*(London, 1855).

[10] A. D. Gilbert, *op. cit.,* contains an excellent bibliography. Most of the essential problems are raised in B.I. Coleman. *The Church of England in the Mid-Nineteenth Century. A Social Geography,* Historical Association Pamphlet No. 98 (1978), which also contains

a good bibliography. The best study of rural religion yet to have appeared is James Obelkevich, *Religion and Rural Society. South Lindsey 1825-1875* (Oxford, 1976).

[11] Ieuan Gwynedd Jones, *Explorations and Explanations. Essays in the Social History of Victorian Wales* (Gwasg Gomer, 1981), pp. 217-35.

[12] *Yr Adolygydd,* III (1850).

[13] Thomas Stephens, 'Sefyllfa Wareiddiol y Cymry', *Y Traethodydd,* XIII (1857), t. 397.

[14] *Baner ac Amserau Cymru,* 7 Mawrth 1860.

[15] Harold Carter, 'Transformations in the spatial structure of Welsh Towns in the Nineteenth Century', *T.H.S.C.* (1980), pp. 175ff: and *idem* with Sandra Wheatley, 'Some Aspects of the Spatial Structure of two Glamorgan Towns in the Nineteenth Century', *W.H.R.,* 9, 'No. 1 (June 1978), pp. 32-56. See also John Gwyn Davies, 'Industrial Society in North-West Monmouthshire 1750-1850', unpublished Ph. D. thesis, Wales, 1980, pp., 89ff.

[16] On rural disturbances see David Williams, *The Rebecca Riots* (second edn., J. P.D. Dunbabin, *Rural Discontent in Nineteenth-Century Britain* (1974), and David W. Howell, *Land and People in Nineteenth-Century Wales* (1977). For the persistence of overt violence and disorder see David Jones, *Before Rebecca. Popular Protests in Wales 1793-1835* (1973), *passim.,* and the same author's articles, 'A Dead-loss to the community: the Criminal Vagrant in Nineteenth Century Wales', *W.H.R.,* 8, No. 3 (June 1977), 'Crime, Protest and Community in Nineteenth Century Wales', *Llafur,* 1, No. 3 (1974) and 'The Second Rebecca Riots: a study of Poaching on the River Wye', *Llafur,* 2, no. 1 (1967).

[17] The periodical literature of the time abounds with references to this major theme, as do the transactions of the 'sassiynnau' etc. For some classic statements see quotations in the present author's 'Merioneth Politics' in *Explorations and Explanations,* pp. 83ff.

[18] For a fuller discussion and some statistics see the present author's 'Religion and Society in *Explorations and Explanations,* pp. 217ff.

[19] On the role of religion in urban areas see W. R. Lambert, 'Some Working Class Attitudes towards organized religion in nineteenth century Wales', *Llafur,* 2, No. 1 (1976), pp. 4-15.

[20] Christopher Turner, 'Revivals and Popular Religion in Victorian and Edwardian Wales', unpublished Ph.D. thesis, Wales, 1979.

[21] On this huge theme, see, in general, Glanmor Williams, *Religion, Language and Nationality in Wales* (Cardiff, 1979), the following articles by W.T.R. Pryce, 'Wales as a Culture Region: Patterns of Change 1750-1950', *T.H.S.C.* (1978), 'Welsh and English in Wales', *Bulletin of the Board of Celtic Studies,* 28 (1978), 'Industrialization, Urbanization and the Maintenance of Culture Areas', *W.H.R.,* 7 No. 3 (1975), and the present author's 'Language and Community in Nineteenth Century Wales', in David Smith (ed.), *A People and a Proletariat* (1981).

[22] See the title essay in Glanmor Williams, *op. cit.*

[23] R. W. Morgan, *Amddiffyniad yr Iaeth Gymraeg, cyfeiriedig at Bob Dosbarth o Genedl y Cymry (A Defence of the Welsh Language, addressed to all Classes of the Welsh Nation)* (Caernarfon, 1858), Rhagymadrodd. Cf. an article by 'Mab Dewi Ddu, Tredegar' in *Y Gwyliedydd* (1825) tt. 47-8, 'Nid hawdd gennyf gredu fod y Creawdwr wedi ein cynnysgaeddu, fel cenedl, ag iaith mor odidog, heb fod ganddo ddybenion arbenig yn hyny, sef ein cael ato, a bod o wasanaeth iddo, a buddioldeb i eraill' (I cannot readily believe that the Creator has endowed us, as a nation, with such a wonderful language, without a special purpose in so doing, namely, that we should belong to him, be of service to him and useful to others).

[24] Radnorshire was a 'pagan' county according to *Y Methodist,* 1 (1852), tt. 57-62. Cf. the sad note in the introduction to the histories of the county churches in Rees a Thomas, *Hanes Eglwysi Annibynnol Cymru,* II (Liverpool, 1872), tt. 526-7.

[25] *Cynllun o Gymdeithas Gennadawl Gartefol, a Fwriadwyd gan Gymdeithasiad y Methodistiaid Calfinaidd yn Neheudir y Dywysogaeth yn y flwyddyn 1826* (Caerfyrddin, d.d.), tt. 1-5

[26] See John Hughes, *op. cit.,* III, tt. 469ff.

[27] T. M. Bassett, *The Welsh Baptists* (Swansea, 1977), *passim.*

[28] The first attempt at a scientific, objective study was by E.G. Ravenstein in his paper 'On the Celtic Languages of the British Isles' in *Journal of the Royal Statistical Society,* 42 (1879), pp. 579-639. For references to subsequent work see the works cited above in note 23.

[29] John Gwyn Davies, *op. cit.,* pp. 67ff. and the statistical tables, pp. 115-17.

[30] P. N. Jones, 'Some Aspects of Immigration into the Glamorgan Coalfield between 1881 and 1911', *T.H.S.C.* (1969).

[31] I am indebted to Sian Rhiannon Williams's research into the history of the Welsh language in Gwent for her study of a language shift in the industrializing parts of Monmouthshire. Her doctoral disseration is a major contribution to the subject. See Siân Rhiannon Williams, 'Rhai agweddau cymdeithasol ar hanes yr iaeth Gymraeg yn ardal ddiwydiannol Sir Fynwy yn y bedwaredd ganrif ar bymtheg'. Unpublished Ph.D. (Wales), 1985.

[32] I have developed this idea in my essay in David Smith (ed.), *op. cit.*

[33] 'Nid cymaint o regwyr yw y Cymry onid ymysgant â chenhedloedd ereill . . . Mae y Gymraeg megis ped fyddai yn iaeth rhy gysegredig i'w defnyddio yn y fath iselwaith' (The Welsh people are not generally users of bad language until they came into contact with other nations . . . The Welsh language is as it were too sacred to be used in such depraved ways), T.E. Watkins (Eiddil Ifor), *Effeithiau Moesawl a Chyneddfawl* (1838).

[34] *Adroddiad Blynyddol Gymdeithas Genhadol . . . am 1864* (Aberystwyth, 1864), t.4.

[35] *Adroddiad . . . 1873*

[36] Parch. David Hughes, *Yr Achosion Saesneg yng Nghymru* (1868). He added, 'Y mae yn alarus i gyfaddef, nad yw eu gorchwyl a'u hamcan fawr amgen na chloddio bedd i'r Gymraeg a'r eglwysi Cymraeg yn ein plith, a hynny cyn bod y naill na'r llall yn hollol barod i'w chladdu' (It is sad to admit that their effort and primary aim is no other than to dig a grave for the Welsh language and the Welsh churches in our midst, and that even before neither the one nor the other is ready for interment).

[37] Cymdeithas Dynolwyr . . . Nantyglo, *Seren Cymru* Tachwedd, 1829). For Edward Lewis who consistently refused to sell his land to the 'Anglo-Saxon invaders', see E. Price, *History of Penuel . . . Ebbw Vale* (Wrexham, 1925), p.24.

[38] See the annual reports of the English Calvinistic Methodist Churches (Presbyterian Church of Wales). For Lewis Edwards see *Y Goleuad,* 21 Gorff. 1871.

[39] See, for example, the five essays on the theology of nation and language in *This Land and People. A Symposium on Christian and Welsh National Identity,* edited by Paul H. Ballard and D. Huw Jones (Collegiate Centre of Theology, University of Cardiff, 1979), pp. 74-136.

Part 3

Understanding Politics

MERTHYR TYDFIL: THE POLITICS OF SURVIVAL*

*"For Man is most ingenious in polluting the best gifts of Nature"**

In taking this as my title I do not wish it to be thought that I am
taking out a patent in a new popular catch-phrase. We already
have 'politics of confrontation', 'politics of consensus', 'politics
of detente', 'politics of cultural despair', and probably others
that I know not of: and it is enough. Such a gesture of academic
entrepreneurship would be entirely pointless, and my purpose
is very simple and modest: it amounts to nothing more than an
attempt to examine a primary theme in the life of the town of
Merthyr in the last century, and in so doing to draw attention
to the basic simplicities underlying the complex nature of
politics in the central decades of the Victorian era. By
'survival' I mean precisely that, the actual physical continuance of a known, historic community of people. I have in mind
also certain rhetorical or metaphorical usages of the word. An
essential part of my problem is to understand the language of
survival, for, as a general rule, it is the language of interest
groups or of classes in the community. Often it is revealing of
the underlying presuppositions, the preconceptions, the un-
spoken assumptions of different groups as they come to
enunciate for themselves views of their predicament that were
specific to themselves even though the language might be the
language of common good. Such views, also, particularly when
they are highly articulated, become the ideologies which
provide the justification for, and determine the direction of,
social movement and action. By politics I mean precisely this
movement of the community; the ways in which a community
and its constituent parts organize in order to ensure survival;
the ways in which that community faces up to what it conceives
to be a threat to its existence. Now, there were many such
threats in the course of the history of Merthyr Tydfil, in particular, those occasions when the continuance of its industrial
base was in question. The middle decades of the century were
such a time. For some years the closure of Dowlais Iron Works
was imminent as Sir John Guest and the Second Marquis of

Bute negotiated the renewal of the leases. The same elephantine struggle was repeated a few years later with regard to the Cyfarthfa leases, and again in the mid-1870s when Robert Thompson Crawshay actually closed the works. Penydarren Works and Plymouth Works did close for ever in the 1859-1868 period. So survival of the industrial base was a recurring threat to the existence of the town. I would argue that the struggle over the leases produced a particular kind of politics—or, if you like, of non-politics or, as some would argue, that it provided the kind of psychic condition of dependence which led to the abandonment of working-class radicalism such as had flourished in the 1830's in favour of the 'politics of embourgeoisement' or of liberalization. Such crises were real enough, and to them we might add others of the same kind: that engendered by the failure of Cyfarthfa to change over from iron to steel production, and finally, of course, the closing of all the main works after the 1914-18 War, culminating in the late 1930s with the recommendation of Political and Economic Planning that the town of Merthyr Tydfil should be abandoned altogether. But it is not these crises of existence that I want to discuss but something possibly more fundamental, namely, the continued existence of life itself in Merthyr, and my theme is the politics engendered by the public health movement.

However rhetorical and pointless it may on reflection sound, the question which sticks in the mind as one studies the sanitary condition of Merthyr in the mid-nineteenth century is, could the place possibly have survived much longer without major public sanitary undertakings? One can understand the gloom and despair with which, from time to time, some of the inhabitants of the place contemplated their future. For certainly the question was asked, and if not by them, then by others, notably by the government, the Health of Towns Association, and, in particular, those marvellously able and dedicated men whose work in the Local Government Board from 1848 and in the Medical Office of the Privy Council from 1858 was slowly but surely breaking down the atrocious individualism of the localities and subsituting mild forms of collectivism and state-direction for laissez-faire. To the evidence of their eyes and noses contemporaries could add the ob-

High Street, Merthyr Tydfil in 1840.

jective information collected in the official Reports on the health and sanitary state of the town. There was De la Beche's in 1845, Rammell's in 1850, William Kay's in 1854, and the annual series of local reports by the Dr. T. J. Dyke, the Medical Officer of Health, which started in 1866.[1] Historians have the advantage of unpublished reports, such as that of Dr. Holland in 1854, and the continuous series of letters which passed between individuals and the Local Board of Health in Merthyr and the General Board in London.[2] He has the advantage, too, of the minutes of local government bodies,[3] and above all, perhaps, he can get some pretty sound notions of the general cultural and political background, of the movements in men's minds, of which a preoccupation with health and sanitation was one, but seen and felt as part of and in relation to a whole complex of other interests and attitudes. Against such a background the question 'Can Merthyr survive' became a question not merely about health and the conditions of life, but also a question about politics, that is to say, about the possession and exercise of power and initiative in the comunity, of the growth and organization of opinion regarding the nature of society, questions about conflicting interests. Merthyr, it seemed, could expire in diseases of its own creation, or be torn apart by class conflict of the bitterest kind in a hideous apocalypse of horror.

Of course, the kind of answer you would have got in Merthyr would have depended on whom you asked the question of, and when you asked it. The ironmasters, with the possible exception of Lady Charlotte Guest and her Trustees, H. A. Bruce and G. T. Clark (after the death of Sir Josiah) would have given fairly optimistic answers. Anthony Hill of Plymouth and Alderman Thompson of Penydarren certainly: for both of these any interference in what they regarded as the natural relations in society was anathema. Robert Thompson Crawshay readily would have recognized the force and urgency of the question, and he would have pointed unhesitatingly to the remedies available, namely, individual self-help encouraged and gently sustained by the paternalism of the masters. The Guests were different from the other ironmasters, more ready to accept urgent and quite sweeping interference by public bodies probably because the evidences of physical and moral decline were most pronounced in parts of Dowlais than elsewhere. The doctors, as well-qualified, skilful and efficient as any, it was said, to be found outside the metropolis,[4] were likewise deeply pessimistic, and the evidence they gave to the Inspectors of the General Board and to the Local Board of Health would seem to have indicated that catastrophe was nigh. Nor would there seem to have been any doubt in the minds of the officials of the General Board that their views were fully justified. So pessimistic and scarifying was the report of Inspector Holland in December 1853,[5] that the President of the General Board asked Dr. William Kay of Bristol to check on his observations,[6] and his answer [7]—elaborated in a *Report* to the Local Board a few months later[8]—was to the effect that it would be difficult to speak of the place in the language of exaggeration: Holland's report was factually correct and a model of restraint. The medical men, then, shared a common view, based on an agreed method of observation and analysis of basic facts, and they were united also in that their prognostications were always of the disjunctive type—*either* Merthyr faces the problem of public health squarely and applies the remedies of sanitary engineering, *or* disaster will follow.

The pessimists were always in a majority, their words most listened to, at times of disaster—either natural disaster, such as occured during particularly virulent visitations of fever or plaque, or during times of political upheaval. The correlation between disease and the spirit of improvement, between the death-rate and investment in health, was close, and at no time closer than during cholera epidemics. At such times, as in 1848/9, and again in 1854 and in 1866, the Great Fear descended upon all classes in the community and action to ameliorate the physical conditions of the town invariably took place, though not, as we shall see, with any kind of unanimity as to the means to be adopted. There was a correlation also with political movements. It was not cholera alone which lay behind the petition from Merthyr to the government to apply the Local Government Act, but also political movements of an alarming kind among a resurgent working class. More immediately, it was Chartism and renascent trade unionism as the grim prospects of depression became evident. It was the general economic condition of the time which strained social relations, and it was the threat of public disorder which aroused the middle-class ratepayers into action. It was not so much cholera or even typhus and smallpox as the generally appalling state in which the bulk of the population had to live and the dangers to public order consequent upon this which was the first stimulus, and it is no accident, as I hope to show, that the first decisive actions to clean up the town were taken immediately after and during a prolonged period of social unrest.

But it was the facts concerning the state of the town and its population—observable facts and facts to be inferred from the growing body of statistics—which strengthened the arguments of the pessimists. First of all there was the evidence of one's own eye and noses—particularly one's nose. Every visitor, whether an official making an investigation or newspaper correspondent looking for copy, business man or tourist or peripatetic minister, was agreed on one thing, that Merthyr was an excessively offensive town.[9] Rammell, reporting to the General Board of Health in 1849/50, concluded that there was no system of drainage and virtually no surface drainage in any parts of the town. The roads, none of which were paved or macadamized, were thus made the receptacles for all the refuse and dirt—human ordure—produced in the adjacent houses. The so-called "ash-tips" which abounded were in fact heaps of cinders and vegetable matter mixed up with manure, and these were left lying in the streets to be carted off at long intervals and dumped on any convenient open space or in the river. "The first circumstance that most strikes every visitor at Merthyr is the extreme and universal dirtiness and wetness of the town", wrote Dr. Holland in 1853. "I have visited many dirty places, and have generally been taken to see the worst parts of the worst towns in England; with the worst parts of London and Manchester I am familiar, that extremely dirty City of Bristol I have recently examined but never did I see anything which could compare with Merthyr. It is not merely mud that is a cause of constant annoyance and discomfort, not merely that there are no proper footpaths and the roadways generally abominable, rendering clean shoes an impossibility;

not merely that in many parts nothing can fairly be called a road exists at all, mere tracks worn by horses wheels and passengers into a puddle, but *everywhere,* even along road and paths constantly frequented are visible indications of the absence of those places of accommodation generally thought indispensible".[10] One is inclined to question whether Merthyr in these respects was any worse than most other towns, and Holland's quite emphatic statement that it was worse than the worst parts of London, Manchester and Bristol should perhaps give us pause. Nor is there any point in locating Merthyr in a sanitary league, and it is sufficient to observe that the descriptions we have of other town, and the sanitary reports on other places suggest strongly that Merthyr, taken as a whole, did present an appalling state of sanitary neglect. Most other towns had areas or quarters which were just as bad: Swansea, for example, is often described at the same time, as a neat and clean town except for certain areas around the docks and the Dyfatty and Greenhill areas.[11] What appalled the visitors and inspectors was the fact that the sanitary condition of large areas of Merthyr was as bad as the worst parts of the worst cities in England, and they were baffled to explain why so relatively small a place, located in a naturally healthy environment should have such an unenviable record.

Lack of surface drainage, a total absence of sewage disposal and of private and public conveniences was one set of observable facts. Another fact was the total lack of any water supply. In Merthyr the water, like every other creature, was made to work, and the river in the judgement of the ironmasters was of course just another factor of production, like coal, or mine or labour. The Taff had been harnessed by Crawshay above his works and its waters drove his mills and supplied his steam-engines before being channelled to supply Anthony Hill with the power required by him. The residue was supposed to keep the canal water in a reasonable liquid state. That portion of the flow of the Taff which escaped Crawshay's weir turned rapidly into an open sewer: by the time it reached Troedyrhiw it was black and thick, as offensive to the eye and nose as to the tongue. Yet this was one of the main supplies of water for domestic use by the inhabitants. The other sources were water spouts in various parts of the town at which women were compelled to queue for hours during the summer droughts for as long as eight to ten hours—themselves heavily polluted by adjacent cesspools, ash-tips and the revolting flow of surface drainage. This, possibly, was the most dreadful observable feature of the sanitary condition of the town, and one which filled visitors with terror. "I can hardly expect credence for such facts as the following", wrote Holland, "yet it is perfectly free from exaggeration. I saw a young woman filling her pitcher from a little stream of water gushing from a cinder heap the surface of which was so thickly studded with alvine deposits that it was difficult to pass without treading on them, in some of which I saw intestinal worms, and the rain then falling was washing the feculent matter into the water which the girl was filling into her pitcher, no doubt for domestic use."[12]

The consequences of these notorious deficiences were likewise evident, and were to be found in the cold statistics of the Registrar General, in various housing and sanitation commission reports, in the Minutes of the Guardians and their Inspector of Nuisances, and later in the annual reports of the local Medical Officer of Health and the annual reports of Sir John Simon from 1859.[13] Merthyr was a disease ridden town. Typhus, smallpox, scarlet-fever were endemic, and from time to time diarrhoeal diseases of one form or another swept through the town. This latter was particularly vicious in its visitations and was much feared because its early symptoms closely resembled those of cholera. Epidemics of one or other of these diseases came almost annually, and it is difficult to believe that the almost excessive religiosity which was such a marked characteristic of the town was not stoked and fired by these visitations. The crude mortality figures confirmed the melancholy facts that were so depressingly present.[14] The death-rate from all causes in the 11 years between 1846 and 1855 before any sanitary works were in operation was 332 per 10,000 inhabitants. More precisely, average mortality between 1847 and 1852 was 29 per 1,000 without cholera, 34.7 with cholera, or 1 in 34.5 and 1 in 28.8 respectively of the population. To get this in perspective, the Registrar General's statistics suggested— and this was taken as a norm by the inspectorate and local

The river Taff running through the Cyfarthfa Iron Works. *Photo: Cynon Valleys Libraries.*

Boards of Health—that a 2 per cent mortality rate (20 per 1,000) was taken as "the mortality in districts of an *average* degree of salubrity". The 1848 Public Health Act could be enforced when the mortality rate exceeded 23 per 1,000. Merthyr's 33 per 1,000 was therefore far in excess of the norm: it was higher than any other town or district in Wales and ranked next to Manchester and Liverpool where the mortality rates were the highest in the kingdom as a whole.

But that was not all: the crude mortality rates concealed two other sets of facts. First, and most important, that it was the deaths of children under the age of five which gave to Merthyr its horrifying precedence in the mortality stakes. On an average, of every five children born in the years 1848-53 two died before reaching the age of 5 years: in fact, most of these died before their first year. For instance, in those years 1900 children were born: 367 (19%) died under 1 year, 286 (15%) under 3 years, and 105 (5.5%) under 5 years. As Dr. Kay expressed it, "More than half of the funerals that take place in Merthyr are those of children under 5 years of age; and more than one-fourth of infants under 1 year",[15] adding that this was only 0.2% worse than Liverpool, the worst sanitary town in the kingdom. Complementary to these facts was another, namely the relative short durations of the lives of those who did survive infanthood. The general average in 1851 was calculated at 17½ years—somewhere between the average for Manchester (20 or 18) and (the worst in the kingdom) Liverpool with 17 years. People did not live long in Merthyr.

How successfully you survived infancy and how long one lived thereafter could be equated also with two other considerations. The first is what Dr. Dyke, the first permanent Medical Officer, referred to in 1866 as "the sanitary topography of Merthyr".[16] The early investigators had found plenty of evidence in the mortality and sickness statistics to prove that Upper Merthyr was a far more dangerous place to live in than Lower Merthyr. Tydfil's Well, where the houses were small and dilapidated, huddled together, and occupied by the very poorest sort of people, was thought to be the worst district of all, but throughout the whole of the town there were pockets of grossly inadequate housing, noisome courts and alleys unventilated, unwatered, undrained. These places were centres of disease and infection and they were identified as the pestilential sources of the epidemics which so decimated the population from time to time, and as the permanent abiding places of the endemic and infectious diseases which carried off the infant part of the population. In this respect, Dr. Dyke's work on the sanitary topography of Merthyr was the exact equivalent of that of the General Board of Health for the country as a whole: it fastened attention on the physical and external conditions of life and established clearly and unequivocally the essential equation between those conditions and public health.

The other considerations, or set of factors in the equation, was the unmistakable identification of disease with occupation and relative poverty. Merthyr was the 'working-class' town *par excellence,* the *exempla* of one-industry towns and as such unique in industrial experience. Of its total population in, for example, 1861 over 15,000 were directly employed in iron-making or coal mining. There were nearly 7,000 coal miners, 2,000 iron-miners, 4,500 ironworkers, and 2,000 craftsmen and labourers.[17] For each person thus employed it was calculated that there were two at home dependent upon him for food and shelter, so that out of a population of 54,000 at least 45,000 were dependent upon the coal and iron trades. Most of the workmen, with the exception of labourers and women and children, earned, in the language and by this standards of the day, good wages and yet they were, as a class, poor. What made them poor was irregularity of labour, and the effects socially of this can be seen in the physical or social conditions, the housing in particular, of the various classes of workmen.[18] What made the iron-miners as a class, more respectable, what enabled them to live in better cottages, in relatively healthier districts, was not high wages, but regularity of employment. Colliers—ironworks and sea-sale—and ironworkers were far more subject to the vagaries of the market and the trade cycle, and it was this which kept them as a class on the edges of poverty. Yet all these occupations demanded strength and endurance as well as skill, but strength was the product of food rich in proteins—meat and cheese—and it was this that was lacking in the diet and which brought them to premature old age and an early grave. The diseases endemic in Merthyr were diseases of malnutrition—typhus, certainly tuberculosis, and mysterious disease later identified as Relapsing Fever or Famine Fever.[19] When the contagious and infectious diseases struck from their breeding places in Tydfil's Well, Ponty-store-house and 'China', they struck usually in times of unemployment and distress and wreaked havoc among a population debilitated by want of food and the basic essentials for existence.

Can we now pose the question, Could Merthyr survive? It survived mainly by reason of the constant inflow of young adults, "rosy-cheeked", said contemporaries, from the country districts round about and from a distance.[20] It was not natural increase from within, despite the almost unprecedented high birth-rate. Contemporaries understood as well as today's demographers, that endemic sickness and high mortality, especially in plague conditions always lead to high birth rates as the communities involved endeavour to renew themselves. As Dr. Kay observed, ". . . the mortality consequent upon the outbreak of severe epidemic . . . though it temporarily diminishes, by an excess of deaths, the members of the community, subsequently, by an augmentation of births, increases the population." "And," he added, "this increase is an unproductive increase; an increase of children for the most part born to die".[21] That is why, on 8 November 1848, the Poor Law Guardians decided to adopt the Public Health Act.

The 1848 Act, despite its many weaknesses—especially its largely permissive character and its lack of centralized compulsive power—did provide places like Merthyr Tydfil which lacked any but the most rudimentary forms of local government with the essential machinery to carry out basic sanitary reforms. In particular, it might enable such Local Boards to carry out essential drainage, to lay down sewerage systems, and to provide adequate supplies of piped water. To pay for all this, local boards were empowered to levy General District Rates and to raise capital for works of a permanent nature they might be authorized to raise a mortgage either with Exchequer or with private companies on the security of the rates. To provide water supplies they could either come to agreement with existing water companies or themselves undertake the pro-vision. All this had to be done with the guidance of, and under the close supervision of, the Central Board of Health—after the Local Government Act 1858, of the Medical Office of the Privy Council (1854) and the Home Office, and after 1872 of the Local Government Board.

It is important, if we are to understand the impact of the Act on Merthyr, to note the chronology of events. The Guardians petitioned for permission to adopt the Act in November 1848. Rammell, the Inspector, came down in April 1849, and his Report was published in May. In the meantime, cholera had arrived, breaking out in Pontystorehouse on 26 May, in Pedwran-fach the following day, and in the 'China' district on the 28th. Between then and September a total of 1389 died of the disease, two thirds of them in Upper Merthyr. If one adds the 41 who died of diarrhoea, then the total was over 1430 in the space of four months. Yet it was not until October 1850 that the Local Board was elected, and another two years went by before a medical officer was appointed, and that only on a temporary basis.[22] As has been remarked, "Cholera seemed easily forgotten and its immediate effect astonishingly small".[23] In fact, cholera was to come again in 1854 before anything substantial was done, and even then there was a further delay of six years before an adequate water supply was provided for most parts of the town, and yet another four years before the main sewerage works were begun.

The cause of these incredible delays must be sought in the nature of the social relations which had been generated over a long period in this iron-town which epitomized the rawest and most brutal forms of capitalism. But before examining that it is necessary to point out that the two basic needs of the town, namely, the provision of adequate supplies of clean water at appropriate pressures and a system of sewage disposal, presented no great engineering problems. It could even be argued that the delays before taking the decision may paradoxically even have been to the advantage of the community. A snap decision on the water supply, for example, would undoubtedly have resulted in the siting of the main reservoir not in the Taf Fechan, where geology and economics were most favourable, but in the

Taff Fawr. More seriously, the delay in commencing sewage works was of the utmost importance since almost certainly in the early 1850s the sewers would have been constructed according to Chadwick's notion involving the creation of what his critics called "Elongated cesspits" pouring the effluence into the rivers. Most scientists at the time and the vast majority of medical men believed that cholera and typhus were air-borne diseases, and that they were spontaneously generated in the noxious gases emitted by accumulations of filth.[24] The medical men of Merthyr were certainly miasmatists as against contagionists, and it is certain that they would have advised the engineers to construct systems accordingly—that is to say, large brick sewers leading to the river at some convenient point below the town which would be flushed out periodically by water under pressure. By 1864 these ideas had changed; the diseases were known to be water-borne, and the major problem faced by the engineer in charge of the operation was that of dis-posal. Samuel Harpur, the engineer in charge of the design and construction, had already constructed systems at Coventry and Cheltenham, and these, with other similar systems, had not proved satisfactory since they depended upon filtration methods designed to separate the solids from the liquids before discharging the latter into the rivers.[25] The outcry this had caused from people who depended upon the rivers for their water supplies had led to the setting up of a Select Committee, and this committee had come down strongly on the side of those—including our own Samuel Roberts of Llanbryn-mair—who advocated the liquifying of town sewage and con-veying it by pipes (and if necessary in trains of specially designed tankers) in liquified form to adjacent farms for agri-cultural purposes.[26] Agreeing with this, Harpur then had to do his sums. Rugby, he discovered, applied their sewage at 20 persons to the acre, Worthing at the rate of 167 persons to the acre, and with a nice calculation he decided that ratio of 50 to 1 would do for Merthyr. He therefore needed about 1,000 acres of agricultural land, and he found it (since it would not all be required at once) in plots of varying size above and below the town. Three quarters of Dowlais sewage could be spread on fields on the Penydarren estate and to the west of Dowlais, the remainder to join the Merthyr system. This would be delivered onto 350 acres of flat land in the valley between Quakers Yard and Troedyrhiw. The main sewers were to be oval-shaped and built of brick 30" in diameter, the connecting pipes of glazed enamel. The total cost was estimated at £27,000. It was this scheme which was sanctioned in March 1865, and a year later 10½ miles of main sewers and drains had been laid down. This was undoubtedly the greatest advance ever in purifying the town, but one wonders what would have been the reactions of people living within sight and smell of the main disposal and dispersion areas at Troedyrhiw and Penydarren: what is the direction of the prevailing wind? And one can sympathize with the inhabitants of Pontypridd who objected strongly to the acquisition by Merthyr Local Board of further land between Navigation (Abercynon) and Pontypridd, and in particular the small farmer just below Mountain Ash who could observe his farm rapidly being engulfed in the effluence of the iron-town.

The effects of these two basic provisions were almost instantaneous. Water was available from standpipes from 1860 and in 1862 nearly every house in Dowlais and Merthyr received a constant, separate supply: 68½ miles of main and branch water pipes had been laid. This, with the sewerage completed in the same decade resulted in the death rate being reduced by 1865 to 271 per 10,000 and of infants to 67: during the next ten years, with the completion of the sewage scheme (1868) and the abandonment of the agricultural method of disposal in favour of filter beds (constructed in 1871), the death rate fell to 256, that of infants to 65, and the average age at death rose from 17½ years to 25 years. Much remained to be done, of course. One of the engineering problems was how to prevent the escape of gas from the sewers which inevitably happened when a sewer drain or pipe broke, for example—not forgetting that the summits of the main drains were in any case provided with openings to allow the escape of gas. These were danger points and cases of fever invariably occurred when this happened. The engineering answer was to apply to the sewage system the up-cast and down-cast ventilation systems of collieries. This was eventually done, and that is how industrial landscape of

Dowlais and Merthyr came to be variegated with stark, brick chimneys 30 feet high.[27]

Yet, when all is said and done, what we are really discussing is not sanitary engineering but social engineering, properly so called, and to seek to understand motivations, aspirations and reactions is immediately to embark upon an anatomy of the town, to seek to expose the intricate nexus of social relations as they were developing. Let us try to answer the obvious and apparently simple question, Why the delay of fourteen or more years before recommendations of the 1850 Report were carried out? We know that there was delay and procrastination everywhere, but Cardiff and Newport and Swansea for example had at least begun their improvements by 1854: why should the delay have been most prolonged where the need was greatest? The very comparisons provide a clue: those other towns were chartered boroughs possessing corporations and systems of representative democratic government, albeit restricted, in which the various interests and classes could be represented and in which final decisions could be taken. Opinion could be organized and given a voice. They had their lords, of course: Newport its Sir Charles Morgan and Cardiff its Marquis of Bute, but it was precisely issues of common concern, such as sanitary reform, which stimulated the organizations of progressive and radical parties consisting of the new bourgeoisie and shopocracy and dedicated to the capture of power and to the progressive development of their towns. It was precisely these things that Merthyr lacked. Rammell has been astonished to find a town of 50,000 inhabitants "as destitute of civic government as the smallest rural village of the empire".[28] He divided the populations into two groups only, the iron-masters, their agents and workmen, and "such professional men and tradesmen as are necessary for supplying the wants of the former". Dr. Kay, three years later, distinguished a three-class system, the working classes, "the middle rank of tradespeople, shopkeepers and others, and the upper class of ironmasters, professional gentlemen, clerical and lay", in the ordinary proportion incident to a populous community.[29] All were connected, directly or indirectly, with the trade and commerce of the place. Later in his paper he tried to put figures to these categories. Of the population of 46,378 he thought 40,000 belonged to the labouring classes and 4,000 to the middle and upper ranks. There is no need, at this point, to question his estimates, except to suggest that this figure for the size of the middle class, even if we include all shopkeepers and all beer-house keepers (and I suspect that his estimates were based on the rating books) is too high. But, like Rammell and all other observers, he also remarked on the absence of the *residential* middle class, men, that is, of independent means and position actually living in the town. Even if there had been small gentry estates in the vicinity it is extremely improbable that they would have maintained town houses in Merthyr. For most of these observers it was not a town: it did not fit in to their definitions of 'urbanism'. It was like some kind of chemical reaction, "a condensation of people", as Dean Conybeare said, rather than the slow organic experience that was a town. It was to these factors together that analysts attributed the quite extraordinary development of the place. The function of a middle class, it was believed in Victorian England, was to stand between the four ironmasters and their lackeys and the overwhelming working-class bulk of the population. The middle-class itself, given the relatively small measure of its wealth, its large component of shopkeepers and the inevitable role within it of professional men who were few in number and mostly connected by interest with the iron masters, was difficult to organize and, as we have seen, they had no forum for debate, no machinery of government which they could hope to control. They were, therefore, unorganized and massively apathetic and pessimistic, finding in religion and campaigns for moral improvements an outlet for their frustrated ambitions. As the Registrar General put it. "The population, suddenly collected by mining operations, is exposed to all the evils of dense districts with few of the alleviations which spring up in towns of slow growth, having well-organized and intelligent municipal councils".[30]

What of the working classes—that mass of labouring men, anonymous, born to slave in atrocious conditions and to live and die in pitiful neglect? What voice had they? What initiatives were open to them? What could be expected of them? Their history proclaimed the answers. "A population living in such a state of constant discomfort as that of Merthyr . . . cannot be safe. I am no longer surprised at the violent and apparently purposeless outrages which have produced similar results, but here the cause is more aggravated the effect more violent: as Blackburn is to Merthyr, so is a Lancashire riot to a Newport rebellion; making allowance for the difference in the density of population the contrast of violence is perhaps as great as of condition".[31] "The equation of dirt, disease, and political disturbance", as Professor Briggs puts it,[32] was assuming an increasingly important place in the moral arithmetic of the times, and there were some among the middle classes who could no longer accept what would appear to be the basic political philosophy of such as Anthony Hill of Penydarren, that local government should be confined to two "only objects . . . to tax and to punish". It might also have an ameliorative function, and insofar as epidemic diseases added panic and hysteria to masses of people already alienated, investment in sanitary reform was only a form of insurance against disorder. It there was to be a convergence of the classes there could be no better way to begin the process than here.

But sanitary reform, wherever it took place—whether in far-off Bala or the black-holes of Trevethin—involved politics, and the conflicts between interests, and the alignments of opinion which ensued stimulated the very nerves of the communities. Right at the beginning, at the time of the original inquiry, opinion was sharply divided.[33] For petitioning were the minor capitalists, such as Kirkhouse, David Williams, some mineral agents, the official spokesmen of the Guardians and, of course, the surgeons. Against were a motley crowd, but including a draper, a coal-dealer and, in political terms, at least five chartists. Among them, also, were those sinister figures, Thomas Lewis and George Overton, the latter a lawyer whose father had made his fortune in coal at Hirwaun and invested a great deal of it in cottages in Dowlais.[34] Standing aloof were the ironmasters. Vociferously present and in mutinous mood were the workmen. The ironmasters could safely stand by and watch: their agents were well briefed. But what of the workmen? Why their opposition? The reasons are not difficult to understand. Matthew John, William Gould, John Beddow,

David Evans, the leaders of a mature Chartism, and the leaders whom the constant strikes threw up, had taught them already to understand that, as Sir Edwin Chadwick put it, the local government proposed would be "Local Government of a Class" . . . and "that Class the well-to-do-Class".[35] In any development they would be excluded. Election to the Local Board would be confined to the ratepayers and in the total population of 40,000 there were only 1377 ratepayers. Whatever happened, therefore, would depend upon the goodwill of that privileged group of men. They knew also that though nominally the burden of the rate would fall upon the rate-payers, in fact it would be passed on to them in the form of a higher rent. And finally, in any case, only the wealthy would qualify to sit on the Board, for the property qualification was designed to exclude any members of the working class.

In fact, of course, they were proved utterly right. The unlikely alliance between the Chartists and Lewis Lewis and George Overton could not affect the issue and when, after sundry delays, the Local Board was formed, it consisted of Guest, Hill and Crawshay, the chief agents of the four ironworks, a banker, lawyer, a farmer, and big businessmen.[36] That was to remain the pattern throughout its history; the whole democratic operation, from the point of view of the workman, was an indecent farce, as offensive to reason as polluted water was to the taste. Nor was this disillusionment characteristic only of the disenfranchised: ironmaster control of affairs was exercised through the voters. As one sarcastic Dowlais voter put it in a letter to the Local Board,

"The next time you send voting papers to Dowlais, please to leave them all at Dowlais office, for it will spare you and them a great deal of trouble. For the man who was distributing this time could not find out the Voters' residences because he was a stranger to the place. Then the Dowlais Agents had to call in every house to tell the Voter who he was to vote for.

So the easiest way is the best way to accomplish everything that will answer the same purpose in the end. Therefore I beg to call your attention to the above plan,

for it will answer the same purpose, and save a great deal
of bodly exercise to both parties, the time spent without
doing any good. Which the late renowned Benjamin
Franklyn said was Money.
Wishing you success in all your endeavours."[37]

Nothing illustrates better this overwhelming power of the
ironmasters than the way in which they were able to delay the
bringing of piped water to the town. When they acted in
concert they were irresistible—and act in concert they did.
Lady Charlotte Guest constantly threatened to act independently—i.e. to do so as she thought fit for Dowlais.[38] But on the
key question of whether to proceed along collectivist
principles—to have a publicly owned and democratically controlled water works—or to set up a private joint stock enterprise, run on business lines and designed to produce a profit,
they were united. For years they worked through their agents
and at the level of parliamentary committees to achieve this
end. The proclaimed justification was public service, the
efficiency of private enterprise, and the sacrosanct nature of the
profit-motive. The concealed motive was the protection of their
own interests and the superiority of private right over public
good. But even after that particular method of provision had
been rejected by the sceptical officials of the Home Office, they
were either singly or in concert able to delay and frustrate the
taking of decisions. Crawshay and Hill between them acted as
if they had sovereign rights over the waters of Taf Fechan, and
resisted to the bitter end any scheme to construct a reservoir
higher up the valley. They even demanded compensation of
£10,000 each should they be over-ruled. Truly, "There is a
great dread of the Ironmasters in this place, and their power is
so extensive, and so sure to be hostiley applied, that public duty
and christian obligations are alike forgotten", as Mr. Simmons
so eloquently wrote in 1855.[39]
    Yet, on reflection, one realizes that the ironmasters were the
predominant voices only because the rest of the town was
divided, and that on the basic issues of politics, or rather, on
issues of local government involving political views and commitment, a predominant section of the middle classes could be

relied upon for their support. At such time conflicting private interests coalesced and formed temporary alliances against the common danger—the attack on property and privilege alike. The cottage owners, headed by Overton, were desperately afraid that the 2d per week per house would have to be borne by them. Normally it would be added to the rents, but working men were in a militant mood, and that decade after 1850 marked the most sustained effort since the thirties to bring sophisticated forms of trade unionism into the valleys. There were bitter strikes in Aberdare in 1850 against wage reductions, violence against blacklegs, talk again of 'Scotch Cattle', threats of "Stopping the supplies" of ministers of religion who would not support them. Above all, a colliers' union, to be called the Glamorgan Union of Colliers was in process of formation—the seed from which grew the first massive united movement of colliers of 1857-8.[40] No wonder that 1839 and earlier movements of the working class were remembered by the authorities, and that these critical years saw not only sanitary reform taking on a new urgency but also that it saw a kind of rejuvenation of the church, and that archdeacons and bishops should now agree that one could not expect those who lodged like pigs to live like Christians.

I started with the question, Could Merthyr survive? It did survive, and I hope I have said enough to suggest that the reasons for its survival are very complex and mysterious, and that the pipes layed underground were only one element, albeit an important one, in its survival.

NOTES

*This article was first published in *Llafur: Journal for the Study of Welsh Labour History*, 2. no 1 (Spring 1976).

*Alfred Haviland, 'The Geographical Distribution of Typhoid Fever in England and Wales', *British Medical Journal*, 10 February, 1872, p. 148.

[1] *Report on the State of . . . Merthyr Tydfil . . .*, by Sir Henry T. de la Beche (1845); *Report to the General Board of Health . . . into . . . the sanitary condition . . . of Merthyr Tydfil*, by T. W. Rammell (1850); *Report of the Sanitary Condition of Merthyr Tydfil* (Merthyr Tydfil, 1854). See also *Fourth Report of the Medical Officer of the Privy Council* (1862).

[2] PRO, MH 13/125. All the correspondence between Welsh local authorities and Government departments relating to health, sanitary and other services between 1847

and 1871 has been transcribed and edited by A. H. Williams, *Public Health in Mid-Victorian Wales* (University of Wales, Board of Celtic Studies, 1983).

³e.g. the Minute Books of the Board of Guardians, Glamorgan Record Office, U/M.

⁴'The Mining and Manufacturing Districts of South Wales', Letter VI and VII, *Morning Chronicle*, 8 and 15 Ap. 1850. There is a list of medical men in Charles Wilkins, *The History of Merthyr Tydfil* (1908), pp. 502-3.

⁵P.R.O. MH/13/125, Holland to Macaulay, Secretary to the General Board, dated Whitehall, 15 December 1833.

⁶*Ibid.*, memo dated 24 December, and draft C. Macaulay to Kay of same date.

⁷*Ibid.*, Kay to Macaulay, dated from Clifton 26 December 1853.

⁸*Report on the Snaitary Condition of Merthyr Tydfil . . .* by William Kay, M.D. Published by the Local Board (Merthyr Tydfil, 1854).

⁹Notable examples would include the *Morning Chronicle Letters* referred to in note 4 above, T. E. Clarke, *Guide to Merthyr Tydfil in (1848); Edwin F. Roberts, A Visit to the Ironworks and Environs of Merthyr Tydfil in 1852* (London 1853); *Two Days on the Welsh Border (n.d., but probably 1853); 'A Peep into a Welsh Iron valley,' The Shilling Magazine,* October 1847; H. A. Bruce, *Merthyr Tydfil in 1852* (1952) and 'On Amusements' in *Letters and Addresses by Lord Aberdare* (n.d.), pp, 1-36, and 'The Present Condition and Future Prospects of the Working Population in the Mineral Districts of South Wales', *ibid,* pp. 37-70 and *The Bristol Times,* 7, 14, 21, 28 February and 13 March 1852.

¹⁰Holland to Macaulay, 15 December 1853, MH13/X/K513.

¹¹The Appendix to the 'First Report of the Commissioners of Inquiry into the State of Large Towns Populous Districts', paints a much more sombre picture. See P.P. 1844, XVIII (572), 8.

¹²Holland to Macaulay, f.3. Cf. also *Morning Chronicle,* Letter I March 1850 (pp. 22-3 in the above edition).

¹³The Annual *Reports on the Sanitary Condition of Merthyr Tydfil* by Dr. T. J. Dyke begin in 1866 and are invaluable source for the medical history of the town. Of the annual *Reports of the Medical Officer of the Privy Council* the most important are the Second (''On Cholera and Diarrhoeal Mortality'') P.P. 1860, XXIX, 201, pp. 111-121, the Fourth, containing Dr. Hunter's Report on Merthyr Tydfil and Abergavenny, P.P., 1862, XXII (179), 160ff., Dr. Dyke's evidence before the Sanitary Commission also repays close study. First Report, 1870, Qs. 6275-6425. See also the medical reports in the Poor Law Commission Reports.

¹⁴The statistics which follow are taken from *The First Report on the Sanitary Condition of Merthyr Tydfil . . .* by Dr. T. J. Dyke (1866). Cf. also his paper to the British Medical Association, *British Medical Journal* (1855), pp. 192-196, and Kay's *Report, op. cit.*

¹⁵Kay, *op. cit.,* p. 16.

¹⁶Dyke, *First Report,* (1866).

¹⁷Harold Carter and Sandra Whearley, *Merthyr Tydfil in 1851. A Study of the Spatial Structure of Welsh Industrial Town* (Cardiff 1983).

¹⁸For a detailed and exceptionally well illustrated study of housing in Merthyr Tydfil see H. Bolwell, 'The Urban Geography of the north eastern rim of the Glamorganshire Coalfield', Univ. of Wales unpublished thesis, Aberystwyth, 1960. For descriptions of housing in various parts of Merthyr, see Dyke's evidence before the Royal Sanitary Commission of 1869, First Report (1870), Qs. 6275-6425. Cf. also F. J. Ball, 'Housing in an Industrial Colony: Ebbw Vale, 1778-1914', S. D. Chapman (ed.), *The History of Working-Class Housing. A symposium* (1971).

¹⁹For an excellent discussion of this point see M. W. Flinn's introduction to his edition of *Report on the Sanitary Conditions of the Labouring Population of Gt. Britain* by

Edwin Chadwick (Edinburgh 1965). See also his introduction to *The Medical and Legal Aspects of Sanitary Reform* (Leicester 1969).

[20] *Fourth Report of the Medical Officer of the Privy Council*, P.P. 1862, XXII (179), p. 160. But compare the paper (by the same person) on mortality in rural South Wales; *Seventh Report*, P.P. 1864.

[21] Kay, *op. cit.*, p. 35.

[22] There is a brief survey in Dyke. *art. cit.;* the most comprehensive study is a splendid thesis (unpublished), by Tydfil Davies Jones (M.A. Cardiff, 1961): see also her article, 'Poor Law Administration in Merthyr Tydfil Union 1834-1894'. *Morgannwg*, VIII (1964), pp. 35-62.

[23] Asa Briggs, 'Cholera and Society', *Past and Present*, 19 (1961).

[24] Compare, for instance, Dr. Kay in the report cited: "cholera is the direct result of sanitary neglect—the direct infliction and penalty entailed by dirt, filth, and impurity. it is not in itself a poison; its influence, *per se*, being comparatively harmless. It is only when attracted by local causes—noxious agencies—elements of malaria—within and around, that it becomes the malignant and deadly scourge which decimated your population in 1849". *Report*, pp. 9-10. Samuel Harpur, *Report to the Merthyr Tydfil Local Board of Health on the Sewage of the District and Development of the Sewerage* (1864). Also, *Copy of a Letter to William Lee, Esq., C.E. and his report on Sewerage at Merthyr Tydil 30 June 1865* (1865). For a report on the sewage outfall and earth filtration works, dated 8 November 1872, see Edward Smith *Manual for Medical Officers of Health* (1873), pp. 185-189. *The Morning Chronicle* correspondent visited Merthyr in the immediate aftermath of the cholera epidemic, and his account, in Letter VII, 15 April 1850, is invaluable.

[25] *Minutes of Information collected on the practical application of sewer water and town manures to agricultural purposes*, P.P. 1852 (1472).

[26] Samuel Roberts, 'Railroads against Sewers', in *Pregethau, Areithiau a Chaniadau* (Utica, 1864). This particular paper was written to persuade the railway companies of America and Britain to organize the collection of "gu", in specially designed containers, from the major points of production for distribution to rural areas for use as manure by the farmers.

[27] For this and other details see Thomas Jones Dyke, 'The Sanitary History of Merthyr Tydfil', *British Medical Journal*, 1 August 1885, pp. 192-196. Tydfil Davies Jones, *art cit.*, provides a more comprehensive treatment.

[28] Rammell, *op. cit.*, p. 12.

[29] Kay, *op. cit.*, p. 4.

[30] *Second Annual report of the Registrar General of Births, Deaths and Marriages*, P.P. 1840, XVII (276), Appendix, pp. 49-50.

[31] Holland, *op. cit.*, ff. 11-12.

[32] Asa Briggs, *art. cit.* For an excellent and comprehensive discussion of the literature, see Malcolm I. Thomas, *The Town labourer and the Industrial Revolution* (1974).

[33] The names are to be found in Rammell. *op. cit.*, in the newspaper reports of the inquiry, especially in the *Cardiff and Merthyr Guardian*, March, April, May, 1849, and in P.R.O., HO13/125, Frank James, clerk to the Guardians, to the G.B.H., 27 November 1848 *et. seq.*

[34] For Lewis, who was deputy chairman of the Guardians, see Tydfil Davies Jones, *op. cit.*, and for Overton, *see* Wilkins *op. cit.*

[35] Quoted in R. A. Lewis, *Sir Edwin Chadwick and the Public Health Movement*, (1952).

[36] There were 39 candidates and the following were elected: Sir John Guest (835 votes), Anthony Hill (851), Robert Thompson Crawshay (833), William Thomas,

Esq., landowner (821), Benjamin Martin agent to Penydarren Works (826), John Evans, manager of the Dowlais Works (737). D. W. James, merchant (807), Walter Thomson, banker (696), Edward Purchase, farmer (780), David Evans, banker (747), Edward Morgan, landowner (676), William Merrick, Lawyer (688), Lewis Lewis, merchant (700), James Ward Russell, solicitor (633), Samuel Thomas, coal owner (607). Guest was elected Chairman.

[37] MH13/125, letter (n.d., probably early April 1853), anonymous voter to Merthyr Tydfil Union and Board of Health. John Jones, a Dowlais grocer, wrote to the Beneral Board of Health. 7 April 1853, as follows: "Will you be so kind as to inform me whether it is legal for the Iron Masters or any other party to send their Agents to follow the deliverers of the Voting papers dictating to the voters how to fill them—and not only that but to fill them out for them, *and cross the names of other candidates out,* the abuse here has been very great—plenty of evidence to prove it—ready and willing."

[38] At a slightly later date G. T. Clark, the senior trustee of the Dowlais Works successfully blocked the fourth attempt to incorporate the town on the grounds that "what would be good for Merthyr would not be good for Dowlais". The whole history of the movement for incorporation is eloquent testimony to the massive power of the iron-masters and the inffectiveness of the middle classes. In general, consult H. W. Southey's essay in Wilkins, *op. cit.*

[39] MH 13/125, Williams Simmons to the G.B.H., dated 2 March 1855.

[40] For the literature regarding these movements consult E. W. Evans, *The Miners of South Wales* (Cardiff, 1961), J. Morris and L. J. Williams, *The South Wales Coal Industry,* 1841-1875 (Cardiff, 1958).

DR. THOMAS PRICE AND THE ELECTION OF 1868
IN MERTHYR TYDFIL

A STUDY IN NONCONFORMIST POLITICS*

PART I

'There is something in the history of this election', wrote
Gohebydd (John Griffith) with reference to the general election of
1868 at Merthyr Tydfil, 'which makes it a kind of "public
property"—as if everyone had a voice in it; and the representatives of those boroughs (i.e. Merthyr Tydfil and Aberdare)
are regarded not as the representatives of Merthyr and
Aberdare only, but of the Principality itself . . . and here alone
of all the Welsh boroughs, it is permissible to say that the
election is almost entirely in the hands of the people, and that
these are almost exclusively Nonconformists'.[1] This had been
Gohebydd's view of the significance of this election since its
earliest stages when he had argued that in the formation of a
public opinion Aberdare and Merthyr were to Wales what
London was to England.[2] Later, when the election was over,
he was still of the same opinion, and attributed the courageous
victories of the north Walians to the splendid example of
Merthyr in returning Henry Richard at the head of the poll.[3]
This was by no means the view of all Welsh Nonconformists:
the breakdown of local particularisms in general elections
which such a view implied was resented in some quarters, and
nowhere more so, as we shall see, than in Merthyr Tydfil itself.
Nevertheless, it was distinctively the attitude adopted by the
generality of Welsh Nonconformists leaders such as Thomas
Gee and Henry Richard himself,[4] and it is this displacement of
local by 'national' issues which is the most important symptom
of a change in the nature of Welsh politics at this time. The
antecedents of this change and the nature of some of the
agencies which helped to create and to make effective the new
public opinion in the country at large, I have discussed in
another place.[5] The object of this study is to examine the role
of one of the main exponents of the new view of Welsh politics
in a context of time and place which appeared to be uniquely

suitable for the successful application of those principles in practice. This will enable us to assess with some confidence the relative importance of 'national' as against local interests and issues in the most important of the Welsh constituencies, and so to assist us towards an understanding of the nature of Welsh politics in the mid-nineteenth century.

*   *   *

By Easter of 1867, when the general election of 1868 in Merthyr Tydfil can be said to have begun,[6] the Rev. Thomas Price, M.A., Ph.D. (or Price Penpound, as he was universally known), may be said to have reached the zenith of his influence in the social and political affairs of Aberdare and Merthyr and of the Principality at large. His local influence was such that it was inevitable that he should play a dominant role in the election; his reputation in the country was such that the nature of this role could be confidently predicted. In the event, not only were his attitudes and actions the reverse of what had been expected of him, but they were, in addition, repudiated by the classes of people in his community whose leader he was. To understand how this situation came about it is necessary, before examining in detail his role in the election itself, firstly to analyse the nature of his power in the constituency both as regards local and parliamentary politics, and secondly, his standing in the Principality as Nonconformist political leader. These two aspects of his reputation are, of course, organically related; nevertheless, they can be clearly distinguished in this way, because such a distinction was inherent in the parliamentary politics of the time, and it was his refusal so to distinguish which accounts for the failure of his leadership.

*   *   *

Thomas Price[7] arrived in Aberdare to take charge of the Baptist church at Carmel (or Penpound as it was then known) towards the end of 1845 when he was 25 years of age, after having spent three and a half years at the Baptist College at Pontypool. For some five years previous to entering College he had been employed as a painter by the contractors Peto and

Dr. Thomas Price in youth and age.
Photo: Cynon Valleys Libraries.

Gazelle, having before that completed his apprenticeship at Brecon. Little is known about his early years, either at Brecon or London, but is relevant to note that at a very tender age this son of a peasant of Maes-y-cwper, Breconshire, had shown unusual initative in that he had managed to save sufficient from his wages as a servant boy in the Clifton family to pay his indentures. There, also, he had broken with family tradition by joining the Baptist church at Watergate, and it was during this time that he evinced an interst in learning and in public speaking. His apprenticeship completed, he walked to London where he followed his trade as a painter for some four years. At London he continued to educate himself, and evidently to take an active and intelligent interest in affairs both secular and religious. He enrolled in Dr. Birkbeck's Mechanics' Institute, and he seems to have attracted sufficient attention to himself as an opponent of Owenite socialism for this fact to be remembered to his credit in later years.

In 1845 the parish of Aberdare was experiencing a population explosion.[8] The census returns of 1841 had shown that its population had increased five-fold since the beginning of the century—from 1,486 in 1801 to 6,471 in 1841. Twenty years later it had trebled again, until by 1871—roughly the period covered by this essay—the parish contained more than 40,000 people; that is to say, an increase of the order of twenty-seven times in the course of the century. Price's arrival coincided with the second and most marked phase of this growth which began in the early 1840s and which was caused by the rapid development of the sale-coal industry in the parish. In the previous decade, from about 1818, people had been attracted into the valley by the growing prosperity of the older ironworks which were being taken over and reorganized by established firms of ironmasters from outside the parish.[9] Thus, in 1818, Richard Crawshay, of Cyfarthfa in the Merthyr valley, purchased the almost defunct ironworks at Hirwaun, subsequently enlarging them and placing them under independent management. The Abernant Ironworks, established in 1800 by F. and R. Tappington, were taken over in 1819 by Rowland Fothergill, whose company already owned flourishing works at Tredegar and Pont-hir, near Chepstow. In 1823 he also took over the sole management of the Aberdare Iron Company at Llwydcoed, purchasing it outright in 1846. Both these concerns passed into the ownership of his nephew, Richard Fothergill, the future member of parliament for Merthyr. The Gadlys Iron Company was founded in 1827 by Matthew Wayne, who had previously managed the Cyfarthfa furnaces for Richard Crawshay and enjoyed a profitable partnership with Sir Joseph Bailey at Nant-y-glo. Although small by comparison with Llwydcoed and Abernant it was, nevertheless, expanding throughout our period, and this despite the fact that from the late '30s onwards the Waynes were increasingly turning their attention to the production of sale-coal. Population growth in this first period was associated with this resurgent activity in the iron industry. Thus Hirwaun expanded very rapidly, and the hamlets of Llwydcoed and Abernant became small townships, while Aberdare village itself, where the Gadlys works and its associated colliery were sited, grew in importance as well as in size. Nevertheless, the parish as a whole, compared with its neighbouring parish of Merthyr Tydfil, was still not significantly industrialized in this early period. The census returns of 1831 showed that 13.8 per cent. of the total numbers employed were in agriculture as compared with 3.2 per cent. in Merthyr, and only 1.2 per cent. as against 19.8 per cent. directly engaged in manufacture.[10]

The second period in the industrial history of the parish opened in 1837 with the sinking of a pit to the Four Foot steam coal seams by the Waynes in association with three others, on land belonging to one of the partners, William Thomas David, at Aber-nant-y-groes, Cwm-bach.[11] This venture was distinct from the iron interests of the Waynes, and was planned for the production of steam coal for export to London and other markets. Its success stimulated others to emulate these pioneers. Three years later Thomas Powell, who had been in the coal trade as producer and shipper for twenty years, began sinking a pit in Cwm-bach, and two years later struck the same seam. This was the first of five pits sunk by Powell during the 1840s, but in addition others had been sunk by local capitalists, notably by David Williams at Ynys-cynon, and David Davis at Blaen-gwawr, and by immigrant industrialists such as Crawshay Bailey at Aberaman, Thomas Nixon at Werfa, and George Elliot in the lower region of the valley.

This was the turning point in the industrial history of the valley, and the cause of the second and greatest period of population growth through which Thomas Price lived. A study of the enumerators' returns for the censuses of 1851 and 1861 shows clearly that it was the new colliery districts which were attracting the immigrants.[12] In particular, the two southern hamlets of Fforchaman (west of the river Cynon) and Cefn-pennar (east of the river) which previously had been agricultural, supporting but a sparse population, saw the creation of new townships in the vicinities of the new pits. The valley bottom itself, along which the canal ran and, from 1846, the railway, came to be completely built up, as did most of the tributary valleys of the river. Meanwhile, the town itself was expanding and taking on its character as the nucleus of a much greater, straggling conurbation filling the whole valley.

It was estimated by de la Bèche in 1845 that one-third of the population increase was by birth and two-thirds by immigration.[13] The vast majority of these latter appear to have come from the adjacent counties of Glamorgan and Breconshire, but a substantial and increasing proportion came from counties further west. The long post-war agricultural depression, the bad harvests of the '40s, and the continual pressure of a rising population on inadequate resources compelled these people to move in search of a livelihood. The expanding industrial areas such as Merthyr and Aberdare were insatiable in their demand for labour, and the immigrants flocked into these areas in ever-growing numbers. The attractive forces of the 'Awstralia Morgannwg' ('the Australia of Glamorgan'), as one inhabitant called it,[14] were probably no less enticing that the repellent ones of life in the countryside in the motivations of these immigrants. Certainly, wages could be high, and the opportunities for a higher standard of living mor available. But the immigrants were in effect colonizing their own country, and they came to townships which were characterized by 'an absence of those civic relations and institutions which exist in more mixed commercial communities'.[15] T. W. Rammell, from the Board of Health, noted in 1850 that 'there were no men of middle station, none of the ordinary class of "residents" who are to be found more or less in number, in every other town in England, however they may be disconnected from the ordinary commerce of the place'.[16] Rammell saw only the ironmasters, their agents and workmen, and such tradesmen and professional men as were necessary to supply the needs of these groups. In fact, a nascent middle class consisting of the agents and professional people, the lesser industrialists and the shopkeepers, existed, but in the early decades of the growth of the town there was lacking that sense of community of interest and of aim which might enable it to build traditions of civic duty and function, which was probably what Rammell saw to be lacking. Aberdare, like Merthyr, was likely to be a place to escape from once a man had made enough to retire.[17]

These facts, the too-rapid growth of the town, and the absence of an established, indigenous middle class, help to account for the fact that 'to all intents and purposes, (Aberdare) was as destitute of civic government as the smallest rural village in the empire'.[18] There was a complete absence of proper sanitary arrangements, no permanent sewage disposal, no adequate water supply, so that in some places 'the lower classes seemed in danger of being engulfed and poisoned by their own excretions'.[19] The death rate was consequently inordinately high—2.17 per cent. (as compared with 2.6 per cent. in Merthyr Tydfil), and the average expectation of life low—for the children of colliers and artisans, 17½ years, for tradesmen, 32 years.[20] Conditions began to improve in the late '50s, but even then, with the Public Health Acts in force, the men who controlled local government were extremely dilatory in their actions, and it needed a succession of typhus and cholera epidemics to awaken the public conscience in these matters.

The religious life which Price entered into was also changing rapidly. The basic denominational pattern already existed and, taken together, it is probable that the percentage increase of the main denominations was not far short of the population increase in the parish. This was particularly true of the Baptists among whom Price had come to work. According to him, the growth of his denomination up to 1860 had been proportionately greater than that of the parish in general.[21] For this denomination the period of greatest expansion, involving the foundation of new churches, was between 1846 and 1866.[22] In Aberdare parish itself at the latter date there were no less than eleven Baptist chapels in addition to Calfaria, with a total communing membership of over 3,500.[23] The features to be noted about this growth are, first, that all these chapels, either directly or indirectly, owed their existence to the expansionist policies of Price and were offshoots of the mother-church at Calfaria, and second, that the connection between the mother- and daughter-churches was closely maintained and cultivated.[24] Thus, from 1854 onwards, the Sunday Schools held an annual festival, and, in addition, quartely meetings became a regular feature of their organization. There was an annual *eisteddfod,* the profits of which went, in turn, to the participating Sunday Schools.[25] From time to time baptismal services were held at convenient places in the river Cynon, which was attended by all the associated churches.[26] At all such gatherings and functions Dr. Price presided—indeed, their great success was due to his extraordinary organizing and administrative talents. In a very real sense most of the chapels associated with Calfaria were his creations. They had all hived-off in accordance with a carefully conceived procedure, by which the authority of the mother-church was maintained long after, it might be, they had achieved full independence. Most of them had started as branches of Calfaria, their executive bodies being chosen from among the Calfaria diaconate.[27] In this way the overall organization was the expression of a more personal organization—a complex of kith and kin relationships dominated by Price himself. He was known to all, his authority accepted in all matters pertaining to the well-being of the denomination in Aberdare—so much so, that he was often known affectionately, but perhaps a little ironically, as *Father Price.*[28]

It follows that Dr. Price, as the acknowledged head of the strongest denomination in the Aberdare side of the Merthyr Tydfil constituency, should have exerted an influence in denominational and religious affairs in his locality far greater than that wielded by any other minister. Apart from the Unitarians, who were numerically weak though socially and politically strong,[29] the other denominations lacked the central organization and social cohesion which Price had given the Baptists. Among the Independents, for example, though there were some outstanding personalities, there were no ministers with the kind of extra-ecclesiastical authority possessed by Price.[30] The Independents had increased by parthogenesis like the Baptists, but there does not seem to have been the same continuing cohesion between the mother and sister-churches in that denomination, with the result that no one minister could be said to enjoy a larger measure of prestige than his fellows or exert a more compelling influence. The various Methodist connections,[31] though numerically powerful as a whole and accustomed to acting together, were governed by constitutions which militated against active political and social action. What influence they exerted as denominations was determined more by the dictates of the county Associations to which they belonged rather than by the exigencies of local conditions.

Calfaria Chapel, Monk St., Aberdare.
Photo: Cynon Valleys Libraries.

This leadership in a well-organized cohesive denomination in a rapidly expanding community provided the basis for an equal authority within the body of Nonconformity as whole in Aberdare, and, to a lesser extent, in the constituency in general. In Nonconformist politics Price first came into prominence both locally and nationally in 1847, on the occasion of the publication of the famous *Reports of the Commissioners of Inquiry into the State of Education in Wales,* when his name was coupled with that of Rev. Evan Jones (*Ieuan Gwynedd*), Rev. William Rees (*Gwilym Hiraethog*), Henry Richard, and others

as one of the most effective critics of those *Reports*.[32] The
inhabitants of Aberdare had been particularly incensed by the
'evidence' submitted to the commissioners by the vicar of the
parish, the Rev. John Griffith, who had entered into his living
only shortly before the commissioners arrived.[33] In his memorandum Griffith had drawn attention to the degraded character
of the women of Aberdare relative to the men, to the fact that
sexual promiscuity was an accepted social convention, to the
drunkeness and improvidence of the miners, and to the em-
otional levity of the religious observances of the Nonconformists. Price had immediately challenged the vicar to a
public debate, and although Griffith had declined, saying that
he would never give Price that honour, the meeting arranged
for that purpose had been held, and Price had emerged as the
undoubted champion of Nonconformity in Aberdare. His
speech on that occasion brought him to the forefront as a formidable controversialist and orator, while the fact that it was he
who had initiated the agitation and arranged the demonstration indicated that here was a politician with the ability to
give practical effect and expression to the feelings and aspirations of the, as yet, unorganized body of Nonconformists.
Moreover, it gave him a kind of parity, if not yet of leadership.
among the new rising generation of Welsh coalowners and
colliery proprietors who were also Nonconformists, and who
were later, with Price, to form the core of the Liberal Nonconformist caucus in Aberdare. His marriage in that same year to
Mrs. Anne Gilbert, daughter and heiress of William Thomas
David, Aber-nant-y-groes, one of the six partners in the
sinking of Wayne's first pit, brought him into a closer relationship with this group. Thus David Davis, Maes-y-ffynnon, and
David Williams, Ynys-cynon (*Alaw Goch*), both on the thres-
holds of their industrial careers, and both destined to play
dominant roles in the cultural and political life of the locality,
were official speakers at the meeting.[34] Others who took part
included a prosperous business man and, of course, ministers
of religion.[35] Shortly after, Price was publicly thanked at a
special meeting for the leading part he had taken in this
contest.[36]

'Yn amser brad y llyfrau gleision.'

Of the resolutions passed at that meeting to protest against the Blue Books, two were explicity directed at the vicar or the parish. The first denied the accuracy of his views and expressed disapproval of his conduct, while the second called for the publication in Welsh of this memorandum 'it being but fair that Mr. Griffith should tell his parishioners in their own language what he has already told the Government respecting their state of morals'.[37] In fact, this represented a climacteric in the growing church *versus* chapel controversy out of which a distinct body of political opinion was to emerge in the constituency. Ieuan Gwynedd and others had already demonstrated, or were in process of demonstrating, that the commissioners were guilty not only of procedural errors and systematic confusions of method, but also of sectarian bias in so far as they relied on the evidence of church people who were not only unsympathetic to the aspirations of Dissenters, but incapable by reason of their vested interests of appreciating them.[38] Arguments such as these dealing with the Reports as a whole were effective catalysts of opinion in the country at large. In the localities they were made politically potent by being 'personalized' as at Aberdare, where Price and the vicar came to embody two apparently incompatible religious and political points of view.

If the contest with the vicar had marked the emergence of a redoubtable champion of Nonconformity subsequent contest of a similar nature[39] served not only to consolidate and enhance this reputation, but also to bring Price into the centre of local politics. The Reports themselves inevitably stimulated such a movement since they were of the widest political significance, not only centrally, at Westminster, but also locally. They had described in details the deficencies in the educational facilities provided by the various organizations, public and private, in Aberdare, and had related these deficiencies to the kind of society emerging in the valleys. The commissioners had found, for instance, that in Aberdare there was accommodation in the ten existing schools for only 1,317 children, and that apart from the National schools (accommodating 135) there were no workmen's schools[40] and more provided by the Dissenters. By implication, they considered the failure of the ironmasters to give a lead in this respect to be a serious criticism of their social morality since it was they who were creating a new type of society in which the ironworks were replacing the ancient units of social structure in which their employees had previously moved.[41] By implication, too, Dissent was indicted for its failure to provide British schools. Price, while rejecting some of the social analysis of the commissioners, accepted the validity of their criticism of the Dissenters, and it was largely due to his energy and vision that a committee of Nonconformists was immediately formed, charged with the task of founding a school under the aegis of the British and Foreign School Society. Price was appointed secretary and included on it were David Williams (*Alaw Goch*), chairman; John Jones, a druggist, treasurer; Evan Griffiths of Hirwaun, a businessman; and three ministers representative of the major denominations.[42] Seven months later the Park Schools (or *Ysgol y Comin*) had been built on land provided by the trustees of the Bute Estate, and shortly afterwards were officially opened.

From the point of view of the political life of the parish this was an event of great significance. It was the first time the Nonconformists had acted together in response to a common stimulus and towards the realization of common aspirations. Moreover, since the venture, if it were to succeed, demanded a continuing organization, involved in this event was the creation of what came to be—or could easily be contrived to become—a kind of political caucus well adapted to the furtherance of Nonconformist aims in other directions and spheres. Its membership, as we have seen, was representative of the emerging political classes, of the newer industrial interests and the 'shopocracy', as well as the leaders of the old pattern of society—the farmers and small landowners.[43] It is important to notice, also, that the iron interest was not represented. The owners of all three iron-making concerns—Rowland Fothergill of the Aberdare Iron Company, the Waynes of the Gadlys Iron Company, and W. T. Crawshay of the Hirwaun Iron Company—were members of the established Church and supporters, therefore, of the National schools, which were likewise responding to the same stimuli. The major land and royalty owners were likewise adherents of the Church, and although ready—like the Bruces of Mountain Ash—to be associated with the British School committee, were, if anything, atipathetic to the extra-educational activities in which the committee was soon involved.

But if the ironmasters were excluded by religious persuasion—and perhaps by political antipathy—from the Nonconformist school committee, in all other respects they were a predominant and established influence. This was particularly true of the sphere of local government. When Price arrived in Aberdare late in 1844 the functions of local government were

divided between the Parish Vestry and the Poor Law Guardians of the Merthyr Tydfil Union, into which the parish of
Aberdare had been assimilated when the Poor Law Amendment Act had been applied in 1836. The most important
functions of local government had thus been removed from the
cognizance of the Vestry, and its subsequent history follows
closely those of similar parish governments overwhelmed by the
multifarious problems which rapid industrialization brought in
its wake—that is to say, the creation of special boards for the
more efficient administration of the more vital sectors of local
government, functioning as independent statutory bodies,
separately elected on a democratic franchise. In Aberdare, in
both of these instruments of local government—in the
administration of the Poor Laws and in the Vestry and its
offshoots—the ironmasters occupied positions of great, but not
of undisputed, power. Moreover, as during the thirty years with
which we are concerned in this essay the industrial pattern of the
valley was chagning, iron giving place to coal as the leading
industry so, too the pattern of political power changed cor-
respondingly. This political change, reflecting a social and
industrial shift, took place gradually during the first twenty
years of Price's domicile in Aberdare. It was a transition from
the older traditional social pattern characterized by the absence
of any powerful social group mid-way between the ironmaster
and the freeholder farming class, and the new emerging pattern
in which a middle class of indigenous coal proprietors allied with
the shopkeepers and tradesmen, the professional men, and the
Dissenting ministers, had come to predominate over both the
old groups. The histories of both the Vestry and the Union
illustrate this change. For instance, up to 1837, no business of
the slightest importance was transacted by the Vestry without
the ironmasters, or their agents, being present. On less important occasions the majority of men signing the minutes were freeholders and farmers.[44] This remained true even after the
Vestry had largely lost its powers to the Union and the other
statutory bodies. When these latter come to be formed, Fothergill, Wayne, or Crawshay Bailey invariably headed the lists of
elections, as, for instance, the Board of Highway Surveyors,[45]
or the Board of Health provisionally formed in 1853.[46] But by

the middle '50s the power-shift was pronounced, and the major organs of government were being run by the 'new men'. From this time forward it is these who predominate; indeed, they succeed in engineering the retirement from public life of the leading iron-master, Richard Fothergill.[47] Decisions respecting such diverse and controversial matters as health, highways, social and cultural amenities—ranging from the decision to levy a rate for a new burial-ground, the Church-rate question itself, the creation of a gas company, the decision to enclose common land as a public recreation ground administered by the local Board of Health—decisions such as these were, in fact, being taken by the 'new' industrialists and their allies. It is these who were determining the slant of social progress. And among these Thomas Price was an acknowledged leader.

Richard Fothergill.
Photo: Cynon Valleys Libraries.

The history of the Vestry, in this context, is less important than that of the Union, but here again, both in the elections of Guardians and in the work of the Guardians elected, the same shift of power and decision-making to the emerging middle class allied with the Dissenters is clearly to be seen. In the first election in 1836, and annually until 1850, one ironmaster and two freeholders or farmers were elected by the parish.[48] In 1851, when the number of Aberdare Guardians was increased to four,[49] there is a significant change. The elections of that year resulted in the return of an ironmaster (Richard Fothergill), the vicar, a farmer, a coal-proprietor. This remained the pattern until 1852 when the ironmaster was replaced by his agent, the vicar by a Dissenting minister. The agent returned was Rees Hopkin Rhys, agent at one time to Fothergill, but also a businessman in his own right and soon to become a coal-proprietor,[50] and destined to excercise a powerful influence in

Rees Hopkin Rhys ('Blind Rhys') 1819-1899.
Photo: Cynon Valleys Libraries.

local affairs. The Dissenting minister who ousted the vicar was Thomas Price. Two years later—in 1855—there is another slight adjustment, Price being replaced by a tradesman. In 1860, there was a further change with the granting of two additional Guardians. The pattern now was: three coal-proprietors, one farmer, one tradesman, and the vicar again. In 1861-62 the coal-proprietors number four, having gained the seat occupied by the farmer. Thus, by the early '60s local government in Aberdare was firmly in the hands of the indigenous coal-proprietors allied with the tradesmen, and having a strong Dissenting character.

It will be noticed that Dr. Price sat as a Guardian for only two years—from 1853 to 1855—a short period of service compared with most of the other Guardians. But the length of his service in that capacity should not obscure the importance of those two years in his career and in the developing political life of the community. First, it is essential to stress that his election was evidence of the emergence into politics of organized Nonconformity. The election of a Nonconformist minister was unprecedented in the Union, and in a way it was more remarkable than the contemporaneous emergence of the coal-owners—although it must be remembered that from 1847 he had been closely associated with them. Second, we must stress that Price appears to have been highly successful and popular as a Guardian. One admirer, with more poetic exaggeration than can be pardoned, thought of him as 'a second Howard to the poor', and of his residence, Rose Cottage, as a haven for the destitute.[51] Third, he appears to have given up his Guardianship in order to devote himself to the local Health Board. He had been indefatigable in persuading the community to adopt the Health of Towns Act, and during the period between 1852, when formal application was first made, and 1854 when the Act was applied,[52] Price was one of those made responsible for seeing that the details of the Act were anyway applied.

To sum up thus far, it is clear that Thomas Price's influence was based, apparently securely, first on his position as a leading Nonconformist minister and particularly among the Baptists, and second, on an alliance with the middle class coal-proprietors and tradesmen who, by the middle '50s had come to form the most important social group in the valley. Such an association between the 'clerical' leadership of Dissent and the rising wealthy classes was perhaps typical of most of the industrial communities in Wales at that time. Certainly, it seemed to be accepted as an organic part of those new urban societies, and recognized by some astute observers as a social phenomenon peculiar in Wales.[53] In some respects, however, Price was untypical of clerical Nonconformist leadership in so far as he had become himself a man of property and, to a limited extent, an entrepreneur in his own right. By his marriage to Mrs. Anne Gilbert, the daughter of Thomas David, Esq., Cwmdare, a landowner at Aber-nant-y-groes, he had allied himself to a substantial local family. When she died two years later, in 1849, Price inherited her quite considerable property.[54] Not only so, but her son, Edward Gilbert, who took the name of Price, became a prominent businessman, setting up as a broker and accountant, and later establishing a woollen mill in Aberdare—the South Wales and Glandare Woollen Manufactory (Ltd.), Aberdare, with a capital of £20,000.[55] Thomas Price was director of this concern. He was, also, at one time, a director of the Aberdare Gas Company.[56] He was, therefore, a man of substance, and, in this respect, on an equality with the businessmen with whom he associated, sharing some of their interests, understanding and sympathizing with their social and economic aspirations. It is, perhaps, understandable that his residence, Rose Cottage, Aberdare should be a large, detached house, much more the home of a prosperous professional man than of a one-time penurious Baptist minister.

Thomas Price's relations with other social groups, and particularly with the working classes, are most difficult to define. His ministerial authority was clearly effective here also, since the bulk of Nonconformists were working-class people. There can be no doubt either that although fortune and an aggressive, driving personality and a more than average intelligence had enabled him to climb out of the class into which he had been born, he felt, nevertheless, a genuine affinity with the workers. In his relations with them, although gruff and sometimes domineering, there was no suggestion of 'class' superiority or of aloofness. His language was forceful and picturesque, very often, according to his biographies, scarcely becoming a minister of the gospel,[57] but, at least, it was the language of common discourse. Moreover, he never forgot his peasant origins, his tough working class youth and early manhood in London. Nor did he allow his congregations and audiences to forget these autobiographical facts: indeed, the tale of his walk to London from his home in Brecon at the age of 16 with 13s. 4d. in his pocket to work as a journeyman painter was a kind of saga in the Samuel Smiles tradition—as it were, 'a spiritual' counterpart to the Crawshay saga.[58]

Nevertheless, his influence with the working class, and particularly among the colliers and ironworkers, did not depend exclusively on denominational or ministerial factors, on his place in the formal politics of the parish, or on his connections with trade and industry. It was based rather on two other aspects of his career which grew in importance as time went on, namely, his enthusiasm for Friendly Societies, and his work and policy as an editor of newspapers and magazines.

His association with the Friendly Societies began soon after his arrival in Aberdare, at a time when the fraternal orders were absorbing the older multiplicity of ill-organized and insecure societies which had characterized South Wales in the previous decades.[59] He belonged to all the major orders—to the Oddfellows, the True Ivorites, the Alfredites, the Foresters—but it was to the well-being of the Oddfellows and the Ivorites that he devoted most of his time and energy, and in whose councils he attained highest eminence.[60] He became head of the South Wales Unity of Oddfellows at a time when there were 16-18,000 members, and in 1864 he was elected vice-president of the Order, and in the following year, Grand Master, being the first Welshman to be so honoured. He had already served as president of the Ivorites—the only Welsh Order—in 1859, and there is no doubt that the expansion of the Order in the years following owed much to his dynamic energy and drive.[61] His knowledge of the law relating to friendly societies was detailed and profound: he was known as the Welsh Solicitor-General of Friendly Societies, was consulted even by professional lawyers in these matters, and himself often conducted cases involving societies in the courts of law.[62] In these ways he became almost indispensable and, by transference of fame, as it were, enhanced his reputation among the working classes in other directions as well.

Of scarcely less importance as establishing and strengthening these ties was his work as editor of various periodicals. From 4 June 1855 he edited *Y Gwron*[63] with W. Williams (*Caledfryn*), and A. J. Davies of Aberaman. Previously, from its foundation on 21 December 1854 by John Josiah Jones,[64] at that time of Carmarthen, *Y Gwron* had been edited singly by W. Williams. The transfer of the paper to Jones's new publishing offices in Aberdare, in April 1854, and the appointment of the two new editors, probably saved the paper from extinction. By July 1855, it appeared weekly instead of fortnightly as before, and its circulation had increased greatly.[65] The transfer of the paper to Aberdare, at the centre of the most populous part of the coalfield, would have ensured an increased circulation, but its success was due largely to the editorial policy of Price and Davies. It became a livelier paper, reflecting the interests and points of view of an industrial, rather than an agricultural, society, even though it circulated in the rural districts as well. Considerable space was given to local affairs, particularly those affecting the interests of workmen, such as safety, compensation, insurance, master and man relationships, and it always provided a forum for discussion in which they could publicize their views, even when the editors were totally out of sympathy with them. This was of inestimable value to the workmen, particularly during times of depression when *Y Gwron* remained almost the only paper in which they could be sure of a fair hearing, or have their views published without unfair comment or in a garbled manner.[66]

The same is true of the other paper edited by Price, the denominational *Seren Cymru.* He became sole editor of this magazine in 1860, and soon turned it into something quite distinctive and unusual in such publications. It devoted, on the whole, less space than most of its contemporaries to denominational and ecclesiastical affairs and more to current politics and ideas. Both in appearance and purpose it resembled the weekly newspaper-cum-magazine, reflecting the radical politics of the locality, giving a firm guide in current affairs, carrying much educative and 'elevating' material and, again, providing the working classes with a forum. It is quite clear that these classes had confidence in the editorial policy of these papers, and looked to them for the publication of their views, and for articles and other material reflecting their own particular interests and concerns.

Complementary to these journalistic activities was Price's work as a lecturer. In this he was indefatigable and enjoyed a tremendous popularity. Current affairs were his speciality,[67] and though his lectures were, more often than not, long and elaborate, they were always carefully prepared and illustrated by maps and diagrams of his own design. In the fields of foreign affairs, politics, and industrial topics he was extremely well-informed, and since, as one observer noted, the Welsh worker 'was fond (there is no accounting for taste) of hearing lectures'[68] it is probable that he reached a much wider audience in this way than if he had confined himself to writing. In politics he expounded the views of the radical wing of the Liberal Party and of the 'political' Nonconformists led by the Liberation Society. His interest in industrial affairs lay less in the economics of the subject than in the more sociological aspects—questions of safety and inspection, of the double versus the single shift, and master-man relationships generally. These were all important issues in the coalfields, and came to a head in the crisis of 1867-68, during the elections, at which time both Price and the colliers were compelled to define more closely than heretofore their attitudes to the problems involved, and to bring out into the open, therefore, the latent differences between them.

What these latent differences were we can discover by studying the history of Price's relations with the men on the question of safety, the double shift, and strikes. Up to 1867 it is fairly clear that on the question of safety in the mines the colliers and Price saw, more or less, eye to eye. After that date, the question of the double shift made it well-nigh impossible for them to agree any longer, for, on this important question, the men were fiercely and diametrically opposed to the policy advocated by Price. His interest in safety dated from the Lletty-Shenkin explosion of 1849 when fifty-two men and boys were killed.[69] The steam-coal pits of the Aberdare area were peculiarly liable to explosions because of the volatile nature of the coal, the increasing depth at which it was mined, and, above all, the effects of the rate of expansion in production which involved inadequate safety measures (even by the requirements of the Act of 1850) and the employment of insufficiently trained and technically ill-equipped officials.[70] In 1856, Price drew up a memorandum on the subject, which he submitted to the Inspector of Mines. In this he advocated an improvement in underground communications, and an improved system of inspection, involving the appointment of six sub-inspectors charged with visiting every colliery at least once a month. They would be paid a maximum salary of £200 per annum from a Consolidated Fund set up for the purpose to which masters and men would contribute. In addition, he advocated the creation of a Perpetual Fund, financed in the same way, out of which compensation to the victims of explosions, or their dependent relatives, would be paid. The colliers were unenthusiastic. They agreed on the need for a sub-inspectorate, and wanted more and not less governmental supervision, but they wished the sub-inspectors to be chosen from among themselves, experienced colliers rather than general engineers, 'of the people' rather than 'of the masters'.[72] From time to time, Price returned to this theme, especially in the '60s, but without eliciting much support from the workmen who, for other reasons, may have been somewhat suspicious of his motives and disinclined to be led by him on this issue. Not until 1867 did safety become once again a great cause of discord in the coalfield, and by that time, as we shall see, it was complicated by the related question of shift working, and of politics, in both of which the colliers were taking a very independent line.

If we are correct in inferring a certain lack of confidence between Price and the colliers with respect to working conditions, there is clearer evidence that his attempts to act as an independent conciliator in industrial disputes were not wholly acceptable to the working men. The evidence is of two kinds. First, and indirectly, Price was a whole-hearted subscriber to the view that trade unions, of whatever kind, were against the 'real' interest of the workmen. Believing in the economic doctrines of the Manchester School, he taught that any kind of organization among the workers designed to compel the masters to improve working conditions, or to raise the price of their labour, was a dangerous interference with the mechanisms of trade which, when allowed to function freely, would best ensure prosperity for both sides and for the community at large. Trade unions were invariably the creations of vicious and evil men, importations from over the border, and invariably wedded to the hated doctrines of socialism. Thus, in September 1863, he had written a leading article in *Seren Cymru* condemning the attempt to form a National Miners' Union, and arguing that in the nature of the economic processes such an organization could not achieve more for the men than was inherently theirs already if they but exercised restraint and devoted themselves to self-help through education. The gradual improvement in wages which had taken place in the early '60s, and, later, the so-called Sheffield trade union outrages of 1867, seemed to vindicate his arguments.[73] Nevertheless, the workmen refused to adopt these attitudes, and in times of industrial disputes, strove to create unions which they hoped would be permanent.

Perhaps they suspected Price's attitudes and doctrines as being more favourable to the masters than to the men, and here they believed they had direct evidence of his real views. Generally speaking, when the men were striking for a rise or, as was more often the case, striking against a wage reduction, Price invariably argued in favour of a return to work. The classic example of this—apart from 1867, which will be described later—occurred in the great winter strike of 1857-58. This strike against a penal reduction of 20 per cent, is of great importance in the history of the coalfield, not merely because it largely determined what the political attitudes of the workmen would be in the election of 1868. Briefly, the situation was this. By the autumn of 1857 the post-war depression was such that it was rumoured that the soft-coal proprietors had determined on a 15 per cent. wage reduction. This was a half of the 30 per cent. rise granted during the three previous boom years, and a delegate meeting of the colliers involved, while agreeing that some reduction was inevitable, determined to send a delegation to the masters to argue for a smaller reduction. A full report of this meeting was published in *Y Gwron*,[74] and in a guarded leader Price gave measured support to these views while stressing the inadvisability of striking. Nevertheless, the reduction of 15 per cent. was officially announced on 26 November and, almost immediately, between 6,000 and 8,000 colliers brought out their tools.

The strike, which lasted well into January, and soon involved the Monmouthshire colliers as well, was a peculiarly bitter and memorable one. Soldiers were quartered in the town, and there was rioting, violence, and looting throughout the coalfields. It was memorable, too, for the way in which it was conducted on the colliers' side. The violence was not as prolonged or as endemic as, in such a protracted strike, it might have become. This must be attributed to the quality of leadership. There was no directing central organization as such: each colliery was free to negotiate as it would, but there were recognized leaders, men of character and of intelligence who, while they could not negotiate on behalf of the men with the united body of masters, could and did arrange mass meetings and use the press to publicize their views. There was movement towards union in the South Wales coalfield in those days, and the men had produced their own leaders, who were well equipped intellectually and morally to lead the men.

Price was involved as editor of one of the few papers in which the men had any confidence, though it was noticeable that, while claiming to be independent of party and calling for rational behaviour, his comments could often be constructed as being highly critical of the men.[75] He interfered more directly on the occasion of a public meeting of colliers in Aberdare addressed by H. A. Bruce the Member of Parliament for the borough. A little previously Bruce had persuaded the Home Secretary to recall the troops[76] and intervened with the master, persuading them to postpone the imposition of an additional 5 per cent. reduction. With these eminently wise achievements to his credit, Bruce now addressed the striking colliers on the floor of the Market. He made two speeches. In

A. H. Bruce (1st Lord Aberdare).
Photo: Cynon Valleys Libraries.

the first, he expounded impeccably the economics of the situation, and argued that on his occasion the masters were not acting unjustly. The miners were visibly impressed; after all, they had been prepared for a reduction from the beginning of the depression. After some discussion, Bruce then went on to make a second speech, in tone and content utterly different from the first. Now he launched into an attack on the colliers for demanding, not only more than the industry could afford to pay, but more than they could with equity expect to receive. Why should Aberdare colliers demand 20s. a week while farm labourers in Glamorgan and Carmarthenshire reared their families on 11s. to 12s.? From his own experience of colliers at Mountain Ash it was perfectly easy for them to live on less than they were demanding. He ended with denunciation of strikes in general, pointed to their ineffectiveness, and illustrated their demoralizing effects from the events of the strike of 1849-50.[77]

This was a disastrous speech: it did nothing to ease the situation as was shown by the continuation of the strike till desparation ended it on 15 January 1858, while it merely confirmed the men in their hatred of Bruce. Price was associated with this and shared some of the odium, since he was with Bruce on the platform and translated what he had said into Welsh for the benefit of the monoglot.[78] It was actions such as these which tended to generate in the men's minds attitudes of scepticism with regard to Price's real opinions and sympathies.

It scarcely needs pointing out that Price was most successful and influential when crusading on issues upon which his middle class allies and the working classes saw eye to eye. There had been one such issue in his early career, one which, coming soon after his campaign against the Blue Books and before his entry into the formal politics of the town, even further enhanced his authority—namely, his successful campaign against the introduction of a Truck Shop in Aberdare by the Aberdare Iron Company. It appears that soon after his appointment as general manager of the Company in June 1850, Richard Fothergill, succeeding his uncle Rowland in that capacity, determined 'to alter the system of paying workmen which had been prevalent up to that time',[79] by which the men had had their 'pay', their 'large draw' after the pay, and a 'draw' every week if required, both 'pays' and 'draws' being in the coin of the realm and in the office of the works cashier. The opportunity came in October, when John Lewis, a grocer, vacated his shop on premises owned by the Company, which were thereupon occupied by another firm of grocers (with whom Fothergill was connected by marriage), who used it as Truck shop. At the same time, the old 'draw' was abolished, and both 'pay' and 'draw' transferred from the cashier's office to the new shop, and it was alleged that pressure was being put on the workmen to deal there.[80]

These proceedings were viewed with 'universal execration' by the shopkeepers, coal-owners, and workmen alike, for Aberdare prided itself on the fact that it was almost unique among ironworks town in being free of the scourge of Truck, and of never having experienced its full rigours.[81] A public meeting was called on 9 April in the Town Hall, which 'was crammed to suffocation', at which Price was the main speaker. His purpose was to propose the establishment of an Anti-Truck Society, and he did so in one of the most remarkable speeches of his career. The organization thus set up consisted of shop-keepers, all the independent coal-proprietors, workmen, the vicar, and dissenting ministers. Its object was to procure evidence against the Abernant Company, to collect funds to sustain the costs of prosecution, and to defend any workman who might be victimized by the Company for giving evidence for the prosecution. [82]

The first case to be brought was on 20 April before H. A. Bruce and two other magistrates, but as the Abernant solicitor refused to plead and paid the trivial fine, no decision was reached on that occasion. But at the Aberdare petty session on 10 May, the case was at least publicly argued, and judgment entered against the Abernant Company and the minimum fine imposed in the hope that (in the words of H. A. Bruce) 'the system we have declared to be illegal, he (Richard Fothergill) will think proper to discontinue for the future'. [83] Fothergill responded by refusing to pay the fine, and by instructing his solicitors to remove the case to a higher court, while the Society, on its part, immediately filed further information against the Company. Not until 7 June was the matter finally determined when, at the Aberdare court, the Company 'having been convinced of their course in acting contrary to the law, were determined to give up the truck system entirely'. [84] This was a notable victory for the Society, and for no one more so than Dr. Price. In fact, the understanding given by the Company appears to have been agreed in separate negotiations between Price and Fothergill. Certainly, Price later claimed the credit for it. [85]

There is no doubt that Price was justified in attaching considerable importance to this episode in his career. It is undeniable that the workmen as a whole, and especially the 'respectable' elements among them, were deeply grateful to him for his leadership on that occasion. Politically, however, the benefit accruing to his esteem among the working classes may not have been as unequivocal as one might have expected. The agitation against the shop had been managed throughout by the shopkeepers and tradesmen, and it could be argued, as some work-men did argue, that the Anti-Truck Association was nothing but a middle class conspiracy by 'a body of unprincipled persons' determined to exclude from the distributive trade company-controlled grocers who regularly undercut the local tradesmen.[86] Colour was given to this when shortly afterwards 1,500 to 2,500 workmen attended a demonstration to deplore the attacks on Fothergill, and an attempt by Price to persuade Fothergill's Treforest workmen of the benefits of Truck-free society ended in fiasco.[87]

One of the unexpected and paradoxical by-products of this contest was an alliance in local and parliamentary politics between Price and Fothergill. It is noticeable that in his con-duct of the anti-Truck crusade Price had been careful to avoid personalities. The stipendiary magistrate, H. A. Bruce, had been far more outspoken than Price, and, characteristically, Bruce and Fothergill were thereafter political enemies. Not so Dr. Price. If anything, he and Fothergill came closer together, and, subsequently, the latter found no warmer supporter in Aberdare then the man who had led the prosecution in 1851. During the general election of 1868, for example, when past records were critically reviewed, it was Bruce who publicly attacked him on the Truck issue and Price who defended him.[88] But by then the association between Fothergill and Price—the Nonconformist minister and the Anglican iron-master—had become alomst a traditional element in Aberdare politics. Both served on the local Board of Health, Fothergill as its first chairman until hounded out of active participation in public affairs after the scandal of the 1857 local election.[89] On that famous occasion—a contest which occasioned great excitement—Fothergill, Dr. Roberts, Dr. Price, and Phillip John had been re-elected with an overwhelming majority.[90] The opposition, led by Thomas Evans, a mineral agent, there-upon examined the voting papers, and initiated proceedings against Fothergill for unfair practices, 'in an effort', as they put it, 'to clean up corrupt local elections'.[91] The award of the magistrate in dismissing the case had been that, although there was a clear factual basis for the charges against Fothergill, the prosecution had failed to prove intent. Consequently, the opposition pressed charges against Fothergill's agent, Rees Hopkin Rhys, a Guardian, but these also failed, as did *quo warranto* proceedings in Queen's Bench.[92] It seems fairly clear, from the records, that Fothergill and his party were technically guilty of the misdemeanours attributed to them, and since Price had, as it were, been returned 'on the same ticket' he was obliged to defend Fothergill. But he could do this only at the cost of alienating a section of the Nonconformist party among whom he had emerged ten years previously.

Similar tensions existed in parliamentary politics, but until 1868 they never became explicit. The reason for this is two-fold. In the first place, the Aberdare side of great Merthyr constituency was very much the weaker in terms of population, voters, and industrial strength. In 1831 the population of Merthyr was 22,083, that of Aberdare 3,691.[93] But by 1871 the difference was much less considerable, Aberdare having grown to 40,305, while Merthyr stood at 54,741. The most spectacular increase in population had, therefore, been in the Aberdare area, the period of greatest increase being between 1851 and 1871, when 26,000 had been added, Merthyr increasing by only 8,000 in the same two decades. The same applies to the numbers of voters—or, until 1867, of potential voters. In 1831 there had been an estimated 569 £10-householders in Merthyr parish, and only fifty-six in Aberdare.[94] But by 1868 Aberdare was providing almost half of the registered voters in the constituency.[95] Industrially, also, Aberdare was growing at a higher speed than Merthyr, but with this difference, that the growth was most spectacular in the independent coal industry After the closure of the Aberaman Iron Works in 1858, Fothergill was the most substantial ironmaster in the town and precincts of Aberdare, although, of course, by comparison with the two giant concerns at Merthyr (and the two lesser ones) his works at Llwydcoed and Abernant were small.

It follows, therefore, that until the 1860s and the Second Reform Act the growing communities of the Aberdare valleys were obliged to accept the political dominance of the richer and more populous Merthyr valleys. Thus, we find that in the early years of the history of the newly-enfranchised borough—from 1832 to 1852—there scarcely existed any regular party caucus in Aberdare independent of that of Merthyr, and that its role in parliamentary politics during those years when Sir J. J. Guest occupied the seat was insignificant. This is not to say that it was a negligible role, since the one occasion on which an opposition candidate actually forced a poll was in 1837 when Guest was opposed by John Bruce (Pryce) of Duffryn, Mountain Ash, landowner and first stipendiary magistrate for the borough. In the event Bruce polled 135 out of a total of 444 cast, of which 67 were polled in Merthyr, and 68 in Aberdare. He polled none in Dowlais. Guest, on the other hand, polled 87 in Bruce's territory alone. Bruce was clearly the forlorn hope of the anti-Guest caucus, the choice of Merthyr rather than Aberdare, and invited to run only after the more obvious canditates. Meyrick and the two ironmasters, Alderman Thompson and Thomas Forman, had declined.[96]

The first indication of the growth of a regular caucus in Aberdare came immediately after the general election of 1852 and, characteristically, Price was in the van of this movement. J. J. Guest had been returned unopposed, being, in fact, seriously ill at the time of the election, and nearly 700 voters of all parties, led by D. W. James and Robert Jones [97] (both of whom had consistently opposed Guest in the past) had agreed to an address to the member 'begging him not to expose himself to the fatigue of canvassing' or even of appearing on the hustings, and assuring him that he should be returned without any trouble.[98] But immediately after the election formalities were over, serious preparations for a by-election, which all anticipated in the near future, were begun, and these included a public dinner at Aberdare, in the course of which D. W. James toasted the town and trade of Aberdare, stating that there was a party of independent men forming in that town, who would be able to render valuable assistance in the event of a contested election. Thomas Price responded on behalf of the town.[99]

Clearly, the 'James Party' in Merthyr, who had managed the opposition to Guest both in local and in parliamentary affairs since the enfranchisement of the borough,[100] anticipated and early election. They were not disappointed for Guest, who had recovered sufficiently to give a public dinner to his supporters in Dowlais in August, suffered a relapse in November, and on 26 November he died.[101] Before the corpse was cold, as some cynics gladly recorded, the James machine went into action while a decent gloom descended on Dowlais House. William Milbourne James, first cousin to J. W. James, and a barrister, issued his *Address* on the 27th, announcing that his political principles were identical with those of the late member, that he was in favour of free trade, parliamentary reform, a considerable extension of the franchise, and the protection of the ballot. In the meantime, handbills with a mourning border were circulated by the other side, condemning this indelicate and premature electioneering, and promising that a worthy successor to Guest was about to come forward. On 6 December, after the funeral, the *Address* of H. A. Bruce appeared, and on the same day a second *Address* by James withdrawing from the contest.[102] On 14 December Bruce was returned unopposed.[103]

The James party retired for the simple reason that the two previous contests had shown that Dowlais and their Merthyr supporters together could carry the representation against the united opposition of all the other ironmasters in the constituency. This had been the lesson of 1835 when the Cyfarthfa lawyer, William Meyrick, standing as a Tory, had enjoyed the enthusiastic support of W. Crawshay, backed by Thompson and Hill.[104] Now, in December 1852, all the Merthyr ironmasters supported Bruce, and W. M. James claimed in his second *Address* to have been told by William Crawshay that 'there would be determined opposition to me on the part of the four Iron Works, on the grounds that my return as a Member for Merthyr would give greater strength to that Independent Party, which had in parochial matters successfully opposed the Iron Masters'. James ended his *Address* by proclaiming that it would be the duty of the independent party so to increase and organize their strength 'that they will use it to teach even Merthyr Iron Masters that property has its duties as well as its rights'.[105]

Whether justifiably or not, Bruce would henceforward be regarded as the nominee and, therefore, the tool of the reactionary iron interest, and a party already existed in the borough,

with its centre in Merthyr, which would never cease to make
political capital of that fact, But, however vociferous it might
become, as a party it was well-nigh helpless in the Merthyr side
of the constituency while the ironmasters remained united. But
in Aberdare circumstances were somewhat different. There the
sole ironmaster was opposed to Bruce, and Fothergill gave the
James party his immediate and consistent support. [106] Fothergill's opposition may have been personal: only a few months
previously Bruce had condemned him for introducing Truck to
Aberdare. It was given an ideological appearance by Price,
who claimed then and later that he and Fothergill had opposed
Bruce because they did not consider him to be sufficiently
liberal. At any rate, Price was among those who organized a
deputation to Fothergill after the election to thank him for
opposing Bruce. [107] It is clear, therefore, that by 1852 Aberdare
Liberals were beginning to organize themselves and to be
active in constituency affairs. At that time, and until 1867,
Richard Fothergill, as the leading ironmaster, was their unofficial candidate being 'presented' to the electorate as an advanced Liberal with a good record in constituency affairs, and
Thomas Price was the acknowledged spokesman for the
caucus.

It is equally clear, however, and by no means contradictory
to assert, that Price and the Liberal group, except in the early
stages of Bruce's tenure of the seat, never once presented
Fothergill as an *alternative* member to Bruce. There was no
question of this. They were realists enough to accept the fact
that even the James family in Merthyr would be unable to un-
seat Bruce while he retained the confidence of Dowlais or a
majority of the Merthyr ironmasters. Moreover, except on the
question of the ballot, Bruce soon proved himself by his votes
in Parliament and activities within the constituency, to be
perfectly acceptable as the representative of the borough. Like
his predecessor, he tended to become more liberal as time went
on, reflecting more accurately, and responding more sensitively to, the majority opinion and political complexion of the
valleys. At no time did any movement to displace him originate
in Aberdare. Thomas Price, in particular, soon came to be an
enthusiastic, though discriminating, supporter.

These arguments can be briefly illustrated by the course of events during the general election of 1857, which followed the dissolution consequent upon the failure of Palmerston to carry the House of Commons with him on the China question. This was the first opportunity the opposition to Bruce had had of testing its strength. It was also a highly favourable opportunity, for the prerequisite conditions for the defeat of Bruce seemed to be present, namely, the fact that three of the four iron-masters—Crawshay, Hill, and Forman—were highly critical of Bruce for opposing Palmerston. James and the opposition party in Merthyr since 1852 had been consistently justifying their opposition to Bruce on the ground that the electoral history of the borough proved it to be a pocket borough and that Bruce was a nominee of the ironmasters. Here was an opportunity for the townsmen to put up their own candidate. Finding a candidate who should please both Crawshay and James was another matter. There was a certain sad realism (and perhaps some sound history) in their choice of William Crawshay, senior, who had retired to Caversham Park. But he declined. So did William Thomas, the Court, a prominent businessman and property owner. In the event, the most the opposition could do, since they applauded Bruce's vote on the China question, was to attack him in his public meetings on the only issue on which they could honestly attack him, namely, his views on the ballot.[108]

Price had no part in these meetings. By now he would do nothing to endanger the sittimg member even though he also remained highly critical of Bruce on the question of the ballot. His energies, and those of Fothergill, were devoted to assisting in the return of the two Liberal candidates for the Glamorgan county seats, C. R. M. Talbot of Margam and H. H. Vivian of Swansea, who were running in harness. Committees 'for the return of two Liberals for the County' were set up at all the important polling centres, including one at Aberdare, and others at Merthyr and Dowlais.[109] Fothergill was chairman of the Aberdare committee, and Price was a member along with a majority of the men we have seen to have been associated with him in the past. But not all. The Tory candidate, Nash Vaughan Edwards—Vaughan of Rheola, also had his committee for the county, and included on it were some of the more prominent names in Aberdare and Merthyr. In fact, when the county election results are analysed it is surprising to discover that Vaughan received 23 per cent. of the votes cast in the Aberdare district, and 17 per cent. in the Merthyr districts.[110] This unexpected strength of the conservative county vote in Aberdare parish may have been a principal reason why Price showed no desire to disturb the sitting member, and why he should have placed so much emphasis constantly on keeping the register up to date, and encouraging registration societ- ies.[111] Shortly after the election, one of the most important in the electoral history of Glamorgan, the importance of Price was officially and publicly recognized when he attended, as a vice- chairman, a dinner given in honour of the successful Liberal candidates at which Fothergill presided.

Two years later the election of 1859, fought on the question of parliamentary reform, was to demonstrate that the organiz- ation of the Aberdare Liberals had reached the stage of mat- urity, and that Thomas Price was now in a position of some au- thority. It also demonstrated that, although Aberdare Liberals were somewhat to the left of Bruce on some aspects of reform, they were not disposed to abandon him at the behest of Merthyr radicals in favour of a virtual 'carpet-bagger'. Whether they would remain loyal to him should the town produce it own rival candidate, was a question which did not arise. Fothergill had retired from politics, and there was no one else of comparable stature to whom they could have appealed had they been so minded.

The election had been preceded by the formation in the con- stituency of a Reform Association for the purpose of supporting John Bright's proposals for parliamentary reform which he had been advocating in a series of speeches during the autumn of 1858, and which he and his associates placed before the House of Commons in the form of a Bill in November of that year.[112] The Association had been formed at a meeting, very thinly attended, at Merthyr presided over by J. W. James, at which resolutions calling for the ballot, triennial parliaments, the re- distribution of seats, and household fracnhise had been passed.[113] A similar, but larger, meeting at Aberdare on 19

January passed the same resolutions and led to the setting up of a committee to co-operate with the Merthyr Association. It consisted of all the town's leading Liberals, including Price. These were all moderate men, and not disposed to accept the extreme demands of the non-electors who, in any case, held their own meeting shortly afterwards.[114] Apart from the ballot, they all saw eye to eye with Bruce.

The consequences of these meetings was that when a candidate for Bruce's seat appeared he could not be certain of much support except from the extreme radical wing, or from those whose hatred of Bruce was stronger than their principles. The candidate who offered himself was E. M. Elderton, a London solicitor, with vague local connections, in his political aims unimpeachable on the ballot but less radical than Bright on the suffrage question. Obviously not a formidable rival to Bruce and not particularly attractive to either the malcontents or the radicals, his adoption meeting almost turned into one in support for Mr. Overton, the local coroner.[115] At Aberdare there was scarcely any support for him at all, as Price had foretold would be the case when Elderton consulted him before commencing his canvass.[116] Here, the feeling of the constituency was put by Price at Bruce's election meeting, to the effect that while approving generally of Bruce's conduct and votes in Parliament, and particularly of his vote against the second reading of Derby's Reform Bill, 'no gentleman can fully and fairly represent this borough in the next parliament without being fully prepared to support a £10 rental as a voting qualification in counties and a large extension of the suffrage in boroughs, a considerable amount of redistribution of parliamentary seats, and protection to the voter in the excercise of his rights by means of ballot'.[117] At the election in May, Bruce polled 798 to Elderton's 106. And of those votes for Elderton only seven had been polled in Aberdare.[118]

*   *   *

It was from this time forward that the political stature of Price began to expand beyond the confines of his own constituency. We have already seen that he was becoming well known in Wales, and, indeed in England as well, [119] as a leading Baptist minister, as prominent supporter of Friendly Societies, as an editor and publicist, and popular lecturer on current affairs. His political fame, however, grew as a result of his dedication to the cause of Welsh Nonconformist politics as defined by the Liberation Society. The essence of this Liberationist views was simply that the Welsh people being predominantly a Nonconformist people, their political energies should henceforth be concentrated on the return to parliament of men of their own convictions, who would 'represent' them on the main Nonconformist grievances. [120] The Society had had supporters in the constituency since the year of its foundation in 1844, [121] and from 1848 Aberdare names begin to appear in the annual transactions of the Society. [122] Thomas Price seems to have joined in 1850 when, characteristically enough, his name, with that of the Rev. William Edwards, appears in the list of council members appointed at the Second Triennial Conference. [123] Thereafter he remained a constant member of the Society, faithfully publicizing its views and activities in his magazines, and in other ways disseminating its principles. From time to time he took part in the meetings and demonstrations of the Society in Aberdare having, no doubt, helped to arrange them. [124]

The year 1862 saw an intensification of the work of the Society in Wales as part of the more general policy of attempting to change the complexion of Parliament itself by the return of members pledged to further and support Liberationist policies at Westminster. [125] This new phase in the relationship of the Society to Wales was inaugurated at a two-day conference in Swansea, attended by Edward Miall, the Society's founder, Henry Richard, its expert on Welsh affairs, and Carvell-Williams, its secretary and expert political analyst. Dr. Price was present, and on the second day spoke to a resolution proposed by Dr. Evan Davies of Haverfordwest [126] His speech, considered within the context of the whole conference, was remarkable for its quality of political realism, distinguished in this respect from most of the other speeches, and, by implication, critical of that of Carvell-Williams who had analysed the shortcomings of Welsh members of Parliament. Price

Henry Richard, M.P., 1812-1888.
Photo: Cynon Valleys Libraries.

began by agreeing that the bulk of the Welsh people were Non-conformist. He wished also to state another fact, namely, 'that three out of every four of the electors of the Principality are under the thumbscrew of one or other of two parties, either the ground landlords, or the iron and coal proprietors so that they can screw three out of every four of the electors from Cardiff to Holyhead'. Moreover, he wished Miall, Richard, and Williams to bear in mind the fact, also, that 'the bulk of the Welsh churches are made up of the poor classes; a very different state of things from what it is in England'. Both land-owners and ironmasters were Church of England men, and their employees and dependants pledged to vote according to their behest, or suffer the consequences. The question was, would the bulk of the Welsh people defy them and vote according to their consciences? The solution lay in a steady and un-spectacular purging of the registers, as had been done in Glamorgan county where both seats were now Liberal. 'It is

impossible for us to get members to vote aright upon our questions while the thumbscrews of the landowners and employers
are exerted in the opposite direction. Let us work for a few
years, and the result will be different from what it is now'. He
was realistic likewise on the question of the supply of candidates. They had been told that Welsh Nonconformists could
return 32 members: where were they to find them? 'We have
but very few men that can spare the time, the money, and the
status to contest our boroughs and counties, and therefore we
must take the best we can. But I very much question whether
we could find two better men than Dr. Dillwyn and Mr. Bruce.
I would not exchange these two men for any other two men I
know in Wales'.[127]

In thus drawing attention to the lack of a ready supply of
suitable candidates, and the need to hold fast to those few who
were true to their constituents despite differences of creed,
Price was drawing attention in a realistic fashion to a neglected
but vital aspect of mid-century Welsh politics. It was politically
unrealistic, and morally and socially dangerous, to whip up
enthusiasm for political causes or to advocate philosophies and
courses of action which could not be personified in actual
candidates as the hustings. And it is to his credit that when an
opportunity offered itself in a suitable constituency to present
the Nonconformist voters with an alternative to that of the
official caucus, he accepted an invitation to stand. This was at
Brecon in January 1866, on the occasion of the by-election
caused by the death of Colonel Watkins of Pennoyre.[128]
Neither of the two candidates to offer themselves for the seat
was considered by some of the Nonconformists to be even
remotely suitable. Hywel Gwyn of Duffryn, Neath, was a
Tory, while John Charles (Pratt), eldest son of the marquis of
Camden, though professedly a Liberal, was so lukewarm and
equivocal or noncommital on the leading questions of parliamentary reform and religious liberty as to be indistinguishable
from his rival. Nevertheless, Dr. Price hesitated to accept the
Brecon Nonconformists' invitation on the grounds that it
would be more appropriate to invite someone with stronger
local connections, or failing such a one, a radical politician of
some eminence—as, for instance, Henry Richard. Alternative-

ly he was quite prepared to see the young earl returned provided he gave satisfactory pledges on parliamentary reform, franchise extension, and religious equality. Neither of these alternatives being realized, by early December Dr. Price had determined to intervene, standing as Welsh Nonconformist Liberal. The *Address* he issued and the speeches he made to the electors received, and indeed deserved, wide publicity, for as he explained, he determined to stand in order to test the high claims which had been made in recent years regarding the necessity of returning at least one Welsh Nonconformist to one of the 32 seats. And he wished to discover what help a practical man could hope to receive without employing half the lawyers and publicans of the constituency. Brecon seemed a good test case, since the town contained eight congregations of Nonconformists and a Dissenting college, and it was estimated that a half of the 200 registered electors were of that religious persuasion. His *Address* and speech were, indeed, very remarkable performances, and were received with so much enthusiasm that the young earl had to step into line and issue a second, more Liberal and specific *Address*. Price regarded this as a victory for himself and the radical cause, and thereupon retired having, as it was later said, rescued Brecon from an honest Tory and a dishonest Whig.[129]

Certainly, Price emerged from this contest with his reputation greatly enhanced, not only in Aberdare, where he was shortly afterwards presented with an inkstand suitably inscribed, but elsewhere in radical Dissenting circles.[130] He himself, however, had no illusions either of personal grandeur or of the nature of the victory, which later events proved to have been pyrrhic anyway. He had probably withdrawn not, as he had publicly stated, because he had achieved a main objective, but because he had realized that however enthusiastic his audiences may have been the Nonconformists would lack the power of their convictions even where they were not already pledged to Lord Camden, and that more than the sound of trumpets was needed to cause the entrenched walls of privilege which encompassed Brecon to fall to the ground. The opportunity to make these misgivings public occurred in the August following the election when the young lord was called to the

Upper House on the death of his father and the Liberal nomination passed to his brother-in-law, Lord Alfred Spencer
Churchill, and not, as Price imagined it would, to Henry
Richard, E. M. Richards, J.P., of Swansea, or Edward Miall.
In a series of leading articles in *Seren Cymru* in August and
September he castigated with bitterness the Nonconformist
leaders of the town, and gave vent to his disillusionment. He
still believed that Liberationist aims could be achieved, but
where in Wales was there a constituency where the voluntary-
ists were sufficiently courageous to practise their principles and
return a Welsh Nonconformist?[131] In the August number he
analysed the contest in which he had taken part. Of the 200
registered voters, a half were professedly Nonconformists,
though, astonishingly enough, not one of the college
tutors—men devoted to teaching ministerial students the
principles of dissent—had the vote. Many of the 100 Nonconformists voters were eloquent on Liberationist platforms, but
when the testing time came they gave exhibitions of political
flunkeyism as debasing as the profoundest Tory in Europe
could desire. As against the eminent and gifted men who were
ready to stand, they had 'hastened, grovelling, to lick the dust
and seek out the brother of the previous Judas'[132]—young, in-
experienced, without a religious or political credo, who could
not even write his own *Address,* whose only qualification was
family connection. Price was forced to account for this servility
by alleging that Lord Camden had bribed the Independents
with grants of land, and the Methodists with money to build
their chapel on the Watton. 'The conduct of these men is a
betrayal of all principles. They should be held to ridicule
throughout Wales. Now, the men like the Nonconformists of
this small town are the curse of Wales.'[133] Dr. Price's anger
had been forgotten by 1867, and his excessive language
moderated; but his disillusionment became a permanent
element in his political philosophy, and played a notable part in
the creation of those attitudes which determined his actions in
the Merthyr Tydfil election of 1868.

   Dr. Price was too intelligent a man and too well-informed to
allow anger to obscure, or disillusionment to undermine, his
faith in the essential rightness of his political doctrines and ob-

COFFADWRIAETH DDAU CAN MLWYDDOL

1662–1862.

ADRODDIAD

CYNADLEDDAU

CASTELLNEDD A DINBYCH.

"Y rhai nid oedd y byd yn deilwng o honynt."

LLANELLI:

ARGRAFFWYD GAN B. R. REES, HEOL-Y-FARCHNAD.

1862.

Pris Pedair Ceiniog.

Cover of Adroddiad Cynadleddau.

WELSH NONCONFORMITY

AND THE

WELSH REPRESENTATION.

Papers and Speeches

READ AND DELIVERED AT THE

CONFERENCES HELD SEPTEMBER and OCTOBER, 1866.

LONDON:

Society for the Liberation of Religion from State-Patronage
and Control,

2, SERJEANTS' INN, FLEET STREET: THOMAS GEE, DENBIGH.

PRICE SIXPENCE.

Cover of Welsh Nonconformity.

jectives. His disappointment did not extend to all Nonconformists, and he evidently came to hope that even apostate Brecon
could retrieve its reputation.[134] It was the middle-class Nonconformists, the tradition-bound, commercially dependent dissenter, who calculated interest against principle, who had disappointed him. Henceforward, he concentrated his energies on
working for parliamentary reform and a wide extension of the
franchise to include all householders, for this was the essential
preliminary to the achievement of all his other aims, and it was
to this and the more efficient organization of the Liberals in the
borough and county that he now devoted himself.

Parliamentary reform, was, anyway, the topic of the hour,
particularly after the preliminary moves towards a comprehensive measure of reform had been taken by the House of
Commons in February 1867. By April, meetings were being
held in the constituency by various bodies sympathetic to the
views expressed by either the National Reform League or the
National Reform Union, and Dr. Price played an important
role in this agitation. His sympathies were with the Union: he
was one of its five Welsh vice-presidents,[135] and he would have
nothing to do with the rival organization's meetings despite the
prominence of the Liberationist plank in their programme.[136]
Instead, Dr. Price concentrated his energies on the more
ambitious and 'national' scheme for a Welsh Representative
Society, the need for which he had suggested at an earlier
meeting called for the purpose of honouring him for his services
at Brecon.[137] What was needed was 'a Society to sow the seeds
of political nonconformity and labour to improve the political
representation of Wales in the House of Commons',[138] and
most of the official speakers, including the chief speaker, Price,
kept to this theme. But it was clear, from some of the speeches
from the floor and from the final resolution proposed by one of
the conveners, that Aberdare Nonconformists had the representation of their own constituency very much in mind, and that
this 'national' society now in process of formation was
admirably adapted to act as a constituency political organization in Merthyr should the need arise.[139] More significantly,
perhaps, this reform meeting, called shortly before the exact
terms of the Second Reform Act had been agreed, but when it

was already certain that Merthyr would benefit from any redistribution of seats, had taken place in Aberdare under the guidance of the constituency's most distinguished Nonconformist leader. In the event of an election the Nonconformists had been provided with an organization, and its leader would be in a very powerful position to determine the attitudes of its members.

This meeting took place at Aberdare on 7 May 1867, and the committee which had been set up consisted of the leading Dissenters of the parish, a group, one would have thought, admirably adapted for the task of putting their principles into practice in their own constituency.[140] Yet, exactly a fortnight later, on 21 May, its acknowledged leader, Thomas Price, was one of a small group of men who approached Richard Fothergill with a view to inviting him to stand for the second seat which would be given to Merthyr under the terms of the Reform Bill then in its final stages. On the same day, Price published a leading article in *Seren Cymru* strongly advocating the offer of the seat to Fothergill in the first place, and only then, in the event of his refusal, inviting a Welsh Nonconformist Liberal to stand.[141] Fothergill's reaction being satisfactory, on the following day a committee was formed to draw up a formal requisition which should be presented, along with a similar one from Merthyr, as soon as possible. By the time this Merthyr committee had been formed, and Fothergill approached on 20 June, the terms of the Bill had been published. Two days later, a joint deputation had visited Fothergill, and finding his political views satisfactory, and receiving from him an assurance that the last vestiges of Truck would be abolished in his works, drew up the final requisitions.[142] These were presented on 30 June, the Aberdare one by Dr. Price, the Merthyr one by William Simmons. According to Price, the Aberdare one had been signed by 2,320 voters, including most of the tradesmen from Hirwaun to Mountain Ash, a large number of registered voters, and a few who would be exercising the vote for the first time. Merthyr's requisition had been signed by 1,200,[143] a clear indication of the amount of support he could expect in that part of the constituency.

The shock of these developments in the constituency, and particularly in Aberdare, was considerable. The Nonconformists had been placed in an extremely awkward situation. Despite his alleged 'political immaturity', his lack of practical politics beyond the confines of his own parish, that he was a Churchman and an Englishman, Fothergill was nevertheless bound to be a powerful candidate. He was a local man, his influence as an industrialist in Aberdare was almost irresistible, and by no means negligible in Merthyr. It was known that the Cyfarthfa interest supported him even to the extent of being represented on his committee by none other that W. T. Crawshay.[144] In the early stages, too, it was open to speculation that the Dowlais interest, while luke-warm, would not be exerted against him. The Wayne family, of the Gadlys Iron Works and collieries, supported him from the beginning, and the other Aberdare coal owners, while for the most part not actively engaged, were known not to be opposed to him.[145] Fothergill's *Address,* also, was in some respects even more Liberal than H. A. Bruce's: it was categorically in favour of relieving the major Dissenting grievances, supported the disestablishment of the Irish Church, and was unequivocally in favour of the ballot.[146] In Aberdare, at least, it would be politically unrealistic, and possibly socially dangerous, to oppose such a candidate. Hence the hesitations with which the Nonconformists reacted initially. Not until the middle of July was there a move in Merthyr to invite Henry Richard to contest the seat, and the form which that meeting took was determined by the situation created by the candidature of Fothergill, for a considerable part of the proceedings was taken up with declarations of fidelity of Bruce whose seat was now to become very insecure.[147] A similar meeting was held shortly afterwards in Aberdare, chaired by David Davis, the son of David Davis, Blaen-gwawr. Price attended this meeting, and argued strongly that the course they were about to adopt could have no other result than to jeopardize the first seat for Bruce. Despite his arguments this stormy meeting proceeded to pass the necessary resolutions, and to set up a committee to co-operate with the Merthyr committee under the chairmanship of J. H. James.[148]

Here was a situation without compare in the annals of Welsh politics, and well might the voices of Price's erstwhile associates be raised in indignation at such a spectacle. Nonconformist leaders throughout England and Wales remonstrated and pleaded with him, pointed to the incongruity of his position, even hinting darkly of treachery, particularly since the overwhelming support being given to Henry Richard inevitably meant that his continued support of Fothergill would cause the defeat of Bruce.[149] Yet Price continued steadfast despite the alienation of his friends and his virtual isolation in Nonconformist circles. Throughout the contest, although he seems to have avoided the public platform, he continued to argue his case, using the columns of his paper to defend himself. In fact, his case was not a good one, since it involved, or would seem to involve, the partial abandonment of those principles which previously he had held to be basic in the political philosophy of Welsh Nonconformity. Thus, when he argued that the contest was between Liberals, and that if Richard were elected not a single vote more would be gained than if Fothergill were elected, he was ignoring what Welsh Nonconformist Liberals had been teaching for more than a decade, namely, that it was not merely reliable votes in Parliament that were expected of the Welsh members, but a positive dedication to the cause of Nonconformity, and of Welsh Nonconformity in particular. He tended to play down the role of religion in politics, too, and this made him cynical of the nature of the support being given to Richard. But this looked as if he were generalizing on the basis of his single experience at Brecon, and including all Nonconformists in the condemnation he had pronounced on the Dissenters of that borough. Finally, he was reluctant to admit as a general principle that local needs and feelings ought to give way to the general interest. He would prefer a local member with local interests, who would do his best for the constituency while not harming the rest of the country.[150] Dr. Price and certainly grown more realistic in his political attitudes, but it was a realism totally out of harmony with the idealistic stage of Welsh political Nonconformity at that time.

There is no direct evidence to show that there was anything personal in this alliance between Price and Fothergill, beyond

The original draft of Henry Richard's Election Address, October 1868.

the fact that they had worked closely together in local and parliamentary politics over a number of years. Nor can any commercial affiliations be detected. As we have seen, Price's commercial interests allied him with the coal owners rather that with the ironmasters, and the interests of these two groups could often be opposed. Despite the fierce contest over Fothergill's Truck shops, indeed, possibly as a result of this contest, Price had come genuinely to admire him. The letter of the agreement they had drawn up together on that occasion had been strictly adhered to, namely, that no workman should be compelled to but at the company shop. This surely shows the imaginative limitations of both men, but at least it enables us to bracket them together, and to show a certain affinity between them. Probably the main motive determining Price's allegations was pride in locality. For the first time Aberdare, which seemed to have been doomed in the past to take its politics from its larger neighbour, had taken the initiative and produced its own candidate. It has the additional advantage of placing the blame for the probable displacing of Bruce on the James party at Merthyr who hitherto had dominated constituency Dissent. He had obviously calculated that Aberdare Dissent would follow his lead, and so break the tradition. In the event, he was proved wrong, for only the Baptists appear to have followed him in any numbers,[151] and in that age of denominational virulence it was only to be expected that he should castigate the choice of Henry Richard, and resent his coming as an intrusion.

Nowhere was the shock of his defection greater than among the working-class organizations he had encouraged. One of the sharpest, and at the same time saddest, letters addressed to him was written by D. R. Lewis, a workman, and secretary of the Aberdare Ivorites. 'We believed', he wrote, 'that when we should have the vote and a second member of the borough, we should have a Welshman—a Welshman from Aberdare, and a nonconformist of advanced political views; but to our disappointment, behold the one we regarded as most suitable turning his back, and supporting an Englishman instead of a Welshman, a churchman instead of a nonconformist . . .'.[152] Moreover, this disillusionment on the score of Nonconformity breached other buttresses in his popularity among the working classes, and encouraged the creation of attitudes hostile to him on purely working-class issues. It was remembered against him that he had supported Bruce and, by implication, the masters in the strike of 1857, that the Fothergill Truck shop which Price claimed to have closed in 1852 still functioned until its closing became a condition of the candidature of Fothergill in 1867.[153] More seriously than even these, Price and the workers could not see eye to eye on the question of inspection and the double shift which soon agitated the coalfield.[154] D. R. Lewis, writing in February, summed up the disappointment which was universally felt at the support which Price had consistently given to Nixon and the other masters in their efforts to compel the colliers to adopt the double shift method of working. They had heard with deep regret 'that the *Defender* of the workmen—Dr. Price—the only person whom we could look to for support in the present difficult situation, had turned his back, and was supporting a system which is of necessity destructive of the workers' health and creative of a social plague in their midst. The sight of a name so well known among the workers of the country printed on such a black page as Nixon's "Treachery of the Worker" seared into our hearts like balls of molten lead'.[155] This was a bitter attack—the ironic reference to Nixon's pamphlet recalled Dr. Price's defence of the Welsh people against the Treachery of the Blue Books of 1846—and Price was clearly hurt. The colliers were disregarding completely the efforts he was currently making to bring masters and men together in a harmonious relationship reflecting the economic harmony which, theoretically, already and of necessity bound them together. He reminded them, in his reply to these attacks, of his appeal in *Seren Cymru* for a statement of their views on the double shift,[156] and informed them that he had translated the letters he had received and had taken them to London where he had placed them before the country's leading men. Despite all these efforts, despite his past record of service, he was being attacked in a mean, unmanly, and dastardly fashion.[157] Nevertheless, the men persisted in their campaign against the double shift and in favour of their own version of mines inspection without him. They still availed themselves of his expertise,[158] but the aims of the campaign were determined by, and its direction entrusted to, representative of the workmen. In fact, even as the decisions of the Nonconformists were being made independently of their one-time *doyen*, so, too, in the industrial and social affairs of the constituency the newly enfranchised were rejecting their old leader, making their own decisions and creating their own independent organizations. In the general election of 1868, it was not only Prices's candidate, Bruce, whom they rejected, but Dr. Price as well.

These conclusions are supported by a comparison of the voting behaviour in the two sides of the constituency on polling day, 11 November 1868. The formal declaration of the poll gave the following figures: Henry Richard 11,683; Richard Fothergill 7,139; and H. A. Bruce 5,776.[159] In both valleys Richard headed the poll with substantially the same proportion of votes—in Merthyr 46 per cent, in Aberdare 49 per cent—but with a higher majority over Fothergill in Merthyr than in 'Aberdare.[160] Clearly, the contest had been for the second seat, and when we study the distribution of the support being given to the two candidates for this seat, several interesting conclusions emerge.[161] Thus we see that Fothergill's majority over Bruce in Merthyr was only 160 in a poll of 13,329, but that in Aberdare it amounted to 1,656 in a poll of 11,446. The explanation for this is two-fold. In the first place it is a reflection of the distribution of the 'interests' of the two men in the constituency. A close analysis of the returns from the individual booths in Merthyr substantiates this. Thus, Bruce polled more than Fothergill in those areas most dependent upon the Dowlais Iron Company, of which he was the senior trustee, that is, in Dowlais and Pen-y-darren, Vaynor, and Georgetown. Fothergill polled most heavily in Abercanaid. Troed-y-rhiw, and the town of Merthyr itself—in the two former places because they were beholden to him, and in Merthyr because he may very well have benefited from an anti-Dowlais vote. In Aberdare the result was determined by more 'political' considerations. Here, Fothergill's power was in any case irresistible, but the margin of his victory over Bruce reflected not merely his industrial power, and almost certainly not his popularity, but rather the determination of the Aberdare colliers to be rid of a member in whom they had no confidence. It is this second reason which is the important one in any assessment of the role of Dr. Price. For although it required no prescience to foresee that once Fothergill was brought forward he could scarcely fail to gain the seat, it could not have been foreseen that this action would make it easier for working-class opinion to cystallize so solidly against Bruce.

The election of 1868 marked clearly the crisis in the political influence and career of Thomas Price both in the constituency and in the country at large. He never quite recovered his old authority in as comprehensive a way as before; indeed, he seems never to have sought thereafter to do so. If he had been in error in refusing to place himself where his past career proclaimed him to belong, at the head of the the political Nonconformity of the Liberationist type in the constituency, he never admitted his mistake. But this study of his developing career has shown that his decisions in 1868 were less surprising that at the time they had seemed. For there is a basic consistency in his political views and actions up to the election: his failure lay in his inability to adapt them to the new conditions created by the Reform Act of 1867. This is most apparent in his relations with the working classes. Here, he refused to see that in the contingencies of a protracted general election campaign the loyalties of the newly enfranchised would not of necessity be given to those middle-class leaders by whose efforts their enfranchisement had largely been won. It was apparent, too, in his relations with Nonconformity. Here, what is significant is that when the time of decision came it was local loyalties and traditions rather than 'national' obligation which determined his course of action. Not only Dr. Price, in fact, but political Nonconformity as a whole, had reached a crisis in its development. To succeed in the future it could no longer assume a necessary congruity between its aims and those of the bulk of its working-class adherents, and, above all, it would need to create a new kind of political organization to replace the old.

NOTES

*This paper was first published in the *Welsh History Review* 2, No. 2 (1964) and No. 3 (1965).

[1] 'Y mae rhywbeth yn hanes hon fel ag yr ystyrir bron yn fath o "public property"—fel pe bai bawb â llais ynddi; ac edrychir ar gynnrychiolwyr y bwrdeisdrefi hyn, ac nid fel cynnrychiolwyr Merthyr a 'Berdâr, ond yn gynnrychiolwyr y Dywysogaeth . . . ac yma, yn unig, o holl fwrdeistrefi Cymru, y gellir dweyd fod yr etholiath bron yn gyfangwbl yn nwylaw y bobl, a'r rheini bron yn

gyfangwbl yn Ymneullduwyr'. *Baner ac Amserau Cymru* (henceforth cited as *Baner*) 4
November 1868. Compare also the same correspondent in ibid., 23 September 1868.

[2] Ibid., 30 October 1867.

[3] See the quotation from his post-election article in Richard Griffith, *Y Gohebydd,
Cofiant a Dyfyniadau o'i Lythyrau* (1905), p. 56: 'oni bai am . . . diysgogrwydd (gwŷr
Merthyr ac Aberdar) o blaid Richard fuasem ni yn y Gogledd ddim wedi gwneyd y
gwrhydri a wnaethom'. Compare also his eve of the poll article in *Baner*, 4 November
1868.

[4] For Thomas Gee's views see, for example, the pre-election survey of Welsh politics
in *Baner*, 2, 9, and 23 September 1868: 'Y mae y mater hwn (y sedd ychwanegol,
hynny yw) o bwys cenedlaethol:—ar ryw olwg, y mae math o lais gan bob Cymro yn
newisiad y cynnrychiolydd chwanegol a roddir i Gymru'. For Richard's view, see his
letter in *Baner*, 28 October 1868, 'At Etholwyr Anghydffurfiol Cymru' which is
couched in the terms of an election address.

[5] See 'The Liberation Society and Welsh Politics, 1844 to 1868', in Ieuan Gwynedd
Jones, *Explorations and Explanations. Essays in the Social History of Victorian Wales*
(Llandysul, 1981), pp. 236 ff.

[6] *Ibid.,* pp. 193 ff. and cf. H. J. Hanham, *Elections and party Management. Politics in the
Time of Disraeli and Gladstone* (1959), pp. 173-5.

[7] For biographical details see *Y Bywgraffiadur Cymreig hyd 1940* (1953), *sub nom.*
Thomas Price (1820-88), and B. Evans (Telynfab), *Cofiant Dr. Price Aberdâr* (1891).

[8] Decennial statistics are as follows:

1801	..	1,486	1841	..	6,471
1811	..	1,338	1851	..	14,998
1821	..	2,062	1861	..	32,247
1831	..	3,961	1871	..	40,305

See *Census Report* and *Merthyr Tydfil Union of Accounts* (1894).

[9] For the growth of the iron industry in the district see, in general, A. H. John, *The
Industrial Development of South Wales* (1950), John P. Addis, *The Crawshay Dynasty*
(1957), Sir John Lloyd, *Old South Wales Ironworks* (1906), and C. Wilkins, *History of the
Iron, Steel and Tinplate Trades* (1903), A. H. John and Glanmor Williams, *Glamorgan
County History Vol. 5 Industrial Glamorgan.*

[10] See *Census* of 1831, Enumeration Abstract, 11, pp. 890-1.

[11] For the growth of the coal industry see, in general, J. H. Morris and L. J.
Williams, *The South Wales Coal Industry, 1841-1875* (1958). For the location of Matthew
Wayne's first pit see C. Wilkins, op. cit., p. 430.

[12] The enumerators' returns are in H.O. 107/2460/1-4, for 1851, and H.O.
RG9/4063-4073.

[13] See Health of Towns Commission, *Report on the State of Bristol, Bath, Frome,
Swansea, Merthyr Tydfil and Brecon* by Sir Henry T. De La Bèche (London, 1845), p. 85.

[14] T. J. Jones, 'Traethawd ar Hanes Plwyf a Phentref Aberdar', *Gardd Aberdar*
(Carmarthen, 1854), p. 87.

[15] *Report to the General Board of Health on a Preliminary Inquiry into the sewerage, drainage,
and supply of water, and the sanitary condition of the inhabitants of the Town of Merthyr Tydfil,*
by T. W. Rammell (London, 1850), p.12.

[16] Ibid., p. 11.

[17] Ibid.

[18] Ibid., p. 12.

[19] R. A. Lewis, *Edwin Chadwick and the Public Health Movement*, p. 41. Quoted by
Tydfil Davies Jones, 'Poor Law and Public Health Administration in the Area of
Merthyr Tydfil Union, 1834-94' (M.A. thesis, University of Wales, 1961), p. 144.

[20] See de la Bèche, T. W. Rammell, and Miss Jones, op. cit.

[21] See Thomas Price, *Jiwbili Eglwys Calfaria, Aberdar* (1862), and B. Evans, op. cit., p. 76.

[22] Statistics are to be found in the *Llythyrau Cymanfa Bedyddwyr Morgannwg,* annually from 1833 onwards, and Ieuan Gwynedd Jones *The Religious Census of 1857. A Calendar of the Returns Relating to Wales.* (Cardiff 1976), pp. 184-90.

[23] According to Price's *Jiwbili,* quoted in B. Evans, *Cofiant,* op. cit., pp. 92 and 96, in 1862 members numbered 3,096.

[24] On these features see B. Evans, *Cofiant,* op. cit., pp. 67-118. In his *Jiwbili* Price claimed that in 1860 there were sixteen chapels and branches associated with Calfaria, with a total membership of 3,096, eighteen ministers and lay preachers, eighteen Sunday Schools, 419 teachers, and 3,272 pupils.

[25] B. Evans, *Cofiant,* op. cit., pp. 121 and 128. And see, for example, *Seren Cymru,* 18 January 1861, for a report of the eisteddfod held at Aberaman when twelve chapels participated.

[26] Richard Fothergill gave assistance in the building of a baptistry on the bank of the river near Abernant. See J. W. Moore, *Hanes Eglwys Bethel, Abernant* (1880), p. 6.

[27] J. W. Moore, op. cit., is a good example of the procedure.

[28] B. Evans, *Cofiant,* op. cit., p. 121.

[28] On the Unitarians in Aberdare see D. Jacob Dafis (ed.), *Gweriniaeth yn Hanes yr Hen Dŷ Cwrdd, Aberdâr, 1751-1951* (1951), and bibliography therein, p. 86.

[28] B. Evans, *Cofiant,* op. cit., p. 121.

[29] On the Unitarians in Aberdare see D. Jacob Dafis (ed.), *Gweriniaeth yn hanes yr Hen Dŷ Cwrdd, Aberdâr, 1751-1951* (1951), and bibliography therein, p. 86.

[30] For the Independents see T. Rees and J. Thomas, *Hanes Eglwysi Annibynnol Cymru,* II, 323 *et seq.* (Liverpool, 1872) and D. Silyn Evans, *Bywgraffiad . . . Barch. David Price, Siloa, Aberdâr* (1896).

[31] These were as follows in 1854: Welsh Calvinistic Methodists—three chapels; Wesleyan Methodists—four chapels; Primitive Methodists—four chapels. See T. J. Jones, op. cit., in *Gardd Aberdâr, p. 78.*

[32] See the *Reports* and Appendices (1848). On the controversy aroused see, in general, J. Rhŷs and D. B. Jones, *The Welsh People* (1900), pp. 484-6. The role of Ieuan Gwynedd is discussed by Brinley Rees in the introduction to his *Ieuan Gwynedd, Detholiad Rhyddiaith* (1957) where the *A Vindication* is printed. Henry Richard's role is discussed in C. S. Miall, *Henry Richard, M.P.* (1889), pp. 21-6, in Henry Richard, *Letters and Essays on Wales* (1884), and in Eleazar Roberts, *Bywyd a Gwaith y Diweddar Henry Richard, A.S.* (1902), pp. 21-6.

[33] For Griffith's evidence see *Reports* Appendix, p. 489 Also B. Evans, *Cofiant, op. cit.,* pp. 48-9 where it is quoted in full.

[34] On these see C. Wilkins, *The South Wales Coal Trade* (1888), J. H. Morris and L. J. Williams, *The South Wales Coal Industry, 1841-1875* (1958), B. Morus, *Enwogion Aberdâr* (1910), and *Y Bywgraffiadur Cymreig.*

[35] W. Williams, London Warehouse, was one of the rising generation of shop-keepers, later to be active in poilitics. See Silyn Evans, op. cit., p. 51 and *Aberdare Times,* 8 August 1868.

[36] Silyn Evans, op. cit, p. 54.

[37] Ibid., p. 51.

[38] See *A. Vindication* in Brinley Rees, op. cit., p. 77 ff.

[39] For instance, the controversy over Rustic Sport held to celebrate a royal wedding, which the church and 'trade' helped to organize but which Price thought to be degrading; and, more importantly, the church rate controversy.

[40] There was a school in Crawshay's Ironworks at Hirwaun. See W. W. Price, *Park Schools Centenary; its History* (1948), pp. 28-9. and *Reports,* but not one in Aberdare.

[41] For this interesting social analysis of Lingren's see *Reports,* op. cit., pp. 20-1.

[42] John Jones was clerk to the Vestry, clerk to the Road Board for north Glamorgan, and was a director later of the Aberdare Water Works. W. W. Price, op. cit., p. 29, gives details of his career and interest. Evan Griffiths was active in the Vestry. See *Aberdare Vestry Books,* vol. I *sub* 5 February 1837. Later committee members and trustees included David Davis, J.P., Maesyffynnon (son of David Davis, Blaengwawr, the coal proprietor), the 'Gladstone of Wales' as he was later called; and Samuel Thomas, founder of the Ysguborwen Colliery and the Clydach Vale Colliery (Father of D. A. Thomas, Lord Rhondda). W. T. Lewis, Lord Merthyr, served as a trustee. For details of these see *Bywgraffiadur,* and W. W. Price, op. cit. Dr. Price gives a list of committee members in his reminiscences in *Seren Cymru,* 4 November 1864.

[43] The committee in 1847 consisted of four ministers, four tradesmen, three coal proprietors, one contractor, and one farmer.

[44] See *Aberdare Vestry Books,* I, Glamorgan Record Office, P/61/5.

[45] *Aberdare Vestry Books,* II, 23 March 1848. Glamorgan Record Office, P/61/2. Ibid., 23 September 1853. It is interesting to note that the Abernant district—where the Aberdare Iron Company was located—was to be left to Fothergill and his agents to administer.

[46] For the history of public health administration in the area see Tydfil Davies Jones, 'Poor Law and Public Health Administration in the area of Merthyr Tydfil Union'.

[47] For this episode see above pp. 288-90.

[48] Merthyr Tydfil Union: Minute Books, I (1836-40); III (1849-51), Glamorgan Record Office, U/M But see *Aberdare Vestry Book* P/61/5, f. 310 where under 30 March 1837 Rowland Fothergill, a farmer, and a freeholder, are recorded as having been returned.

[49] Merthyr Tydfil Union: Minute Books, III (1849-51), 23 March 1850, Minute 2608, f. 185, records the order for the increase.

[50] He is thus described in 1861, Minute Books, 1860-63, f. 67.

[51] See 'Pryddest o glôd i'r Parch. T. Price am ei ofal dros y Tlodion, yng nghyd â'i ymdrechion diflino o blaid crefydd yng Nghwm Dâr' by Gwalch [i.e. John Jones] in *Seren Gomer* (1858), pp. 272-3.

[52] Details of the (repeated) applications can be found in *Aberdare Vestry Books,* II. I am indebted to Miss Tydfil Jones, M.A., for this reference.

[53] Edward Miall, in a speech at Swansea in September 1862, contrasting the socio-religious attitudes of the English middle classes with those of Wales, said that in England when the middle classes gather wealth they tended to fall away from dissent into the established church: 'three generations of carriage folk never continue to be Dissenters'. *Cambrian,* 26 September 1862. This tendency was almost certainly less pronounced in Wales than in England.

[54] For details of the marriage and family see B. Evans, op cit., *Bywgraffiadur, Seren Gomer,* October 1849, p. 310 and ibid., November, p. 350. For a list of Aberdare landowners in c. 1850 see T.J. Jones, op. cit., in *Gardd Aberdâr,* p. 57.

[55] See advertisement in *Aberdare Times,* 4 November 1871. It would appear that the Prices bought this mill as a going concern, since the Glandare Mills were owned by Thomas Roberts in 1868. See *Slater's Directory for 1868, sub* Aberdare.

[56] See *Gwron,* 1 May 1858. Price had been among the foremost agitators for a gas company, see *C.M.G.,* 4 March 1848.

[57] E.g. B. Evans, op. cit.

[58] See his own recollections at a presentation to him as editor of *Y Gwron* in 1858: *Gwron,* 1 May 1858. See also T. R. Roberts, *Eminent Welshmen* (1908), *sub* Thomas Price.

[59] On friendly societies in general, see J. H. Clapham, *An Economic History of Modern Britain* (1926), i. 295-300, 588-91; P. J. J. H. Gosden, *The Friendly Societies in England, 1815-1875* (1961) and Gwyn A. Williams, 'Friendly Societies in Glamorgan, 1793-1832', *Bulletin of the Board of Celtic Studies,* XVIII, 111, (November) 1959), 275-89. According to T. J. Jones, op. cit., p. 78, there were in 1854 six orders, with a total of fifty-nine lodges, and an aggregate membership of 5,162.

[60] The Foresters honoured him with a presentation in 1849, and the Alfredites in 1863. See *Y Gweithiwr Gymreig, 8 March 1888.*

[61] For details of his activities see the whole of chapter XV in B. Evans, op. cit. Statistics of growth between 1859 and 1865 are given in a testimonial presented to Price and printed in ibid., pp. 185-7.

[62] Ibid., p. 239.

[63] For the history of this newspaper, *Y Gwron Cymreig a Chyhoeddwr Cyffredinol Dywysogaeth Cymru* see R. D. Rees, 'Glamorgan Newspapers under the Stamp Acts', *Morgannwg,* III (1959), 78-9.

[64] For W. Williams and J. J. Jones see *Bywgraffiadur.* A. J. Davies was an Independent minister at Aberaman.

[65] According to a letter in *C.M.G.,* 27 December 1857, its circulation in that year was 2,000 copies weekly. That of *Baner ac Amserau Cymru,* formed in 1859, with a 'national' coverage, is put at 4,000 copies weekly.

[66] Colliers' meetings would often end with a vote of thanks to the editors of *Y Gwron.*

[67] In 1855, for instance, he gave a series of four lectures, at the invitation of the management, to the Abernant workmen on the war. See *Gwron,* 15 March 1855 to 12 April 1855 for reports of these lectures. Other topics included 'Hanes y Rhyfel Presennol yn India', 'The Indian Mutiny', 'Y Collier a'i beryglon'.

[68] The quotation is from G. T. Clark's evidence before the Royal Commission on Trade Unions, Fifth Report, *Parliamentary Papers,* 1867-8, xxxix (3980), Q. 125.

[69] On this see J. H. Morris and L. J. Williams, op. cit., p. 183.

[70] Ibid., the whole of chapter VIII is relevant.

[71] These are conveniently, but incompletely, listed in Dafydd Morgannwg (David Watkin Jones), *Hanes Morgannwg* (1874), pp. 63-4.

[72] *Seren Cymru,* 27 March 1867, gives a detailed exposition of Price's views on the safety question. In general, see Morris and L. J. Williams, op. cit., pp. 179-208, but the authors do not discuss the 'sub-inspectorate' plan.

[73] See B. Evans, op. cit., pp. 63-4.

[74] *Y Gwron,* 14 November 1857.

[75] As when he welcomed, in a leader, a detailed statement of the masters, case by Thomas Joseph, in *Gwron,* 5 December 1857.

[76] Actually, he sent a telegram along with that of the Aberdare justices asking for the removal of the soldiers to Cardiff. PRO/HO/45, 7239a and 7239b.

[77] *Y Gwron,* 12 December 1857.

[78] Later, Price denied having heard this second speech of Bruce's, while agreeing that he was on the platform with him. *Seren Cymru,* 8 November 1867.

[79] *C.M.G.,* 24 May 1851.

[80] *C.M.G.,* 12 Arpil 1851.

[81] According to one speaker there had been a Company shop in Aberdare in 1828, but it had not been oppressive. *C.M.G.,* 12 April 1851.

[82] For the resolutions, Price's speech, etc., see *C.M.G.,* 12 April 1851. Cf. also the detailed account of the Aberdare Anti-Truck Society in Tremenheere's Report of the Commissioners appointed under the provisions of the Act 5 and 6 Vict. c. 99, to inquire into the operation of the at Act, and into the state of the population in the Mining Districts, 1852. *Parliamentary Papers,* 1852, XXI (425).

[83] For Bruce's considered views on Truck, in general, and of its social effects in South Wales, see his speech of 16 February 1854 supporting C. Forester's Bill to amend the Truck Acts, *Hansard*, 3rd series, vol. 130, 762-3.

[84] By this understanding there was no agreement to *close* the shop. It needed the candidature of Fothergill in a general election to achieve that. See *Aberdare Times*, 29 June 1868.

[85] In *Seren Cymru*, 13 December 1867.

[86] These points were made by Fothergill in a letter to the *Mining Journal* reprinted in *C.M.G.*, 21 June 1851. Price himself admitted that goods in the Company shop were cheaper than elsewhere, and it was well known that Crawhsay from time to time sold provisions to his Hirwaun workmen at wholesale prices 'in order to bring the tradesmen to heel'.

[87] For a report of the Treforest meeting see *C.M.G.*, *7 June 1851.*

[88] For Bruce's attack see, for example, *Merthyr Telegraph*, 24 October 1868, and for Price's defence see *Seren Cymru*, 13 December 1867.

[89] For Fothergill's chairmanship of the Board see *Aberdare Leader*, 27 June 1903. *Y Gwron*, 28 August 1858, says that he retired from public life and the Board of Health on account of attacks on him by unnamed person. Price was certainly not a party to this.

[90] Dr. Roberts was a surgeon employed by the Abernant Company. Philip John was a grocer; see Slater's *Directory* for 1868, *sub* Aberdare.

[91] See T. Evans's letter accusing Price, in his editorial capacity, of trying to whitewash Fothergill, in *Y Gwron, 14 November 1857.*

[92] Details of this contest can be traced in *C.M.G.*, 9 September 1857, *passim*, and *Y Gwron* of the same dates, with the addition of *Y Gwron*, 23 February 1858.

[93] See Boundary Commissioners' *Reports*, 1832.

[94] See *Census Reports* and *Abstract of Merthyr Tydfil Union*. See also Boundary Commissioners' *Reports*, 1867.

[95] In what was by then a double-member constituency, Merthyr polled 13,329 and Aberdare 11,446 voters. See *Merthyr Express*, 21 November 1868.

[96] The 1837 election is described in Islwyn W. R. David, 'Political and Electioneering Activity in South-east Wales, 1820-1852' (M.A. thesis, University of Wales, 1959), pp. 140-1. C. Wilkins, *History of Merthyr Tydfil* (1908), p. 215 gives details of the polling in Dowlais, Merthyr, and Aberdare.

[97] For D. W. James, see *Bywgraffiadur*, C. Wilkins, op. cit., and Gwyn A. Williams, 'The Making of Radical Merthyr', W.H.R., 1, 161-92.

[98] See *C.M.G.*, 3 July 1852, for the *Address* dated 29 June.

[99] See *C.M.G.*, 17 July 1852.

[100] See Gwyn A. Williams, *art.* cit.

[101] *C.M.G.*, 3 December 1852.

[102] Ibid., 11 December.

[103] Ibid.

[104] The election is discussed by Gwyn A. Williams, *art.* cit., pp. 184-6, and in Islwyn W. R. David, op. cit., pp. 129-31. And see the interesting analysis in the memorir of Guest in *C.M.G.*, 3 December 1852.

[105] Ibid., 11 December 1852.

[106] One newspaper reported 'on tolerably good authority' that Fothergill had privately cvommunicated his regret to Bruce for having given his support to W. M. James, See *C.M.G., 11 December 1852.* There is no direct evidence for this, and Fothergill's subsequent attitudes bo Bruce throw doubt on its validity.

[107] See Price's claims that he and Fothergill had supported James in 1852 in *Seren Cymru*, 28 February 1867, and compare ibid., 13 December 1867.

[108] The election is well covered in the local papers, e.g. *C.M.G.*, 14 March 1857 onwards.

[109] the Merthyr and Caerphilly Committee was chaired by R. T. Crawshay, that of Dowlais by G. T. Clark, with H. A. Bruce a prominent member, *C.M.G.*, 27 March 1857.

[110]

		Vaughan	Talbot	Vivian	Total
Aberdare	..	162	262	285	709
Merthyr	..	174	400	431	1,005

C.M.G., 4 April 1857.

[111] E.g. Y *Gwron*, 17 October 1857. This election is notable as being the first occasion on which the Calvinistic Methodists as a distinct denomination called upon their members 'to support by their votes *no other* candidates but those who consistently advocate and practise the principles of religious liberty, *Cambrian*, 25 April 1857.

[112] For these speeches see J. Thorold Rogers (ed.), *Speeches of John Bright, M.P.* (1868), II, and for his reform Bill see W. N. Molesworth, *History of England* (1874), III, 132.

[113] *C.M.G.*, 1 January 1859. Merthyr would have got two additional members by the terms of Bright's Bill.

[114] The secretary of the non-electors was William Davies, a puddler. See *C.M.G.*, 23 April 1859.

[115] At this meeting, Gould, the Chartist, proposed the nomination of Overton, which was carried. It was J. W. James who objected to this unusual procedure. See report in ibid., 23 April 1859. But see *Merthyr Star*, 29 April 1859, which came out strongly in Elderton's favour, and for reports of rumours that Fothergill and Crawshay would support him, ibid., 24 April 1859.

[116] *Seren Cymru*, 30 April 1859.

[117] *C.M.G.*, 23 April 1859.

[118] Ibid., 7 May 1859.

[119] See B. Evans, op. cit., p. 131.

[120] For an analysis of the relations of the Liberation Society and Welsh politics at this time see my *Explorations and Explanations*, pp. 236-68.

[121] See the list of council members in *Proceedings of the First Anti-State-Church Conference* (1844), and *Report of the first Triennial Conference* (1847). See *Secretary's Cash Book*, L.C.C. MS. A/Lib/89, for subscriptions from Hirwaun and Aberdare in 1848.

[122] The first name to appear is that of Mr. D. E. Williams of Hirwaun in 1848.

[123] See *Report of the Second Triennial Conference* (1850).

[124] E.g. in November 1859 when he was chief speaker with C. J. Foster, LL.D., chairman of the Society's parliamentary committee.

[125] For details of this policy shift see my article, in *Explorations and Explanatins*, pp. 259-63.

[126] The resolution is worth recording *in extenso*. 'That this conference is of opinion that Welsh Nonconformity has never been adequately represented in the House of Commons—that while the population of Wales contains a much larger proportion of Dissenters than is to be found in England, Ireland, or Scotland, the relative number of their parliamentary representatives is much less than in either of those countries; and that, even of those members who attach themselves to the Liberal party, the majority are in the habit of treating questions deeply interesting to the friends of religious liberty with culpable remissness; that this Conference is constrained to admit that, for these reasons, the Dissenting influence exerted by Wales for the advancement of these voluntary principles had been comparatively small, and, having such a conviction, the Conference is earnestly solicitous that practical steps should be taken for so improving

the Welsh representation as to bring ti to harmony with the views and feelings of the population', *Nonconformist,* I (1862), 830.

[127] For the speech see the *Nonconformist,* pp. 831-2. or *Cambrian, 26 September 1862.*

[128] See W. R. Williams, *The Parliamentary History of the Principality of Wales* (1895), for details of the representation of Brecon. The election is described in outline in B. Evans, op. cit., pp. 169-71, and is well covered in *Seren Cymru, Merthyr Telegraph, Merthyr Express, Aberdare Times,* and *Baner.*

[129] See *Aberdare Times,* 13 April 1867. The original manuscript of the speech, corrected for the press, is in N.L.W. MS. 3317B.

[130] B. Evans, op. cit., p. 171.

[131] The following is an example of his language: 'The fact is, Wales is very pleased and surprisingly ready to throw her principles to the moles and bats, in order to have the opportunity of raising the hat, or bending a knee, to some petty lordling (or, indeed, to the lordling's steward or hound); verily, they would be as ready, at the word of command, to abase themselves to the hound as to the lord—to obey is their lot'. *Seren Cymru,* August 1866 (translated).

[132] Ibid., 14 September 1866.

[133] Ibid., 24 August and 14 September 1866.

[134] In 1867 he hoped that at the next election it would be possible for Brecon nonconformists to be in a position to share the seats with the Anglican landed interest, Camden or Somerset the county, and the Nonconformists the borough. *Aberdare Times,* 11 May 1867.

[135] The other four were all North Walians—from Ruabon (two), Wrexham, and Brymbo. See pamhlet in the George Howell Collection, 324. 42/53a-68b in the Bishopsgate Institute. The Brymbo member was Rev. J. Jones, author of the highly interesting *Llyfr Etholiadol Cymru* (1867).

[136] League sympathizers organized a reform demonstration at Merthyr, at which the chartists, Gould and Dr. Jones and the very radical Baptist Rev. Charles White, were prominent, and which was addressed by C. M. Elderton, evidently nursing the constituency. See *Aberdare Times,* 27 April 1867.

[138] Quoted from the requisition convening the meeting which was held on 7 May 1867. See *Aberdare Times,* 11 May 1867, for a full report.

[139] The final resolution, moved by the Unitarian Rev. J. J. George, expressed guarded confidence in Gladstone but was more critical of Bruce: 'From education, habits, and natural prejudices, it was difficult for a man in his position of life to thoroughly understand the wants of the working man', ibid. for a list of the committee members, which included most of the old political associates of Price, see *Cardiff Times,* 11 May 1867.

[140] A preliminary meeting, chaired by C. H. James, had been held in Merthyr on 25 June *(Cardiff Times,* 29 June 1867); for the July meeting see ibid., 27 July 1867, and for the Aberdare meeting ibid., 3 August, where it is reported that Dr. Price dissented from the proposition to invite Henry Richard 'believing (that it) would be rather to jeopardise the seat of Bruce than prevent the election of Fothergill'.

[141] *Seren Cymru,* 21 May 1867.

[142] *Aberdare Times,* 29 June and 6 July 1867. Price gave a retrospective and not wholly accurate account of these transactions in *Seren Cymru,* 11 September 1868.

[143] *Aberdare Times,* 6 July 1867.

[144] *Y Gwladgarwr,* 22 August 1868, and *Merthyr Express,* 21 November 1868.

[145] Some of the Welsh coal-owners, such as David Davis, Blaen-gwawr, and his son and partner, David Davis, Maes-y-ffynnon, sat on both the Fothergill and Richard committees.

[146] *Aberdare Times,* 29 June 1867. A revised *Address,* omitting references favourable to Bruce, was issued in July 1868. See ibid., 25 July 1868.

[147] *Cardiff Times,* 29 June 1867, *Aberdare Times,* 27 June 1867. There is a long and detailed account of these transactions in *Baner ac Amserau Cymru,* 4 September and 30 October 1867.

[148] *Cardiff Times,* 3 August 1867.

[149] See, for instance, letters published in *Seren Cymru,* 13 December 1867, with list of correspondents who had written similar letters. Also the article in *Baner ac Amserau Cymru* already cited: 'if it were possible for Wales to have a say in the matter, I do not think I should be wrong in stating that 94 per cent. would be for Bruce. And it is certain . . . that I doubt whether Wales would ever forgive you if you lent your influence to return Fothergill at the expense of sacrificing Bruce', See also *Seren Cymru,* 8 November 1867, for Price's notice of these articles and of complaints of ill-usage, and ibid., 13 December 1876, for mention of 'a multitude' of letters pleading with him to withdraw from his invidious position, including letters from prominent Englishmen.

[150] *Seren Cymru,* 8 and 15 November 1867, 13 December 1867, and 11 September 1868.

[151] *Baner ac Amserau Cymru,* 4 September 1867.

[152] Ibid., 5 July 1867 (translated). Note that this was written when the candidature of Richard was only rumoured. Later letters are more specific and condemnatory.

[153] For references see my article in *Explorations and Explanations,* op.cit.

[154] Ibid., pp. 278-80, recounts the development of this situation in brief.

[155] *Seren Cymru,* 28 February 1868. The reference is to the pamphlet published by Nixon consisting of his original letters advocating the double shift in the *Mining Journal* (1867), pp. 787 and 794, his correspondence with Lord Kinnaird (chairman of the last Mines Commission), with letters of support from industrialists, inspectors of mines, engineers, agents, and Dr. Price. See John Nixon, *The Single Shift System the Cause of Double the Loss of Life* (Cardiff, 1867).

[156] *Seren Cymru,* 20 December 1867.

[157] *Seren Cymru,* 6 march 1868.

[158] He revised their pamphlet *Double and Single Shift Working Compared* (Aberdare, 1868) for a second edition. *Seren Cymru,* 27 March 1868.

[159] *Aberdare Times,* 21 November 1868.

[160] Votes cast for each candidate in Merthyr and Aberdare:

Merthyr	..	Richard	..	6,095 or 46%
		Fothergill	..	3,698 or 28%
		Bruce	..	3,538 or 26%
			Total ..	13,329

Aberdare	..	Richard	..	5,472 or 49%
		Fothergill	..	3,815 or 33%
		Bruce	..	2,159 or 18%
			Total ..	11,446

These figures are based on the Nonconformist Committee's hourly reports. See *Merthyr Express,* 21 November 1868.

[161] The Bruce Committee returns from individual polling booths in the Merthyr parish are to be found in *Merthyr Express,* 21 November 1868.

HEALTH, WEALTH AND POLITICS IN VICTORIAN WALES*

If I were to choose a text for these lectures it would be part of a sentence from a letter written by a Mr. William Jowett of Morriston 5 February 1859 to Henry Hussey Vivian, Esq., of Hafod and Singleton Abbey, Swansea. And like any good preacher I would then put it into its context and by exegesis arrive at some great practical or doctrinal truths. I shall spare you the exegesis and it will surprise none of my friends that I have no great truths to utter, but the text and the context are highly relevant to what I have to say in these lectures. The words that Jowett wrote are as follows: " . . . certainly not while men are what they are". The immediate context is this. Vivian had bought an old, abandoned zinc spelter works at Morriston and had declared his intention of re-starting the furnaces when trade improved. Our Mr. Jowett, on learning about this, had written to the Secretary of State for the Home Department who, as the political head of the Local Government Act Office was responsible for public health under the 1858 Public Health Act, to ask whether Vivian could be prevented from doing this because of the appalling pollution and danger to the health of the inhabitants of Morriston that would inevitably ensue. On successive occasions and with the greatest possible courtesy he had also written to Vivian who for a long time ignored him until eventually he replied very briefly to the effect that Jowett should mind his own business: his were the only intimations he had received that the Spelter Works at Morriston were considered other than a benefit to the place. It was this brief note that occasioned the letter from which my extract is taken. "You state", wrote Jowett, "that I am the only one who has intimated to you that the works would prove a nuisance. No doubt of it, and let me ask you how many there are who dare do it? Can any man employed by you or through you do so without the risk of being dismissed? or would anyone working at Copper Smelting take upon himself the consequences—certainly not while men are what they are—but apply the Ballot and then see how matters will stand".[1] We can safely

Morriston near Swansea.

assume that Jowett was not intentionally raising philosophical questions about the nature of man, though clearly these were involved, nor that it was his intention to engage Vivian in a discussion on political theory, though this too was involved. But it is equally certain that Jowett could see that the decision to open or not to open a zinc spelter at Morriston was in essence a political question.

Before we ask how this could be so, let us move as far away as possible from the toxic fumes and the deadly industries of the Lower Swansea Valley and go to the apparently unadulterated atmosphere, the rural solitudes and the sweet security of the streets of Bala in Merioneth. There, at his home in Plas-yn-dre, and in the same week exactly George Price Lloyd, Esq., was memorializing the secretary of state on the subject of the adoption of the Public Health Act of 1858 by Bala. The context of his letter was as follows. Earlier that month the ratepayers of Bala had held a properly convened public meeting at which they had decided, with only one dissenting voice, to petition the government to be brought under the 1858 Local Government Act. This would enable the ratepayers to establish a Local Board of Health, to cleanse the town, provide it with sewers and with clean water, light it and generally help to create conditions that would make it a more salubrious and comfortable place to live in. The odd man out in this movement, the single objector, was Richard Watkin Price, Esq., of Rhiwlas, and round about the time that Jowett was having his *contretemps* with Vivian, Price was sending a counter-petition to the secretary of state praying that he would dismiss the ratepayers' petition. Now R. W. Price was the proprietor of an estate of 9,000 acres in the vicinity of the town: an adjacent parish was almost entirely owned by him: he was one of the richest land-owners in Merioneth, was head of an ancient family and lineage going back to pre-Norman times, he was chairman of the bench and the most powerful man in what local government existed. His arguments and the facts he adduced are interesting and revealing. Bala was a small place of only about 1,300 people, "chiefly poor persons earning their livelihood by manual labour with the exception of a few shopkeepers and others of small incomes, there being", he explained, "only two residents whose independent income exceeds £300 per annum". He went on to say that there was only one bank, no staple trade or manufacture, that the death rate was not exceptionally high, and he concluded "That there does not exist within the said Town any occasion for the said Act, owing to the poverty of the Inhabitants and the small amount of rateable Property". Later on, Price gave it as his opinion that the whole movement was nothing by a conspiracy on the part of a few people in the town "merely to get the management of the place into their own hands".[2]

Morriston and Bala were vastly different types of places of course: they were cultures apart you might say: and so they appeared to be, the one an almost archetypal industrial village but recently planted, more blessed than most comparable places perhaps by the vision and initiative of its paternalistic minded founder, the other almost a paradigm of the small rural town, scarcely moving in its deep antiquity, utterly dependent for its livelihood upon the prosperity of small tenant farmers. But there were important resemblances as well. First, in both places political activity, organization and debate originate in local events and local conditions. Public health is the immediate occasion—atmospheric pollution in Morriston, a desire to clean up the town in Bala—but the consequence is a transformation of local government. Then we notice the important role played in this by relative inequalities of wealth. These are as wide and as basic in Bala as in Morriston, and they not only underly the pattern of disease but also largely determine the shape and structure of local government and the debate about politics. Finally, we notice that there are deep similarities in the assumptions about, or attitudes to, politics current in both places. Jowett's ''men being what they are'' (i.e. when it comes to political action) corresponds to Price's arrogant certainty that his judgement of the town's need should prevail over the common voice of its inhabitants.

First of all, the concern with public health and in particular with the sanitary state of urban places. This began in Wales, as in the rest of Britain, with the work of Edwin Chadwick and his great *General Report on the Sanitary Condition of the Labouring Population of Great Britain* of 1842; the Reports of the Royal Commission on the State of Large towns of 1843-5, and the passing of the first Public Health Act in 1848, but it required the frightful cholera epidemic of 1849 to begin the necessary sanitary reforms. Asiatic cholera had reached Britain in epidemic proportions for the first time in October 1831, and the mortality caused by that epidemic has been estimated at 23,000. Relatively few of these deaths had been in Wales, and in any case, the demographic impact of cholera was negligible. But it was a shock disease and unlike most other diseases—so it was imagined—no respecter of persons or of class. As the authorities in Welsh towns had heard of its approach so, in the initial panic, they had set up Boards of Health or Nuisances Committees, and generally had whistled in the dark, for having no idea how the disease was transmitted there could be no clear idea of how to deal with it. In fact, the original panic had been everywhere soon forgotten, and the largely ineffective administrative measure abandoned. Then in 1849 came the next great

visitation, and this time 53,000 people died, and Wales
suffered a major attack. In all the main urban places, and
particularly in Merthyr Tydfil where 1,683 died and another
455 in 1854, there were outbreaks, and it was this visitation
more than anything else which aroused a continuing concern
with the sanitary condition of the main centres of population.
By now the equation of dirt with disease was clearly established
and because the medical profession held almost exclusively to
miasmatic explanations as to its modes of diffusion, the sanitary movement which followed to all intents and purposes
became an attack upon smells and the removal from the abodes
of people of the more obvious causes of smells became a main
objective. Hence the movement for the cleansing of towns, for
sewage removal, and the supply of piped water.

That there was justification enough for this activity no one
who has read the report of public health inspectors and, later,
of local Medical Officers of Health can doubt. Towns were for
the most part unpaved, sewers were open and on the surface of
the main roads or back lanes, there were no arrangements for
the removal (beyond sale to local farmers for manure) of
human effluvia, and the most common form of disposal was the
open cesspool—"that magazine of all the contagious". Running water was invariably in short supply and since rivers, the
most obvious receptacles for industrial and human waste, were
the major source of supply, water for human consumption was
always and everywhere in towns heavily polluted. It was these
fundamental conditions that Sanitarians set out to remove and
as a direct result of the coincidence of disease and legislation in
1848/9—an accidental coincidence—about 25 urban or urban/
/rural places in Wales—17 of them in south Wales—adopted or
petitioned to adopt, the 1848 Public Health Act. By the eve of
the 1858 Act a few more had been added, and by the time of the
Local Government Act of 1872 about 70 places, urban and
rural, had equipped themselves with the powers of the Act.
Local authorities thus set up, either as committees of corporations (as in Swansea) or as distinct bodies (as in Merthyr)
could exercise the power available to them in the two Health
Acts, but could also make use of the provisions of the almost
annual additions to this basic legislation which successive

parliaments passed. Thus, there were a number of Nuisances Removal Acts (1855, 1860, 1866), various Sewage Utilization Acts (1865, 1867), Lodging Houses Acts (1850, 1851), Vaccination Acts (1853, 1861), a Disease Prevention Act (1855), a Sanitary Act (1866), and finally, a Local Government Act in 1872 and the Public Health Act of 1875 which consolidated a great deal of this legislation.

Until the passing of the Sanitary Act of 1866 and the Public Health Act of 1875 the trouble with most of this legislation was that it was largely permissive. The 1848 Act and again the 1854 Act could not be applied except on petition of two thirds of the property owners and ratepayers or when mortality exceeded 23 per 1,000. The 1848 Act and subsequent Acts gave Local Boards authority to borrow money on the security of the rates to pay for the essential undertakings, but there was no means by which the central authority could compel these authorities to proceed with essential works though it considerable powers once an application had been made. Thus, Swansea borrowed a total of £104,000 from the Public Loans Office between the formation of the Local Board in 1849 and 1864. Arriving at decisions to spend money, however, invariably occasioned contests of often furious proportions as parties formed over the issue of the spending of public money. This is a theme we shall examine later. It is sufficient for the moment to make the point that the lack of central direction and control and of powers of coercion, the intricacy of the law involved, and the voluntary nature of the legislation vitiated at worst and seriously delayed at best much of the sanitary reform of the period.

Mortality rates illustrate this melancholy point. Four years after Victoria came to the throne—which was also the year when civil registration of births, deaths and marriages came in—the crude death-rate per 1,000 population in Wales was 20.2. In 1848, on the eve of the passing of the Public Health Act it was 22.0. The following year—the year of the cholera—it rose to 25.8. Not until the last decade of the century did the rate fall and remain consistently below 100.0. It was with the reform of the Board of Health in 1855 and the appointment of Sir John Simon as the first Medical Officer that these statistics of disease and death came to be analyzed and the foundations for systematic studies of public health inaugurated, and one of the first products of his labours and those of his associates in the Medical Department of the Privy Council was the constructing of a kind of topography of death and disease in Britain. At first, in the spirit of Chadwick's Report of 1842, the inspectors looked at urban areas and very soon they had identified the killer diseases and the diseases that debilitated or that ended, when they did not kill, in chronic sickness. Diarrhoeal diseases, diseases of the lung, industrial diseases, fevers, especially scarlet fever, smallpox, typhus—these were located in the sense that it was discovered by investigation on the spot precisely the conditions in which these diseases thrived. Then from 1864 onwards attention was turned to rural districts largely in order to investigate outbreaks of fever in country towns and the discovery was made that sanitation was as necessary in the countryside as in the towns, and that the health of the peasantry in some places was almost as precarious as that of the town dwellers. The incidence of disease may have been different, but the general level of health was little better than in the towns. Thus, the great reports of Dr. Hunter, who moved through industrial and rural south and south west Wales in the 1860s, make melancholy reading. In the towns, to the appalling and ever-present hazards of violent accidents, maiming and death by explosions and from machinery and the steady toll on youth and vigour of a variety of pulmonary diseases casued by working long hours in ill-ventilated places, was added the avoidable sickness caused by dirt, by over-crowding, by bad living conditions generally, while in the countryside he found a people weakened and disease-ridden by lack of food. "The farmer in Wales as well as the (agricultural) labourer", he wrote, "must be taken to mean a person generally badly lodged and insufficiently fed and clothed . . . The evil effects of poverty upon the health is rather increased by the frugal habits of the Welsh farmer . . . it may be truly said of the class that in many districts the farmer himself does not eat fresh meat once a month . . . the farm labourers who board in the house fare proportionately worse . . . A super-intendent registrar in Cardiganshire reported a man who earned sixpence a day, and had no other resources for a wife

Aberdare's first Hospital c. 1875.

Mr. G. T. Clark's Hospital, Dowlais.

Photo: Glamorgan Record Office.

and three children''.[4] If the miner, the iron worker and copper
smelter typically suffered from inflammatory lung diseases due
to lack of ventilation and extremes of heat and cold, the farmer
and farm labourer and his family suffered from phthisis, tuberculosis, other forms of consumption, and typhus, and the
causes were often poverty, lack of nourishment and living conditions sometimes as bad if not worse than in worst parts of industrial towns. In 1864 in Cardiganshire Dr. Hunter found
that commonly children cried for food as soon as weaned and it
was judged that if the climate had been cold the people had all
died. It is probably true to say that, so far as Wales was concerned, the equation or disease with poverty as distinct from
with dirt was based initially on observations of country life. If
the miner and the iron worker were hungry sometimes, as
undoubtedly was the case and sometimes for months on end,
hunger was the condition of life for the workers on the over-
populated land, and two bad harvests in a row could spell
famine and death. This was the conclusion of investigations by
Dr. Hunter into the death rate of the population of south west
Wales.

Nevertheless, it was inevitable and anyway made good sense
to concentrate on the urban districts, for by the mid-century it
was clear that it was to the industrial areas that the excess
population of the countryside were moving and that Wales, like
England, was becoming an urban country—a country of town
dwellers. The industrial areas were growing inexorably at the
expense of the rural districts. By the decade 1851-61 every
county in Wales with the exception of Denbighshire and Glamorgan experienced a net outflow of people. Net migration for
the whole of the country in that decade ran at a rate of 1.67 *per
cent,* in the following decade 3.82 *per cent* and in the decade
1871-81 at the rate of 3.67 *per cent.* Thereafter, the rates fell and
by the beginning of this century Wales was receiving population at the rate of nearly 5 *per cent* for the decade. During the
central decades of the century—from 1841 to 1881—the
pattern as a whole was of consistent loss of population but it is
the county patterns that are most revealing. It was the deep
rural counties of the south west and of mid-Wales where there
was no industry to support their continually rising populations,

where consequently the pressure on available resources was most acute and where living standards were at their worst, that the loss was greatest. Cardiganshire, for example, lost 10 *per cent* throughout the period, and Radnorshire by 1881 was losing 19 *per cent* of its population. This, it must be emphasized, was at a time of rapid population increase—about 11 *per cent* each decade. Natural increase (excess of births over deaths) was rising consistently throughout the period (from 10.42 in 1841-51 to 14.73 in 1871-81) but in some of the rural counties even higher rates than these could not maintain their populations within their boundaries. The rural counties which, as Dr. David Howell shows, were not very efficient to producing food were on the contrary prolific in their production of children. They produced children for export!

The monstrous irony in this situation, of course, was that for the multitudes of young men and women fleeing from the degenerative diseases of the countryside—the products of poverty and malnutrition—the consequence for them in their new abodes were as likely as not to be sickness and early death from some other, perhaps more terrifying, disease. But this could never be foreseen, nor was the evidence before his eyes such as to propose to the imagination that such was the probability. It was moral degeneration rather than physical degeneration that Victorians identified as the chief and characteristic danger of towns. The impression that one gains from the views of contemporaries about levels of general prosperity in the towns is that it was high: standards of living were vastly superior to those in the countryside. The colliers of Aberdare in 1853 were incensed when H. A. Bruce told them that it was their avariciousness rather than need that made them reject a wage of about a £1 a week when their cousins in Carmarthenshire were bringing up families of six or seven children on 7 shillings a week, and G. T. Clark said in 1848 that £10 to £15 a month was not unusual for a puddler. He found it "difficult to reconcile statistics of mortality in the . . . district with the appearance of the people. They appear to be well fed, when off work, warmly clad, and in good bodily condition".[5] Eight years earlier the Registrar General in the introduction to his Second Annual

Report, wondered whether diseases in Wales might not have some 'racial characteristics, and regretted that 'the ordinary laws of mortality are at present disturbed in Wales by the confluence of workmen within the mining districts''[6]. Sir John Simon's inspectors—Dr. Greenhow in 1858, for example—were mainly concerned in their visitiation to the urban areas with industrial diseases, and their reports are filled with graphic descriptions of the conditions under which men laboured and the processes they were engaged in.[7] Yet it is certain that these alone were not responsible for the appalling death rates and the chronic sickness but their existence in combination with two other sets of factors that seemed to be inseparable from urbanization, namely, areas or pockets of bad housing and the existence of a stratum of hopeless and terrifying poverty at the base of society.

All towns, old and new, had their areas of bad housing. In old medieval towns these were invariably streets and enclosed courts of small cottages put up as in-filling in the ancient burgage plots, and in the new towns they were the original cottages erected for or by the first immigrant settlers. In both these categories the death rates were invariably higher than the average for the town as a whole. Swansea had its fair share of the first type. In 1884, ten years after the Artizans and Labourers' Dwelling Improvement Act of 1875, the average annual death rate over a period of five years in Back street was 39 per 1,000, Queen Street 42, Frog Street 40 "with an undue proportion of death from zymotic diseases and phthisis".[8] Merthyr Tydfil is an example of the second type where certain well-defined areas, such as 'China' and Tydfil's Well had death rates exceeding 37 as against the town average of 23.[9] By the end of the 1880s the authorities were beginning to demolish such streets of houses and squares, but the displacement of people which resulted merely created slum conditions elsewhere, sometimes in new houses specially built for displaced families. For example, when the Dyfatty came to be inspected with a view of demolishing that pestilential area it was discovered that it contained 1,753 individiuals, classified into 254 prostitutes and loafers, 1,251 artizans and 248 tradesmen. Where were

Carmarthenshire Cottages.

they to go? No doubt Swansea Corporation acted from the highest motives and for the general good when they demolished such slum-areas, but in this particular—which cost £121,000—the result was merely to create slums elsewhere. "Fifteen houses in one part of the town have been built for artizans, but they are very superior, and none of the artizan class occupy them. In another part thirty houses have been erected, but only eight persons out of 250 who were displaced reside in them; they are too good for one family of the poorer class, and already some of them are occupied as tenements by two families".[10]

This identification and mapping of sources of disease in the midst of towns was the great discovery of the 1860s when the work of the Medical Officers of Health, where they had been appointed by often reluctant authorities, began to bear fruit. What these local topographies of disease achieved was to show more or less conclusively that ill-health, contagion, infection were associated not only with dirt but also with poverty. "As a rule", said Dr. Dykes before the Sanitary Commission, "epidemic contagious diseases affect the poor first".[11] In his discussion on the causes of premature death Dr. Simon put it thus " . . . even with the high civilization of this country, and with its unequalled system of poor-law relief, *privation* still exists as a cause of premature death. Children especially suffer from this cause; and many of their so-called scrofulous ailments are in fact starvation-disorders . . . there are other kinds of privation practically inseparable from poverty. It must have scanty house-room . . . scanty clothing and scanty fuel. It must have a weight of care in its daily struggle for subsistence".[12] It is also clear that where this relationship between socio-economic status and disease was recognized for what it was—as something beyond the possibility of alleviation by the individuals concerned, the moral censoriousness so typical of the time came to be replaced by an enlightened demand for tougher mandatory legislation and central control. The most enlightened Medical Officers of Health wanted the same kind of centralization and rationalization of the complex of competing and jealous authorities as was being slowly achieved in the country as a whole applied in the localities as well: Dr.

Ebenezer Davies of Swansea, for example, and Dr. T. J. Dykes of Merthyr. And there is no doubt that by the 1870s and early 1880s their work was beginning to show results in Wales. I think, that it was the flood of new migrants flowing into the new colliery villages and into the port-towns and old centres of industry that made substantial improvements in the physical condition of people virtually impossible to sustain and which left to later generations a legacy that still poisons the lives of some communities.

If there is an element of doubt as to the actual effects of all this legislation on the physical condition of the people—and the official investigations and reports of the 1920s and the 1930s indicate that it was less than one might at first suppose—there can be no doubt about its effect on local government and the growth of political awareness. G. T. Clark observed that it was difficult to reconcile the high mortality statistics of Merthyr Tydfil with apparent vigour and healthy appearance of the inhabitants of the place. Mr. Clark, in addition to being an engineer and manager at the Dowlais Iron Company (he was soon to become resident and managing trustee) was a fine historian, and a man on whose judgement, power of observation and objectivity the Central Board of Health relied heavily for reports on the sanitary conditions of many Welsh places, and if his essential perplexities are also ours perhaps we should listen carefully also to the explanation that he proposed. One of the reasons he gave for the "monstrous mortality" of the place was what he called "the wretched civic economy of these districts". By that he meant local government, and a year later R. W. Rammell, whose Report of 1850 on the sanitary conditions of the town was to be such a landmark in its social history, likewise thought that this might be the key to understanding the nature of the community. "For all intents and purposes of civil government", he wrote, "Merthyr Tydfil is as destitute as the smallest rural village of the empire".[13] Not mis-government necessarily, but non-government, or a form of government so rudimentary as to be wholly inadequate to the size and importance of the place. That is why the language of visitors to these districts, whether they were official or unofficial, government reporters or London journalists, tended to become rhetorical and florid. They were baffled by what they saw and knew not how to describe it. Dean Conybeare of Llandaff Cathedral, the great geologist, sought for his meataphors in science, and referred to the string of settlements at the heads of the valleys as "condensations of labouring people".[14] Another called them "colonies in the desert".[15] Whatever these places were, they were not towns in the accepted sense, and the people who lived in them were not 'town-dwellers' but the 'inhabitants of the iron-districts'. They might be urban; they were certainly not civic.

The model of town government that observers had in mind as most needed by these mineral districts was that of the municipal corporation—those ancient chartered boroughs whose governmental systems had been reformed and re-modelled by statute in 1835. They had been given forms of democratic self-government in which councils elected on a franchise wider than the parlimentary one, were responsible to the ratepayers for whom they acted. Swansea was one such municipality, and its mayor and twenty four councillors and aldermen, its recorder and seven J.Ps (appointed by the Crown) governed not only the town and franchise but also most of the region of the Lower Tawe, including Morriston, where industrial growth was greatest and population most dense. Cardiff, Newport and Neath had similar corporations. In fact, of course, the possession of institutions of government, however elaborate, was no guarantee of good government, and the sanitary state of most of the small boroughs of Wales which had not been radically reformed was scarcely such as to suggest that they were more fortunately placed than the government-less iron-towns. They were better off only if the institutions they possessed were put to good purpose, or the powers they had used for the common good. It was potentialities that changed when a place was ʾbrought under government.

Pontentialities changed because the institutions of govern-ment current in the towns not only made it possible for them to do desirable things, such as bring clean water to the houses, sewer the place, pave it, light it and so on, but they also pro-vided a framework within which decisions could be properly taken by the people most affected. This meant the possibility of

Cottages near Abergavenny.

political conflict, of a struggle for power among individuals and groups. That is what the municipalities possessed and that the iron-towns lacked. The pattern of politics was different in Swansea from that in Merthyr, and part of the reason was this 'lack of governance' in the latter place. One tends to forget the magnitude of the municipal tasks being undertaken from the 1850s onwards by towns. The expenditure of money on the security of the rate was truly enormous: towns by the 1870s were owners of reservoirs, gasworks, sewage-works etc. on a huge scale: running a corporation was big business and something to be fought for and over. The iron-districts had none of this. Their only experience of formal politics was in elections to the Poor Law Board of Guardians which in the case of Merthyr had replaced the Select Vestry in 1836, and in observing its activities and those of its off-shoots from afar. Its operations were remote because it was a middle class institution: lower class people could be forgiven for believing that it represented a kind of conspiracy against them. Public expenditure was miniscule, even the sum raise annually for the relief of the poor in general. The aggregate of the Sunday collections made in the chapels in 1861 after the adoption of the 1848 Act was greater than that raised by the Guardians for the relief of the poor. In the single year 1861 the 45 chapels in the town and vicinity of Merthyr collected no less than £8,000 for the maintenance of the ministry.[16] The *total* expenditure between 1858 and 1865 on the new water supply was £84,000! It is not strange, when one thinks of it, that politics in Merthyr tended to oscillate violently between the extremes of apathy and rebellion. "A population living in such a state of discomfort", wrote Dr. Holland in 1854, "cannot be safe . . . I am no longer surprised at the violent and apparently purposeless outrages which have occasionally broken out in South Wales. In Lancashire similar causes produced similar results, but there the cause is more aggravated and the effect more violent: as Blackburn is to Merthyr, so is a Lancashire riot to a Newport rebellion".[17] Adopting the 1848 Public Health Act changed nothing overnight: on the contrary, the chronology of improvement, the incredible delays in the provision of clean water and sewage disposal, is exactly what one would expect, because the lack of an a organized political life and of institutions meant that there was no way in which pressure could be brought upon those responsible for the delay. In no place in Wales was oligarchy safer or less under challenge than in Merthyr, the home of working-class radicalism!

Why was this? The answer lies in the fact that this lack of governance was merely a symptom of a much profounder difference between the old-established and the newly-planted towns, namely, differences in social structure. Contemporaries understood this. G. T. Clark and Rammell, for example. The former put it thus. ''The social economy of these districts has suffered severely from the want of a middle-class between the master and labourer. The master is a great capitalist, in many cases non-resident, and having but little opportunity of improving the condition of his people. The agents and managers are dependent upon the masters, and are too commonly raised from the lower classes to retain much intimacy or feel much on their behalf. Hence an absence of sympathy between the rich and the poor, and the spread of secret societies, chartism, and rebellion. The people . . . have nothing in common with their lords, and they are ready, at the instigation of designing men, to rise up against them and government''.[18] Rammel, likewise, saw only two groups in the population, the masters and their agents, and the working men with a small class of tradesmen and professional men to serve their joint needs. Another observer, Dr. Kay, who was also inspecting the place on behalf of the Central Board of Health, distinguished a three-class system, the working classes, ''a middle rank of tradespeople, shopkeepers and others'', and the upper class of iron-masters and lay and clerical gentlemen. They agreed, whether they had a two-class or a three-class model of society, that what was lacking was a class of men of independent means and position, not connected by profession or interest to the main industry or any of its off-shoots, and residing in the towns. The ideal they had in mind was of the landowner, great or relatively small, who maintained a house and who resided either permanently or for part of the year in the town, and in so doing set standards of behaviour—morals as the Victorians said—who expected and got the deference of all other classes whatever the sources of their wealth, and who brought taste and gentility into society as a whole as patrons of building, the arts and education. Without such classes, they thought, and particularly without an aristocratic class, they there could be no ''great exhibition of political things'' as Walter Bagehot put it, on the local scale, no ''theatrical show of society'', no visible government, no incarnation of deference. Government was what an ironmaster (Anthony Hill of Penydarren) said it should be, confined to ''two objects only—to tax and to punish''. Even our Mr. Jowett, who was radical enough and who always claimed in his letters to the General Board of Health in London to speak on behalf of the working-classes of Morriston, made no bones about this. When the ratepayers of Morriston started a movement in 1861 for separation from the Borough of Swansea Jowett opposed it as a conspiracy aimed against the poor. He explained how the Vestry was dominated by these small property-holders. ''It will be quite impossible'', he wrote in 1864 ''to obtain justice by Men solely from Morriston—as we have no *Real* Gentlemen amongst us''.[19]

This model, like most models, grossly over-simplified the real situation in most of the old Welsh industrial towns: so far as the boroughs of south Wales were concerned, from Newport to Swansea and beyond, it was more generally the case that quite early in the century the local gentry had themselves turned entrepreneurs. Thus the Llewellyns of Penllergaer and the industrialist Dillwyns had united their families. In Cardiff, Aberafan, Neath, Bethesda the local landowners had taken a leading part in the industrial development of their towns without, however, actually entering into marriage aliances with the industrialists or financiers. Nevertheless, their presence was a determining factor in the shape of social developments—in the case of Lord Bute and Lord Penrhyn down to the detail of town planning and architectural style. The obverse of this was the adoption by the capitalists in their places of work and residence, of the fashions and ways of life of the gentry. This happened also in iron-towns, in Merthyr and Aberdare, for example, but in those places it involved non-residence—the Guests in Dorsetshire, the Crawshay tribe in their various county seats, and the Fothergills and others in country houses in the Vale. Where they were resident these upper-class families enclosed parks and erected palatial houses which in turn encouraged the creation of socially distinct suburban parts of town—Singleton Park and Sketty in Swansea. And always municipal government was a major pre-occupation. Sometimes it led to massive bourgeois alliances against artistocracy (as in Cardiff against Bute and in Swansea against Beaufort and in Newport against the Morgans), sometimes to bitter inter-class conflicts—but everywhere to politics.

The Concretes, Dinas.   *Photo: Western Mail.*

Cardiff Slums.

But it was not only an upper middle-class of this kind that the industrialized boroughs possessed: they also had a more variegated lower middle-class than that possessed by the iron-districts. In Swansea there were not only many old-established and substantial commercial and trading families, bankers, large numbers of professional men, but also a very extensive and rich shopkeeping class, itself markedly variegated and ranging from the David Evans's, Evan Evans, Lewis Lewis, Edwards, Morgans, etc. to the humble shopkeeper on the street corner. The iron-towns never achieved such variety. Professional men were relatively few and the shopocracy similarly small and ground between the ironmasters and the workers. It was a growing class, being swelled by immigration from outside of more specialized types of retailers and kinds of craftsmen and by recruitment from below, but it never did and never could achieve the power and drive of the equivalent classes in the large towns. And politically in the affairs of the town they were as often as not conservative and reactionary, more sensible of the burden of rates than of the common good.

For these were working-class towns, to all appearances monolithically so. For example, Swansea had just under 5,000 male occupiers of houses (10,636 houses) of which just under a half were below the £10 rateable value. Merthyr had 8,000 occupiers of houses (16,114 houses) of which 9 out of 10 were below £10 rateable value. In a very real sense this did reflect the fact that the bulk of the inhabitants were workers of one kind or another, and that gradations of wealth were not as wide as in towns of a more variegated character, and as I hope to show more clearly in my second lecture, this uniformity of class was a hindrance and not an aid to political activism. In such conditions the politicization of the people was more difficult than elsewhere. It is only when we look more closely that we find differences emerging within the working classes which, though minute in themselves, were of the highest significance within their own social contexts. But here again, the determining factor was the relative diversification of industry. Neath, for example, had not only extractive industries of various kinds, but also engineering works, foundries, manufactories of many types where highly skilled craftsmen were employed. The working classes in those places could produce an aristocracy of labour far more readily than the one-industry places of the coalfield and the quarry areas. Nevertheless, in these latter towns as the century advanced so ironworks became technologically more sophisticated, and society as a whole became more complex and mobile. But for the most of the period we are concerned with it is an undoubted fact that the places where standards of public health were lowest and where wealth was most unevenly distributed were also the places where political activity as it related to local affairs was least in evidence. Jowett, whose words we used as a text to start this discourse, could see no indication that the poor working men of Morriston were ready or able to combine politically against the further pollution that threatened them. Jowett was a man of property—at least of sufficient property to act as Overseer in the 1860s (he was rated at £15)—and could afford to take political initiatives because he was independent of the industrialists. For the workmen in that same polluting industry the receipt of wages necessarily involved dependence and sub-servience, and few there were who could, as individuals, openly protest. "Men being what they are" placed the burden of initiative on the classes who could and would combine against avoidable evils and for a better ordered society.

And what of Merioneth? Its local political life illustrates perfectly that very same point. There, it was predominantly a shopocracy, stiffened by craftsmen and inspired by scholars and religious leaders, that found in the remote history of the town a justification for opposing the tyrannical power of one man and devised a means of doing so. There, the deficiencies in public health led not only to the adoption of the Public Health Act of 1858 but also to the rediscovery of the urban liberties of the past. It was the old, neglected country town that led the way and not "that great Pandaemonium" of the iron-district. Democracy is about ideas as well as numbers.

SECOND LECTURE

Mr. Jowett's aphoristic aside—"certainly not while men are
what they are"—that I took for a text for my first lecture will
serve equally well for this one. He made the remark, you will
recollect, with reference to a particular local situation—the re-
opening of an old zinc spelter at Morriston—the point of his
argument being that it was unrealistic or naïve to expect a
working-class community which by definition was dependent
for its economic well-being on a certain employer to take action
against that employer in defence of its own better intrests.
Moreover, Jowett went to say, " . . . but apply the Ballot and
then see how matters will stand". If local politics is what lies
before the eyes it is national politics and political principle that
come into contemplation. It was in their experience of local
politics either as active participants or as semi-passive observers that Victorian Welshmen everywhere learned their
national politics. Politics, in the sense of the discussion of ideas
as well as the learning and mastery of techniques of agitation,
persuasion and organization invariably began, in country
places as well as in the towns, in people's experience of local
events. Demands for Church rates turned meetings of vestries
into debating chambers, and whether or not to pay a penny
rate to repair a church became a decision involving history and
political and moral principle.[20] Men learned more about representative democracy from the annual elections to Boards of
Guardians, or to municipal councils, or to School Boards than
from parliamentary elections. They understood the meaning of
undue pressure, corrupt practices and intimidation not from
the infrequent parliamentary electoral contests but from how
and by what means 'interests' came to be regularly put into
power in town councils and at whose expense, and they had no
need to study select committee reports and the evidence in
royal commissions to understand the relationship between
property and rights. "Sir", wrote Mr. Williams of the Gadlys
Iron Works, Aberdare to the Local Government Board Office
on 22 August 1857—"Sir, it has been the practice in this
district with regard to the voting papers, in the annual elections

of the members of the Board of Health, for some few influential agents to the Iron Masters and Coal Proprietors to cause those papers to be brought by the voters to such agents' houses— there to be *filled—examined there—*and *delivered en masse* to the Collector and not delivered to the Collector and the several residences of the Voters''.[21] This, I think, is what Jowett had in mind. Men are what they are, he seems to be saying, partly at any rate, because circumstances make them so: but change the circumstances and then see!

What kinds of circumstances did he have in mind? The answer to this depends very largely on the kind of men he was talking about. He was not thinking about the lowest class of men, that 'residue' of society that inhabited the worst parts of the towns, whose existence was plagued by endemic sickness, who knew poverty as Sir John Simon wrote, ''not merely as subject of physical privations; but poverty as complicated with the caduity and helplessness of ignorance''. All towns, even small country towns in Wales, had this 'submerged tenth' (or 'submerged sixth' or whatever, for in size it varied with time and from place to place). Nor was he thinking of middle-class men, professional men, substantial shopkeepers and tradesmen whose wealth was sufficiently secure and large to give them an acknowledged stake in the running of the communities or the places they inhabited. The men Jowett hand in mind were work-men, inhabiting decent houses and possessing gardens—for he points out that the atmospheric pollution from the proposed works would manifest itself first in the death of all vegetation in workmen's gardens. Some would be craftsmen, artizans, skilled in their trades, like mechanics, others whose value lay less in their expertise than in their physical strength, and the majority of the men would be unskilled labourers. Jowett would probably have had in mind also that class of small or medium-size shopkeepers that we have already mentioned who were so closely allied by kin, by interest and by sympathy to the upper reaches of the working-classes, even though they had re-jected some aspects of working-class culture.

We can distinguish a number of circumstances that in various ways conditioned such groups or classes of people in their pursuit of politics. First and foremost were the legal and

constitutional constraints on action. For example, the way the
vote was distributed among the population. Not everyone had
the vote, and it was the possession of property or the occupation of someone else's property as a tenant of a certain kind
that conferred it. Not natural rights or inherited rights (like
being the son of a freeman), but gross annual rentals, rateable
values and receipts for the payment of rates were the criteria
that determined the composition of the electorates. In practice
it meant something like this. In the county constituencies as a
whole in the mid-1860's there were about 45,000 parliamentary voters, of whom about three-quarters were freeholders
or leaseholders, the remaining quarter being tenants mainly
tenant farmers paying rent of £50 and upwards. These numbered just under 11,000 (10,938), and as a class constituted
about one-fifth of the total occupying tenants. There were, that
is to say, just over 50,000 (50,113) adult males occupying land
as tenants, and of these just 11,000 (10,938) had the vote. In
terms of population (910,586 exclusive of the representative
boroughs) this was a proportion of about 4.45 *per cent,* though a
great deal depended on where one lived: you were likely to get
a better chance of a vote in Radnorshire (8.27 *per cent* voters to
population) than in Carnarvon (3.00 *per cent),* and on the whole
a better chance where there was *no* heavy industry or dense
urban areas outside the representative boroughs. For example,
if you were a manual worker and lived in the parish of Trevethin, or Bedwellte, or Llanddeiniolen you inhabited a kind of
electoral 'no man's land', or a voters' limbo. In such places
there was no formal organized political life such as was possible
in parliamentary boroughs, and it was not until 1885 that they
were brought within reach of the system. But the new voters
were thought to be ignorant and naïve, for having never experienced a tradition of self-government they could not be
expected to have a mature understanding of politics.

So far as the towns were concerned, the system in the municipal boroughs—the so-called scheduled boroughs—gave the
vote in local elections to all ratepayers who had resided in the
town for three years and paid the rates. This was less liberal
than one might think, for the population was very mobile and
people constantly on the move. But generally this franchise

under the Municipal Corporations Act was the most democratic to obtain at the time—far more so than the voting system under the Poor Law Act of 1834. Here, the franchise was distributed according to a strict system of classification by wealth. Property rated at less than £50 gave one vote, £50 to £100 two votes and so on to a maximum of six votes for values of £250 and above. The Public Health Act of 1848 and subsequent Acts up to 1872 adopted the pattern of the Poor Law franchise of plural voting, so that in these two essential areas of urban life property was given a built-in advantage, and this remained the case until the great reforms in local government at the end of the century. Moreover, the property qualification for councillors, members of elected Boards, and for Guardians was high (£500 in real property or a private income from such property of at least £15 per annum). This is why in the majority of places that adopted the 1848 or the 1858 Public Health Act the initial elections were invariable hard fought and why almost without exception the Boards so elected were representative mainly of the middle-class property owners rather than the £8 ratepayers and consequently easily dominated and controlled by the industrial or moneyed interests.

The parliamentary franchise—confined to the £10 householder up to 1867 and thereafter to householders irrespective of occupation values (but nevertheless hedged around like a fortress with many spiky qualifications and restrictions)—gave the vote to rather less than 4 *per cent* of the borough populations. The range of difference between them was enormous: you had a better chance of a vote in the rural boroughs of Radnorshire, where 1 in 17 had the vote, than in the industrial boroughs of Swansea, where, if you lived in Aberafan, you had 1 chance in 47, in Neath 1 in 39, and in Swansea 1 in 30. In Merthyr Tydfil, your chances of having a vote would be very slim indeed—about 1 in 70 of the population was enfranchised—or 1.4 *per cent* of the total population. When Jowett was writing it was calculated that about a quarter or less (23.4 *per cent* in 1867) of the total electorate of the five contributory boroughs belonged to the working classes, 'working-class' including not only men who worked for wages but also craftsmen working on their own account and employing other men.

In fact, the working class voter had suffered from the provisions of the 1832 Reform Act, for the majority of working-class voters under the unreformed system had qualified not on property but on rights—as freemen. It was rights that the 1832 Act abolished, and those rights were the rights of working men. This is one of the reasons why growth in the number of voters was so much less than the growth in the population as a whole in the intervening years.

Associated with this was another circumstance that was beyond the control of a substantial proportion of voters, and that was the dependence of the franchise upon economic conditions prevailing in particular places at particular times. The franchise, as we have seen, was tied to property and its extent defined by occupation qualifications, by the payment of local rates. Negatively, receipt of any assistance from the poor law in the previous twelve months disqualified a man. The number of potential voters was therefore always determined by levels of prosperity, and this for the vast majority of workmen, and even for some small shopkeepers and tradesmen, was a matter completely beyond their control. The trade cycle, in itself a major factor from registration to registration in industries that were mainly export orientated, was complicated by such completely uncontrollable factors as climate. For example, prolonged bad weather in the Bristol Channel by closing the ports could have the same practical effect as a temporary down-swing in the trade cycle: it could be tantamount to a minor depression, but still a depression big enough to put some men in occupation of £10 houses who might otherwise qualify on to the poor rates and hence off the register.

Far more subtle and difficult to understand was the undoubted fact that for the most part there was a readiness on the part of the vast majority of men to accept the social structure as they experienced it and to act out their roles in it. Contemporary Welsh radical politicians called this 'apathy', or regarded it as political blindness. They attributed it to ignorance or to failure or a refusal to see into the realities beyond and beneath the appearance. It was even said that it was due to an excess of interest in, and concentration on, religion and religious culture. This was the opinion of Chartist leaders as well and the reason why they devoted so much time and energy to the pursuit of literacy and learning. It seems to have been particularly true of the late '70s and the '80s when discussion about social reform in Wales never or rarely moved beyond the level of cosmetic changes. Even the institutions to which men attached most importance as organs of social change had lost their reformist, radical and, what they had sometimes had in the past, their revolutionary, fervour. The millenarian note had departed, for example, from the temperance movement and its links with early radical movements had been broken. It had become a great propaganda and educational movement, more secular than religious in its psychology and aiming at legislative change by means of organized constituency pressure on members of parliament. As such, like the Anti-Corn Law League, it had to be single minded in its objectives and discriminating in its choice of allies. There was a general acceptance of the benefits of the economic system as a whole, and a distrust of any forms of union or of any ideologies dedicated to the downfall of that system. Middle-class leadership was accepted, even in some working-class industrial movements, and this invariably involved the banishment of politics from industrial relations where the market and only the market reigned supreme. This was as true of Mabon's Cambrian Miners in the 1880s as it was of W. J. Parry's North Wales Quarrymen's Union, and it helps to explain the existence in both parts of the country of working-class conservative voters. If nearly 5,000 Aberdare colliers voted for the trade union leader Thomas Halliday in 1874, nearly the same number six years later voted for the colliers' arch enemy, Sir W. T. Lewis.

How does one account for this? I would suggest that the nature of urbanization in Wales during the early decades of the century, and particularly the nature of migration into them from the Welsh countryside, from near and far partly accounts for it. The entirely new settlements being formed or being added, like encrustations, to the old commercial-industrial towns necessarily involved what was tantamount to the wholesale transfer of rural culture into still developing places. We have said that these urban places springing up in close organic association with ironworks or collieries or quarries in south and north Wales were not civic, but in respect of their functioning as communities, what were they? They were obviously not rural either, and yet in some essential respects they were intelligible in terms of a rural model of society, that model being the proprietorial estate. There was the same—or what looked like the same—bifurcation of society in terms of wealth and status. The ironmasters or the colliery owner corresponded socially to the landed proprietor. The rural estate, like the works, was an economic unit and functioned thus, and the people who lived and worked on it and in it did so in accordance with rules and customs known and tacitly accepted by all. Men looked at the rural estate and saw the proprietor's mansion and park, his agents, bailiffs, managers and the mass of tenant farmers and labourers, inhabiting his property, tilling his land, dependent upon him and according him deference. Likewise they looked at the industrial estate and saw the ironmaster, noticed his mansion and park, observed his agents, managers and the mass of workmen living in his houses, or on land leased from him, all of them dependent upon him and deferring to him. At profounder levels of analysis observers thought that they found the resemblances even more convincing when they tried to look at these places from the point of view of the immigrant from the countryside. "The basis of the old parochial terrier (or rent-roll of tenants) was the manor: the basis of the new one is the works . . . Nor can it be justly deemed an exaggeration to speak of these works as parishes . . . So that, just as when parishes were first instituted, it was in every man's interest to think what parish he belonged to, because his rights of relief, employment, and redress were all parochial or manorial, so now does the same interest make him think of these or those works, and not at all, or very remotely, of the parish. In the works is his sick-fund, sometimes his benefit society; in the works (by a tolerated system of fining) is his ordinary court of justice".[22] In other words, these places were the industrial analogues of rural estates. It may be that the immigrant overcame his feelings of disorientation and of alienation by reading into his present situation his experience of his rural past. Life was made more intelligible by a transfer of values into his new mode of existence. And of course they brought with them the institutions that most perfectly expressed those values and reproduced them in their new industrial settings. It is true that not all the Welsh immigrants into the industrial estates had come from rural estates: not all were exchanging a squire for a master: many would have come from non-proprietorial parishes. But even these, I suggest, would have carried with them the same familiar conceptions of order and degree as pertaining naturally to society. These were the norms, often broken no doubt, and sometimes rejected: these were the inherited beliefs and assumptions that they brought with them. For they clung to their distinctive regional cultures. It seems certain also that movement from the country to the town, from the rural estate to the urban estate, did not involve the destruction of family ties, but on the contrary, their preservation in substantially the same forms. Cardiganshire people in their new abodes in, say Merthyr, were as likely to be living cheek by jowl with Cardiganshire people as before.

In politics they were accustomed to elections and electioneering based more on family and connection than on principle, and for the most part in elections they did what they were told—to vote if they had a vote in certain way or to join the mob under the colours of their master if they didn't. And when they moved to industrial south Wales they found a similar if not an identical system operating there. If they were 'Dowlais men', for example, on election day they marched down the hill through Penydarren to the Market Square to demonstrate their loyalty to the 'house' of Guest and to intimidate any possible opposition. Was there any difference in principle between Bowen of Llwyngwair's tenants descending on Haverfordwest and Vivian's workmen from Landore and Hafod marching through Swansea to the town hall? Surely Henry Hussey Vivian or C. R. M. Talbot or Richard Fothergill were never seriously worried, before the Ballot Act, that their workmen would not vote for them? And if they were worried could they not exert pressure, and that in subtle ways that no lawyer could prove to be illegitimate? In the political history of Merthyr Tydfil after 1831 the crucial factor was Crawshay's lack of political ambition and his refusal to make any sustained effort at any time to disturb the hegemony of Dowlais. Positively this in-activity of one of the most powerful families in the constituency ensured continuity of representation, but negatively it made it virtually impossible for a vigorous formal political life to develop in the borough, and in particular for the working-class electorate to master the techniques of ordered agitation. Working men had to learn first how to organize *themselves* for political ends. Hence it was that their most spectacular achievement in the period between the First and the Third Reform Acts was not in 1841 when they put up Morgan Williams as a Chartist candidate in opposition ot Sir John Guest, but in 1868 when, as a matter of union policy, they decided to oppose H. A. Bruce, or when, as in 1874, again acting as a union, they decided officially to support Thomas Halliday in the Merthyr election of that year. Putting up their own candidate, however splendid as a gesture, was, as everyone knew, an act of despair or at best simply a way of getting at a mass audience. "You may hold up your dirty hands against me today", said H. A. Bruce when he stood unopposed in 1857, "but I'll be your member tomorrow".[23] Hence the concentration on the creation of unions, the shift from the 'politics' of 1831 to the struggle for union in the early 1850s. But unions were fragile and evanescent things in Wales and in the apprehensions of ordinary, respectable workmen deeply suspect, and the characteristic 'union' of the coalfield in the last three decades of the century was a loose federation of self-regarding local organizations designed to ensure, with a minimum of dispute, the automatic operations of the Sliding Scale. And the reason for this? Because of the unending flow into these places of families formed and conditioned not by industry but by agriculture, men whose psychology was that of peasants and not of an industrial proletariat.

This helps to explain a remark I made in my first lecture to the effect that in no place in Wales was oligarchy as safe as in Merthyr Tydfil. That is not intended for a paradox, for it was the combination of two things that made it so, namely, the overwhelming power of the industrialists and this constant stream of poor, possibly ailing, certainly monoglot and probably confused immigrants from the country. The industrialists, we need to remind ourselves—the iron-kings and the copper-kings—mastered not only metals but men and societies. They were capitalists on a scale and in as complete a way as the world had ever known. They owned all the means of production without exception, directing and controlling not only the strategy but also the fine detail of production and of marketing. Typically, they owned all the raw materials, the furnaces, the mills and forges, the reservoirs, the quarries and clay-pits, the brick works, the farms for hay and fodder, the land on which the houses of their men were built, the houses themselves and (in association with partners) canals, tramways, railways and banks. This was economic power at its most absolute, and commensurate with it was the social power that issued from it. How could such oligarchy be challenged? The short answer is that it never was, and politics could exist only in the interstices, as it were, of the main areas of its operation: a petit-bourgeois thrust here against truck, a strike there against a wage reduction, a critical report on housing or health at some other undefended crack in the regime. Frontal attacks on oligarchy were doomed to failure, and all the numerous attempts by the middle-class radicals of the town to incorporate the borough during Victoria's reign were successfully resisted by the ironmasters.

But if there is no paradox to expound there is irony enough. It is this. Oligarchy is first successfully challenged not in the home of working-class industrial radicalism nor at the heart of the new techologically-based urban civilization of the modern world, but in that quiet backwater in the heart of Merioneth where, as I have already briefly explained, the inhabitants of small town decided that self-government was preferable to gentry domination and political principle more important than customary deference. What Jowett's men would not do or could not do, "men being what they are", these men did. Before asking how this could be, let me remind you briefly of the circumstances and give you a short narrative of the events.

Bala, according to a contemporary guide book, consisted "of one wide street and a smaller one, not lighted, but well supplied head of Llyn Tegid where the Dee flowed out of the lake.[23] It was a small place of rather less than 500 houses—almost exactly the same as Morriston—and a population of about

1,300—to put that in perspective, rather less than one eighth of the total numbers of miners and colliers alone in Merthyr! It had no industries to talk of; just two small carding factories and the chief source of income of the inhabitants was knitting, something they did incessantly, men as well as women and children. There were a number of shops, a few inns, and a relatively high number of craftsmen—shoemakers, carpenters, painters and so on—who produced and worked for the farmers of the adjacent parishes. These were quite numerous, not very prosperous, and almost without exception yearly tenants of the two or three great landlords of the district. The farms averaged about 50 or 60 acres, though there were some considerably larger, and in addition there were little communities of agricultural labourers in small villages, such as Llanuwchllyn and Llandderfel. A poor community, not the kind of place to set the world on fire.

Except for two things. First, it was a religious and intellectual centre. It was at Bala that the great Reverend Mr. Thomas Charles had settled, and he had turned it into the spiritual home of Calvinistic Methodism in north Wales, if not in Wales as a whole. It had two colleges, One was Athrofa'r Bala headed by Thomas Charles' son-in-law, Lewis Edwards, M.A., Dr. Lewis Edwards as he later became, the philosopher, theologian, essayist, founder-editor of the quarterly *Y Traethodydd.* The other college belonged to the Independents, and was headed by the remarkable Rev. Michael D. Jones who, not a scholar like Lewis Edwards, was a man of extraordinary talent and a propagandist of rare ability. The other tutors were likewise men of quality and outstanding gifts. The other feature that it is important to mention is the fact that Bala was an ancient borough, long since decayed as to its government, but chartered nonetheless, and what the ratepayers decided to to in that February 1859 was to petition to be brought under the operation of the Local Government Act of 1858 as a preliminary to recovering some of the burghal liberties which, according to charter, were theirs by right. In fact, recovering their charter—something that they had succeeded in doing by the following January—gave them no additional powers, but what it did give them was what they most needed at that juncture, namely, status and prestige.

For what they were proposing and what they did was in direct defiance of some of the largest of the local landlords, in particular, of R. W. Price of Rhiwlas, and this act of defiance was the first in a chain of events that no one could have foreseen and that ended in a political movement of country-wide significance. Merioneth had always been a deeply Tory county, its one parliamentary seat to all intents and purposes the property of—or, at any rate, regarded as the property of —the Vaughan family of Hengwrt and Nannau who had either occupied it or otherwise controlled it for more than a century and a half. In 1859 the sitting member was a relative, W. W. E. Wynne, Peniarth, the great antiquary (to whom Sir Robert Williames Vaughan had bequeathed the great Hengwrt Collection of manuscripts which eventually came into the hands of Sir John Williams who gave them as its foundation collection to the National Library of Wales: but that's another story), and since Wynne had no wish to retire it was assumed that he would be returned unopposed. That is, until the Bala committee for the incorporation of the town thought otherwise. They put up a Liberal candidate, virtually at the last moment, and they came within 38 votes of gaining the seat. At the next elections, when Wynne's eldest son was the Tory candidate, they tried again and again lost, but then in 1868 they won the seat—"Mae Castell deudraeth ar ei draed/A Pheniaeth mewn adfeilion."

There is no time to recount this dramatic story: it has been done many times before, for it remained for generations an inspiration for poet and politician alike.[24] The reason is very evident. Nowhere in the modern political history of Wales had there been such a dramatic confrontation between inherited landed wealth, power and prestige as personified in the persons of R. W. Price of Rhiwlas and Sir Watkin Williams Wynne of Wynnstay on the one hand, and of a dependent tenantry on the other. The very names of the farms involved—Maes-y-gadfa and Fron-goch—seem to have a tragic appropriateness, for the confrontation in 1859 and again in 1865 had involved the evictions of some of the tenants from their farms for refusing to

vote as requested by their landlords. For these elections encouraged not only the tenants of other estates, particularly in
Carmarthenshire and Cardiganshire, to do likewise but also
signalled a bitter campaign or retribution by their Tory landlords. The myth that the essence of Welsh political life in the
last century was to be found dramatized in these events was
founded on fact and not on fiction, and was based not on fortuitous happenings in a back-water but in the deep sufferings of
innocent people and in an extraordinary determination by a
few men to regard politics not as a meaningless and empty
charade but as the highest and most responsible activity of free
citizens. It was not the creation of ruthless Welsh Nonconformist politicans. The elections of 1868 and the subsequent
history of Welsh radicalism and of political developments in
general are scarcely intelligible except against this background
of events in Bala in the ten years between 1858 and 1868.
Thereafter, the political universe of Welshmen was different.

I have been unable to resist the temptation to spend more
time than I can properly spare on this episode. It is time to
explain its deeper significance. Why, we may ask, were those
few Bala people politically "what *they* were"? It would require
more than the tail-end of a lecture to deal adequately with that
question: perhaps the day is coming when Welsh historians will
be as well-equipped as French historians to analyse the past of
their communities at the level that this question demands.
Some of the Bala people's most important characteristics will
have already been mentioned and have occurred to you. As in
Merthyr and Morriston and scores of other places, a preoccupation with health and amenities stimulated political activity.
The relativities of wealth and poverty, of social power and of
impotence were every bit as evident, if not more oppressive,
than in industrial towns. In many ways, Bala was more deprived than any of the places we have mentioned. It is at the
intellectual and religious life of the community that we must
look, and to this I now turn.

There is no need to remind you that Bala was a thoroughly
religious and overwhelmingly Nonconformist place. It was the
spiritual centre of Calvinistic Methodism in north Wales, a
kind of Rome and Mecca rolled into one, a place of pilgrimage,

famous for its 'sasiynnau'—the only place in Wales where a Norman 'motte' had been turned into a pulpit—and it was there, as I said, that the denomination's most presitigious college was located. The other denominations were by comparison very much weaker, and the fact that the Independents also had an academy nearby was a reflection not of their numerical strength in the county (or in north Wales) but was the result of historical accident and the tenacity of its principals, father and son. But Merthyr Tydfil and Swansea were also, judging by purely quantitative criteria, scarcely less religious. Indeed, Wales as a whole, from the mid-1830s onwards was probably the most religious region in the British Isles. It is not, however, the differences between Glamorgan and Merioneth in respect of their overall religiosity that is important: that, for example, Merioneth had seating for every man, woman and child plus another 5 *per cent* of the total population while Glamorgan could only accommodate 87 *per cent* of its population: such quantitative differences are probably important but not entirely to the point. It is the denominational mix in this great amplitude of provision that needs to be explained and that provides the essential clues in our inquiry. In Bala, as in north Wales generally, the most powerful denomination was the Calvinistic Methodist: in industrial south Wales it was the Independents and the Baptists—the old Dissenting denominations rather than the new Methodist ones—and with a spice of Unitarians in the Swansea and Merthyr districts.

This distinction is vital because it directs attention ot important facts about the relation of religion to politics. First it suggests that we should look critically at the familiar generalizations about Methodism being always and everywhere conservative in its social attitudes (or more precisely as inculcating conservative attitudes) to politics, and Dissent being radical and progressive or encouraging such attitudes in its adherents. For we have just seen that the most creative and 'radical' political movement in Victorian Wales took place not where Dissent was strong but where it was weak. And earlier we noted that political oligarchy was most entrenched, apathy and possibly fear most in evidence, where Dissent was strongest. Clearly, religion as a politicizing agent is responsive to, as well as creative of, the culture of the communities of which it is a part. How it worked and to what effect depended on the particular community. Thus, in an industrial community, newly settled, in process of formation lacking institutional of government, peopled constantly by strangers from many corners of the land and from alien and hated places, containing anonymous quarters of disease and depravity, prone to violence, to excesses of drink and infidelity—in such places organized religion almost by definition was a conservative force. It became a civilizing agent, an organ of community discipline, a major instrument of social control, and often—too often—was recognized as such by industrialists who, for obvious reasons, had financial interests in law and order. It allied itself readily with the powers that be and on the side of social order, and consciously provided from among its own members and adherents an elite of respectability and good conduct. In politics it led its massive following into the paths of middle-class righteousness. In such places, it is worth remarking, it is not the chapels that radicalize society but society that radicalizes the chapels; the history of the relations between Chartism and the major dissenting denominations is evidence enough of this.

But in rural towns and in country areas the social role of the chapels might well be reversed or, at any rate, be very different. In such places, in the inherently conservative communities of the ordered and disciplined estates, the chapels might well be the only sources of radical thought and the only begetters of radical political activity. In Penllyn and Llanycil, in Cwm-tir-mynach and Frongoch, the chapels would be the only communities distinct from and outside of the comprehensive community of the estate. There, in Penllyn, the community of the chapel produced an elite also, but an elite which could sensitively express and powerfully direct the hidden and sometimes repressed, but always ancient, resentments of a proud people deprived of their ancient freeholds and expected to defer to their superiors even in the precious and private realm of religion. As these men saw it—these good conservative Calvinists who accepted without question the authority of the men placed over them—they were being asked to betray their most precious beliefs in voting for a Roman Catholic fellow-traveller. On grounds of conscience they would not do so: on constutional grounds they claimed the right not to do so. Nonconformist ministers in nienteenth-century Wales did not create out of their fertile imaginations imaginary grievances: they eloquently expressed what was already there and gave voice and direction to the political aspirations of the people. "Yr hyn ydyw Rhufain i'r Eidal ydyw Bala i Ogledd Cymru. Dyma fam y drwg: dyna'r *city of destruction;* dyma lle y ffurfir brâd y *powdr gwn* yn erbyn yr Eglwys. Dyma lle yr heuir hadau gwenwynig Ymneillduaeth a gwerin-lywodraeth".[25] [What Rome is to Italy Bala is to North Wales. Here is the mother of the evil: here is the city of destruction; here is plotted explosive treachery against the Church. Here are sown the poisonous seeds of Nonconformity and republicanism]. Brush away the rhetoric, dilute the exaggeration and there is quite a little truth in that judgement.

When therefore we study the role of organized religion in making men politically "what they are" it is to the specific and the particular that we must turn our attention—to specific congregations in their particular places and circumstances. And that is precisely the work of the social historian.

Speculation as to what might have been is usually pointless, but one is tempted, in conclusion, to ask, Could this have happened in Swansea or in Merthyr? The answer of the historian must be, Why bother to ask? For the fact is that those political events in Bala profoundly affected political developments subsequently in may other constituencies, including Swansea and Merthyr. Everywhere in Wales Nonconformists of all persuasions came to reflect anew upon their past: those events led the self-taught man as well as the scholar to ponder upon the nature of religious communities and to question, as a matter of political philosophy, the implications of the link with established power: it stimulated discussion about rights and notions of justice; above all, it provided not only this nation but also, throught the mediation of the press and parliament, the rest of the kingdom with deeply moving tales of moral courage. Great pressure movements and societies, both religious and secular, like the Liberation Society and the Reform league, saw

Vote by ballot: sketches at the Taunton Election.

1. Voters giving his name and number on register.
2. Stamping ballot-paper with private mark.
3. Voter marking ballot-paper.
4. All that is visible of voter while marking paper.
5. Voter depositing paper in ballot-box.
6. Policeman taking boxes from polling-booths to Guildhall.
7. Method of folding ballot-paper.
8. Voter's mark. Any other whatsoever disqualifies vote.

the significance of what had happened and renewed their efforts to enlighten the people and to organize them behind common political objectives. And ten years later, in the election of 1868, the reward was great. Mr. Jowett of Morriston, disappears from sight in 1864. Let us hope that he lived long enough to see that, even without the Ballot, ordinary and common men could act with the greatest heroism in the pursuit of political ideals, ''men being what they are''.

NOTES

[1] William Jowett to H. Huseey Vivian, Esq., M.P. dated from Morriston 5 February 1859. P.R.O. MH 13, 178/16.

[2] Memorial of Richard Watkin Price, Esq., to the Secretary of State, dated from Rhiwlas, Bala 23 February 1859.

[3] Williams Farr, 'On the Mortality of Children', *Journal of the Statistical Society,* 49, (1866), p. 9.

[4] Seventh Report of the Medical Officer of the Privy Council, 1864.

[5] G. T. Clark, 'Iron Manufacture in South Wales', *Westminster Review,* 1848, pp. 101-2.

[6] Appendix to the Second Report of the Register General of Births, Deaths and Marriages, P.P. 1840 XVII (276), pp. 49-50.

[7] For Dr. Greenhow's Report on Merthyr Tydfil see Second Report of the Medical Officer, 1859, P.P. 1860 XXXIX (201), pp. 111-121.

[8] Royal Commission into the Housing of the Working Classes, First Report, P.P. 1884-5 XXX (4402), Appendix pp. 700-2.;

[9] For Dr. T. J. Dyke's evidence see *ibid.,* Qs. 12, 974-13, 119.

[10] *ibid.,* Appendix to First Report, p. 705.

[11] Dr. Dykes's evidence is in the First Report of the Sanitary Commission, Qs. 6275-6425.

[12] *Public Health Reports,* ed. E. Smeaton, 2 vols. (1887), p. 433.

[13] T. W. Rammel, *Report to the General Board of Health . . . into . . . the sanitary condition . . . of Merthyr Tydfil* (1850), p. 12.

[14] Sermon, preached before the District Committees of the S.P.C.K. . . . for that part of the diocese of Llandaff situate in the county of Glamorgan . . . (Cardiff, 1830).

[15] Seymour Tremenheere, Report . . . into the State of . . . the Mining Districts (1846).

[16] This is based on calculations ot be found in 'The Scripture Reader's Journal', N.L.W. MS. 4943 B, ff. 54-57.

[17] Dr. Holland to the General Board of Health, 15 December 1853, P.R.O. MH 13/125.

[18] G. T. Clark, *art. cit.*

[19] William Jowett to the Secretary of State, dated from Morriston 26 October 1864, P.R.O. MH 13 178/26 i.

[20] For an example see below pp. 81-2.

[21] P.R.O. MH13 1A/34.

[22] Reports of the Commissioners of Inquiry into the State of Education in Wales (1847), Vol. I, pp. 12-13.

[23] Samuel Lewis, *Topographical Dictionary of Wales* (1848 edn.)

[24] For a full account see Ieuan Gwynedd Jones, *Explorations and Explanations,* pp.

[25] *Y Cymro,* quoted in *Baner ac Amserau Cymru,* 29 February 1860.

INDEX